Working Title Films

For Leah

Working Title Films
A Creative and Commercial History

Nathan Townsend

EDINBURGH
University Press

Edinburgh University Press is one of the leading university presses in the UK. We publish academic books and journals in our selected subject areas across the humanities and social sciences, combining cutting-edge scholarship with high editorial and production values to produce academic works of lasting importance. For more information visit our website: edinburghuniversitypress.com

© Nathan Townsend, 2021 , 2023

Edinburgh University Press Ltd
The Tun – Holyrood Road
12 (2f) Jackson's Entry
Edinburgh EH8 8PJ

First published in hardback Edinburgh University Press 2021

Typeset in 11/13pt Garamond MT PRO by
Servis Filmsetting Ltd, Stockport, Cheshire

A CIP record for this book is available from the British Library

ISBN 978 1 4744 5193 2 (hardback)
ISBN 978 1 4744 5194 9 (paperback)
ISBN 978 1 4744 5195 6 (webready PDF)
ISBN 978 1 4744 5196 3 (epub)

The right of Nathan Townsend to be identified as author of this work has been asserted in accordance with the Copyright, Designs and Patents Act 1988 and the Copyright and Related Rights Regulations 2003 (SI No. 2498).

Contents

List of Figures and Tables	vi
Acknowledgements	viii
Introduction	1
1 Transatlantic British Cinema and the Political Economy of Film	11
2 The Independent Years: Hand-to-mouth Production and Social Art Cinema (1984–8)	42
3 The PolyGram Years Part I: Founding a Studio and Making a Subsidiary (1988–92)	68
4 The PolyGram Years Part II: Development, Green-lighting and Distribution (1993–8)	94
5 Swapping Studios: From PolyGram to Universal (1998–9)	124
6 The Universal Years Part I: Development, Green-lighting and Distribution (1999–2006)	138
7 The Universal Years Part II: Retrenchment and Reorientation (2007–12)	162
8 The Universal Years Part III: New Relationships (2012–)	178
9 The Global Market for Working Title's Films	198
10 Transatlantic British Cinema: Creative Risk, Commercial Risk and the Issue of Diversity	218
Bibliography	234
Filmography	244
Index	257

Figures and Tables

FIGURES

1.1	Total number of UK films by production category, 1992–2017	29
1.2	Total spend on UK films by production category, 1992–2017	30
1.3	Average spend on UK films by production category, 1992–2017	31
1.4	Selective and automatic public funding for film in the UK, 2006/7–2017/18	34
1.5	Top six sources of selective public funding for film in the UK, 2006/7–2017/18	35
1.6	Share of UK and ROI box office by nation of origin, 2002–18	36
1.7	Distributor share of the UK and ROI box office, 2002–18	37
3.1	PolyGram Film Fund procedures flowchart: development and green-lighting	80
3.2	PolyGram Film Fund procedures flow chart: production, sales and revenue	83
3.3	Working Title films funded by PolyGram's Film Fund 1990–2	84
3.4	World music market: competitor market shares, 1991/1992	89
4.1	Working Title operating framework, 1993	99
4.2	The control sheet (sample)	109
4.3	The expansion of PFEI's operating companies by year	116
9.1	Domestic vs international box office for Hollywood films, 2001–18	216

TABLES

1.1	Distributor share of box office, UK and ROI, 2018	38
1.2	Box office results for the top twenty UK films released in the UK and ROI, 2018	39
1.3	Box office results for the top twenty UK independent films released in the UK and ROI, 2018	40
2.1	Channel 4, British Screen and BFI funding for Working Title's films, 1985–8	61

3.1	Working Title's slate by funding, distribution and sales, 1988–9	75
4.1	PFE third-party English-language production deals, 1998	105
4.2	PFE's film and television library acquisitions	117
6.1	Universal's 1999 production deals	141
7.1	Universal's 2009 production deals	173
8.1	Universal's 2016 production deals	185
9.1	PFE slate: box office top fifteen (excluding acquisitions), 1992–8	202
9.2	Working Title's Universal slate: box office top twenty, 1999–2019	205
9.3	Working Title's Focus Features slate: box office top fifteen, 1999–2019	208
9.4	WT²'s slate: box office top ten, 1999–2007	210
9.5	Universal's slate: box office top twenty, 1999–2019	212
9.6	Working Title's Studiocanal slate: box office top films, 2011–19	214

Acknowledgements

In this book I have endeavoured to trace the connections between creativity and commerce at play in the operation of a film production company throughout a series of evolving industrial contexts. In another act of contextualisation, then, it is important to acknowledge the people who have contributed directly and indirectly to its publication. Thanks go to Andrew Higson for his guidance and support throughout both the years of my doctoral research under his supervision and subsequently as a mentor and colleague. Thanks also go to Duncan Petrie for his input on my work at various important junctures over the same time period. I would like to acknowledge the help of former colleagues, Huw Jones and Roderick Smits, who read and commented on earlier drafts of this work and Tim Crosby and Alex Newhouse for their tireless proofreading. More generally, I would like to thank all my colleagues in the School of Arts and Creative Technologies at the University of York for their friendship and support throughout the last decade. It has also been a rewarding place to work because of the students who have passed through the department in that time, many of whom are now contending with issues of creativity and commerce for a living.

While undertaking research for this book, I was very fortunate to be granted access to the privately held archives of PolyGram Filmed Entertainment (PFE) by the studio's former President and CEO, Michael Kuhn, and former COO, Malcolm Ritchie. Thanks go to both for permitting use of this invaluable material and to Malcolm, in particular, for his unfaltering help in clarifying various important points of detail along the way. Equally, thanks go to the former and current personnel at Working Title, PFE and Universal, who agreed to be interviewed as part of this research. This book is derived, in part, from articles published in *Historical Journal of Film, Radio and Television* in 2018 (available online: https://www.tandfonline.com/doi/full/10.1080/01439685.2017.1358415) and 2020 (available online: https://www.tandfonline.com/doi/full/10.1080/01439685.2020.1733204), an article in *Journal of British Cinema and Television* in 2018 (available online: https://www.euppublishing.com/doi/full/10.3366/jbctv.2018.0414) and one in *Studies in European Cinema* in 2019 (available online: https://www.tandfonline.com/doi/full/10.1080/17411548.2018.1501869). Accordingly, I would like to thank Taylor & Francis and Edinburgh University Press for permission to reproduce material from these publications.

It is also important to acknowledge several people who have contributed indirectly to the publication of this book at key points in my life. My interest in film began twenty years ago at Queen Elizabeth Sixth Form College in Darlington. There, I took courses in Sociology and Communications Studies respectively taught by Mike Ellis and Mark Dixon who brought these subjects to life in vivid ways that ignited my interest in academic work. As an undergraduate at the Institute of Communications Studies, University of Leeds, I had the good fortune to take a course called The European Film Industry: Past, Present and Future(s), taught by Graham Roberts. This was my first engagement with an industry-focused version of film studies and it opened my eyes to some of the bigger questions that I pursued years later as a postgraduate student at the Department of American and Canadian Studies, University of Nottingham. There, Paul Grainge was not only an inspirational teacher but also a great mentor who encouraged me to pursue my interest in industry-focused research. Throughout all these periods of my life, I also have my parents, Audrey and Phil Townsend, to thank for their love and support. Finally, the most recent leg of this journey would have been impossible without my wonderful partner, Leah, to whom this book is dedicated.

CREATIVITY AND COMMERCE: A DISAGREEMENT

INT. OFFICE – CAPITOL PICTURES – DAY

Lead actor, Baird Whitlock, reclines in a chair wearing full wardrobe. Eddie Mannix, Head of Production, sits behind his desk listening to Baird explain his recent absence from the set of *Hail, Caesar! A Tale of the Christ.*

> **Baird:** So, I'm thinkin', 'What the hell!' I've woken up in strange houses before but never without a broad next to me.
>
> **Eddie:** Uh-huh
>
> **Baird:** These guys are pretty interesting, though. They've actually figured out the laws that dictate *everything*. History, sociology, politics, morality – everything. It's all in a book called Kapital with a 'K'.
>
> **Eddie:** That right?
>
> **Baird:** Yeah. You're not going to believe this. These guys even figured out what's going on here at the studio, because the studio is nothing more than an instrument of capitalism. So, we blindly follow these laws like any other institution, the laws that these guys figured out. The studio makes pictures to serve the system. That is its function. That's really what we're up to here.
>
> **Eddie:** Is it?
>
> **Baird:** Yeah, it's confirming what they call the 'status quo'. I mean, we may tell ourselves that we're creating something of artistic value or there's some sort of spiritual dimension to the picture business. But what it really is, is this fat cat, Nic Schenck, out in New York running this factory, serving up these lollipops. What they used to call a 'bread and circuses' for the…
>
> **Eddie stands up, walks around his desk, and grabs Baird by his breastplate. He hauls him to his feet and slaps him across the face, forehand and backhand**
>
> **Eddie:** Now, you listen to me, buster. Nic Schenck and the studio have been good to you and to everyone else who works here. If I ever hear you bad-mouthing Mr Schenck again it'll be the last thing you say before I have you tossed in jail for colluding in your own abduction.
>
> **Baird:** Eddie, I wouldn't, I would never do that…

Eddie slaps Baird across the face again, forehand and backhand

Eddie: Shut up! You're going to go out there and you're going to finish *Hail, Caesar!* You're going to give that speech at the feet of the Penitent Thief and you're going to believe every word you say.

Eddie slaps Baird across the face for a third time, forehand and backhand

Eddie: You're going to do it because you're an actor and that's what you do, just like the director does what he does, and the writer, and the script girl, and the guy who claps the slate. You're going to do it because the picture has worth and you have worth if you serve the picture, and you're never going to forget that again.

Hail, Caesar! (2016)

Praise for *Working Title Films: A Creative and Commercial History*:

There ought to have been a studio study devoted to Working Title years ago. Now, thankfully, there is one. And Nathan Townsend's book proves that it's certainly been worth the wait. This is a work of meticulous scholarship which does more than chart the history of what he terms, with customary qualification, 'arguably the most important production company in the history of British cinema'. The story of Working Title, in Townsend's thoroughly contextualised approach, is also the history of the British film industry over the past 40 years. Furthermore, it is an object lesson in how to do production history.

Professor Justin Smith, De Montfort University Leicester.

This is an important book, providing a much-needed history of Working Title, the most successful and influential UK production company over the past forty years. Nathan Townsend's lucid and penetrating analysis, informed by deeply assimilated theory and an abundance of primary research, shows how the company managed to reconcile the competing demands of creativity and commerce to forge what he calls a Transatlantic British Cinema that promotes particular versions of Britishness. Deftly combining the micro and the macro, Townend's authoritative study makes a significant contribution to Media Industry Studies as well as British cinema history and deserves the widest possible readership.

Professor Andrew Spicer, University of the West of England, Bristol.

Essential reading for anyone engaged in the serious study of contemporary British cinema, Nathan Townsend's book provides a long overdue full critical analysis of Working Title's operations and outputs since its inception four decades ago. It traces the company's complex history and surveys the full range of its transnational endeavours, from Oscar-winning highs to critic-infuriating lows, and is nourished throughout by Townsend's conceptual sophistication and granular attention to detail.

Professor Melanie Williams, University of East Anglia.

Introduction

Working Title Films is arguably the most important production company in the history of British cinema. Making such a bold claim, even when tempered with a caveat, requires some careful justification. One set of supporting arguments is related to numbers. At the time of writing, Working Title has been in business for over thirty-six years and has produced more than 120 feature films. Collectively these films have received fourteen Academy Awards and forty BAFTAs, generating worldwide box office revenues in excess of $7 billion in the process. Putting aside longevity, critical acclaim and commercial success for a moment, it is also possible to make a second set of arguments related to cultural impact. In every decade since its establishment, Working Title has produced films which have made defining contributions to British film culture. During the 1980s, for example, the company made critically acclaimed art cinema including films like *My Beautiful Laundrette* (1985), *Wish You Were Here* (1987), *Sammy and Rosie Get Laid* (1987) and *A World Apart* (1988). In the 1990s Working Title produced globally oriented commercial movies such as *Four Weddings and a Funeral* (1994), *Bean* (1997), *Elizabeth* (1998) and *Notting Hill* (1999). This momentum was built upon in the 2000s with the likes of *Billy Elliot* (2000), *Bridget Jones's Diary* (2001), *Johnny English* (2003) and *Hot Fuzz* (2007), while the subsequent decade saw *Tinker Tailor Soldier Spy* (2011), *The Theory of Everything* (2014), *Legend* (2015) and *Yesterday* (2019) added to the Working Title canon.

Even a cursory review of Working Title's credits, however, reveals a more diverse picture. The company has also produced a wide range of films which are quintessentially American in terms of characters, settings and cultural themes. During the 1990s examples include the work of American auteurs like Tim Robbins (*Bob Roberts*, 1992; *Dead Man Walking*, 1995), Mario Van Peebles (*Posse*, 1993; *Panther*, 1995) and the filmmaking partnership of Joel and Ethan Coen (*The Hudsucker Proxy*, 1994; *Fargo*, 1996; *The Big Lebowski*, 1998). This continued in the 2000s and 2010s, with romantic comedies (*40 Days and 40 Nights*, 2002; *The Guru*, 2002; *Definitely, Maybe*, 2008), action movies and thrillers (*State of Play*, 2009; *Contraband*, 2012; *Baby Driver*, 2017), as well many more collaborations with the Coen brothers on films like *O Brother, Where Art*

Thou? (2000), *The Man Who Wasn't There* (2001), *Burn After Reading* (2008), *A Serious Man* (2009) and *Hail, Caesar!* (2016). Equally, further examples such as *Senna* (2010), *Everest* (2015), *The Program* (2015) and *Entebbe* (2018) present a mix of international elements which cannot be squarely aligned with either Britain or America beyond their production in the English language.

This diversity of output is more easily understood when viewed through the lens of Working Title's remarkable industrial development, which is punctuated by three distinct stages of ownership. The company was independently owned and managed following its incorporation in 1984 and largely produced low-budget art cinema. In doing so, Working Title received commissions and investment from publicly funded filmmaking institutions in Britain for much of the 1980s, most notably from the broadcaster, Channel 4. In 1992, however, the company became a subsidiary of PolyGram Filmed Entertainment (PFE), a newly formed film studio which, over the course of the 1990s, became a European-owned competitor to the major Hollywood studios. During this period, Working Title operated simultaneously from offices in London and Los Angeles, actively combining the film industries and cultures of Britain and Hollywood. Despite the premature demise of PFE in 1998, the company continued to work on both sides of the Atlantic as a subsidiary of Universal, one of the so-called 'Big Six' Hollywood studios of the era. This relationship has endured for over twenty years, during which time Working Title also formed a longstanding co-production partnership with the European-owned 'mini-major', Studiocanal, and has more recently made films with other major Hollywood studios including Twentieth Century Fox and Sony Pictures.

This book offers a history of Working Title Films which, as its title suggests, is centrally concerned with both the creative and commercial aspects of the company's development. More specifically, it is concerned with the ways in which the demands of creativity and commerce have been reconciled throughout the successive stages of the company's history. Consequently, the focus remains on the operation of Working Title as business within a series of evolving industrial contexts. On the one hand, this entails focusing on the structures, processes and practices at play within the production company itself. What, for example, is the internal structure of Working Title, and how has it evolved? Who are the company's key personnel, and how do these players explain their roles and responsibilities? How does the company work with the writers, directors and actors directly responsible for creating its films? On the other hand, it also involves understanding Working Title's institutional relationship with other film businesses. To what extent was Working Title reliant upon investment from Channel 4 as an independent? How did PFE decide which of the projects on Working Title's development slate to green-light? What factors influence the distribution and marketing of Working Title's films as a subsidiary of Universal?

Over the past decade or so, questions of this kind have increasingly been addressed within a field known as Media Industry Studies. From the outset, efforts to define the parameters and objectives of this area have noted the diversity of academic traditions which have influenced its emergence and development. For Jennifer Holt and Alisa Perren these include, amongst other disciplines, social theory, studies of mass communication, sociology and anthropology, media economics, political economy, cultural studies and film and television studies (Holt & Perren 2009: 1–16). Refining these observations, Paul McDonald argues that Media Industry Studies is best understood as a 'subfield' of research and pedagogy which specifically focuses on industrial structures, processes and practices and sits within and between the disciplines of cultural, film and media studies. Like Holt and Perren, however, he stresses the 'disciplinary heterogeneity' of Media Industry Studies which appropriates 'cherry-picked ideas, concepts, perspectives, and arguments from many – though highly circumscribed – directions' from the '*über*-fields' of the humanities and social sciences (McDonald 2013: 145–6). More recently, Matthew Freeman has argued:

> ... what is meant by media industry studies today is principally *contextualisation* – it aims to trace connections between the micro and the macro, between production and culture, so as to better understand *how* and *why* the media industries ultimately work the way that they do. All media industries essentially operate as a complex blend of creativity and enterprise, translating culture into economy. Contextualisation affords a valuable insight into the processes and practices of this translation, be they big or small. (Freeman 2016: 12)

While contributing to this growing body of scholarship, this book also embraces the interdisciplinary nature of Media Industry Studies by simultaneously working within the longer established academic disciplines of film studies and political economy. In doing so, the contextualisation that is pursued here is framed by larger questions about the relationship between the film industries and cultures of Britain and Hollywood. Film studies scholarship about national and transnational cinemas, for example, helps to explain this relationship at a conceptual level: what are the creative and commercial strategies that link British and Hollywood cinema? How do they combine in different industrial contexts? What is the impact of these strategies upon the films that are produced? In contrast, political economy sees films as commodities that are produced, distributed and consumed within a capitalist industrial system, and engages with questions of power and control within this system: what are the regulatory frameworks that govern the relationship between the British and Hollywood film industries? How is control exerted along the circuit of production, distribution and consumption? What are the political, social and ideological implications of these power relations?

These many questions, with roots variously in the fields of Media Industry Studies, film studies and political economy, are usefully organised by the work of Amanda D. Lotz and Horace Newcomb. The authors suggest that there are six 'levels of analysis' from which such questions can be pursued, five of which are relevant here: national and international political economy and policy, specific industrial contexts and practices, particular organisations, individual productions and individual agents. These levels can be envisaged as concentric circles with the outermost representing macro analysis (national and international political economy and policy) and the innermost, micro analysis (individual agents) (Lotz & Newcomb 2011: 72–7). While this book is primarily structured around the middle of these levels, namely the history of Working Title Films as a 'particular organisation', analysis at all levels is implicitly or explicitly pursued throughout. Doing so highlights the ways in which the company operates with 'relative autonomy' and 'circumscribed agency' (ibid.: 71) within a wider industrial landscape defined by dynamic interdependence across all these levels.

Chapter 1 engages with analysis at the macro level and considers the relationship between the film industries and cultures of Britain and Hollywood through the disciplines of film studies and political economy. This initially involves critically reviewing orthodox accounts of British cinema as 'national cinema', which emphasise the discrete and oppositional status of British cinema in relation to Hollywood. In doing so, I propose an alternative conceptual space which I call 'Transatlantic British Cinema', which draws on more recent scholarship about cinematic transnationalism to emphasise the transnational and more specifically, *transatlantic*, strategies at play throughout the history of British cinema and in the current operation of Working Title. In the second part of the chapter, Transatlantic British Cinema is viewed through the lens of political economy. Here, the relationship between the British and Hollywood film industries is considered in the light of prevailing economic and regulatory contexts. In turn, distinctions are drawn between the production, distribution and exhibition of Transatlantic British Cinema and its conceptual other, independent British cinema, highlighting the disparity of resources which define these parallel streams of industrial activity.

Chapter 2 begins the extended mid-level analysis of Working Title Films by examining the company's years of operation within the independent sector between 1984 and 1988. Under the leadership of its co-founders, Tim Bevan and Sarah Radclyffe, Working Title emerged from the music video production company, Aldabra, to become one of the most successful production companies of the 1980s, making low-budget films such as *My Beautiful Laundrette*, *Wish You Were Here* and *Sammy and Rosie Get Laid*. Significantly, most of these films received funding from the British broadcaster Channel 4 which, alongside other publicly owned filmmaking organisations such as the British Film Institute (BFI) Production Board and British Screen Finance, contributed to the emergence of so-called 'social art cinema'. With the arrival of a third partner, Graham Bradstreet, Working Title made the transition from a producer-for-hire business model to a company which developed and financed its own films, albeit precariously. This narrative of independent production is also considered in relation to the company's collaboration with a series of international sales agents and independent distribution companies that were responsible for selling, distributing and marketing Working Title's films.

Chapter 3 considers Working Title's integration into PolyGram Media Division (PMD), a subsidiary of the major record company, PolyGram, between 1988 and 1992. During this period, Working Title was transformed from an independent production company to a subsidiary 'label' with its own subsidiary, Working Title Television (WTTV). Moreover, PMD created a prototype studio system around Working Title which included the launch of an international film sales company and a corporate tax structure which jointly funded the production of the company's films. By coordinating the activities of these businesses, PMD developed the so-called 'control sheet', a centralised creative and commercial filter which assessed the risk and reward profile of film projects. As a result, Working Title's output moved into more market-oriented territory, exemplified by the production of films like *Chicago Joe and the Showgirl* (1990), *Drop Dead Fred* (1991) and *Map of the Human Heart* (1992). In turn, these developments led to the departure of Radclyffe and Bradstreet, the formation of Bevan's partnership with Eric Fellner, and the launch of a new film studio, PolyGram Filmed Entertainment.

Chapter 4 examines Working Title's years as a subsidiary of PFE between 1993 and 1998 through the concept of creative and commercial gatekeeping, with gates at the points of development, green-lighting and distribution. Within this nascent studio system, PFE provided Working Title with annual overhead and development budgets and granted the production company creative autonomy at the point of development. Thereafter, PFE assessed the commercial potential of each film project through a more sophisticated version of the 'control sheet', which projected worldwide revenues and, in turn, directly informed the green-lighting process. The final gate, distribution, was also controlled by PFE, which built a worldwide distribution and marketing network over the course of the 1990s through its US operations, Gramercy Pictures and PolyGram Films, and through PolyGram Filmed Entertainment International (PFEI) in thirteen other territories. This period saw the production of Working Title's first major commercial hits including *Four Weddings and a Funeral*, *Bean* and *Elizabeth*, films that set the tone of the company's production agenda in subsequent decades.

Chapter 5 considers the premature demise of PFE following its sale to Seagram and Working Title's subsequent integration into Seagram's major media subsidiary, Universal, between 1998 and 1999. While most of PFE's assets were sold to third parties or closed, Working Title became a component part of Universal, one of the 'Big Six' major Hollywood studios of the era. In the years that followed, Universal made a succession of deals with Bevan and Fellner which have ensured the company's continuous alignment with the studio for over twenty years. The second part of this chapter examines Universal's subsequent changes in ownership, which have seen the studio operate as a subsidiary of several other multinational conglomerates including Vivendi, General Electric and Comcast. During this time a series of deals were struck with companies such as Studiocanal, Relativity Media and Perfect World Pictures to co-finance Universal's film slates, including Working Title's output.

Chapter 6 again uses the concept of creative and commercial gatekeeping to examine Working Title's relationship with Universal between 1999 and 2006. Significantly, the company's transition between studios was marked by continuity as much as change, during which the three key stages of gatekeeping – development, green-lighting and distribution – remained in place. In this way, Working Title's exclusive production deal with Universal ensured that the company continued to receive annual overhead and development budgets from its parent company, and retained creative autonomy at the point of development. Equally, Universal also used centralised market forecasting to inform green-lighting decisions with the so-called 'ten-column' replacing the control sheet. Finally, distribution was also controlled by Universal and its sister studio, Focus Features, in the domestic market and by United International Pictures (UIP) in the international market. During this period, Working Title's output was shaped by Universal's 'portfolio' production strategy, which focused on a combination of low-budget 'portfolio' films, medium-budget 'event' films and big-budget 'tent-pole' films. In practice, Working Title's 'portfolio' films such as *Billy Elliot*, *Ali G Indahouse* (2002) and *Shaun of the Dead* (2004) were largely made through a subsidiary production company, WT^2, while its medium-budget 'event' films like *Bridget Jones's Diary*, *Johnny English* and *Nanny McPhee* (2005) were produced by the company directly.

Chapter 7 considers the evolution of Working Title's relationship with Universal between 2007 and 2012. During this period, the studio's production strategy shifted considerably, with an increased focus on the production of big-budget tent-pole films. For Working Title, this prompted the closure of WT², the increasing production of sequels such as *Mr. Bean's Holiday* (2007), *Nanny McPhee and the Big Bang* (2010) and *Johnny English Reborn* (2011) and a renewed emphasis on American action films and thrillers like *State of Play*, *Green Zone* (2010) and *Contraband*. Significantly, the reorientation of the company's production agenda was underpinned by changes in Universal's senior management, the impact of the global financial crisis and the reorganisation of the studio's international distribution and marketing infrastructure, most notably the break-up of UIP and the launch of its sister company, Universal Pictures International (UPI). Cutbacks at the studio also saw the temporary closure of WTTV and, for the first time, the production of films outside the company's exclusive contractual relationship with Universal.

Chapter 8 continues to examine Working Title's evolving relationship with Universal following the company's transition from an exclusive to a 'first-look' deal with the studio in 2012. This contractual realignment underlined Universal's continuing movement away from low- and medium-budget production and towards the titles of its key blockbuster franchises. During this period, Working Title's slate moved into the periphery of tent-pole territory for the first time with *Les Misérables* (2012) and *Cats* (2019), albeit with markedly different commercial results. Elsewhere, the company's output was defined by further sequels such as *Bridget Jones's Baby* (2016) and *Johnny English Strikes Again* (2018) and an increasing number of 'specialty' releases through Focus Features, including *The Theory of Everything*, *Darkest Hour* (2017) and *Victoria & Abdul* (2017). Significantly, Working Title's first-look deal also permitted the company to work with financing and distribution partners outside its relationship with Universal for the first time. Studiocanal financed and distributed *I Give It a Year* (2013), *Legend* and *King of Thieves* (2018), for example, while Sony Pictures did the same with *Grimsby* (2016) and *Baby Driver*. Finally, the relaunch of WTTV spearheaded Working Title's renewed interest in television production, with offices operating simultaneously in the UK and US for the first time.

Chapter 9 considers the market profile for Working Title's films by analysing the company's output in terms of its box office success in the worldwide marketplace. This begins with an examination of the distribution and marketing strategy behind the company's breakthrough hit, *Four Weddings and a Funeral*, which redefined box office expectations for British films in popular genres and inspired a string of so-called 'Curtisland' romantic comedies which became the bedrock of Working Title's success in the following years. Thereafter, the worldwide market for the company's films is considered in terms of its distribution between the 'domestic' (i.e. US and Canada), 'international' (i.e. all other territories) and UK market segments across the PFE and Universal eras. This analysis demonstrates a strong international market for Working Title's films, with the UK placed as the leading national component within this grouping. Moreover, the market profile for Working Title's films is placed in the context of the growth of the international marketplace, one of the most striking developments within the global film industry in the early twenty-first century.

Finally, Chapter 10 returns to the concept of Transatlantic British Cinema, once again viewed through the lens of political economy. Here, the evolving 'mid-level' industrial structures, processes and strategies which have defined Working Title's history are considered in terms of creative and commercial risk management. In doing so, this chapter examines the ways in which the mitigation of risk circumscribes the representational boundaries of Working Title's films and Transatlantic British Cinema at large, effectively determining the versions of Britain and Britishness which circulate in the mainstream of British and global film culture. Moreover, this translation is viewed in the context of the wider political, economic and social power dynamics which surround it. In turn, such factors raise the issue of diversity within the British film industry and British film culture, including the ways in which film policy has intervened in the production of Transatlantic British Cinema and its conceptual other, independent British cinema.

Some Notes on Methodology

The chapters which open and close this book cover a theoretical terrain which includes film studies, a discipline typically situated within the arts and humanities, and political economy, a subject area usually aligned with the social sciences. In doing so, both chapters are reliant upon a wealth of secondary material drawn from these fields to build a conceptual framework – Transatlantic British Cinema – through which to view both the history of Working Title and the history of British cinema. In contrast, the intervening chapters rely largely on the selection and use of primary research materials from four main sources: the national and international trade press; previously unpublished archival material; production and box office data and interviews with key industry players.

Using such primary data presents both opportunities and challenges. As Kenton T. Wilkinson and Patrick F. Merle (2013) point out, trade press coverage is a rich source of information that often provides detail that is unavailable elsewhere. This includes blow-by-blow accounts of the constant deal-making that surrounds the development, production and distribution of films as well as the mergers and acquisitions which structure the broader context within which such activity happens. Using trade press coverage uncritically, however, may serve to perpetuate industry myths, as this material often also acts as an extension of the public relations departments of powerful industry interests (ibid.: 419). Accordingly, it has been used in this book as a means of evidencing the factual granular details of the industry, rather than some of its more hyperbolic claims. In doing so, the BFI Library's collection of discontinued trade publications such as *AIP & Co.*, *Producer*, *Screen Finance* and *Monthly Film Bulletin* has been invaluable in researching Working Title's years as an independent production company. In contrast, later chapters rely more heavily on the major extant publications *Screen International*, *The Hollywood Reporter* and *Variety*.

The historical detail provided by the trade press has been further enhanced by access to two privately held archives which contain a wealth of material about both PolyGram Media Division and PolyGram Filmed Entertainment. These collections include, amongst other things, internal business reviews, acquisition contracts, company memos and box office reports. Such resources have, of course, proven especially valuable as they offer uniquely detailed insights into this period of Working Title's development. As a point of contrast, generating a historical account of Working Title's subsequent history as a subsidiary of Universal has relied to a much greater degree on publicly available information, particularly the trade press, a research context that is common to the study of most extant businesses. This account is also supplemented with the use of production and box office data which comes from the PolyGram archives, the BFI's Research and Statistics Unit and the most comprehensive publicly available sources, namely the Amazon-owned companies IMDb and Box Office Mojo.

Finally, this book makes extensive use of over thirty interviews with key industry players who have contributed, directly or indirectly, to the development of Working Title. As a matter of design, I did not pursue interviews with the writers, directors and actors directly responsible for the creation of Working Title's films. Instead, subjects are limited to the key members of staff who managed, or continue to manage, the day-to-day operations of the company and its successive parent companies, PFE and Universal. This includes Working Title Co-Chairmen, Tim Bevan and Eric Fellner, and its former directors, Sarah Radclyffe and Graham Bradstreet. Interviewees also include current and former Working Title departmental heads such as Liza Chasin, Jon Finn, Jane Frazer, Debra Hayward, David Livingstone, Angela Morrison, Alison Owen, Paul Webster, Natascha Wharton and Michelle Wright. Additionally, key PFE executives Michael

Kuhn, Malcolm Ritchie and Stewart Till have also been interviewed, as well as former Universal and UIP/UPI executives such as Andrew Cripps, David Kosse, Paul Oneile, Peter Smith and, once again, Stewart Till. Collectively, the voices of these industry players have greatly enhanced the story that this book sets out to tell.

CHAPTER 1

Transatlantic British Cinema and the Political Economy of Film

> [N]ational identity is by no means a fixed phenomenon, but constantly shifting, constantly in the process of becoming. The shared, collective identity which is implied always masks a whole range of internal differences and potential and actual antagonisms. The concept of national cinema is equally fluid, equally subject to ceaseless negotiations: while the discourses of film culture seek to hold it in place, it is abundantly clear that the concept is mobilised in different ways, by different commentators, for different reasons. (Higson 1995: 4)

> In its simplest guise, the transnational can be understood as the global forces that link people or institutions across nations. Key to transnationalism is the recognition of the decline of national sovereignty as a regulatory force in global coexistence. The impossibility of assigning a fixed national identity to much cinema reflects the dissolution of any stable connection between a film's place of production and/or setting and the nationality of its makers and performers. This is not in itself a new phenomenon; what is new are the conditions of financing, production, distribution and reception of cinema today. (Ezra & Rowden 2006: 1)

Constructing conceptual categories is one of the most pervasive forms of discourse within film studies and across the arts and humanities generally. It is also among the most problematic as established, revised or new conceptual boundaries become subject to scrutiny for their inclusions, exclusions and omissions. As the above quotations demonstrate, the categories of national and transnational cinema are no exceptions. In the first instance, 'national cinema' concedes substantive definition to its fluid, negotiable and variously mobilised nature. In the second, 'transnational cinema' identifies only the 'decline of national sovereignty as a regulatory force' and the 'impossibility of assigning a fixed national identity' as determinants. The possibility of imposing essentialist structures which regulate the boundaries of 'national cinema' or 'transnational cinema' have thus been met with the realisation that such monolithic categories are inherently diverse and unwieldy.

This problem has typically been dealt with by asserting particular mobilisations or sub-categories of national cinema by applying the label of nation, explicitly or implicitly, alongside one or more additional criteria such as genre (e.g. drama, comedy, documentary), authorship (directors, studios, writers) or period (silent cinema, World War II, 1960s). Discourse about British cinema has, for instance, generated various sub-national conceptual categories which use such markers. Well-known examples include the British Documentary Film Movement, the Gainsborough melodrama, the Ealing comedy and the British New Wave. Equally, the work of veteran filmmakers like Ken Loach and Mike Leigh, and more recently established talents such as Shane Meadows and Andrea Arnold, have ensured social realism remains a perennial feature of contemporary British cinema. Significantly, it is the very idea of national distinctiveness or specificity which has underpinned the conceptual construction of, and critical debate about, such film movements, cycles and canons. They are sub-categories of national cinema defined first and foremost by their deep-rooted connection to Britain.

Other well-known cycles of British cinema, however, demonstrate a transnational or, more specifically, transatlantic orientation. The longstanding dominance of the Hollywood film industry in the global marketplace has encouraged British studios and production companies to collaborate with Hollywood in the production and/or distribution of British films which seek to appeal to, and generate revenue from, global audiences. Well-known examples include the historical epics produced by London Films during the 1930s (*The Private Life of Henry VIII*, 1933; *The Four Feathers*, 1939) or the literary and theatrical adaptations of the Rank Organisation during the 1940s (*Great Expectations*, 1946; *Hamlet*, 1948) which were respectively distributed by United Artists (UA) and Universal in the US. Further examples are found in the James Bond films produced by Eon Productions during the 1960s (*Dr No*, 1962; *You Only Live Twice*, 1967) and the literary adaptations of EMI Films in the 1970s (*Murder on the Orient Express*, 1974; *Death on the Nile*, 1978), which were respectively distributed by UA and Paramount. More recently, the fantasy films produced by Heyday Films in the 2000s (*Harry Potter and the Philosopher's Stone*, 2001; *Harry Potter and the Half-Blood Prince*, 2009) and the historical dramas made by Working Title Films during the following decade (*Victoria & Abdul*, 2017; *Mary Queen of Scots*, 2018) were respectively financed and distributed by Warner Bros. and Universal and thus add further examples to this trend.

Remarking upon this distinction is not, of course, new in and of itself. Academic discourse about British cinema has repeatedly acknowledged the national or transnational market strategies open to British cinema (Higson 1989, 1995; Crofts 1993; Hill 1997; Street 1997). Despite the persistence of transatlantic activity between the film industries and cultures of Britain and Hollywood, however, it is the concept of national cinema which continues to dominate debates about British cinema. Dudley Andrew, for instance, stresses that the 'institution of film historiography' has long privileged 'the national' as 'textbooks, university courses, and museum screenings continue to parse cinematic output mainly by nation'. Foregrounding 'the national' has enshrined the belief that 'Every country – the mature ones at least – was thought to have its distinct industry, style, and thematic concerns' (Andrew 2009: 65). Indeed, the dominance of the national cinema paradigm ensures that its conceptual other, 'transnational cinema' is used far less frequently as an organising principle.

In this chapter, I propose a transnational conceptual category which I call 'Transatlantic British Cinema'. This space is defined, in the first instance, by a spectrum of interaction between the film industries of Britain and Hollywood which stretches from collaboration at one end to integration at the other. Secondly, Transatlantic British Cinema also entails hybridity between British and Hollywood cinema at a textual level, whereby the film cultures associated with each are, in various ways, merged. Thus, Transatlantic British Cinema straddles the conceptual divide between national and transnational cinema by suggesting a way of understanding the transnational cinema most closely related to a particular nation – Britain – and, more specifically, a way to interpret a particular orientation of that transnationalism: the transatlantic. This conceptual reinterpretation, in turn, relies upon more recent scholarship in the field of transnational cinema. Prior to undertaking this discussion, however, it is first necessary to consider the conceptual construction of British cinema as national cinema.

BRITISH CINEMA AS NATIONAL CINEMA

The concept of national cinema and more specifically British cinema as a form of national cinema enjoyed a significant wave of scholarly interest in the late 1980s and 1990s (Higson 1989, 1995; Crofts 1993; Hill 1997; Street 1997). Throughout this wealth of discourse, Hollywood has consistently been cited as an important determinant in the conceptual construction of British cinema. Hollywood's influence has, however, typically been understood as an external force which shapes British cinema from without, not within. In this way, the broader implications of Hollywood's global presence are acknowledged while primacy continues to be afforded to 'the national' by asserting a British film industry and culture which remain largely discrete from, and oppositional to, Hollywood. Thus, while the authors cited above each bring a distinct perspective to the debate they are, nonetheless, united by their adherence to positions which define British cinema in these terms.

Stephen Crofts' article *Reconceptualising National Cinema/s* is, for example, typical in its construction of national cinemas. He argues that most national cinemas, especially in the West, are 'defined against Hollywood' and consequently use strategies designed to combat the 'transnational reach' of the major studios (Crofts 1993: 49–50). Drawing on Crofts, John Hill identifies three such strategies which define the British experience. Firstly, there is the 'Imitating Hollywood' model in which British cinema attempts to 'beat Hollywood at its own game' by deliberately targeting a worldwide mass audience (ibid.: 56). As an industrial approach, international competition with Hollywood is, according to Hill:

> ... a strategy which has been tried at various junctures in the history of British cinema: by Alexander Korda in the 1930s, by Rank in the 1940s, by EMI in the 1970s, and by Goldcrest in the 1980s. Given the competitive advantage which Hollywood enjoys over other national industries by virtue of its scale of production, size of domestic market and international distribution and exhibition network (amongst other factors), this has proved an economically unviable strategy and, despite some success with individual films, all such attempts have resulted in financial disaster. (Hill 1997: 246)

A second category of national cinemas identified by Crofts, and appropriated by Hill, are 'European Commercial Cinemas', which 'compete, with varying degrees of success, with Hollywood product in domestic markets' (Crofts 1993: 54). For Hill, a cinema based upon this market-strategy existed in Britain between the 1930s and the 1970s before disappearing in step with the declining theatrical market (Hill 1997: 246). Prominent examples include genre films from studios such as Gainsborough Pictures, which specialised in melodramas (*The Man in Grey*, 1943; *The Wicked Lady*, 1945), Ealing Studios, famous for its comedies (*The Lavender Hill Mob*, 1951; *The Ladykillers*, 1955), popular comedy series like the *Carry On* films (1958–78), the *Doctor...* series (1954–70) beginning with *Doctor in the House* (1954) or the *Confessions...* series (1974–7), originating with *Confessions of a Window Cleaner* (1974).

The final category of national cinemas identified by Crofts and used by Hill are 'European-Model Art Cinemas'. This mode of production aims to 'differentiate itself textually from Hollywood, to assert explicitly or implicitly an indigenous product' and to reach domestic and international markets via 'those specialist distribution channels and exhibition venues usually called "art-house"' (Crofts 1993: 51). This model of production, however, only emerged within British cinema during the 1970s, and came to prominence in the following decade. Prior to this, histories of British cinema have typically identified the 'documentary-realist tradition', exemplified by the British Documentary Film Movement (*Drifters*, 1929; *Fires Were Started*, 1943) and the 'quality cinema' of theatrical and literary adaptation (*Henry V*, 1944; *Oliver Twist*, 1948) as substitutes (Hedling 1997: 178). From the 1980s onwards, however,

Hill argues that three strands of British filmmaking can be grouped under the umbrella term 'art cinema' (Hill 1997: 246–7). These include the realist tradition, expressed in the work of directors like Ken Loach (*Riff-Raff*, 1991; *My Name is Joe*, 1998), Mike Leigh (*Meantime*, 1983; *Secrets and Lies*, 1996) and Shane Meadows (*TwentyFourSeven*, 1997; *This is England*, 2006); the postmodern or avant-garde film, which is also the domain of auteur filmmakers like Derek Jarman (*Caravaggio*, 1986; *Wittgenstein*, 1993), Peter Greenaway (*The Cook, the Thief, His Wife & Her Lover*, 1989; *8 ½ Women*, 1999) and Patrick Keiller (*Robinson in Space*, 1997; *Robinson in Ruins*, 2010); and the 'heritage' category which remains dominated by adaptations of classic theatre and literature and historical films like *Henry V* (1989), *Sense and Sensibility* (1995) and *The King's Speech* (2010).

The tendency to conceive of British cinema as a set of oppositional industrial strategies defined against the transnational influence of Hollywood is further embedded by both Andrew Higson (1995) and Sarah Street (1997) in their respective monographs on the subject. Street repeats the assertion that British cinema may attempt to 'beat Hollywood at its own game', while acknowledging the 'profound impact' of Hollywood on the conception of British cinema. She suggests that domestic producers are caught in a 'perpetual bind' of market-related decision-making in which they must target a national or international audience via product differentiation or direct competition in response to Hollywood's dominance (Street 1997: 2). While Higson notes the strategies of product differentiation and direct competition, he also identifies two transnational strategies open to British filmmakers: collusion with Hollywood and other (non-US) forms of international co-operation. It is worth noting the choice of terminology here. The word 'collusion' carries connotations of secrecy or even treachery and is conceived of as the joint Anglo-American exploitation of the UK distribution and exhibition markets for the benefit of Hollywood companies. The much more conciliatory term 'co-operation' is, however, used to describe the potential European alliances that might be forged as a challenge to Hollywood's dominance (Higson 1995: 9–13).

Significantly, the discrete and oppositional status of 'the national' has endured when the relationship between the film industries and cultures of Britain and Hollywood has been considered in a direct manner. In *Britain and the American Cinema* (2001), for example, Tom Ryall examines US involvement in the British film industry, British success in the US market and the appropriation of British culture in Hollywood films. Similarly, in *Transatlantic Crossings* (2002), Sarah Street explores, amongst other things, patterns of economic negotiation between the British and Hollywood film industries, issues of cultural exchange and cross-cultural reception. Thus, while both studies examine transnational exchange, they do so from the perspective of national cinema. This insistence on using national markers of interpretation and enquiry, albeit in the context of transatlantic exchange, fails to capture the inherently transnational properties of what I am calling Transatlantic British Cinema.

Other than Higson's narrow interpretation of collusion with Hollywood, the dynamic which persists in governing all of these conceptions of British cinema is their oppositional relationship to Hollywood. The claim that British cinema has intermittently competed with Hollywood in the international marketplace is often asserted but rarely scrutinised. In privileging the strategies of competition and differentiation, accounts of British cinema have typically misrepresented, underplayed or omitted the transnational, or more specifically the *transatlantic*, as an important and sometimes defining element in much of British cinema. While not explicitly contributing to a conceptual debate, Paul McDonald comes the closest to reorienting the discussion in this direction by acknowledging that:

> Hollywood is internally part of the very substance of the film industry in Britain. So deep and long-standing are the interactions between Britain and Hollywood that any sense of a cinema industry or industries in Britain can only reasonably be defined as the collection of commercial actions and reactions by which British producers, distributors, exhibitors, and cinemagoers have embraced, willingly collaborated with, unwillingly collaborated with, or actively resisted the involvement of Hollywood in the film culture of the UK. (McDonald 2008: 220)

To effectively examine the relationship between the film industries and cultures of Britain and Hollywood from this perspective requires a conceptual approach that integrates more recent scholarship about cinematic transnationalism. What follows draws extensively on the work of Mette Hjort (2009), which substantially informs the conceptual construction of what I call Transatlantic British Cinema.

TOWARDS A TYPOLOGY OF TRANSATLANTIC BRITISH CINEMA

It is helpful to define what I mean by 'British' before addressing the 'Transatlantic' in Transatlantic British Cinema. As Higson (1989) argues, the concept of national cinema can be mobilised in four ways, namely from economic, text-based, consumption-based and criticism-led perspectives. Two of these are relevant here. Firstly, Transatlantic British Cinema is British in its legal status of origin, which establishes a 'conceptual correspondence between "national cinema" and "the domestic film industry"' (Higson 1989: 36). As John Hill (2016) points out, British cinema has been defined in such economic terms by UK government film policies since the 1920s in response to the dominance of Hollywood. Secondly, Transatlantic British Cinema is also British in a 'text-based' sense insofar as any given example must demonstrate a commitment to the national onscreen (Higson 1989: 36). I use this marker in a relatively loose sense to indicate films which, to a greater or lesser degree, feature British characters and/or settings and/or cultural themes. Examples of Transatlantic British Cinema, then, are British products from both economic and textual perspectives.

In contrast, explaining the 'Transatlantic' in Transatlantic British Cinema, requires an engagement with the study of cinematic transnationalism. The preferred conceptual approach within this area of scholarship has been to develop broad typologies which act as matrices through which specific examples or cycles of cinema might be interpreted. Mette Hjort, for instance, argues that transnational cinema can be understood as several different (and potentially overlapping) strategies which operate at both industrial and textual levels. Three of the strategies which she identifies are relevant to my discussion of Transatlantic British Cinema, namely opportunistic, globalising and affinitive transnationalism. 'Opportunistic transnationalism' entails simply 'responding to available economic opportunities at a given moment in time' (Hjort 2009: 19). For the purposes of this book, however, Hjort's term will be substituted for the more general category 'economic transnationalism', to acknowledge the prioritisation of economic matters without necessarily implying the expediency or short-term gain suggested by the word 'opportunistic'. Secondly, 'globalising transnationalism' involves making films which have 'spectacular production values secured through transnational capital flows' and which operate in tandem with 'many of the genre- and star-based vehicles of transnational appeal' (ibid.: 21–2). Finally, 'affinitive transnationalism' is epitomised by efforts to communicate across borders with similar nations and peoples. In this case similarity or 'affinity' is understood in terms of 'ethnicity, partially overlapping or mutually intelligible languages, and a history of interaction giving rise to shared core values, common practices, and comparable institutions' (ibid.: 17).

Taken together, the strategies of economic, globalising and affinitive transnationalism define the substance of Transatlantic British Cinema and respectively work to reduce the industrial, formal and cultural distance between British and Hollywood cinema. It is worth asserting here that combining these strategies does not necessarily constitute a recipe for commercial success, but rather the ambition to achieve this end. Equally, any given example of Transatlantic British Cinema may display a greater or lesser degree of orientation towards each or any of these three inclinations. Accordingly, the strongest examples will explicitly embrace economic, globalising and affinitive strategies, whereas weaker cases will do so at a more implicit level, or foreground one strategy while another recedes.

Positioning Working Title Films within the conceptual framework of

Transatlantic British Cinema does not suggest that these strategies are new or unique. As I have argued elsewhere (2014), British studios operating in the 1930s and 1940s such as London Films, the Rank Organisation and MGM-British can also be positioned within this conceptual framework. These film businesses were, of course, very different from Working Title precisely because they were studios rather than production companies. Accordingly, they owned and operated the production facilities in which their films were made and, to varying degrees, the distribution and exhibition infrastructures through which they were released. Nonetheless, the strategies of economic, globalising and affinitive transnationalism remained common to the operation of these studios, a fact which places Working Title within a broader history of continuity, rather than exception.

As the chapters in this book suggest, Working Title has moved between three major states of ownership: the independent years (1984–8) the PolyGram years (1988–98) and the Universal years (1998–present). During the first of these, the company produced films within an industrial context that broadly aligns with the 'European-Model Art Cinemas' described above and is thus separate from a discussion of Transatlantic British Cinema. What follows, then, outlines the creative and commercial history of Working Title Films during its years as a subsidiary of PolyGram and Universal in order to align both the company and its output with the strategies of economic, globalising and affinitive transnationalism and thus the concept of Transatlantic British Cinema.

Economic Transnationalism

As a business strategy, economic transnationalism relates to the industrial relationships which link British studios or production companies to financing and/or distribution and marketing for their output via the major Hollywood studios. Occasionally, however, economic transnationalism has also been pursued by studios outside this grouping which have briefly emulated the business functions of the majors. Such relationships are transatlantic in the first instance because these institutions are based in the US, primarily in and around Los Angeles. In the second instance, however, the relationship is global as the industrial infrastructures which these businesses support distribute and market their products on a worldwide basis. Such relationships effectively align Transatlantic British Cinema with Hollywood cinema from an industrial perspective.

Working Title's first parent company, PolyGram Filmed Entertainment (PFE), was launched by PolyGram, one of the 'Big Six' major record companies of the era. As a subsidiary of PFE, Working Title was provided with annual overhead and development budgets and operated as an internal business within a nascent studio system. Despite its European ownership, PFE was headquartered in Los Angeles and, over the course of the 1990s, built a distribution and marketing infrastructure with worldwide ambitions. Significantly, the initial stages of this process were undertaken in collaboration with Hollywood majors. This included, for example, the establishment of the US distribution company, Gramercy Pictures, as a joint venture with Universal for the company's 'specialty' output and so-called 'rent-a-studio' deals with other Hollywood studios for its mainstream fare. In its final years of operation, however, PFE briefly competed with the major Hollywood studios directly by acquiring Gramercy outright, launching a second US distribution company, PolyGram Films, and establishing direct distribution and marketing subsidiaries which covered thirteen international territories. This remarkable example of studio-building came to an end in 1998, however, when Universal's former parent company, Seagram, acquired both PolyGram and PFE.

Working Title was one of the key assets integrated into Universal following Seagram's acquisition of PFE. Accordingly, the company also received annual overhead and development budgets from its new parent company and continued to operate as an internal business within a studio system. Unlike PFE, however, Universal was one of the so-called 'Big Six' Hollywood studios, a global entertainment oligopoly that also included Disney, Paramount, Sony, Twentieth Century Fox and Warner Bros. Universal Studios, for example, originally consisted of three major divisions – Universal Pictures, Universal Parks & Resorts and Universal Music Group – the former of which included the US distribution and marketing operations, Universal and Focus Features, in addition to international distribution and marketing subsidiaries in thirty-five territories. In the years that followed, ownership of Universal passed between a succession of multinational conglomerates including Vivendi, General Electric and Comcast, each of which reconfigured the studio's position within a new corporate landscape. In 2004, for instance, General Electric subsumed Universal into NBCUniversal, which combined the studio with the assets of the major US television network, NBC. More recently, Comcast acquired another studio, Dreamworks Animation, and Sky, the largest media conglomerate headquartered in Europe.

GLOBALISING TRANSNATIONALISM

As a production strategy, globalising transnationalism relates to film form and involves producing films in popular genres, with star actors and high production values. The relationship is transatlantic in the first instance because the strategy of combining these creative precepts originated with, and is most consistently pursued in, Hollywood cinema. In the second instance this relationship is, once again, global, because these features ensure a broad appeal to worldwide audiences already familiar with and receptive to such qualities in Hollywood films. These textual strategies effectively link Transatlantic British Cinema with Hollywood cinema from a formal perspective.

The Transatlantic British Cinema produced by Working Title has, for example, largely conformed to the conventions of four popular genres: romantic comedy, family films, period dramas and comedies. Undoubtedly the most commercially successful and high-profile of these genres is the romantic comedy. At the centre of this success is a canon of Working Title romcoms written by Richard Curtis including *Four Weddings and a Funeral* (1994), *Notting Hill* (1999), *Bridget Jones's Diary* (2001), *Love Actually* (2003), *Bridget Jones: The Edge of Reason* (2004), *About Time* (2013) and *Yesterday* (2019). This is followed by such titles as *About A Boy* (2002), *Wimbledon* (2004) and *Bridget Jones's Baby* (2016) as well as lesser-known films like *What Rats Won't Do* (1998) and *I Give It a Year* (2013). In contrast, Working Title's family films, many of which are also comedies, are led by the extraordinary success of the Rowan Atkinson vehicles *Bean* (1997), *Mr. Bean's Holiday* (2007) and a trilogy of spy spoofs: *Johnny English* (2003), *Johnny English Reborn* (2011) and *Johnny English Strikes Again* (2018). This list is supplemented with such titles as *Nanny McPhee* (2005) and *Nanny McPhee and the Big Bang* (2010) as well as *Loch Ness* (1996), *The Borrowers* (1997), *Thunderbirds* (2004) and *The Kid Who Would Be King* (2019).

The period drama is Working Title's next largest genre output and includes both biographical films and adaptations of classic or contemporary literature. The life and times of monarchs is, for example, the essential subject matter of *Elizabeth* (1998), *Elizabeth: The Golden Age* (2007), *Victoria & Abdul* (2017) and *Mary Queen of Scots* (2018), while *Frost/Nixon* (2008), *Rush* (2013), *The Theory of Everything* (2014) and *Darkest Hour* (2017) portray a range of great twentieth-century lives with subjects that include David Frost, James Hunt, Stephen Hawking and Winston Churchill. Less frequently, Working Title has adapted classic literature including the Jane Austen novels *Pride & Prejudice* (2005) and *Emma* (2020) or very occasionally contemporary literature with a period setting such as *Atonement* (2007). Working Title comedies which sit outside of the romcom or family film categories include *Hot Fuzz* (2007), *Paul* (2011) and *The World's End* (2013) as well as titles like *Plunkett & Macleane* (1999), *Wild Child* (2008), *The Boat that Rocked* (2009) and *Grimsby* (2016).

The star power associated with these films is, of course, another highly significant factor in their global appeal. The films listed above, and the broader Working Title canon, feature the most prominent British stars of multiple generations, many of whom have given career-making or -defining performances in the company's films. Male actors range from Gary Oldman, Hugh Grant,

Colin Firth and Rowan Atkinson to James McAvoy, Benedict Cumberbatch, Eddie Redmayne and Tom Hardy. The list of their female counterparts is no less impressive. Judi Dench, Julie Walters, Emma Thompson and Kristin Scott Thomas are accompanied by the likes of Keira Knightley, Rosamund Pike, Felicity Jones and Lily James. Such names are, of course, supplemented by a myriad of well-known supporting actors including Jim Broadbent, Brenda Blethyn, Tom Hollander, Rachel Weisz, Bill Nighy, Shirley Henderson, Rhys Ifans, Kelly Macdonald and Alan Rickman, to name a few.

The production values associated with Working Title's films are perhaps best indicated by the range of production budgets within which the company works. While the company's largest-scale American productions like *The Interpreter* (2005), *State of Play* (2009) and *Green Zone* (2010) were budgeted between $60 million and $100 million, Working Title's Transatlantic British Cinema is typically more modestly budgeted. Romantic comedies, family films and comedies, like *Notting Hill*, *Johnny English*, *Paul*, *Nanny McPhee and the Big Bang* and *Bridget Jones's Baby* fall within the $30–$45 million bracket, for example, whereas period dramas like *Elizabeth*, *Pride & Prejudice*, *Atonement*, *The Theory of Everything* and *Darkest Hour* remain in the $15–$30 million range.[1] Such budgets ensure that Working Title's films attain the production values typical of Hollywood films in the same genres.

Working Title's films are, however, less easily grouped in terms of globalising transnationalism when the output of its former low-budget subsidiary, WT[2], is also considered. Films such as *Billy Elliot* (2000), *Mickybo and Me* (2004), *Inside I'm Dancing* (2004) and *Sixty Six* (2006), for example, mix the genre conventions of the comedy-drama with British social realism, while the comic origins of *Ali G Indahouse* (2002) and *Shaun of the Dead* (2004) can both be found on British television (as, indeed, can the origins of *Bean* and *Mr. Bean's Holiday*). In turn, most of these films feature actors who were, at the time of release, either untried or familiar only to UK audiences, including Jamie Bell, Romola Garai, Sacha Baron Cohen, Billie Piper and Simon Pegg. Similarly, diminished production values are also associated with these titles, with each film realised on a budget of $5 million or less.

AFFINITIVE TRANSNATIONALISM

As a production strategy, affinitive transnationalism relates to content and involves producing films which forge links between similar cultures and people through the representation of characters and/or settings and/or cultural themes which draw on and enhance existing affinities. As Hjort notes, transnational strategies may be 'marked', whereby attention is intentionally drawn towards the transnational elements in the text, or they may be 'unmarked' where transnationalism remains a contextual factor (Hjort 2009: 13–14). It is useful to draw on this distinction in relation to Transatlantic British Cinema at a purely textual level to highlight the spectrum of available affinitive strategies. In doing so, it is possible to differentiate between marked affinitive transnationalism, which is explicitly transatlantic, and unmarked affinitive transnationalism, which is only implicitly so. Such strategies are, once again, transatlantic in the first instance because they form a dialogue, directly or indirectly, between British and American culture onscreen. They are, however, global in the second instance because the films that emerge from this process are calculated to appeal to audiences worldwide. Such affinities effectively link Transatlantic British Cinema with Hollywood cinema from a cultural perspective.

The relationship between Britain and the United States is, of course, inherently affinitive in the way that Hjort describes, including the use of a shared language, a long history of interaction, common core values and practices and comparable institutions. Such affinities are most directly drawn upon in Working Title's romantic comedies, which often exemplify *marked* transatlantic affinity by placing American characters in British settings. Prominent examples include *Four Weddings and a Funeral*, *Notting Hill*, *Love Actually*, *Wimbledon*, *I Give it a Year*, *About Time* and *Bridget Jones's Baby*. As Annabelle Honess Roe (2009) notes, the relationships between such characters in Working Title's romcoms use the dramatic premise of the culture clash to play out the 'special relationship' between the two nations. In doing so, many of the stereotypical cultural tropes associated with each are enacted, typically leading to a successful romantic and national union. This strategy is also occasionally used in the opposite direction, when British characters are placed in American settings. This is true of comedies like *Bean* and *Paul*, the romantic comedy *Yesterday* and the period drama *Frost/Nixon*, all of which also use the transatlantic culture clash as a comic or dramatic foil, albeit in different ways. Expanding upon these themes, Tobias Hochscherf and James Leggott suggest that:

> … Working Title has been at the forefront of establishing ways of working with and according to the models of major Hollywood studios in order to produce profitable films with high production values aimed at largely middle-class, affluent audiences. As a potpourri of British and American characteristics, its films have repeatedly used an array of American and British performers in lead roles, often connected with Hollywood genres such as romantic comedy and horror, whilst also extending and exporting indigenous traditions of comedy and costume drama. Some of its most popular films also deal with Anglo-American culture clashes on both an aesthetic and narrative level, thematising cultural difference whilst adopting a formally populist approach. (Hochscherf & Leggott 2010: 9–10)

In contrast, the strategy of affinitive transnationalism can also be used in *unmarked* ways. One common approach within the Working Title canon is the reproduction of the dominant versions of Britain and Britishness that have long circulated in both Transatlantic British Cinema and Hollywood cinema. This is evident in many of Working Title's period dramas, which draw upon the established fame or notoriety of British (or English, Scottish, etc.) historical figures, events and eras as a means of enhancing transnational affinity. As James Chapman argues, the British historical film often promotes the popular 'myths' of the historical experience which tend to align with 'narratives of national greatness', including, most prominently, the Tudor period, the Victorian era and World War II (Chapman 2005: 6–7). *Elizabeth*, *Elizabeth: The Golden Age* and *Mary Queen of Scots* are, for example, set in the Tudor period, *Victoria & Abdul* in the late Victorian era and *Atonement* and *Darkest Hour* before and during World War II. While *Pride & Prejudice* and *Emma* are set in the lesser used Regency era, any deficit in period familiarity is eclipsed by the pre-sold status of Jane Austen's novels and their multiple adaptations on film and television. Interestingly, the family films *Nanny McPhee* and *Nanny McPhee and the Big Bang* are respectively set during the Victorian era and World War II, and underline the preference for such historical representations outside the period drama.

Several of Working Title's contemporary comedies, however, ostensibly buck the trend towards affinitive transnationalism. The films of the so-called 'Three Flavours Cornetto Trilogy', for example, which includes *Shaun of the Dead*, *Hot Fuzz* and *The World's End* are all set in decidedly ordinary regional and suburban English locales and feature characters with equally ordinary working- and middle-class lives. In each case this sense of the everyday is, however, soon disrupted by extraordinary events which ignite extended genre parodies. *Shaun of the Dead*, for example, spoofs the zombie movie, while *Hot Fuzz* sends up the buddy cop genre and *The World's End* lampoons the apocalyptic science-fiction film. In this way, the trilogy uses unmarked transatlantic affinity by engaging with archetypal Hollywood genres and applying them to British settings. In reference to *Shaun of the Dead*, for example, Lindsey Decker (2016) describes this situation as an instance of 'transnational genre hybridity', noting the numerous homages to American popular culture as well as the debt to traditions of British comedy. Genre parody is also used as an affinitive strategy in the *Johnny English* trilogy, for instance, which harnesses the spy genre, most notably the James Bond film series, as its comic foil. Elsewhere, the 'pre-sold' appeal of British popular culture in America and globally is used in a more direct way with the appropriation of Arthurian legend in *The Kid Who Would be King* (2019), the music of The Beatles in *Yesterday* (2019) and the adaptation of an internationally successful stage musical in *Cats* (2019).

On first inspection, much of WT²'s output also appears to eschew affinitive transnationalism as a textual strategy. *Billy Elliot*, *Mickybo and Me*, *Inside I'm Dancing* and *Sixty Six*, for example, all draw on the tradition of British social realism by depicting the troubled lives of adolescent boys or young men in a range of metropolitan, regional and national settings. As Samantha Lay argues, social realism has 'always been a somewhat marginal, sometimes oppositional mode of expression that has relied – to varying degrees – on its otherness from more mainstream film products as a distinguishing feature' (Lay 2007: 233). Such 'otherness' is, however, mitigated by the application of Hollywood dramaturgy to these films, which foregrounds universalistic triumph-over-adversity narratives. Under these conditions, the range of settings on offer do not prove to be deterministic. Indeed, the protagonists situated within them are either propelled out of these problematic environments or reshape them according to their needs. In this way, the natural inclination of social realism towards social critique is curbed and these films are reoriented towards mainstream film culture.

FROM TRANSATLANTIC BRITISH CINEMA TO THE POLITICAL ECONOMY OF FILM

As I have argued, Transatlantic British Cinema employs three strategies – economic, globalising and affinitive transnationalism – which respectively reduce the industrial, formal and cultural distance between British and Hollywood cinema. This conceptual category, however, remains broadly descriptive, offering a typology through which to identify various transnational characteristics rather than addressing deeper questions about the power relations which shape its production, distribution and consumption. In order to delve further into this area, it is necessary to take up a different set of conceptual tools, namely those provided by political economy. As Vincent Mosco explains, political economy can be defined as the study of '*the social relations, particularly the power relations, that mutually constitute the production, distribution, and consumption of resources*' (Mosco 2009: 24; emphasis original). Classical political economy, he notes, began during the Enlightenment and focused on applying scientific methods to the study of eighteenth- and nineteenth-century capitalism. Thereafter, this intellectual terrain has been occupied by various schools of thought, including Marxist, conservative, neoclassical, feminist and environmental positions (ibid.: 37–64).

Despite the diversity of critical perspectives that have been pursued within the ambit of political economy, Mosco outlines a set of 'central qualities' that characterise the approach, which include the study of social change and history, social totality, moral philosophy and praxis. Focusing upon social change and history, for example, involves examining the 'dynamic forces of capitalism' that are responsible for growth and change in society in the long and short term. In contrast, social totality takes a holistic approach that seeks to combine various disciplines in order to understand the relationship between the political and the economic, including the connections between institutions, commodities, social relations and the forces of hegemony. Moral philosophy, on the other hand, insists that analysis of the economic system must be accompanied by a consideration of the moral issues associated with it. Finally, praxis orients the work of political economy away from theory and towards practice with the ambition of actual social change (ibid.: 26–36). When the political economy approach is applied to the 'products of communication', Mosco argues, it raises important questions about the underlying structures and processes which shape their production, distribution and consumption:

> This formulation has a certain practical value for students of communication because it calls attention to fundamental forces and processes at work in the marketplace. It emphasizes how a company produces a film or a magazine, how it deals with those who distribute the product and market it, and how consumers decide about what to watch, read, or listen to. Finally, it considers how consumer decisions are fed back into the process of producing new products. But political economy takes this a step further because it asks us to concentrate on a specific set of social relations organised around *power* or the ability to control other people, processes, and things, even in the face of resistance. This would lead the political economist of communication to look at shifting forms of control along the circuit of production, distribution, and consumption. (Ibid. 2009: 24)

In her book *How Hollywood Works*, Janet Wasko draws on this conceptual framework to develop a sub-discipline which she describes as the 'political economy of film'. Here, the focus is on the study of films as commodities which are produced, distributed and consumed within a capitalist industrial system, namely the Hollywood film industry. Moreover, this approach questions the political and ideological implications of this system by insisting that film must be 'placed within an entire social, economic, and political context and critiqued in terms of the contribution to maintaining and reproducing structures of power' (Wasko 2003: 10). In pursuing these ends, Wasko identifies four prominent 'illusions' at work in the film industry, which she expresses in the form of well-known aphorisms that demand critical interrogation. 'There's no business like show business', for example, relays the common assertion that the film industry is a unique and inherently risky business. In contrast, 'It's a dog-eat-dog business', suggests that the film industry is extremely competitive. Related to the notion of competition, '… a supremely democratic form of entertainment' implies that the film industry offers a wide range of choice, the demand for which is determined by the audience. Finally, 'That's entertainment!' highlights the assertion that Hollywood films merely entertain audiences, rather than functioning as ideological products (ibid.: 222–4).

The approach of political economy within the field of media industries research has, however, been subject to criticism in recent years for its perceived limitations. Timothy Havens, Amanda D. Lotz and Serra Tinic (2009), for example, argue that the discipline is not only too far removed from the immediate industrial structures, processes and practices which collectively create media texts, but also from meaningful assessment of the texts which emerge from this activity. The authors favour a research approach which they call 'critical media industry studies', which uses 'mid-level' fieldwork to achieve a 'helicopter' level view of the media industries. This allows, they contend, 'much finer detail, albeit with narrower scope' when compared to the 'jet plane' perspective provided by political economy, from which 'many details are obscured' (Havens et al. 2009: 239). As they go on to argue:

> The limitation we find with critical political economy approaches to the media industries results from their consistent focus on the larger level operations of media institutions, general inattention to entertainment programming, the incomplete explanation of the role of human agents (other than those at the pinnacle of conglomerate hierarchies) in interpreting, focusing, and redirecting economic forces that provide for complexity and contradiction within media industries. Overall, there is a general neglect of quotidian practices and competing goals, which are not subject to direct and regular oversight by corporate owners, and which define the experiences of those who work within the industry. Similarly, if and when popular culture is considered within a political-economic analysis, there is a reductionist tendency to treat it as yet another form of commodified culture operating only according to the interests of capital. (Ibid.: 236)

Such criticism prompted a robust defence of political economy by some of its leading proponents. Eileen R. Meehan and Janet Wasko, for example, argue that such attacks 'caricature' political economy by misrepresenting the scope and diversity of research conducted under its ambit. Amongst other things, they point to the growing body of scholarship which draws on political economy traditions to examine such industries as film, television, social media and digital games, as well as labour at various levels of the industry (Meehan & Wasko 2013: 48–9). Moreover, the authors note a fundamental distinction which separates political economy approaches from those of media economics and more recently established fields such as Media Industry Studies and production studies. For Meehan and Wasko, media economics 'celebrates the individuals, working cohorts, companies, and markets constituting the entertainment-information sector' while political economy of the media 'contextualizes those individuals, working cohorts, companies, and markets within the ongoing development of capitalism' (Wasko & Meehan 2013: 150). In doing so, the authors argue that those working in the contextual tradition are 'keenly aware that research must address not only media corporations and markets but also the people whose collective labour creates media artifacts, the artifacts themselves, and the people who engage with or are exposed to those artifacts' (ibid.: 153).

Accordingly, the tradition of political economy is used here to situate the concept of Transatlantic British Cinema within the larger context of its production, distribution and consumption, namely capitalism. This task is undertaken by working primarily at the 'mid-level' of analysis which involves examining the structures, processes and strategies which have defined the operation of Working Title as a business throughout a series of evolving industrial contexts. In doing so, many of the criticisms of political economy are addressed by providing a historical account of a production company which deals squarely with 'the role of human agents' in the production, distribution and consumption of 'entertainment programming'. Indeed, Working Title's journey from an independent to a subsidiary of a major Hollywood studio is charted in the chapters which follow before the concept of Transatlantic British Cinema is reintroduced in the final chapter, which considers the company's output at a textual level. Here, conclusions are drawn which transcend the 'reductionist tendency' to view such texts as 'operating only according to the interests of capital'. Rather, Working Title's films are placed within the wider social, economic and political contexts from which they have emerged and, in line with the broader objectives of political economy, are critiqued in relation to their role in maintaining the power relations inherent within these contexts.

In what remains of this chapter, however, Transatlantic British Cinema is positioned within the tradition of political economy at the macro level of analysis. Initially, this involves drawing a distinction between Transatlantic British Cinema and its conceptual other, independent British cinema. Thereafter, a range of the British Film Institute (BFI) data is used to illustrate the ways in which these parallel industrial modes of production are subject to starkly different conditions along the circuit of production, distribution and exhibition. In doing so, two of Wasko's (2003) film industry 'illusions' are invoked – 'It's a dog-eat-dog business' and '… a supremely democratic form of entertainment' – when considering the fundamental issues that arise from this discussion, namely competition and diversity in the marketplace. Moreover, this situation is considered in relation to the evolution of British film policy over the last thirty years, which has involved a notable shift in emphasis from 'interventionist' to 'market-friendly' strategies which have served to exacerbate the disparity of public resources available to Transatlantic British Cinema and independent British cinema. In sum, the picture is one of increasing Hollywood domination of both the British film industry and of British film culture.

A Divided Industry: Transatlantic British Cinema and Independent British Cinema

From an industrial perspective there are, broadly speaking, two versions of British cinema which run in parallel: Transatlantic British Cinema and independent British cinema. As I have argued, the former is defined by economic transnationalism, which links British production companies to the integrated financing, distribution and marketing functions of the major Hollywood studios. In contrast, the latter is defined by unintegrated configurations of smaller companies which inhabit a wide range of industrial contexts. At one end of the spectrum, are the myriad of production companies, financiers, sales agents, distributors, broadcasters and public funding bodies which typically combine around the production of a single film. At the other, are the so-called 'mini-major' studios, which combine some of the financing, production, sales, distribution and marketing functions of the Hollywood studios, albeit at a much reduced scale. While Transatlantic British Cinema and independent British cinema often remain discrete modes of production, they also intermittently intersect. The Hollywood studios may, for example, acquire distribution rights to independently produced films, while independent distributors, on occasion, acquire the distribution rights to Hollywood films.

The diversity of industrial contexts within the independent sector is, of course, accompanied by a diversity of production strategies. Independent British cinema continues to encompass the British commercial and art cinemas identified by Crofts (1993) and Hill (1997). Since the 2000s, the British commercial cinema has been partially revived through the intermittent production of films based upon popular television shows like *The Inbetweeners Movie* (2011), *Mrs. Brown's Boys D'Movie* (2014) and *Absolutely Fabulous: The Movie* (2016) as well as low-budget crime film series including *Green Street ...* (2005–9), the *Kidulthood* trilogy (2006–16) and the *Rise of the Footsoldier ...* (2007–19) films. Simultaneously, various shades of British art cinema continue to be created by filmmakers like Ken Loach (*I, Daniel Blake*, 2016; *Sorry We Missed You*, 2019), Mike Leigh (*Mr. Turner*, 2014; *Peterloo*, 2018), Clio Barnard (*The Selfish Giant*, 2013; *Dark River*, 2017) and Shola Amoo (*A Moving Image*, 2016; *The Last Tree*, 2019). In contrast, mini-majors such as Entertainment One, Studiocanal and Lionsgate often pursue the strategies of globalising and affinitive transnationalism associated with Transatlantic British Cinema in an attempt to compete with the output of the major Hollywood studios. Studiocanal has, for example, been particularly active in this area in recent years with titles such as *Paddington* (2014), *Shaun the Sheep Movie* (2015) and *Early Man* (2018).

The broad distinctions between Transatlantic British Cinema and independent British cinema can be seen in the data produced by the BFI's Research and Statistics Unit (RSU), which records UK production activity in the three constituent categories: 'Inward Investment', 'Domestic' and 'Co-production'. Here, inward investment designates a film which is 'substantially financed and controlled from outside the UK and which is attracted to the UK by script requirements (e.g. locations) and/or the UK's filmmaking infrastructure and/or UK film tax relief'. In contrast, a domestic 'indigenous' film is 'made by a UK production company that is produced wholly or partly in the UK', while a co-production is a film made by 'companies from more than one country, often under the terms of a bilateral co-production treaty or the European Convention on Cinematographic Co-production'[2] (BFI 2019a: 173). Significantly, inward-investment films broadly align with the activity of the major Hollywood studios, while domestic films and co-productions are typically the preserve of independent British cinema.

Figure 1.1 shows all UK films produced between 1992 and 2017 divided into the three constituent categories. Despite a change in the methodology used to collect this data, which divides the time frame into two distinct periods, it is possible to establish some underlying trends across the entire period.[3] The total rate of production increased dramatically between 1992 and 2010, rising from just thirty films to 374, with an average annual output of just over 200 films per year across the entire period. Within this landscape, domestic

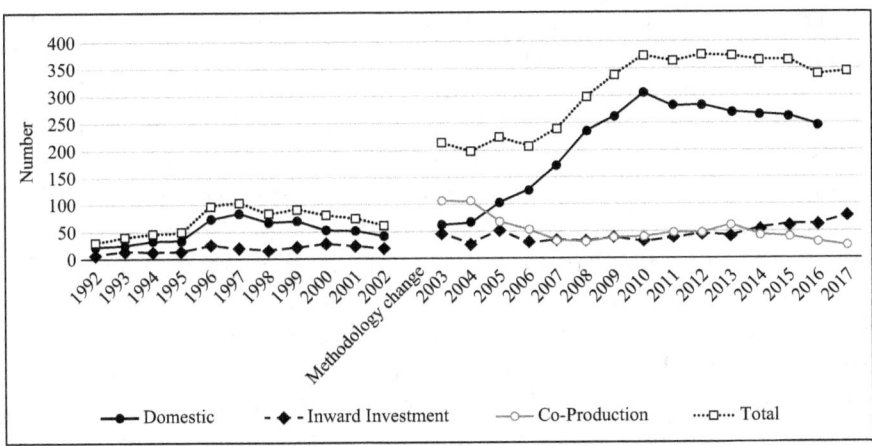

Figure 1.1 Total number of UK films by production category, 1992–2017.
Source: BFI RSU 2020

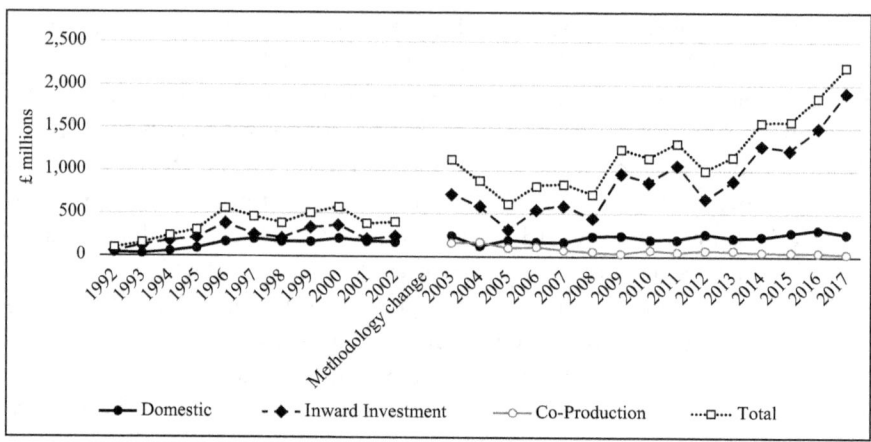

Figure 1.2 Total spend on UK films by production category, 1992–2017.
Source: BFI RSU 2020.

films have virtually always been the most frequently produced category, with numbers rising from just twenty-two in 1992 to 305 in 2010, with an average of 143 per year. In contrast, the number of inward-investment films has risen more modestly, ranging from eight in 1992 to seventy-eight in 2017, with an average of just over thirty-three per year. Finally, the number of co-productions has fallen over time, with a high of 106 in 2003 and a low of twenty-three in 2017, with an average rate of just over fifty films a year between 2003 and 2017.

As Figure 1.2 shows, total spending on UK production has also increased dramatically over time, rising from £98.4 million in 1992 to just over £2.2 billion in 2017. The disparity in resources available to the three categories of production is, however, substantial. Total spending on domestic films, for example, rose from £30.3 million in 1993 to £320.5 million in 2016, with an average annual spend of £186.7 million. In contrast, total spending on inward-investment films rose sharply from just £58.5 million in 1992 to £1.9 billion in 2017, with an average annual spend of £624 million across the entire period. The only category to see a decline in total spending is co-production, which fell from a high of £169.1 million in 2004 to just £32.2 million in 2017, with an average annual expenditure of £77 million between 2003 and 2017.

As Figure 1.3 shows, there are, unsurprisingly, also marked differences between average spend per film across the three categories of production. The average spend on domestic films, for example, rose to a high of just over £4 million in 2000 before falling to a low of £0.6 million in 2010, with an average spend of just over £1.8 million across the entire period. In contrast, average spend on inward-investment films rose from just £7.3 million in 1992 to £29.1 million in 2010, with an average spend of £16.9 million across the

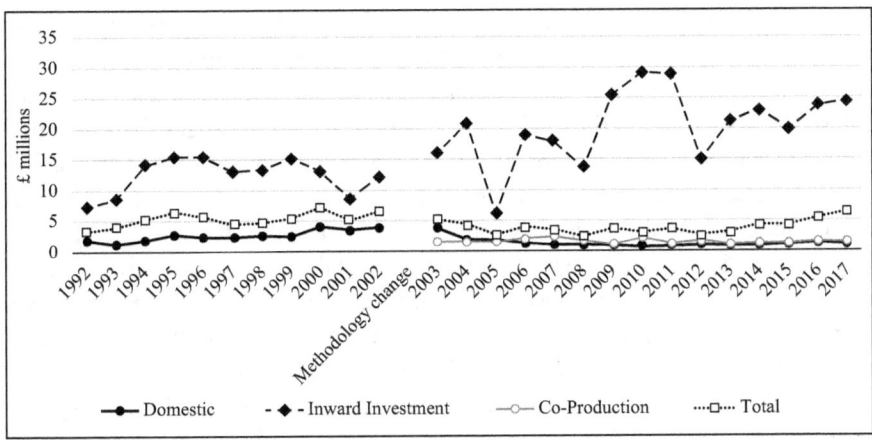

Figure 1.3 Average spend on UK films by production category, 1992–2017.
Source: BFI RSU 2020.

entire period. Finally, the average spend on co-productions was similar to that of domestic films, fluctuating between a high of just over £2.3 million in 2007 to a low of just over £1 million two years later, with an average spend of just over £1.5 million between 2003 and 2017.

The remarkable growth of the UK production sector over the last thirty years must, however, be understood in the context of the successive film policies pursued by successive UK governments. As John Hill argues, the history of film policy in Britain can be understood as a series of strategic responses to Hollywood dominance which have evolved in three 'fairly distinct phases' defined by 'protectionist', 'interventionist' and 'market-friendly' approaches (Hill 2016: 719). Beginning in the 1920s protectionist policies required both distributors and exhibitors operating in Britain to adhere to minimum quotas of British films. This figure fluctuated between 5 and 20 per cent during the 1920s and 1930s, increased briefly to a high of 45 per cent in the 1940s, before finally settling at 30 per cent from the 1950s onwards (Dickinson & Street 1985: 5 & 196–8). Interventionist policies were also introduced to provide a combination of loans and subsidies. This was initially coordinated through the National Film Finance Corporation (NFFC), a specialised investment bank founded in 1949, which provided loans for British film production. The following year, the so-called Eady Levy was introduced as a temporary measure before being made statutory in 1957. In practice, the Levy returned a proportion of box office receipts to producers of British films in proportion to the commercial performance of their output (ibid.: 216–26).

During the 1980s, however, all of these measures were dismantled by the Thatcher government, which suspended the quota in 1983 and abolished the

Eady Levy and the NFFC with the passage of the 1985 Films Act. In the same year, the NFFC was replaced by British Screen Finance, a public body which was funded partially by private investment and given the remit of achieving financial self-sustainability (Hill 1993: 205–7). These seismic changes firmly aligned British film policy with the imperatives of the free market and it was not until the following decade that policy was decisively reoriented towards 'market-friendly' fiscal incentives which were explicitly designed to attract inward investment (Hill 2016: 719). While Hill's periodisation usefully describes a shift in policy emphasis over time, it is important to note that successive UK governments have continued to pursue both market-friendly and interventionist strategies since the 1990s, albeit with a varying degree of commitment.

The first substantive movement towards a market-friendly film policy was enacted by John Major's Conservative government which, under Section 42 of the 1992 Finance Act (No. 2), introduced an accelerated tax write-off for films with production budgets over £15 million. This trajectory was enhanced in 1997 by Tony Blair's incoming Labour government, which introduced tax write-offs for films with budgets below £15 million under Section 48 of the Finance Act (Hill 2012: 344–5). Significantly, both the Conservative and Labour governments regarded the Section 42 and Section 48 tax incentives as 'an investor relief system' rather than 'state aid' and thus sidestepped the involvement of the European Commission (EC) in approving the legislation (Magor & Schlesinger 2009: 314). Consequently, eligibility for both schemes required meeting only the legal definition of a British film established in the 1985 Films Act, which was based upon entirely economic rather than cultural factors. This included the nationality of the maker (an individual or company), the location of the studio in which the film was made and the percentage of labour costs which accrued to British or Commonwealth citizens. While an amendment in 1999 placed greater emphasis on production spend rather than studio location, eligibility for the Section 42 and Section 48 tax incentives remained tied only to economic criteria (Hill 2016: 710).

In addition to these market-friendly incentives, however, both Conservative and Labour governments also pursued interventionist strategies which provided direct financial support for film production and distribution in the form of grants and loans. Under the Major government this was initially administered through British Screen Finance. From 1994 onwards, however, the government also began to allocate funding for film from the National Lottery through the Arts Councils of England, Scotland, Wales and Northern Ireland (Hill 2012: 336). This funding was redirected three years later when the Labour government created the Department for Culture, Media and Sport (DCMS), which oversaw the launch of the UK Film Council (UKFC) in 2000. This new body assumed responsibility for the functions of the Arts Council's Lottery

Film Department and British Screen, which were subsumed into it. Thereafter, the UKFC distributed grant-in-aid funding to the BFI and the British Film Commission, which continued to pursue remits respectively centred around film education and culture and attracting inward investment (Doyle 2014: 132).

By the early 2000s, the objective of the UK film tax relief was, according to Margaret Dickinson and Sylvia Harvey, to 'enable the British industry to compete, not against Hollywood, but against potential rivals for Hollywood investment' (2005: 427). The Section 42 and Section 48 fiscal incentives, however, became increasingly associated with tax avoidance, which initially prompted the closure of various legal loopholes, before a decision was taken to overhaul the entire system in 2004 (Hill 2012: 345). The result was the introduction of the UK film tax credit in 2007, which required a minimum UK expenditure of 25 per cent of the total production costs and, in turn, offered a tax write-off at 20 per cent for all qualifying UK expenditure (Hill 2016: 713–16). The new scheme was, however, subject to European Commission approval for the first time. Under Article 87 of the EC Treaty any use of state resources which distorts competition is deemed incompatible with the common market, with the exception of cultural content supported on the basis of 'verifiable national criteria' (Hill 2012: 347). For this reason, non-economic criteria were introduced to the rules governing the certification of a film as 'British' in the form of the 'Cultural Test'. Under the initial points-based system, each film had to attain a pass mark of 16 out of 31 accrued from four categories: 'Cultural Content' (16), 'Cultural Contribution' (4), 'Cultural Hubs' (3), 'Cultural Practitioners' (8). As John Hill argues, however, the Cultural Test provides a definition of British film that 'demands very little by way of national-cultural specificity' and has proven to be highly 'Hollywood-friendly' in application (Hill 2016: 713–19).

The Conservative–Liberal Democrat coalition which replaced Labour following the 2010 general election continued to support both interventionist and market-friendly film policies, albeit with substantial changes at an institutional level. In 2011 the UKFC was disbanded in an effort to reduce public spending and its functions were assumed by the BFI. Notably this included the administration of both market-friendly and interventionist measures in the form of the film tax credit and the distribution of National Lottery funds for film-related activities. Significantly, however, the tax incentives initiated by Labour were enhanced by the Conservative-led coalition, which increased the rate of relief from 20 to 25 per cent for the first £20 million of qualifying expenditure, with 20 per cent applied thereafter. In addition, the minimum UK expenditure was lowered from 25 per cent to 10 per cent and the Cultural Test was effectively watered down with a requirement of 18 out of 35 points, with additional points available in the 'Cultural Content' and 'Cultural Hubs' sections as well as for

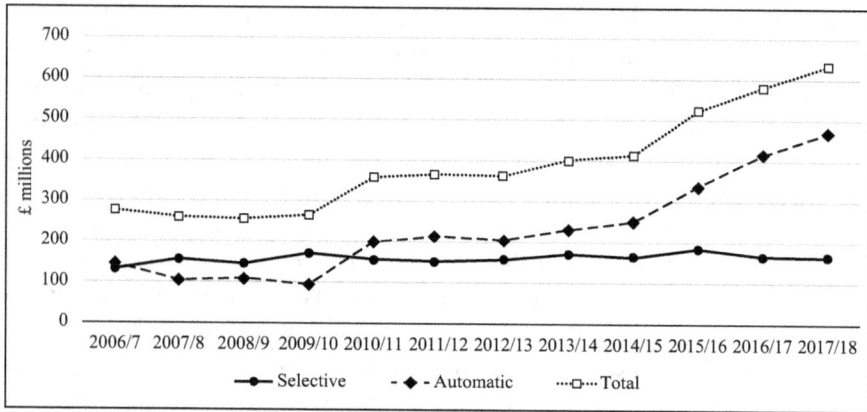

Figure 1.4 Selective and automatic public funding for film in the UK, 2006/7–2017/18. Sources: UKFC 2009–10; BFI 2011–19a.

visual effects and special effects. Simultaneously, the tax credit was extended to also cover 'high-end' television, animation and video games (ibid.: 716–18).

Since the introduction of the UK film tax credit, the BFI has published annual data about public expenditure on film. As Figure 1.4 shows, public funding for film more than doubled between 2006/7 and 2017/18, rising from £276.9 million to £633.7 million. This funding is, however, composed of both 'automatic' and 'selective' streams. The former is awarded as tax credit and represents the 'market-friendly' strand of UK film policy, while the latter is partially used to fund film production and distribution in the form of grant-in-aid and thus aligns with the 'interventionist' strand of film policy. Significantly, it is the rise of automatic funding which accounts for the overall increase in public funding of film. This strand has increased dramatically from a low of £95 million in 2009/10 (35.7 per cent) to £469 million in 2017/18 (74 per cent). In contrast, selective funding has fluctuated much more modestly, rising from £131.9 million (47.6 per cent) in 2006/7 to a high of £184.6 million in 2015/16 (35.3 per cent) before falling again to £164.7 million (26 per cent) in 2017/18.

This situation has led Jack Newsinger and Steve Presence (2018) to argue that the film policies of successive Labour and Conservative governments have created a 'corporate welfare system' for the major Hollywood studios. Elaborating on this theme, the authors suggest:

> That tax relief is by far the single largest source of public funding for film in the UK is indicative of the extent to which the film industry is valued in primarily commercial terms by the state. Rather than using public funds to mitigate market failure, tax relief transfers those funds to the private sector

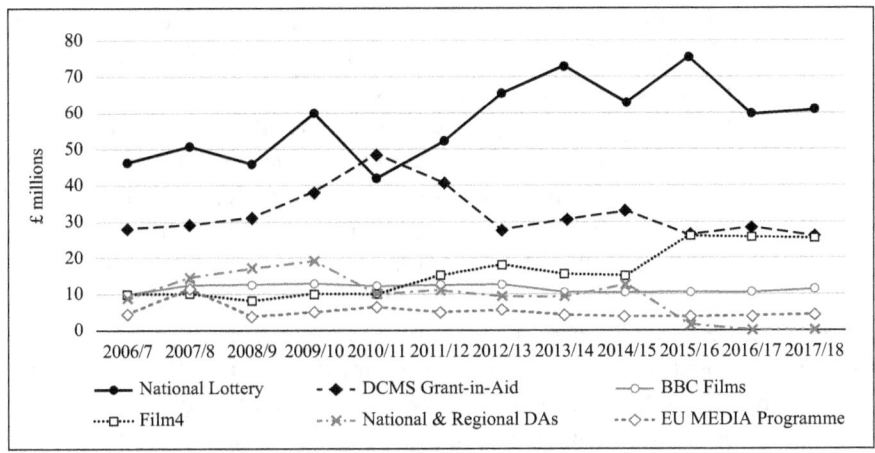

Figure 1.5 Top six sources of selective public funding for film in the UK, 2006/7–2017/18. Sources: UKFC 2009–10; BFI 2011–19a.

and thereby boosts the commercial operation of the industry by reducing the costs and risks involved in private investment. Of course, the tax relief was ostensibly designed to benefit indigenous producers, and, to the extent that all films which qualify can claim back 25% of the first £20 million (24 million euros) spent and 20% of any subsequent spend, it does. However, because tax relief is proportionate to production spend, levels of subsidy for big-budget films far exceed anything available to indigenous filmmakers because the latter make films with considerably smaller budgets. (Newsinger & Presence 2018: 450–1)

Significantly, independent British cinema remains highly dependent upon funding available through the various forms of 'selective' public funding for film. Figure 1.5 shows the top six sources of selective public funding between 2006/7 and 2017/18, which comprise the National Lottery, DCMS Grant-in-Aid, BBC Films, Film4, National and Regional Development Agencies and the European Union (EU) MEDIA programme. Collectively, these funds account for an average of just over 80 per cent of selective public funding for film across the entire period. By far the largest contributor is National Lottery funding, which ranges from £42 million in 2010/11 to £75.4 million in 2015/16, with an average of £57.8 million over the entire period. Significantly, however, this funding is divided between several film organisations including the BFI, Creative Scotland, Northern Ireland Screen, Film Cymru Wales and the Heritage Lottery Fund. Similarly, the second largest public source of funding, DCMS Grant-in-Aid, is distributed to the BFI, the Arts Council of England (ACE) and the National Film and Television School (NFTS) in support of their core activities. This funding has decreased over time, falling from a high of £48.7 million in 2010/11 to a low of £26.1 million in 2017/18 with an average of £32.4 million across the entire period.

Beyond these largest tranches, the filmmaking arms of the BBC and Channel 4, BBC Films and Film4, provide the next largest sums of selective public funding for film. Over the last decade, for example, the annual budget of BBC Films has remained relatively stable, increasing from £10 million in 2006/7 to just £11.3 million in 2017/18. In contrast, Film4 has increased its funding of film from a low of £8.2 million in 2008/9 to a high of £26.1 million in 2015/16. The final major sources of public funding for film come from the National and Regional Development Agencies and the EU MEDIA Programme. Both have decreased over time, with Development Agency funding falling dramatically from a high of £19.1 million in 2009/10 to just £0.1 million in 2017/18, while MEDIA funding has declined more modestly, from a high of £11.5 million in 2007/8 to a low of just £3.8 million in 2014/15 and 2015/16.

Finally, the division between Transatlantic British Cinema and independent British cinema is also evident at the points of distribution and exhibition. Figure 1.6 shows the UK and Republic of Ireland (ROI) box office between 2002 and 2018 divided according to nation of film origin. Perhaps unsurprisingly, 'US' films is the largest constituent group and contains almost exclusively films produced by the major Hollywood studios. The market share for this category ranges from 81.6 per cent in 2003 to 51.1 per cent in 2015, with an average share of 66.6 per cent across the entire period. The second largest category,

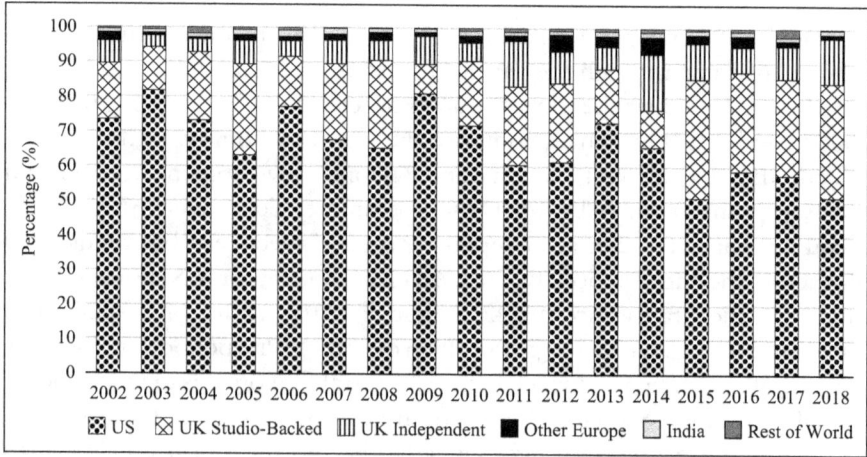

Figure 1.6 Share of UK and ROI box office by nation of origin, 2002–18. Sources: UKFC 2010; BFI 2018.

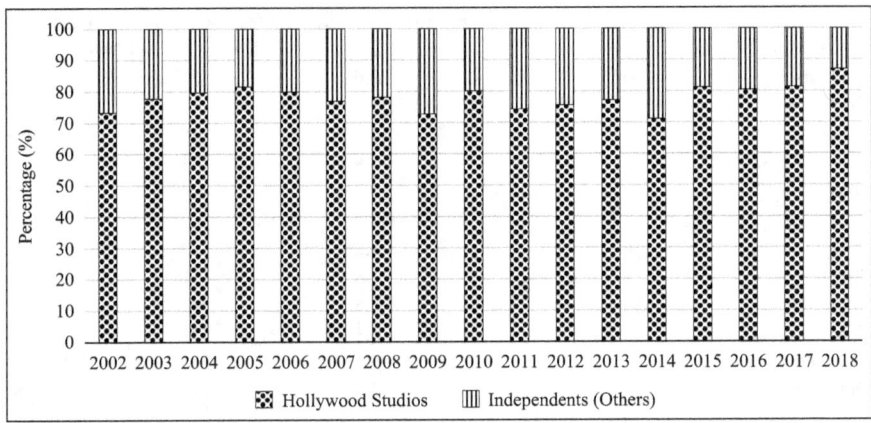

Figure 1.7 Distributor share of the UK and ROI box office, 2002–18.
Sources: UKFC 2002; BFI 2011, 2018.

'UK Studio-Backed' films, comprises both Transatlantic British Cinema and Hollywood films. The market share for this category fluctuated between 8.5 per cent in 2009 and 32.9 per cent in 2018, with an average of 21 per cent across the entire period. Collectively, then, these figures account for an average of 87.6 per cent of UK and ROI market between 2002 and 2018 and underline the dominance of the Hollywood studios in this area. In contrast, the market share of 'UK Independent' films has varied between 3.4 per cent in 2003 and 16.1 per cent in 2014, with an average of 8 per cent across the entire period. Yet smaller market shares are attained by the remaining categories, with films from 'Other Europe', 'India' and 'Rest of World' accounting for an average of just 2 per cent, 1.2 per cent and 0.8 per cent respectively (see Jones 2017 for a more detailed account of this phenomenon).

The dominance of the major Hollywood studios is further underlined by the division of market share between distributors. As Figure 1.7 shows, the UK operations of the 'Big Six' major Hollywood studios – Disney, Paramount, Sony, Twentieth Century Fox, Universal and Warner Bros. – has accounted for between 71 per cent (2014) and 87 per cent (2018) of the UK and ROI theatrical market between 2002 and 2018, with an average share of 78 per cent across the entire period. In contrast, the market share of the 'Independent' distributors outside this grouping has fluctuated between 29 per cent (2014) and 13 per cent (2018), with an average market share of 22 per cent over the period.

Table 1.1 shows the top ten distributors in the UK and ROI in 2018 ranked by market share. The 'Big Six' Hollywood studios collectively accrued almost £1.2 billion in gross box office revenue, accounting for 87 per cent

Distributor	Market share (%)	Films on release in 2018	Box office gross (£ millions)
Walt Disney	23.6	24	325.6
Universal	19.5	40	268.5
Twentieth Century Fox	14.5	28	199.3
Warner Bros.	13.9	31	191.4
Sony	10.7	33	146.8
Paramount	4.8	12	66.0
eOne Films	3.2	22	43.9
Studiocanal	2.8	31	38.4
Lionsgate	1.5	21	21.2
Entertainment	1.1	9	15.6
Top 10 total	95.5	251	1,316.8
Others (128 distributors)	4.5	715	61.4

Table 1.1 Distributor share of box office, UK and ROI, 2018. Source: BFI 2019a: 70.[4]

of the entire theatrical market. Of the remaining distributors, eOne Films, Studiocanal and Lionsgate are typically classified as mini-major studios, while Entertainment is one of the largest independent UK distributors. Significantly, these four companies shared just over £119 million in box office revenue, some 8.6 per cent of the UK and ROI theatrical market. The remaining 128 distributors outside the top ten, however, shared just £61.4 million in box office revenue, 4.5 per cent of the UK and ROI theatrical market.

Table 1.2 shows the commercial performance of the top twenty UK films in the UK and ROI theatrical market in 2018. The combined gross box office of £508 million was generated by examples of both Hollywood cinema (e.g. *Avengers: Infinity War*, *Jurassic World: Fallen Kingdom* and *Solo: A Star Wars Story*) and Transatlantic British Cinema (e.g. *Bohemian Rhapsody*, *Mary Poppins Returns* and *Darkest Hour*), which generated average box office grosses of £25.4 million. Significantly, 18 out of the top twenty titles were distributed by the major Hollywood studios and took £490.7 million of the total revenue. The exceptions, *Early Man* and *King of Thieves*, were distributed by Studiocanal and took just £17.3 million collectively.

In contrast, Table 1.3 shows the commercial performance of the top twenty UK independent films in the UK and ROI theatrical market in 2018.[5] This combined gross box office of £60.9 million, which equates to an average box office gross of just over £3 million, is comprised largely of commercially oriented films in popular genres (e.g. *Early Man*, *Finding Your Feet*, *Robin Hood*) and those which more readily align with the art-house market (e.g. *Peterloo*, *Yardie*, *On Chesil Beach*). Significantly, 15 out of the top twenty titles were distributed by three mini-major studios – Studiocanal, eOne Films and Lionsgate – and collectively took £52.3 million. In contrast, the remaining five films, *The Festival*, *The Wife*, *Adrift*, *Cold War* and *They Shall Not Grow Old* were distributed by smaller

Rank	Film	Nation of origin	Box office gross (£ millions)	Distributor
1	Avengers: Infinity War	UK/USA	70.8	Walt Disney
2	Mamma Mia! Here We Go Again	UK/USA	65.5	Universal
3	Bohemian Rhapsody*	UK/USA	53.3	20th Century Fox
4	Mary Poppins Returns*	UK/USA	43.4	Walt Disney
5	Jurassic World: Fallen Kingdom	UK/USA	41.6	Universal
6	Fantastic Beasts: The Crimes of Grindelwald*	UK/USA	34	Warner Bros
7	Mission: Impossible – Fallout	UK/USA	24.4	Paramount
8	Darkest Hour	UK/USA	24.1	Universal
9	Venom	UK/USA	20.2	Sony
10	Solo: A Star Wars Story	UK/USA	19.4	Walt Disney
11	Johnny English Strikes Again	UK/Fra	17.7	Universal
12	Ready Player One	UK/USA	16.1	Warner Bros
13	Three Billboards Outside Ebbing, Missouri	UK/USA	15.3	20th Century Fox
14	Christopher Robin	UK/USA	14.9	Walt Disney
15	Early Man	UK/Fra	11.2	Studiocanal
16	Sherlock Gnomes	UK/USA	9.5	Paramount
17	Tomb Raider	UK/USA	7.7	Warner Bros
18	Widows	UK/USA	6.4	20th Century Fox
19	Red Sparrow	UK/USA/Hun	6.4	20th Century Fox
20	King of Thieves	UK/Fra	6.1	Studiocanal
Total			508	

* Film still on release on 21 February 2019.

Table 1.2 Box office results for the top twenty UK films released in the UK and ROI, 2018. Source: BFI 2019a: 25.

independents outside this grouping such as Picturehouse, STX Entertainment, Curzon and Trafalgar and collectively generated just £8.6 million.

Reviewing the distinctions between Transatlantic British Cinema and independent British cinema along the circuit of production, distribution and exhibition suggests that competition for resources and revenue within the UK film industry exists at two starkly different levels. Films in the Hollywood-dominated 'Inward Investment' production category, for example, have average budgets of £16.9 million. In contrast, the budgets of the 'Domestic' and 'Co-production' categories, which are largely associated with independent British cinema, average just £1.8 million and £1.5 million respectively. In turn, the level of public funding directed towards film is now dominated by market-friendly 'automatic' expenditure via the film tax credit, which is largely accrued by the Hollywood studios and accounted for 74 per cent (£469 million) of public funding for film in 2017/18. In contrast, interventionist 'selective' funding, which is almost exclusively directed towards independent

Rank	Film	Nation of origin	Box office gross (£ millions)	Distributor
1	Early Man	UK/Fra	11.2	Studiocanal
2	King of Thieves	UK/Fra	6.1	Studiocanal
3	The Guernsey Literary and Potato Peel Pie Society	UK/Fra/USA	5.9	Studiocanal
4	Finding Your Feet	UK	5.9	eOne Films
5	The Commuter	UK/Fr/USA	4	Studiocanal
6	Show Dogs	UK/USA	3.5	eOne Films
7	The Festival	UK	3.4	Entertainment
8	Nativity Rocks!	UK	3.1	eOne Films
9	The Children Act*	UK/USA	2.9	eOne Films
10	Robin Hood	UK/USA/HK/Hun	2.8	Lionsgate
11	The Wife	UK/Swe/USA	1.7	Picturehouse
12	Ghost Stories	UK	1.6	Lionsgate
13	Adrift	UK/USA/HK/Ice#	1.5	STX Entertainment
14	Peterloo*	UK	1.3	eOne Films
15	Yardie	UK	1.1	Studiocanal
16	Cold War*	UK/Pol/Fra	1.1	Curzon
17	You Were Never Really Here	UK/Fra/USA	1	Studiocanal
18	On Chesil Beach	UK	1	Lionsgate
19	Journey's End	UK	0.9	Lionsgate
20	They Shall Not Grow Old*	UK/NZ	0.9	Trafalgar
	Total		60.9	

* Film still on release on 21 February 2019.

Table 1.3 Box office results for the top twenty UK independent films released in the UK and ROI, 2018. Source: BFI 2019a: 27.

British cinema, has stagnated, accounting for just 26 per cent (£164.7 million) of public funding for film in the same financial year. Equally, the UK and ROI theatrical market is dominated by the 'US' and 'UK Studio-backed' films of the Hollywood studios, which collectively account for an average of 87.6 per cent of the theatrical market. In contrast, the average market share of 'UK independent' film is just 8 per cent.

The disparity in production resources and market share associated with Transatlantic British Cinema and independent British cinema has profound consequences for both competition and diversity in the marketplace. One level of competition takes place between the major Hollywood studios, which distribute both Transatlantic British Cinema and Hollywood cinema while vying for the vast majority of the UK and ROI theatrical market. Another level of competition is played out between the mini-majors and independents, which distribute independent British cinema while vying with one another for a greatly diminished share of the UK and ROI theatrical market. In turn, the versions of Britain and Britishness available to cinema audiences at home and abroad are, in effect, circumscribed by this situation which effectively ensures that Transatlantic British Cinema dominates the mainstream of British and global film culture, while independent British cinema remains at the periphery. Drawing such contrasts between Transatlantic British Cinema and independent British Cinema at the level of national and international political economy and policy is important not least because it also highlights the broad distinctions which have marked Working Title's journey between these two parallel modes of industrial activity.

Notes

1 Data about Working Title's production budgets is taken from the most comprehensive publicly available source, IMDb.com, but the provenance of this data is not otherwise verifiable.
2 In addition to being a signatory to the European Convention on Cinematic Co-production, the UK currently has bilateral co-production treaties with eleven nations: Australia, Brazil, Canada, China, France, India, Israel, Jamaica, Morocco, New Zealand and South Africa.
3 The BFI Research and Statistics Unit have a production database dating back to 2002; data prior to that is based on information sourced from the British Film Commission, *Screen Finance* and *Screen International*. Different methodological process were used in the collation of this data. The data in figures 1.1, 1.2 and 1.3 is derived from personal email correspondence between the author and the BFI RSU, 1-4-2020.
4 It should be noted that there is an error in the figures published in the BFI Statistical Yearbook 2019, p. 70 that has been amended here. The total box office gross was double counted as £2,695 (million), whereas the accurate figure is £1,378.2 (million). Confirmed via email correspondence with the BFI RSU 19-8-20.
5 These films are drawn from the 'Top Thirty' list of independent films as classified by the BFI. However, the BFI's definition of 'independent' encompasses 'Film made with independent (non-studio) US support or with the independent arm of a US studio', and thus includes ten films distributed by the major Hollywood studios: *Darkest Hour, Johnny English Strikes Again, Phantom Thread* (Universal); *Three Billboards Outside Ebbing, Missouri, Widows, Red Sparrow, Isle of Dogs, The Mercy* (Twentieth Century Fox); *Overlord* (Paramount) and *Patrick* (Walt Disney). For this reason, these films have been removed from Figure 1.9 to give a more realistic account of independently distributed films, i.e. those distributed outside the Hollywood studio system.

CHAPTER 2

The Independent Years: Hand-to-mouth Production and Social Art Cinema (1984–8)

Working Title Ltd was established in early 1984 by the aspiring feature film producers Tim Bevan and Sarah Radclyffe. In the years that followed, the production company became one of the most prolific and successful in Britain, responsible for a series of notable art-house films including *My Beautiful Laundrette* (1985), *Wish You Were Here* (1987), *Sammy and Rosie Get Laid* (1987) and *A World Apart* (1988). As the title of this chapter suggests, Working Title was an independently owned and managed business throughout this period. In his study of British filmmaking during the mid- to late 1980s Duncan Petrie uses the term 'independent' to describe the work of 'producers and directors who do not have access to a regular source of finance; who are not under contract to a major studio' (Petrie 1991: 63). While this definition accurately describes Working Title's situation throughout the decade, a literal interpretation of independence is, nonetheless, unhelpful. Like many other British independents during the 1980s, Working Title operated within a filmmaking landscape defined largely by the influence of Channel 4. Each of the films listed above, for example, received complete or partial production funding from the broadcaster's filmmaking subsidiary, Channel Four Films, which has remained a dedicated investor in low-budget feature films ever since.

Working Title's relationship with Channel 4 throughout this period is thus an apt reminder that the designation 'independent' is frequently used to describe a range of industrial contexts within the film and television industries which are more accurately characterised by *dependence* or *interdependence* (Blanchard & Harvey 1983: 227; emphasis added). Equally, viewing the early development of Working Title through the lens of Channel 4's influence alone underplays the reality of independent British film production which continues to be characterised by complex networks of interdependence across audio-visual sectors. As Bevan explains, the emergence of Channel 4 was one among three broader industrial developments which profoundly influenced Working Title's early years:

What was going on then, at the end of the '70s and the early '80s, was there was a collision course of several things which created a sort of magic opportunity, which I can talk about in retrospect, but you didn't know, obviously, at the time that that was the case … The unions were losing their grip and power because of Thatcherism, so that was the beginning. ACTT ceased to be the force that it was, and BETA, so in the course of those two or three or four years, film ceased to be a closed shop. There was the advent of the music video business, which was attracting a lot of young people into making small films that were sort of below the radar, and the powers that be couldn't keep their fingers on, as it were, which was a spin out of the commercials business, but it was less regulated than the commercials business and it was a kind of good, really good, free for all. And then thirdly, in the early '80s was the beginning of Channel 4, which was explicit in terms of its film remit but also in terms of getting independent people to make television and film for it. So, there was a collision course of these three things that was creating a wave of opportunity, a bubble of opportunity.[1]

This chapter examines Working Title's years as an independent production company through the prism of these developments. The advent of both the music video business and Channel 4 had a direct impact upon the formation and expansion of the company, while the steady beat of Thatcherism made its presence felt in more indirect ways. These ranged from the raft of changes that the Thatcher administration made to film policy, to Thatcherism becoming the underlying subject matter of several Working Title films. While an examination of the creative and commercial interrelationships which Working Title forged helps to illuminate the many intricacies of independent filmmaking in Britain during the 1980s, the individual and collective agency of the company's key players is, of course, equally essential to understanding Working Title during this period. Before taking up this narrative, however, it is first necessary to examine the industrial infrastructure which supported the British film industry in more detail. In addition to Channel 4, this also included two other state-supported institutions, British Screen Finance Ltd and the British Film Institute (BFI) Production Board, which collectively supported the production of 'independent' British cinema throughout the decade.

THE THREE PILLARS OF INDEPENDENT BRITISH CINEMA: CHANNEL 4, BRITISH SCREEN AND THE BFI PRODUCTION BOARD

Upon its launch in November 1982, Channel 4 became the first broadcaster to challenge the BBC/ITV duopoly that had defined the television landscape in Britain for over twenty-five years. Within this dichotomy, the BBC and ITV continue to operate at opposite ends of the public broadcasting spectrum. The former is funded by public subscription in the form of a licence fee and has a comprehensive public service remit to 'inform, educate and entertain'. The latter is financed by advertising revenue and combines a commercial agenda with more limited public service obligations. The introduction of a third broadcaster (and fourth channel) proved to be a divisive issue that took shape over several years and across both Labour and Conservative governments. Rather than entrench the existing public/private binary, the Labour-era Annan Committee recommended the establishment of a broadcaster that could balance these imperatives and, in so doing, increase the plurality of both programming and programme producers. These objectives were subsequently set in motion with the publication of a White Paper in 1978 and a Broadcasting Bill the following year, which initiated the construction of a new transmission network. Conservative victory at the 1979 general election, however, ensured that the ultimate configuration of the new channel rested with the incoming government (Lambert 1982: 70–84).

Significantly, several of the principles which underpinned the Annan Committee's recommendations also proved appealing to the Thatcher administration. In the first instance, the idea of independent production promoted the ideals of entrepreneurialism and competition and suggested a strategy for weakening trade union power in the television industry. In the second instance, if the public/private divide could be successfully reconfigured, the apparent demand for greater plurality could be paid for by the market. Ultimately, the 1980 Broadcasting Act, which established both the legal basis for Channel 4 and defined its public service remit, ensured that the new broadcaster would operate as an autonomous and non-profit subsidiary of the Independent Broadcasting Authority (IBA), the government body which also regulated ITV. Like ITV, Channel 4 would be entirely funded by advertising revenue, however, this income was to be administered by the existing ITV companies on behalf of Channel 4 in return for an annual subscription determined by the IBA (ibid.: 84–94). In practice, the new model ensured that Channel 4 was free to pursue its public service obligations without the direct commercial pressure to deliver audiences to advertisers.

It was, however, the specific commitments of Channel 4's public service remit that most clearly distinguished it from its rivals. Firstly, the new channel had to broadcast a 'suitable proportion of matter calculated to appeal to tastes not generally catered for by ITV'. Secondly, a 'suitable proportion' of programmes had to be of an 'educational nature'. Thirdly, the channel was required to 'encourage innovation and experiment in the form and content of programmes'. Finally, and most significantly for the changing structure of the television industry in Britain, Channel 4 would act as a 'publishing house' by commissioning independent production companies or the existing ITV companies to make its television programmes (Harvey 1989: 63–5). Indeed, it took the launch of Channel 4 to induce a structure within the British television industry which resembled the longstanding structure of the British film industry. Independent film production had become so pronounced by the 1980s that 342 companies were involved in the making of just 454 films throughout the decade. By 1990, the television industry eclipsed this marker of plurality, and could count over 500 independent production companies (Paterson 1992: 43–7).

The increasing structural alignment of the film and television industries suggested that they might complement one another, a possibility that Channel 4's management had pursued from its inception. In his successful application for the post of Chief Executive of Channel 4, Jeremy Isaacs stated his desire to make and help make 'films of feature length for television here, for the cinema abroad' (Isaacs 1989: 146). His reluctance to fund theatrically released cinema in Britain was in part due to rules imposed by the Cinematograph Exhibitors' Association (CEA), which insisted on a three-year gap between theatrical release and television broadcast. Channel 4, however, negotiated with the CEA, which agreed to waive the clause to allow limited theatrical releases for some of the first films that the channel funded. A more formal agreement was reached in 1986 permitting theatrical exhibition and a broadcast delay waiver to films with production budgets under £1.25 million, a figure which was raised to £4 million in 1988 (Hill 1996: 157). In this respect, one of Channel 4's major achievements within the British film industry and more broadly within British film culture, was to close the gap between the made-for-television and theatrically released film by opening up the possibility of a domestic theatrical release prior to broadcast (Pym 1992: 8).

Concurrently, the Thatcher administration presided over a raft of policy changes which profoundly changed the film industry be eliminating the last vestiges of 'protectionist' legislation. At the start of the 1980s, the national industry was underpinned by three longstanding support mechanisms: the film quota system, the Eady Levy and the National Film Finance Corporation (NFFC). Unsurprisingly, the new government looked to the free market for an answer to the problems it perceived in the film business. In line with the broader objectives of reducing both public expenditure and regulation of industry, all three measures were dismantled over the course of Thatcher's first two terms. The quota was initially reduced from 30 per cent to 15 per cent in 1982 before being withdrawn at the start of the following year. The publication of a White Paper in 1984 recommended the abolition of both the Eady Levy and the NFFC, both of which came to pass with the implementation of the 1985 Films Act (Hill 1993: 205). Taken together, the removal of the quota, the levy and the NFFC severed the state-supported connection between domestic production, distribution and exhibition.

British Screen Finance Ltd was established to replace the NFFC, and continued to operate as a specialised bank for the provision of loans in support of indigenous film production. Significantly, however, the annual £1.5 million grant which British Screen received from the government was guaranteed for only a five-year period, with the mandate to achieve self-sustainability thereafter. This figure was then supplemented by annual subventions from three industry investors in the form of loans. Thus, Channel 4 and the two dominant national cinema chains, Cannon and Rank, respectively contributed £300,000 per annum for five years, £300,000 per annum for three years and £250,000 per annum for three years. Thereafter, however, Channel 4 remained the only consistent supporter of British Screen (ibid.: 206–7). Like the NFFC before it, British Screen supported British film production by providing loans to independent production companies. On the one hand, this provision of direct government aid to the film industry had to be oriented towards commercially viable projects, on the other, it could not merely be used as a substitute for investment available from existing commercial sources. Elaborating upon this balancing act, Simon Relph, British Screen's first Chief Executive explained:

> The NFFC set out in a fairly catholic way to support the work of young producers and directors who needed and deserved a start but could not get it from the majors here or in the States. I'm very anxious to continue that tradition. But projects must make sense financially: how much they are going to cost must be balanced against how much they are likely to bring in. I'm not in favour of subsidising a filmmaker to do something which is uncommercial but I am keen on taking risks that a more purely commercial entity might not be prepared to take. (Petley 1985a: 14–15)

The only state-sponsored mechanism for filmmaking to survive Thatcherism, albeit not unscathed, was the BFI Production Board. The Board, which was largely funded by the Eady Levy, was established in 1966 to replace the Experimental Film Fund. By the mid-1970s, it had become increasingly aligned with the Independent Filmmakers' Association (IFA) and thus typically supported the production of short films that reflected the IFA's interests in non-commercial filmmaking with an emphasis on the avant-garde. By the end of the decade, however, the Production Board became more purposefully involved in funding the development and production of low-budget feature films intended for theatrical distribution (Dupin 2012: 205–7). The increasingly aligned filmmaking remits of Channel 4 and the BFI led to a co-production agreement between the two under which the former claimed first option on the broadcast rights to the latter's output in return for an annual subvention. This grant, which was initially set at £420,000 a year, almost doubled the Board's filmmaking budget and was later enhanced to coincide with the abolition of the Eady Levy (ibid.: 209–11). As Tony Smith, the former Director of the BFI, observed, debates about the balance of public and private funding within the independent sector were often misleading:

> ... Is Channel 4 by virtue of its decision at Board level to allocate some of its really rather uncommercial money, IBA money in fact, to filmmaking, taking a 'commercial' decision or a 'subsidy' decision? ... All this talk about the market place is really camouflage for various forms of cross subsidy and, in the case of television, various forms of direct subsidy. We are all in the subsidy business. Furthermore, what people completely fail to understand is that the bigger and shinier full-length features often consume less public money than the highly experimental films because they have far greater access to co-production, pre-finance and pre-purchase monies. (Petley 1985b: 17)

While the mandates of Channel 4, British Screen and the BFI Production Board were somewhat disparate, they each worked to correct 'market failure', by ensuring that low-budget independent production remained viable through the judicious use of public funds. Indeed, it quickly became apparent that the three organisations could not operate in a mutually exclusive manner. Already bound by their partial economic dependence on Channel 4, British Screen and the BFI Production Board frequently collaborated with the broadcaster by co-producing films. Channel 4 and British Screen co-productions typically occupied the more commercial end of the spectrum, including films like *Prick Up Your Ears* (1987), *The Dressmaker* (1988) and *Scandal* (1989). In contrast, Channel 4–BFI co-productions such as *The Draughtsman's Contract* (1982), *Caravaggio* (1986) and *Distant Voices, Still Lives* (1988) often directly embraced the avant-garde. Nonetheless, such films collectively contribute to the conceptual construction of 'social art cinema', a term which Christopher Williams uses to describe 'the substance of Channel 4's contribution to British film-making'. For Williams, social art cinema combines many of the tropes of European art cinema – 'individual identity, sexuality, psychological complexity, anomie, episodicness, interiority, ambiguity, style' – with other prominent themes in British cinema, including the depiction of social issues and the use of realism as a representational mode (Williams 1996: 198–200).

In addition to the constraints imposed by the CEA waivers, Channel 4 was, of course, also limited by its budget. The broadcaster's first annual filmmaking allocation, for example, was £6 million, a figure which, along with co-financing from other sources, produced twenty-three films with an average cost of £400,000. Subsequent rises in production costs, however, ensured that an increased annual budget of £9.5 million in 1987 yielded only sixteen to seventeen films, with an average cost of £1.2 million (Kent 1987: 263). The funding that plugged any remaining gaps was typically raised by pre-selling distribution rights to films via a sales agent. In practice, Channel 4 managed this interface with the private sector by establishing an in-house sales agent, Film Four International, which conducted the majority of its business at major international film festivals and markets.

Taken together, Channel 4, British Screen and the BFI maintained a state-supported interest in filmmaking which, to varying degrees, opposed the free-market doctrine of Thatcherism. Significantly, the creative milieu which they supported was characterised by independence from the commercial forces of the market, most clearly embodied by the Hollywood film industry. This independence was, however, simultaneously defined and prescribed by the creative agendas of these institutions. As Petrie argues, such organisations acted as gatekeepers which were responsible for 'effectively determining what British cinema is; what subjects are worth producing and even what the final product will look like'. In turn, the filmmakers – writers, directors and producers – directly responsible for producing British cinema must 'initiate and develop their ideas in relation to existing patterns of funding and production' (Petrie 1991: 107). What follows charts Working Title's journey through the landscape of independent film production during the 1980s, beginning with the establishment of Aldabra, the music video production company which preceded it.

From Aldabra to Working Title

The origins of Working Title can be traced back to a chance encounter between its founding partners, Tim Bevan and Sarah Radclyffe, in 1982. At the time, Radclyffe was working as a production manager on *The Comic Strip Presents…* (1982–2016), the alternative comedy show which was first broadcast on Channel 4's opening night. Despite Bevan's unsuccessful application for a position on the show, the two stayed in touch and began to discuss their mutual ambition to produce feature films. An opportunity to work together soon emerged through Radclyffe's friendship with the film director Derek Jarman, who had been asked to direct a music video and needed a producer to get the ball rolling. Significantly, Radclyffe had acted as Associate Producer on Jarman's third feature film, *The Tempest* (1979), while working for the producer, Don Boyd. As she recalls:

> Don raised quite a lot of money and needed to make about five films before the end of the tax year, it was one of those things. I'd met Derek Jarman through mutual friends and when Don said, 'Does anybody know any interesting directors and interesting projects?' I said, 'Yes! Derek's trying to do *The Tempest*'. So, I introduced that, which Don then funded and I got a producer credit. I was on set the whole time and that's probably where I learned the most. I knew nothing at the beginning of that. If somebody told me the lens

didn't fit the Nagra, which was the sound equipment we used in those days, I would have had no idea. It was quite a hippy production. We put the call sheet on the door in the morning and everybody helped build the set and nobody came near us because it snowed quite heavily and we were stuck in Stoneleigh Abbey in Warwickshire.[2]

The idea of establishing a music video production company on the back of this opportunity was immediately appealing to Bevan, who was at the time employed by Video Arts, a production company which specialised in corporate training videos. 'I was thinking "Oh my God", at Video Arts, there were these five or six guys who run it and that job doesn't look too difficult,' he recalls. 'Why don't I try doing that, rather than work my way up through the system?'[3] Acting on this impulse, the new partners incorporated Aldabra Ltd in May 1983 and took up residence in a small office on New Oxford Street. Aldabra initially built its business by working with Jarman, who directed music videos for acts such as Orange Juice, Lords of the New Church, Wang Chung, Carmel and Marc Almond in quick succession (Peake 1999: 312). As Radclyffe explains:

To start with, most of the early ones came to us through Derek, because he'd been contacted by the bands themselves who'd seen his films. He was absolutely idolised by certain groups of people. Then Tim and I started to become a bit more calculating about it and started to work with other film directors because that seemed to us a good way of getting to meet them. When you're starting out, you can't exactly say to Stephen Frears or Nic Roeg, 'I'd really like to produce your next film'. But you can say, 'Would you like to do a music video?'. It was something that nobody else had done at that stage. Nobody had approached those sorts of film directors. A lot of people were asking them to do commercials, but commercials were a very precise art, and the client had creative control and they took quite a lot of time to make. They were quite grown up, whereas music videos were quite fun.[4]

Over the course of its first year in operation, Aldabra joined an expanding list of rival music video production companies such as Jump Productions, Midnight Films, MGMM (Mallet, Grant, Mulcahy & Millaney) and Fugitive Films, which were all seeking a slice of what quickly became a £30 million a year industry with its own trade body, the Music Film and Video Producers' Association (*Screen International* 1985: 34). 'It was a cowboy business then. So, it was one, personality; two, directors; three, concept; four, connections; five, anything you could make sexy,' Bevan explains. 'Aldabra was by no means the biggest of these companies ... There were a group of people running around town taking meetings with the five or six record companies trying to get work.'[5] Significantly, this period saw the first contact between Aldabra and PolyGram through its subsidiary PolyGram Music Video Ltd (PMV), which commissioned music videos for the various acts signed to PolyGram's record labels. As Radclyffe recalls:

> After we'd done a few, we got to know the execs in record companies, and that's how we met Michael Kuhn, who was at PolyGram. In those days Michael was very much trying to make us dot the i's and cross the t's of our contracts, and deliver them on budget ... It was an amazing training for producers because your fee as a production company – and by that stage we'd got an assistant and an office – was a percentage of your budget. So, if you went over budget it came out of your fee. You learned very quickly that you have a contingency, and then you have your fee, and you have to work at keeping it. That's where it was a problem when the bands were not ready in the morning and you'd go into overtime. However, the record companies wouldn't pass a budget that had a lot of overtime in it. They would say that it was our job as the producer to make sure that you didn't go into overtime. So, it was quite hard to keep them on budget and it was really good training. It made you really aware of where the pennies were spent.[6]

After a year in business, Bevan and Radclyffe began to shift their focus onto feature filmmaking and to this end incorporated Working Title Ltd in early 1984.[7] Aldabra's continuing success in the music video business, however, proved to be an important factor in underwriting the new venture. 'We started Aldabra as a way to make money and learn how to run a company ... but we decided to have a different label for our film activities,' Bevan explains. 'They were concurrent for quite a while because there was no real business going through Working Title.'[8] Shortly thereafter, Working Title relocated to a one-room office on Little Russell Street, just minutes away from Aldabra. Perched between Soho and Holborn in London's West End, the location was apt for a new filmmaking enterprise in the 1980s. The epicentre of the British film industry historically converged on the nearby Wardour Street, a road which connects the theatres of Shaftesbury Avenue with the shops of Oxford Street. While restaurants, bars and a gaudy array of sex shops had long since replaced many of the more obvious markers of a film industry, the centripetal pull of Soho remained powerful for independent production companies, not least because of its proximity to Channel 4's headquarters on Charlotte Street.

WORKING TITLE AS A PRODUCER-FOR-HIRE

Channel 4's mandate to be different was channelled, most notably, through David Rose, the channel's first Senior Commissioning Editor for Fiction. Rose and his Assistant Commissioning Editors, Walter Donohue and Karin Bamborough, were jointly responsible for Channel Four Films, a subsidiary which invested in independent production, and Film on Four, the slot in the broadcasting schedule which hosted its output. Rose joined Channel 4 after a long career at the BBC, most recently as Head of Regional Drama at the BBC's Pebble Mill studios in Birmingham. Steeped in the public service tradition, he used the creative autonomy granted to him at the BBC to help realise the work of young dramatists like Mike Leigh, Willy Russell, Alan Bleasdale and David Hare on the BBC's drama anthologies *Play for Today* and *Second City Firsts* (Mayne 2012). In line with Channel 4's public service responsibility towards innovation and experimentation, Rose described his editorial priorities for the channel as follows:

> If you pick up a script and you immediately feel you have been there before, that it's derivative, then I would rather find something else. Frankly, I just want a script that makes me keep turning the pages. I certainly favour original work ... I have reservations about adaptations from the novel. I think you start with a burden and that it's only a very clever writer who can successfully shed that burden. And I favour contemporary work. That is partly because I see quite a few period pieces on the other channels. I think the audience responds extremely well to contemporary drama. On occasion, it can illuminate a subject more clearly and with more effect than current affairs programmes. (Kent 1987: 262–3)

Working Title's first feature film, *My Beautiful Laundrette*, featured all these elements, and would later be described by Jeremy Isaacs as 'the archetypal *Film on Four*' (Isaacs 1989: 160). Significantly, the film began life at Channel 4 when Bamborough commissioned Hanif Kureishi to write an original screenplay. Acting on the advice of a friend, Kureishi delivered the completed script to Stephen Frears to solicit his interest in the project (Kureishi 1986: 41–4). As Radclyffe acknowledges:

> With *Laundrette*, we were in the right place at the right time. We knew Stephen, because we'd done music videos with him. Hanif had written it and Stephen and Hanif had developed it and it was way down the development line, practically ready to go when it came to us, and Channel 4 were funding these sorts of films. Tim and I were the luckiest producers on the planet because we started at exactly the right time and it fell into our lap. We didn't originate it, but we get credit for it in the outside world. Producers would die to have a project like that, at that stage of development, just dropped into their lap nowadays.[9]

The film was commissioned and Working Title began production in February 1985, shooting on location in South London with a schedule of six weeks and a budget entirely funded by Channel 4 (Pym 1992: 170). The extent to which Rose and his team were involved in the production process in the case of fully or majority funded projects was, however, significant. As well as having final approval on all key appointments in the development and pre-production stages – director, line producer, cameraman, editor, designer, composer and leading players – the editorial team at Channel 4 also viewed rushes and monitored cost returns during production (Kent 1987: 263). As Bevan explains, however, the oversight of Channel 4 also devolved a substantial amount of responsibility to the production company once the shoot began:

> What David Rose and Karin Bambrough and the people who ran Channel 4, and Simon Relph who was at British Screen did, was they really gave producers a lot of string, basically. The reason that we learned so quickly was they weren't micromanaging what we were doing ... Obviously they monitored what we were doing creatively. They'd watch dailies, and all the rest of it, and made sure we were shooting the script, but how we spent the money, as long as we did it to budget, and as long as ... their production people were happy with what our production people were doing, they left us to get on with it.[10]

Set in an impoverished and crime-ridden South London, the drama follows an unemployed former skinhead and his developing relationship with a British Pakistani who employs him in the eponymous laundrette and eventually becomes his lover. What leapt off the screen was both original and provocative, and seemed to embody the nascent creative ethos of Channel 4. Significantly, Working Title's relationship with the editorial team at the broadcaster also extended to post-production, and took the form of a creative mentorship with a light touch. As Radclyffe recalls:

> David Rose and Karin Bamborough at Channel 4 were just so wonderful. They were very intelligent and very good with scripts. Their comments were always comments that you wanted to include, whether that was at the script stage or editing stage, and during the shoot they were just incredibly supportive. It was very much that you were given a suggestion as to what might work in the script and in the edit, unlike now when you're told what to do. But that's possibly to do with the fact that there's a lot more money involved now. With any of the Channel 4 films you weren't guaranteed theatrical release, which in a way was a really good thing, because we were all so arrogant as filmmakers that we absolutely believed that our film would be good enough to either get great festival recognition or prove itself in some way to be good enough to go into the cinema. That was the criteria, you were making it for Channel 4 but if it got the kind of reaction that *Laundrette* got then it would go into the cinema.[11]

My Beautiful Laundrette was screened at the Edinburgh Film Festival in August and was subsequently sold for distribution by Film Four International.

After initial sales to Mainline Distribution in the UK and Orion Classics in the US, the film made its first market appearance at MIFED (Mercato Internazionale del Film e del Documentario), in Milan in October alongside a Film on Four line-up which included *Letter to Brezhnev* (1985), *She'll Be Wearing Pink Pyjamas* (1985) and *Wetherby* (1985). 'Slowly but surely I start placing this film ... I kept dragging it everywhere and screening it and it kept doing sales,' explains Carole Myer, former Head of Film Four International. 'I must have dragged it around for at least a year, a year and a half.'[12] The experience proved to be a breakthrough for the company's reputation within the independent sales business. 'Once you have something where it appears in major film festivals, some people are going to want to buy it from you,' Myer continues. 'Your whole credibility changes, you're somebody that they're not going to want to miss when they're at a market.'[13]

This steadily expanding international exposure soon combined with mounting critical acclaim, including awards from the New York Film Critics Circle and the National Society of Film Critics as well as an Academy Award nomination for Best Original Screenplay. In a 1985 opinion piece entitled 'Charity or Business?' Bevan reflects upon the state of the British film industry. Written in the form of a manifesto, he first identifies the role of a British producer as providing a visible platform for native talent. As he goes on to suggest:

> The next question must be what should producers be doing in order to provide for and guide this talent into film production? They should start by ensuring that we are regarded as a business rather than a charity. Film production is too readily associated with people bemoaning the fact that government or taxation incentives are being removed. We must show an optimistic and healthy structure of film production so that the business of film making can attract the financial stimulants it needs.
>
> In order to achieve a healthy business, producers should be guiding the creativity in the film world into making films that are of a broad interest and entertaining. It should be spelt out that filmmaking, because of its inherent expense, has to appeal to a wide audience. If there is a statement to be made of limited appeal then writing a book or painting a picture costs a great deal less. This need not mean that the product has to be overtly 'commercial' – the beauty of film production is that the canvas is extremely broad.
>
> In order to justify finance for films at the moment it is necessary that they should cross over to the US. This guarantee of American distribution is sufficient in the eyes of many to make a film commercially viable. If *My Beautiful Laundrette*, a film about a gay Pakistani laundrette owner, can find US distribution, the area for commercial success is very wide.
>
> Existing sources of finance must be provided with product which is at least going to make its money back. Further to this, if we are to attract healthy and realistic production investment from the city then we must prove that we

are in the business of film – which, like any other business, means making a profit. (Bevan 1985: 32)

Bevan's declared prioritisation of films which cater for 'broad interest' and 'appeal to a wide audience' sits somewhat uneasily next to the example of *My Beautiful Laundrette* and the ethos of Channel 4 as an institution. Indeed, the film's production was entirely reliant on public funds which were guided by non-profit and public service mandates. Nonetheless, the breakthrough success of *My Beautiful Laundrette* proved to be the starting point of a sustained period of activity for Working Title predicated largely on the wider ascent of Channel 4 and, more broadly, the developing project of 'social art cinema' within the independent sector. 'Really, *Laundrette* was the only film that Tim and I produced together. After that, the other one had to like a project but if either of us wanted to do something passionately, we would go off and do it,' Radclyffe explains. 'So, we kind of dovetailed, and tried to have one of us in the office and the other making a film.'[14] Within a week of *My Beautiful Laundrette*'s appearance at Edinburgh, Radclyffe reunited with Derek Jarman to begin production on *Caravaggio*. The film would not, however, be produced directly by Working Title and was instead a co-production between the BFI and Channel 4. Describing the genesis of the project, Radclyffe recalls:

> *Caravaggio* was developed by Derek and Nicholas Ward-Jackson, art dealer, and a passionate Caravaggio devotee, and a friend of Derek. There was a wonderfully lavish version set in Italy and written by an Italian, but it was about what you could get financed in those days. Ultimately it was financed by the BFI and shot in a warehouse in Wapping for very little money. It was a question of moving it into something that we could finance, with Derek attached to direct and largely unknown talent. It was Tilda Swinton's first film, Sean Bean's first film and Nigel Terry meant a little bit.[15]

Bevan also took a hiatus from Working Title to produce *Personal Services* (1987) for Zenith Entertainment. Zenith was established in 1984 by Charles Denton and Margaret Matheson and had already produced such films as *The Hit* (1984), *Wetherby* and *Insignificance* (1985). '[Tim and Sarah] were obviously flavour of the month after *My Beautiful Laundrette*,' Matheson explains. 'They were movers and shakers, they'd have probably made it their business to meet me because we [Zenith] were thought of as money, we were money.'[16] Prior to the establishment of Zenith, Matheson had been Controller of Programmes at Central Independent Television, the ITV franchise holder for the Midlands. Significantly, Zenith was established as a subsidiary of Central, a factor which afforded the company greater stability than most of its contemporaries. An ongoing output deal with Central guaranteed Zenith ten hours of programming a year, which included the long-running *Inspector Morse* (1987–2000). In turn, the fees from this television output paid for the company's overhead at its offices on Great Titchfield Street. The decision to set up Zenith as independent from Central was, according to Matheson, a strategic one:

> By making television and, of course, feature film, through a company which was not the main broadcast company, you could avail yourself of infinitely more suitable union agreements for production purposes. The second and more governing reason for forming Zenith was that there was then a tax structure whereby independent television companies paid a levy on profits, but some income was excluded from that calculation, and the excluded income was essentially overseas pre-sales, so you could structure an agreement whereby you maximised the overseas pre-sale element of a project, thereby saving a significant amount of levy and making it very good value-for-money production.[17]

Working from a commercial model which prioritised international sales positioned Zenith at a tangent to the non-profit and public service remit of Channel 4. In contrast, the filmmaking process at the company was based on a combination of personal and commercial factors. 'It's often chaos theory. It's partly collaborators who I already either knew or had actually already worked with,' Matheson explains. 'It's partly the kind of things I like, and it's partly what the market will bear.'[18] Indeed, Matheson commissioned David Leland, who had previously written made-for-television films such as *Made in Britain* (1982) and *Birth of a Nation* (1983) for Central, to write *Personal Services*. Inspired by the later life of Cynthia Payne, Britain's most notorious madam, the cross-over market potential of the project attracted investment from British Screen (North 1986: 10). In the process of writing the film, Leland also produced a second screenplay, *Wish You Were Here*, based on Payne's early life. The project soon attracted funding from Channel 4 and became the first co-production between Zenith and Working Title. 'I was both happy and keen to credit Working Title because they were clearly a force, a growing force, and credits helped them,' Matheson explains. 'It seemed to me quite wrong for people in fully paid jobs to be [credited]. I'm not personally credited on most of those Zenith films.'[19] As Radclyffe argues, there were distinct advantages to producing films with a limited number of investors, particularly if one or more of those investors had a public service remit:

> There weren't so many voices on the creative side. That was partly because there weren't so many investors and partly because the investors tended not to have conflicting voices. If there were only two – Channel 4 and British Screen – that was easy. The trouble with too many voices is that it's too

easy to go down to the lowest common denominator. What works for one investor doesn't necessarily work for another and that becomes a complex issue. With Channel 4 and British Screen, you didn't have to pre-empt what each individual investor and market would think of a film.[20]

On the one hand, consistent financial input from state-supported institutions continued to insulate the filmmaking process, to a greater or lesser extent, from the commercial pressures of the market. On the other, working within the creative ambit of 'social art cinema' involved running a business within consistently tight financial parameters. Significantly, Channel 4 commissioned on a 'cost-plus' basis which entailed calculating the producer's fee based on a percentage of the total production budget. A sliding scale permitted fees of 25 per cent on projects with budgets of £50,000 or less, for example, while projects budgeted between £500,000 and £1 million were eligible for a fee of 12.5 per cent (*Producer* 1988: 25). As Bevan explains:

> On those early films you'd start at 10 per cent but get whittled down to five, probably, by the time you'd got it made ... You'd try to run your business off it so ... all these lovely people you have around the place, you'd make one of them the assistant accountant, you'd make another of them assistant production manager, and you'd pay for them off the budget ... It was very much a hand-to-mouth existence, basically. One of the problems with that period of time was ... we had to be in production all the time in order to stay afloat. We were also trying to finance a little bit of development, and this and that, so that's why we kept the music video business going because we were robbing that, basically, to pay for our film overhead ... The classic independent model is not a very good one, is the long and short of it.[21]

During this period, the administrative workload at Working Title began to pile up, suggesting that the company needed to expand. Two producers, Luc Roeg and Elizabeth Trafford, were employed to manage Aldabra while Working Title relocated to larger premises on Livonia Street, a small alley in the heart of Soho. Within the close-knit world of the British film industry it was not long before one association led to another. Luc's father, Nic Roeg, suggested that Bevan contact Graham Bradstreet, a chartered accountant with whom he had worked at United British Artists (UBA), the production company behind his most recent film, *Castaway* (1986). 'I got a call out of the blue from Tim, along the lines of ... "I gather you're an accountant, we should meet". "OK, when?" and that was it,' Bradstreet recalls. 'I met Tim, and we had a chat over a period of a couple of months, I guess we met several times and in the end he said, "I think you should meet my partner."'[22] The working relationship between Bevan, Bradstreet and Radclyffe soon developed and a new company, Working Title Films Ltd, was incorporated in July 1986.

Equity in the new venture was split evenly between the three new partners, with Bradstreet assuming the position of Finance Director.

DEVELOPING AN INDEPENDENT BUSINESS MODEL

Working Title's success in its first two years of operation owed a great deal to Bevan and Radclyffe's ability to successfully align their company with projects already in development within the wider industry. Notably, the four films which they had produced by the summer of 1986 – *My Beautiful Laundrette, Caravaggio, Personal Services* and *Wish You Were Here* – were all developed and funded by third parties. Bradstreet's experience in accountancy and finance, however, suggested that Working Title might now develop on its own terms. The three partners naturally gravitated towards the aspects of film production which best suited their skills. Radclyffe remained largely involved in the creative side of the business, Bradstreet concentrated exclusively on financing and Bevan worked across both areas. 'It proved the logic that one plus one plus one made more than three,' Bradstreet explains. 'We all specialised in what we did and that's what made it work.'[23] Shortly after his arrival, Bradstreet prioritised the establishment of an in-house development fund, setting up numerous meetings with potential investors. As he recalls:

> We had a pretty good business plan, we had a pretty good track record and we needed development money, because Tim and Sarah and I took a view that we wanted to own the projects that we had going forward. Previously they had pretty much worked as guns for hire on projects and hadn't owned them. So, we wanted to own the projects ourselves, develop them ourselves and fund them ourselves. So, that was a sea change ... It was immediately post-Goldcrest, so it wasn't easy to raise [money] ... We tried everything from advertising companies, to private individuals, to corporates, to people who had previously invested in Goldcrest and other film companies. We had spoken to our lawyers, which was then Marriott Harrison ... and, in fact, it was [through] a recommendation from Marriott Harrison that we found the Frye brothers.[24]

The Frye brothers were industry outsiders who nonetheless had an interest in filmmaking and money to invest. The result of this rare find was the incorporation of a sister company, Working Title (Developments) Ltd, which was capitalised with £250,000 in August 1986. 'They had a right to invest in any film that we were developing,' Bradstreet explains. 'That company was repaid on the first day of principal photography with a premium on the amount of development money that had been spent on that production ... and a back-end net profit position in the movie.'[25] The capital now at Working Title's disposal underpinned the creation of the company's own development slate. The first opportunity to develop a film in-house came with the arrival of Kureishi's next screenplay, *Sammy and Rosie Get Laid*. The project reteamed Kureishi with Frears and, in doing so, leveraged the established success of *My Beautiful Laundrette* by offering investors the same creative team. The film, which follows the lives of the eponymous couple through a contemporary vision of London sharply divided along lines of race, social class and poverty, attracted investment from the US independent distributor Cinecom, Channel 4 and British Screen in quick succession (Bradstreet 1988: 50). As Bevan explains, securing a substantial presale from a US distributor became an increasingly important part of the funding package for each film:

> What existed in America at the time were the studios, but also there were some proper independent distributors, there were probably half a dozen at least, maybe a dozen ... There were places who were buying these films, and it was quite competitive for distribution in America, and what I quickly learned was that, actually, if you had the right package – not dissimilar to a music video – if you had a script that people liked, and you had a director people liked and a couple of actors that people liked, you might be able to pre-sell the rights to that movie and they'd give you a million bucks, or whatever it was, as a pre-sale price and you'd then take that contract to a merchant bank and they'd discount that contract and you'd put that towards the production.[26]

This steadily growing interest in British cinema was predicated upon the health of the independent sector on the other side of the Atlantic. The major Hollywood studios had, it seemed, turned towards big-budget films, leaving a gap in the market for more creatively ambitious smaller films. Indeed, an unprecedented number of independents involved in production and distribution – Miramax, Cinecom Pictures, Skouras Pictures, Atlantic Entertainment, Island Pictures, Orion Classics and Vestron Pictures – were regularly filling this vacuum with alternative product. Equally, Working Title formed an important distribution relationship in the UK with Palace, a company that was based in Wardour Mews, just a stone's throw from Livonia Street. Under the leadership of Nik Powell and Stephen Woolley, a group of companies, including Palace Pictures, Palace Video and Palace Productions, evolved to cover the bases of theatrical distribution, video distribution and film production. While Palace Pictures had a well-established reputation for distributing European and American art-house cinema, the ambition which Palace and Working Title had for their films was not restricted to independent venues alone. As Paul Webster, Palace's former Head of Theatrical Distribution, explains:

> We made it absolutely one of the central tenets of what we did to work within the existing structures. The independent cinema circuit, as such, didn't

really exist. There was the Curzon Mayfair, there were the Academy cinemas on Oxford Street, a few independents in London – Phoenix East Finchley, Screen on the Green, Screen on the Hill – but outside of London it was basically the RFTs, it was the Regional Film Theatres, that was it, so you *had* to work with the main chains ... It was our idea to do a kind of belt and braces, root and branch approach to things. So you would work very, very assiduously to court the attention and affections of the cinema bookers.[27]

Working Title also began to work with The Sales Company, a sales agent established as a joint venture between British Screen, Palace and Zenith (Ilott 1986: 1–2). Based on Shaftesbury Avenue, the new company was managed by Carole Myer, who had left Film Four International to run it. As she explains, The Sales Company operated on a break-even basis by charging its parent companies a considerably lower percentage of commission on completed sales. Rates of 7.5 per cent and 5 per cent were respectively set for international (non-US) and US sales, which amounted to less than half the typical rate charged by external sales agents.[28] Working Title's involvement with the new sales venture was a natural progression, given the company's established links with its parent companies. '[Working Title] got offered percentages that were lower, and they agreed that everything, if it was available, was going to go through me,' Myer explains. 'Almost all the agreements I had that weren't with film distributors, were just little letters that [state] we agree to be responsible human beings together.'[29] As she goes on to explain:

> Sarah and Tim ... valued what I did really well, which was not true for everyone, but they ... understood that I never did a deal without them knowing what was involved and what the distributor could do for them. So, it's not like [they were] appointing me and I was out there doing things without them knowing about it, which is how most producers ... [experience it]. They just feel as though their sales agent is ripping them off, basically. I also paid them every month any money that came in. That was unheard-of in the film business. If you were lucky, you got statements every six months.[30]

The 1987 Cannes Film Festival, which featured five Channel 4-funded films, proved to be a moment of affirmation for the Film on Four project. *Prick Up Your Ears* and *The Belly of an Architect* (1987) were in competition for the Palme d'Or, *A Month in the Country* (1987) featured in the Un Certain Regard category and *Wish You Were Here* and *Rita, Sue and Bob Too* (1987) appeared in the Directors' Fortnight. Channel 4's *annus mirabilis* was further underlined when David Rose received the Roberto Rossellini Award on behalf of the boradcaster at the climax of the festival. Simultaneously, the business conducted on behalf of Working Title at Cannes that year underlined the importance of the affiliated film market as the site of deal-making. The sales agent, Gavin Film, completed international sales on *Personal Services* and began international pre-sales on *Sammy and Rosie Get Laid* (*Screen International* 1987a: 61). Simultaneously, Film Four International sold the US distribution rights to *Wish You Were Here* to Atlantic Entertainment. As part of a separate negotiation, Atlantic agreed a two-picture co-production deal with British Screen which included acquiring US distribution rights and making an equity investment in Working Title's next film, *A World Apart* (*Screen International* 1987b: 2).

More than any other Working Title film during the 1980s, *A World Apart* stretched the company's resources to the limit. Radclyffe had developed the anti-apartheid period drama in collaboration with its writer, Shawn Slovo, who based the screenplay on the lives of her parents, the activists Ruth First and Joe Slovo. With a shoot in Zimbabwe and a projected budget of over £2 million, the funding secured from Atlantic and British Screen proved insufficient. To close the gap, Bradstreet raised funding on location through various tax structures. 'These were tax structures, not like we consider them now, with tax credits and where governments have formal treaties and all the rest of it,' he explains. 'It tended to be, I'd find a piece of legislation that I could apply a film to and then use that legislation.'[31] Despite these efforts, the production of the film was a strained process. As Radclyffe recalls:

> Finance on *A World Apart* never really closed and the money kept running out constantly. There was a moment when we needed to do some re-shoots, and I'm sure that the financiers didn't know this, but we were completely out of money and we'd all reached our credit card limits. There was a wonderful girl called Clarissa who was the assistant accountant and she realised that money was very tight and every time we got money from the bank she would hide about five per cent of it right in the back of the safe. So, when we were completely out, she said 'Sarah, come here …' I could have hugged her. Literally, the whole thing would have fallen apart without her. There was always a gap in the financing. How we got started and how we got cash-flowed, I don't know.[32]

As Table 2.1 shows, five of the first six films produced by Bevan and Radclyffe between 1985 and 1988 had financial input from Channel 4. This ranged from 100 per cent of the budget for *My Beautiful Laundrette* (£650,000) to just 10 per cent of the budget of *A World Apart* (£275,000). Similarly, three of this number also received investment from British Screen, ranging from an estimated 50 per cent of the budget for *Personal Services* (£1,000,000), to 19 per cent of the budget for *A World Apart* (£500,000), while *Caravaggio* received 47 per cent of its budget (£225,000) from the BFI Production Board.

Working Title's alignment with Channel 4 and the ascent of 'social art cinema' more broadly began to be acknowledged in the trade press. One

Title	Year	Budget	Channel 4	%	British Screen	%	BFI	%
My Beautiful Laundrette	1985	650,000	650,000	100				
Caravaggio*	1986	475,000	250,000	53			225,000	47
Personal Services*	1987	2,000,000			1,000,000	50		
Wish You Were Here	1987	1,132,000	849,000	75				
Sammy and Rosie Get Laid	1987	1,370,000	400,000	29	325,000	24		
A World Apart	1988	2,675,000	275,000	10	500,000	19		

Table 2.1 Channel 4, British Screen and BFI funding for Working Title's films, 1985–8 (all figures £GBP).
Sources: All Channel 4 and BFI data: Pym 1992. All British Screen data: North 1986: 10–11; Bradstreet 1988: 50; Romer 1992: 71–2.
* Films produced by Bevan and Radclyffe for other companies.

article, for example, summarised the company's remit as the production of 'British films with new and radical directors who will take up themes, treatments and acting that are on the edge of film convention' (Mackie 1986: 22), while Bevan later declared his company's commitment to 'socio-economic and political movies with a strong narrative' (Pearson 1988: 23). In many ways, the filmmaking culture at Working Title also began to broadly mirror these sensibilities by embracing attitudes and practices which typically eschewed strictly commercial imperatives. As Radclyffe explains:

> Everyone was given profit participation and I think at Working Title we gave more people profit participation than some of the other companies did. We always gave the heads of department something because then, psychologically, they felt it was theirs too. It sounds rather naïve, but you wanted to have a good time as well. So we fed everybody well and had parties. I don't think it's looking at the past through rose-tinted glasses, but it didn't feel nearly as hard as it does now. We were also dealing with people at the beginning of their careers as well and there weren't that many independent films being made. I think everybody did it because they loved it. I never remember going through the agony of trying to persuade somebody to accept a deal to be on a film, whether that was cast or crew. Nobody would ever turn anything down in those days for the money.[33]

In contrast, the relationship between Working Title and Britain's emerging art cinema was, for Bevan, largely based on accepting the creative parameters of producing independent films within an industry dominated by Channel 4. 'That was the last period of absolute change,' he recalls. 'If you were working in the arts and if you were working in cinema, and if you were working in television, you were reflecting that in many ways.'[34] Recalling the political outlook at Working Title in relation to the company's output, he explains:

> We were pretty apolitical. Nobody liked Thatcher very much, but there was rub in the air and there was change afoot, there is no doubt about that … I think when you're in the middle of something you don't take too much time to consider it, which is something I still feel. You consider carefully what you embark upon, but then, when you're doing it, you don't think too much about it. Then you get it done, and you come out the other side of it, and it takes a long time before you can look at it with the benefit of hindsight … It just so happens that the *Laundrette* was the film that came out of that era that happened to be the one that, historically, now represents that era.[35]

In just four years, Working Title had earned a position at the forefront of Britain's nascent 'social art cinema', a creative movement which was largely initiated and sustained by Channel 4 and, to a lesser extent, British Screen and the BFI Production Board. During this period Working Title moved from a producer-for-hire business model to operating as a company which developed and produced films on its own terms, albeit precariously. In turn, this transition was underwritten by a fundamental shift in the way the company's films were funded. The third-party financing packages behind *My Beautiful Laundrette* and *Wish You Were Here* were replaced by the equity investments, distribution deals and tax structures which financed *Sammy and Rosie Get Laid* and *A World Apart*. Nonetheless, sustained public investment throughout this period ensured that the production of such films was, to a greater or lesser extent, shielded from market forces. By the time *A World Apart* was screened at Cannes Film Festival in May 1988, however, a new era of filmmaking was on the horizon for Working Title.

Notes

1. Tim Bevan, interview with the author, 6-8-2013.
2. Sarah Radclyffe, interview with the author on 26-3-2015 and subsequent email correspondence on 22-4-2015.
3. Tim Bevan, interview with the author, 6-8-2013.
4. Sarah Radclyffe, interview with the author on 26-3-2015 and subsequent email correspondence on 22-4-2015.
5. Tim Bevan, interview with the author, 6-8-2013.
6. Sarah Radclyffe, interview with the author on 26-3-2015 and subsequent email correspondence on 22-4-2015.
7. It has not been possible to determine the exact date of incorporation of Working Title Ltd. However, the company is first mentioned in the trade press in

July 1984 and described as a 'wholly owned subsidiary of Aldabra'. See 'Comic Doc from Working Title', *The Stage and Television Today*, 26 July 1984, p. 16.
8 Tim Bevan, interview with the author, 6-8-2013.
9 Sarah Radclyffe, interview with the author on 26-3-2015 and subsequent email correspondence on 22-4-2015.
10 Tim Bevan, interview with the author, 6-8-2013.
11 Sarah Radclyffe, interview with the author on 26-3-2015 and subsequent email correspondence on 22-4-2015.
12 Carole Myer, interview with the author, 27-11-2013.
13 Ibid.
14 Sarah Radclyffe, interview with the author on 26-3-2015 and subsequent email correspondence on 22-4-2015.
15 Ibid.
16 Margaret Matheson, interview with the author, 17-9-13.
17 Ibid.
18 Ibid.
19 Ibid.
20 Sarah Radclyffe, interview with the author on 26-3-2015 and subsequent email correspondence on 22-4-2015.
21 Tim Bevan, interview with the author, 6-8-2013. Working Title retained only a small net profit share in its early films. This figure, for example, amounted to only a 5 per cent share with *My Beautiful Laundrette* and a 4 per cent share with *Wish You Were Here*. This potential income was, however, typically only recouped following the lapse of the original distribution contract, a period which could be as much as ten years. Source: PolyGram, (1995) 'Documents relating to the reorganisation of Working Title Films Limited including the sale of certain assets to Working Title Limited: Volume 1' PolyGram Filmed Entertainment (PFE) Archive (hereafter, 'PFE Archive').
22 Graham Bradstreet, interview with the author, 9-10-2013.
23 Ibid.
24 Ibid.
25 Graham Bradstreet, interview with the author, 30-10-2013.
26 Tim Bevan, interview with the author, 6-8-2013.
27 Paul Webster, interview with the author, 10-5-2013.
28 Carole Myer, interview with the author, 27-11-2013.
29 Ibid.
30 Ibid.
31 Graham Bradstreet, interview with the author, 9-10-2013.
32 Sarah Radclyffe, interview with the author on 26-3-2015 and subsequent email correspondence on 22-4-2015.
33 Ibid.
34 Tim Bevan, interview with the author, 6-8-2013.
35 Ibid.

Johnny (Daniel Day-Lewis), Tania (Rita Wolf) and Omar (Gordon Warnecke) listen to Rachel's story in *My Beautiful Laundrette*.

Lynda (Emily Lloyd) attracts admirers at the seafront promenade in *Wish You Were Here*.

'The usual social deviants, communists, lesbians, blacks and a sprinkling of the mentally subnormal': Rosie (Frances Barber) and Sammy (Ayub Khan-Din) draw up a guest list in *Sammy and Rosie Get Laid*.

Diana (Barbara Hershey) and Molly Roth (Jodhi May) join the protest in *A World Apart*.

Dexter (Jeff Goldblum) and Kate (Emma Thompson) celebrate at the opening night of *Elephant!* in *The Tall Guy*.

Betty (Emily Lloyd) and Karl (Kiefer Sutherland) make deadly plans in *Chicago Joe and the Showgirl*.

'If for these dignities thou be envied, I give thee more': Piers Gaveston (Andrew Tiernan) receives gifts and titles from King Edward (Steven Waddington) in *Edward II*.

Elizabeth (Phoebe Cates) attempts to ignore her imaginary friend (Rick Mayall) in *Drop Dead Fred*.

CHAPTER 3

The PolyGram Years Part I:
Founding a Studio and Making a Subsidiary (1988–92)

Between 1988 and 1992, Working Title was transformed from an independently owned and managed production company to a subsidiary 'label' of the nascent film studio, PolyGram Filmed Entertainment (PFE). Significantly, PFE was a subsidiary of PolyGram, one of the 'Big Six' major record companies, which was, in turn, a subsidiary of the consumer electronics manufacturer, Philips. PolyGram's diversification into the film industry began within the confines of PolyGram Music Video (PMV), a division of the company managed by Michael Kuhn, a lawyer by training, and PolyGram's Director of Legal and Business Affairs. Working from PolyGram's headquarters in London, Kuhn gradually gained approval to make 'long-form music videos' which featured PolyGram artists and played heavily on the links between music and film. Such projects were given an official home with the creation of PolyGram Media Division (PMD) in February 1987. Kuhn was appointed CEO and President of the new venture and recruited Malcolm Ritchie, a chartered accountant, to act as CFO. Over the next five years, the two men began laying the foundations of a substantially larger film business which ultimately became PolyGram Filmed Entertainment.

Kuhn's interest in Working Title began to take shape following a chance encounter with Tim Bevan in Los Angeles. Already acquainted with one another from their time working in the music video business, the pair discussed the ambitions they harboured for their respective companies. Kuhn explained that he wanted to expand PMD's production capability and was considering a range of investments. In turn, Bevan described the capricious nature of independent production in Britain and his attendant desire to transform Working Title into a more stable and better resourced company. PMD subsequently acquired a 49 per cent equity stake in Working Title Films and simultaneously built a prototype studio around the company. This included establishing an international film sales company and devising a corporate tax structure which jointly funded the production company's films. In doing so, Kuhn and Ritchie initiated the development of the so-called 'control sheet': a centralised creative and commercial filter which assessed the risk and reward profile of film projects and began to shift Working Title's filmmaking in a more commercial direction.

Accordingly, this period of Working Title's history saw a substantial transition in the company's output which included both its final contributions to 'social art cinema', such as *London Kills Me* (1991), *Edward II* (1991) and *Dakota Road* (1991) and its initial forays into commercial filmmaking with the likes of *Chicago Joe and the Showgirl* (1990), *Drop Dead Fred* (1991) and *Bob Roberts* (1992). Simultaneously, Working Title began to operate from offices in both London and Los Angeles for the first time, an arrangement which continues to define the company's essential structure. The straightforward narrative of corporate diversification outlined above, however, belies a much more extensive and complicated history which, when taken into account, better explains PolyGram's overall business strategy during the 1990s.

THE LONG SHADOW OF POLYGRAM PICTURES

Philips was founded in 1891 by the Dutch industrialists Frederik and Gerard Philips to manufacture electric lamps and light bulbs. Over the next half century the company evolved into a large multinational corporation which produced a range of consumer electronics including radios, gramophones, electric shavers and television sets. By the 1940s the company saw diversification into consumer 'software' as an increasingly important strategy in enhancing its market presence. The acquisition of several companies which manufactured, recorded and distributed gramophone records soon followed. The post-war boom in recorded music sales led to the establishment of an umbrella company, Philips Phonografische Industrie, into which Philips consolidated its music assets. Siemens, Europe's other leading electronics manufacturer, found itself in a similar position and established its own consolidated record company, Deutsche Grammophon. Seeing the potential advantages of collaboration, the two conglomerates merged their music interests in 1962 by exchanging a 50 per cent share in one another's record companies and renaming the combined venture Grammophon-Philips Group. The amalgamated record company was merged at an operational level in 1972 and renamed PolyGram (Bakker 2006: 102).

Throughout the 1960s and 1970s, Grammophon-Philips Group/PolyGram expanded its assets in the record industry by establishing or acquiring artists-and-repertoire (A&R) companies, commonly known as record 'labels', including Polydor, Decca, Mercury and London Records. PolyGram managed its labels as semi-autonomous businesses which developed distinct musical identities. Generic business functions such as financing, manufacturing, publishing, marketing and distribution were, however, centralised within PolyGram (ibid.: 105). The natural synergies between the record and film businesses began to take effect when a disco label, RSO Records, produced a string of highly profitable musical films, including *Jesus Christ Superstar* (1973), *Saturday Night Fever* (1977) and *Grease* (1978). A similar situation evolved at the Los Angeles-based Casablanca Records and FilmWorks which, under the leadership of the producers Peter Guber and Jon Peters, evolved into PolyGram Pictures. Between 1980 and 1983, the company invested $80 million in film production, of which $62 million were spent on the production of seven feature films: *Endless Love* (1981), *An American Werewolf in London* (1981), *The Pursuit of D.B. Cooper* (1981), *Deadly Blessing* (1981), *Six Weeks* (1982), *Missing* (1982) and *Split Image* (1982). PolyGram's first attempt to enter the film industry was, however, widely considered a financial disaster and recorded an estimated loss of $50 million.[1]

The failure of PolyGram Pictures coincided with a looming crisis in the record business. The popularity of disco music was over and PolyGram's distribution and marketing infrastructure became an undersupplied and costly liability. A management exodus ensued which saw the appointment of Jan Timmer as CEO and President of PolyGram in 1983. Significantly, Timmer was recruited from Philips, where he had presided over the market launch of the Compact Disc (CD) in collaboration with Sony. This situation enabled the two conglomerates to license the manufacture of both CDs and CD players to their competitors (McGahan 1993: 179). In turn, PolyGram was able to reissue its extensive back catalogue on the new format. The boom in sales of CDs and CD players which followed saw PolyGram's net profit margin soar by 60 per cent between the mid-1980s and early 1990s, a period during which Philips consolidated its ownership of PolyGram by acquiring Siemens' shares in the company. Capitalising on this success, PolyGram staged an initial public offering (IPO) in 1989 with 20 per cent of the company's stock. The exercise raised $400 million and revealed the company's value to be $2 billion (Bakker 2006: 116–17). Explaining PolyGram's long term strategic thinking at this moment of buoyancy, Kuhn explains:

> The management at PolyGram saw a time when everyone had bought a CD player and renewed their entire catalogue, and as we became a public company, albeit only 20 per cent, they were all saying, 'Well, what's your next trick? What are you going to do next?' They'd all got used to 15 per cent year-on-year growth in profits throughout the 1980s. That's where the plan for a film division came from, simply because 50 per cent of the revenues from film came from video. Videos were bits of plastic being distributed around the world through retail shops, which is what we did on the record side. We had the infrastructure in forty countries and we knew that we were quite good at financial control of creative business, which is what the film industry is as well. So, what we'd have to do is get a supply line of films and then learn how to market them.[2]

The legacy of PolyGram Pictures, however, cast a long shadow over the development of PolyGram Media Division. 'It was certainly useful to look back and see what they had done and how it had been done, and we were constantly reminded of the errors in the past,' Ritchie recalls. 'PolyGram was nervous ... about overextending the operations and ending up with the sort of disaster that PolyGram Pictures had been.'[3] Accordingly, each business plan that PMD produced contained a section dedicated to explaining the reasons for the failure of PolyGram Pictures. One such example noted that the collapse had been the result of six interrelated factors. Three were related to the lack of ancillary markets for films. Both the home video and pay-TV markets were virtually non-existent at the time, while the dominance of state broadcasting monopolies diminished the value of product in the international market. Two further problems were structural. Firstly, the lack of an established back catalogue of films meant that failure at the box office could not be absorbed by other income streams. Secondly, there were no 'efficient tax arrangements' with which the cost of production could be sheltered, a factor which coincided with a 20 per cent rise in interest rates during the period.[4] Part the reason for the failure of PolyGram Pictures was, for Ritchie, also the result of ineffective corporate oversight:

> At that time PolyGram was effectively split between Eindhoven, London and Hamburg ... It wasn't until later that PolyGram effectively had the head office in London. It would have been incredibly difficult to manage a Hollywood venture with the structure that PolyGram had, it just wasn't set up for it and, I think that the truth is as well, a lot of people took advantage of these European owners, and stretched the business – took investments, took risks – and they could have been incredibly lucky and it could all have come good ... some of the projects subsequently became very successful ones, notably *Batman*, but we didn't have the distribution structure or anything to take advantage of that. It was the wrong venture at the wrong time and had not been properly planned out.[5]

By the late 1980s, however, several of the market conditions that had been disadvantages for PolyGram Pictures had become advantages for PMD. 'From a business point of view, there was no such thing as video in those early days, and secondary revenues were really limited to television,' Ritchie explains. 'The whole market was changing through the '80s with VHS and ... the growth of cable television ... everything was different.'[6] By 1987, for example, the worldwide market for film was estimated to be $13.3 billion, of which $3.7 billion came from theatrical releases, $6.3 billion from home video and $3.3 billion from television.[7]

Expanding PMD was, however, dampened by personnel changes at the top of the company. At the end of 1987 Jan Timmer accepted a position on the Group Management Committee at Philips and was replaced as President of PolyGram by David Fine, the former CEO of PolyGram's UK operations. 'David Fine had been, under Jan Timmer, the guy who'd had to be the nuts and bolts manager. He wasn't a visionary, but the guy who had to deliver the results and make the numbers work,' Kuhn explains. 'He was a fantastic manager in that regard, but anything that looked risky and dangerous like the launch of CD in the first place and certainly films later, he inherently felt – probably quite rightly – resistant to and nervous about.'[8] Consequently, the investments made by PMD were both modest and keenly observed in its first years of operation. This activity did, however, allow Kuhn and Ritchie to begin laying the foundations of a film studio which, like the existing PolyGram 'label system', was initially built by acquiring independent companies.

EXPANDING POLYGRAM MEDIA DIVISION: TWO PRODUCTION LABELS, A SALES COMPANY AND A TAX SCHEME

Immediately prior to the establishment of PolyGram Media Division, Kuhn began investing in low-budget feature films with funds made available through PolyGram Music Video. The first of these efforts, *P. I. Private Investigations* (1987), was co-produced by Steve Golin and Sigurjón 'Joni' Sighvatsson, owners of the LA-based music video production company, Propaganda Films. In January 1988 PMD made its first substantial investment by acquiring a 49 per cent stake in Propaganda for $3.25 million.[9] Significantly, the company represented a natural fit with PolyGram's existing business interests and, as importantly for Kuhn, had independent feature films in development and production including *The Blue Iguana* (1988) and *Fear, Anxiety and Depression* (1989). In July PMD made its second significant investment with the incorporation of Working Title Television Ltd (WTTV), a joint venture in which Working Title assumed a 51 per cent stake and PolyGram took 49 per cent. PolyGram subsequently capitalised the company with an unspecified investment 'up to a maximum limit of £2 million'.[10]

Establishing WTTV was, in part, motivated by the prospect of the 1990 Broadcasting Act, which would ensure that UK broadcasters had to commission at least 25 per cent of their programming from independent producers. The governing reason for the investment, however, was to forge a relationship with Working Title Films. With Propaganda and Working Title identified as partners, Kuhn and Ritchie began considering how the companies might be integrated into PMD as production labels. A 1988 business plan proposed the creation of a 'Financial Services Division' and outlined five opportunities for investment in the film industry which would avoid the risks of direct investment in production. Options included home video acquisition and distribution, a P&A (prints and advertising) fund, completion bonds, banking services for independent producers and establishing an international sales company. With each option, it was envisaged that a 'critical mass of production activities' would be achieved by 'grouping together a number (say 5) independent producers – two of whom would be Poly-Gram associates – (Propaganda Films and Working Title Films and TV)'.[11]

The increasingly intertwined relationship between Working Title and PMD soon suggested more tangible ways in which the two could mutually develop their filmmaking capacity. Shortly before PolyGram's investment in WTTV, Wendy Palmer, the former Director of Marketing and Distribution at Handmade Films, had approached Working Title and a second independent, Initial Film and Television, with a business proposition. Palmer wanted to establish an independent film sales company and to do so, she required something to sell:

> I realised during my years at Handmade that having only one production entity [meant that you] really didn't have enough [films], with the ebb and flow of film production. Sometimes you'd have three or four films on the go and sometimes, frequently, you'd have none and so the idea of having more than one producing entity, it seemed to solve that problem ... [Working Title and Initial] were both seriously undercapitalised, was the basic problem. That was a more pressing issue for them than independent sales at that point ... [Tim Bevan] felt quite strongly that they needed an American production company ... and the problem with Initial was that they were basically producing in the same area. So, we started looking around for an American company and finding the ideal marriage – the companies that were in the States that were at the same [stage of] evolution or development as Working Title – was quite tricky.[12]

The idea of having an in-house film sales company was immediately appealing to PMD and, with Propaganda already identified as a US-based partner, Palmer was brought back into the conversation. Simultaneously the lack of financial incentives for film production in Britain prompted Working Title's Finance Director, Graham Bradstreet, to search for suitable fiscal opportunities further afield. 'There were no transferable tax credits or anything else like that in those early days,' he explains. 'You had to make the movie, either totally commercially, so you had to convince people ... [to] essentially fully fund it, or alternatively we found tax structures that would benefit an investor outside of the industry.'[13] As he goes on to note:

> There was a structure that I had developed under which German companies could get an accelerated write-off on movies, and PolyGram was one of those companies that could access this ... You had to be a corporate and you had to

> be in a similar business, it was something called Organschaft and it meant that they could write off the cost of the movies at an accelerated rate and a high rate and get a tax advantage. We told Kuhn about this and he 'instructed me' ... to see their in-house tax counsel about it ... We then spent a significant amount of time fine-tuning it to make it work for PolyGram.[14]

By March 1989, PMD settled on a strategy which involved combining the tax structure which Bradstreet had introduced with the establishment of an in-house sales company. The initial business plan envisaged that Propaganda and Working Title would use the funding raised by these new companies to collectively produce twenty-one films over a five- to six-year period. Significantly, the plan was accepted on the basis that the tax structure and sales company would, in combination, limit PolyGram's risk of investment to approximately £1 million at any one time, with a ceiling set at £2.5 million.[15] Initiating the plan required the incorporation of two new companies. The first of these, PolyGram Filmproduktions GmbH, was incorporated as a subsidiary of PolyGram Germany and was thus able to take advantage of its parent company's tax liabilities. While an accountant was employed part-time to manage the business affairs of PolyGram Filmproduktions in Hamburg, Wingolf Mielke, a German executive at PolyGram's London office, was appointed as Managing Director. Thus, in practice, PolyGram Filmproduktions operated under the operational auspices of PolyGram Media Division.

In June, Manifesto Film Sales BV was established as a subsidiary of the Netherlands-based PolyGram NV, but once again fell within the operational auspices of PMD in London. The new venture, managed by Wendy Palmer, offered a systematic method of raising production finance through pre-selling the distribution rights to the films in development at both Propaganda and Working Title. The new company's first home was in a shared room at Working Title's Livonia Street offices, before these were traded for a dedicated office on Wardour Street. As Malcolm Ritchie explains, operating an international film sales company offered several advantages:

> If we'd have used a third-party sales company we might have paid a 15 or 20 per cent fee, but if we had enough throughput the effective cost of Manifesto might have been about 5 to 7 per cent. It made sense to do that, plus, an important fact was that we had control of the sales process. We could go to the AFM, Cannes and MIFED ourselves and start meeting the buyers, and in doing that we began to get an idea of the sort of product that worked. We became much smarter about the sort of projects that we should be doing. I think both Working Title and Propaganda felt more empowered as well because they were then closer to the ultimate distributors and began to get a better feel about how their projects might do in the marketplace.[16]

As PMD expanded its operations, Working Title's need for direct investment was underlined by a mounting crisis within the independent sector. The ascent of 'social art cinema' appeared to be a short-lived phenomenon. In October 1988, Channel 4 publicly announced the difficulties it was experiencing in attracting US finance to its productions. According to the broadcaster, almost any British film with a budget of £1.5 million or over required a US pre-sale, a goal which had been achieved by 50 per cent fewer films in 1988 than in 1987 (Dawtrey 1988: 1). The change in the US market was attributed to a more cautious approach to acquisitions in the independent sector, as several of the leading independent distributors including Atlantic, Cinecom and Vestron experienced financial difficulties. The situation snowballed into the following year, at which point British Screen and Channel 4 began to directly fund distribution to help secure UK releases for the films they had invested in (Dawtrey 1989: 1). As Table 3.1 shows, however, Working Title had largely moved away from Channel 4's creative ambit by producing films with commercial partners.

Title	Year	UK funding	US distribution	UK distribution	Int'l sales
A World Apart	1988	Channel 4/British Screen	Atlantic	Palace	The Sales Co.
Paperhouse	1988	–	Vestron	Vestron	Vestron
For Queen and Country	1989	Zenith	Atlantic	UIP	The Sales Co.
The Tall Guy	1989	LWT	Miramax	Virgin Vision	The Sales Co.
Diamond Skulls	1989	Channel 4/British Screen	Circle Films	Virgin Vision	The Sales Co.

Table 3.1 Working Title's slate by funding, distribution and sales, 1988–9.

Notably, the four films which Bevan produced in this period were all in broadly commercial genres, including the fantasy film *Paperhouse* (1988), the crime-drama *For Queen and Country* (1989), the comedy *The Tall Guy* (1989) and the thriller *Diamond Skulls* (1989). Moreover, only *Diamond Skulls* received funding from the state-supported sources of Channel 4 and British Screen. In contrast, *Paperhouse* was entirely funded by Vestron, while *For Queen and Country* and *The Tall Guy* both made use of the ITV levy through Zenith and London Weekend Television (LWT) respectively. The latter proved to be a significant film in Working Title's history insofar as it was the company's first collaboration with the writer Richard Curtis. It was also the first instance of the company outsourcing the role of the producer to a third-party, in this instance, Paul Webster. As Webster recalls, despite its poor commercial performance, the financing structure behind *The Tall Guy* made it one of the most profitable films of Working Title's independent years:

> It was financed almost entirely by London Weekend Television, who brought the TV licence ... It was made for £1.2 million and was in profit before it was finished ... London Weekend Television paid for the UK television

rights and they paid, I think, £850,000 for it. The bulk of the money was paid up front by Nick Elliot, who was head of LWT at the time, and it was a brilliant deal that Tim did ... The business reason that Richard stayed loyal to Working Title ... was that within a few months of that being finished, a substantial cheque was on Anthony Jones's [Curtis's agent] desk. He said, 'OK, these people must be straight, this doesn't happen.' Working Title were absolutely straight and made the best decision of their careers.[17]

In lieu of a direct investment from PolyGram, Working Title continued to develop its own business strategies. In May 1989 the company secured a three-year distribution agreement with one of the most successful remaining US independents, New Line Cinema. The deal covered theatrical and television distribution for eight Working Title films in the US and Canada. A separate deal was agreed for US video rights, while Palace signed a four-film theatrical deal for the UK market (Groves 1989: 3). Such deals did not, however, directly fund development, the area in which the company was most consistently undercapitalised. Indeed, recouping development expenditure in the independent sector typically only happened when a film went into production. As Bevan explains:

> We realised that in order to produce movies you need to run an overhead and you also need to develop material and that all costs money, particularly in terms of developing material. You need to get to a point when developing material where if you've spent quite a lot on it, but if it's not going to turn itself into a film, you need to be able to write that off. No independent company can really afford to do that and so the only way to get our money back was to get the film made, by charm and brute force and by all the rest of it. We got a number of films financed which should probably never have been made in order to get our fees out and in order to get the development money out of it. That was not a sustainable or a sensible model.[18]

An investment in Working Title Films itself became inevitable by the end of the 1980s. Supporting the financing and selling of Working Title's films through PolyGram Filmproduktions and Manifesto Film Sales made little sense for PolyGram Media Division if the production company remained the sole beneficiary. The percentage of equity which PMD acquired in Working Title Films amounted to a strategically determined 49 per cent. 'PolyGram didn't want to consolidate a company that was showing losses,' Ritchie explains. 'It wanted to invest money and if it lost that money, that was fine, they would write it off, but they didn't want to carry anything more.'[19] From Working Title's perspective, the remaining 51 per cent equity would ensure, in theory at least, that the three partners retained overall control of the company. For Bevan, the prospect of relinquishing equity in Working Title was an acceptable price to pay for the investment that PMD could offer in the longer term. The idea of ownership is, of course, inextricably wedded to the idea of independent film production and, in turn, the creative and operational autonomy such a label suggests. As Bevan explains, however, the reality of Working Title's years as an independent often bore little resemblance to the ideals of the label:

> If you are asking me now what the three most important things are, I'd say, the capital to run the business – to run my overhead and my development; creative freedom to be able to do whatever I want to do in terms of developing the sorts of films I want to make; and thirdly, when I get a film made, single source worldwide distribution ... In the late 1980s, we didn't have the capital and we certainly didn't have the single source worldwide distribution because every film was sold off to different companies all around the world. Arguably because of that, we didn't have the creative autonomy either, because our situation was always dictating what we did next, rather than us dictating what we did next.[20]

The rationale for investing directly in Working Title Films was, for Kuhn, both pragmatic and personal. 'There wasn't a lot of choice, was number one. Number two was we needed to have a company here who knew their way around making low budget or relatively low budget films,' he explains. From this point on, however, Working Title's relationship with PMD was also primarily routed through Kuhn's relationship with Tim Bevan. 'We always hit it off from day one and we're still great friends to this day. Like most things in business, personality is a big part of it, and if you can't get on with somebody then it's normally not a good idea,' he elaborated.[21] The dice were cast, and Working Title became a production label within PolyGram Media Division's prototype film studio.

POLYGRAM MEDIA DIVISION AND THE PROTOTYPE FILM STUDIO

In February 1990, PolyGram Media Division and Working Title Films reached an agreement that saw the production company take its first step towards becoming a subsidiary. PMD invested £1.5 million in a new holding company, Working Title Group Ltd, which acquired 100 per cent of Working Title Films Ltd from Tim Bevan, Graham Bradstreet and Sarah Radclyffe. In return, the three original shareholders received a 51 per cent stake in the holding company via a separate company called Passport Film Services Ltd. The remaining 49 per cent of Working Title Group was acquired by PMD. The business plan which accompanied the acquisition included a breakdown of anticipated expenditure which, while relatively modest, covered all the company's principal areas of activity. Of the £1.5 million total investment, £900,000 was earmarked for four key areas, including £250,000 for pre-production finance, £150,000 for working capital, £100,000 towards new offices and £400,000 for development, distribution and marketing finance. This recapitalisation also allowed the company to arrange overdraft facilities secured against the business and, in specified circumstances, PolyGram could make additional funding available to Working Title of up to £1 million in the form of secured, interest-bearing loans.[22]

Thereafter, Bevan, Bradstreet and Radclyffe were contracted exclusively to the company and responsible for its day-to-day management. The company's new board of directors, however, now included the three original partners and three representatives from PolyGram. Significantly, board level agreement was now required for a range of actions, including major project initiation, employee hiring, and approval of accounts, forecasts, cash flows and loans.[23] Crucially, the new partnership was subject to an initial period of two and a half years, which allowed both PMD and Working Title to test the new relationship within a defined time frame. As the proposal document reveals:

> The new venture will run for an initial period from 1-6-90 to 31-12-92, after which time PolyGram may elect to extend for at least a further 2 years. Termination by PolyGram alone may be sought after 31-12-92 in the event that the audited results up to that period are significantly below the business plan estimates. If the agreement is terminated after 31-12-92, or at a later date, various buy-out options for PolyGram and/or Passport come into play.[24]

In August 1990 Working Title moved into a three-storey office building on Water Lane in Camden and was soon joined by a significantly expanded Manifesto Film Sales. In this new setting, the disparity between the working practices of an independent production company and a multinational entertainment conglomerate quickly came to the fore. As Ritchie recalls:

> Creatively they had a lot of talent but their finance and business affairs were almost non-existent. The way we had been brought up within the PolyGram ethos was to run things in a fairly organised way, with monthly reporting and balance sheets. If we were going to invest in something, we knew what potential return we could expect. They had nothing like that at all, they were very much hand-to-mouth. I'm not necessarily blaming them because that's the way they had grown up, and clearly they had learned a lot along the way and had their successes. From a PolyGram point of view it was very clear, very quickly … that they couldn't continue with an operation like that. They would have to start preparing reports, getting their accounting systems up to scratch and just operating in a more professional manner than they had previously done.[25]

From this point onwards, Working Title was integrated into a dynamic system of PolyGram-owned companies. With pre-sales financing generated by Manifesto on the one hand, and equity financing raised by PolyGram

Filmproduktions on the other, Working Title and Propaganda became filmmaking 'labels' positioned between the two companies. These subsidiaries did not, however, raise funding on an ad hoc basis. Instead, the essential processes of the film business – development, financing, green-lighting, production, marketing and sales – were systematised within PolyGram Media Division. This was realised by directly linking the label's filmmaking activities with those of Manifesto and PolyGram Filmproduktions. Figure 3.1 shows the development, financing and green-lighting procedures of PMD in the form of a flow chart. The green-lighting procedure began when a label developed a film project, a stage at which each label maintained creative autonomy. The proposed film package, which typically included a script, preliminary budget and attached talent including producer, director and cast, was subsequently distributed to both Manifesto and PolyGram Filmproduktions.

Next, Manifesto opened initial sales discussions with international distributors based on the package. Shortly thereafter, PolyGram Filmproduktions initiated loan discussions with investment banks which specialised in film financing, most notably Pierson, Heldring & Pierson and Guinness Mahon & Co. Securing a bank loan, however, depended upon Manifesto's ability to pre-sell the projects in development at Working Title and Propaganda. 'For a film to get green-lit we had to draw-down from a bank, so we had to have sufficient signed sales, and sufficient sales estimates for the bank to start advancing production funding,' Palmer explains. 'I had to get a certain percentage of my estimates as signed contracts and then they would advance money against the remaining countries, based on what I had estimated them being worth.'[26] Starting in the UK, the company also began to forge 'cornerstone' output deals with various distribution companies, which built longer-term contractual relationships into the system:

> I eventually set up deals where we segregated the rights, so we sold theatrical, video, pay TV and free TV separately. I had what we call output deals. I had an output deal with the BBC, an output deal with Sky, an output deal with Rank and CBS/Fox were doing video... I set up output deals in a lot of other countries in Europe too. If you do an output deal you can get a discountable contract really quickly which was a much more efficient and effective way of getting the bank finance drawn-down... It was really important to keep the term as low as possible, five to seven years was ideal, because that was time to give two years theatrical, 12 months video, two to four years on TV and then the rights would revert back to Manifesto. That was a big selling point for PolyGram because they were big on building up catalogues, that's where they had made all their money with music.[27]

In all cases, secured sales were 'subject to contract' agreements payable by the distributor upon receipt of the completed feature film. When presented to

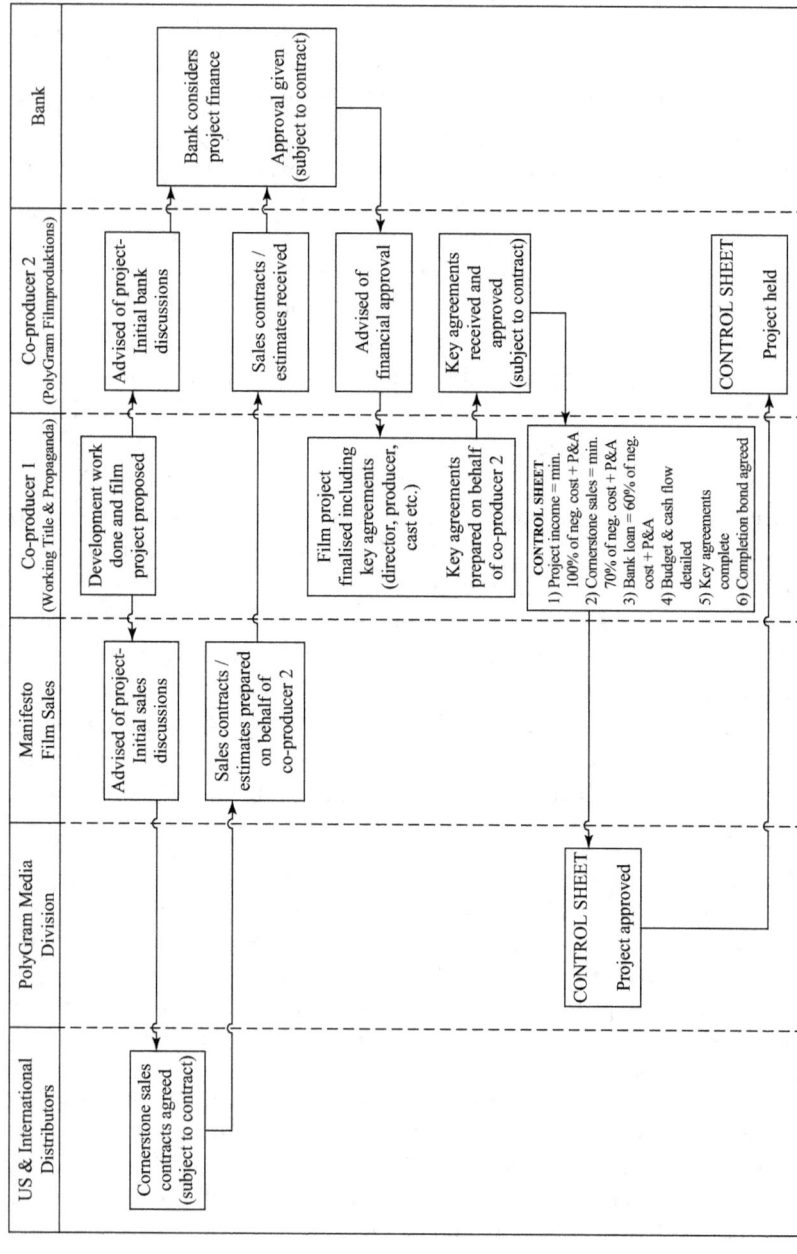

Figure 3.1 PolyGram Film Fund procedures flowchart: development and green-lighting. Source: PolyGram (1989), 'PolyGram Film Fund Procedures Flowchart', PFE Archive.

the bank, however, the total income guaranteed by signed sales and suggested by estimated sales amounted to a figure which could be lent against. Once this figure was established, the contractual elements of the film could be finalised by the production label, before being reviewed by PMD. Significantly, the contracts of above-the-line personnel (writers, directors, producers, cast) had the potential to affect the overall return on investment for PolyGram if they included clauses relating to profit participation.

The final stage of the green-lighting process entailed filtering the amassed contractual detail through a centralised creative and commercial filter known as the 'control sheet'. The control sheet laid out the terms for the green-light decision in six stages, the first three of which involved an examination of project income and expenditure. Firstly, the entire anticipated income of the project had to equal a minimum of 100 per cent of 'neg. cost + P&A', or rather negative cost (the cost of production and post-production up to the printing of the first film negative) and prints and advertising (the cost of additional prints and advertising materials supplied to the distributor). Within this overall figure, the cornerstone sales had to equal a minimum of 70 per cent of neg. cost + P&A, against which the bank would loan 60 per cent of neg. cost plus P&A. The disparity of at least 10 per cent between the income from cornerstone sales and the bank loan acted as both a contingency and a buffer to cover the cost of the interest and fees payable on the bank loan. Finally, the control sheet required that the production label complete key production agreements, produce a detailed budget and cash flow and secure a completion bond. Reflecting on the development of the control sheet, Ritchie explains:

> The control sheet came about because, not long after we set up and started making films in 1987 and 1988, Michael said to me: 'As part of this whole venture, we've got to keep the PolyGram board happy. They've got to see that we're managing the process, they've got to see that we know what the risks are and that they're manageable risks. How best can we present this?' I came up with the idea for what became the control sheet. The concept was simple, it was to try to project how well a film would do in terms of its pre-sales and ultimately, when we were in direct distribution, what the actual sales in particular territories might be. The whole goal of it was to try to come up with projects that were commercial, that would make money, or at least we wouldn't lose money ... Did it help the commerciality of projects? Yes, it did. Nobody is going to say at the end of the day that you can decide which film to make by virtue of what an accountant had come up with. That's not how it should work, and that's not how it does work, but what it does do is [make you] ... better informed when you're looking at a project as to whether or not it has commercial appeal.[28]

Once a film project passed through the control sheet, the processes of production, sales and revenue collection began. As Figure 3.2 shows, the labels kept PolyGram Filmproduktions advised of the financial requirements of the production, which were then transferred from the bank directly to the production label, or a subsidiary vehicle company incorporated for the purpose of the particular production. The gap in financing, which amounted to approximately 40 per cent of neg. cost + P&A, was then funded by PolyGram Germany via PolyGram Filmproduktions. The associated tax write-off which sheltered PolyGram's direct investment would then come into effect when PolyGram Germany completed its annual tax return.

With the requisite funding in place, the production label completed production and post-production on the film, before delivering the master negative to Manifesto. Manifesto subsequently arranged duplicate prints and produced marketing materials which would accompany the prints when delivered to the distributor. Upon receipt of the film, the terms of the signed sales contract would come into effect, triggering payment and the preparation of a royalty statement by the distributor. Manifesto subsequently deducted its commission and expenses from the sales contract, before the balance and royalty statement were transferred to PolyGram Filmproduktions. In turn, PolyGram Filmproduktions repaid the bank loan and accrued any profit yielded. In cases of commercial success from the distribution of a film, the production labels would receive a commission from Manifesto in addition to their production fee, which was factored into the original production budget.

In practice, the films which Working Title produced between 1990 and 1992 fell into two categories: those which passed through the control sheet and were funded by PMD, and those which were funded with third-party finance. Figure 3.3 shows the former case, noting the financial positions of the six films which Working Title produced before PolyGram Filmproduktions applied the tax write-off for which the company was set up. Significantly, five out of six cases indicate a loss-making position from pre-sales alone, ranging from $3,279,000 for *Chicago Joe and the Showgirl* to $243,000 for *Map of the Human Heart* (1992). As Ritchie goes on to explain, the tax write-off was an essential part of PMD's financing strategy:

> It was a timing thing, because if the projects were fantastically successful, then you end up paying tax, [and] you're going to pay tax at 55 per cent, but I think there was always the perception that these project were never going to be break out massively profitable films. So, [on a] film costing £5 million, you effectively were getting a tax write-off of 55 per cent, so the actual risk for PolyGram, the group, was 45 per cent of £5 million and provided you could bring in some revenues through presales, you could bring the risk down to a very low position.[29]

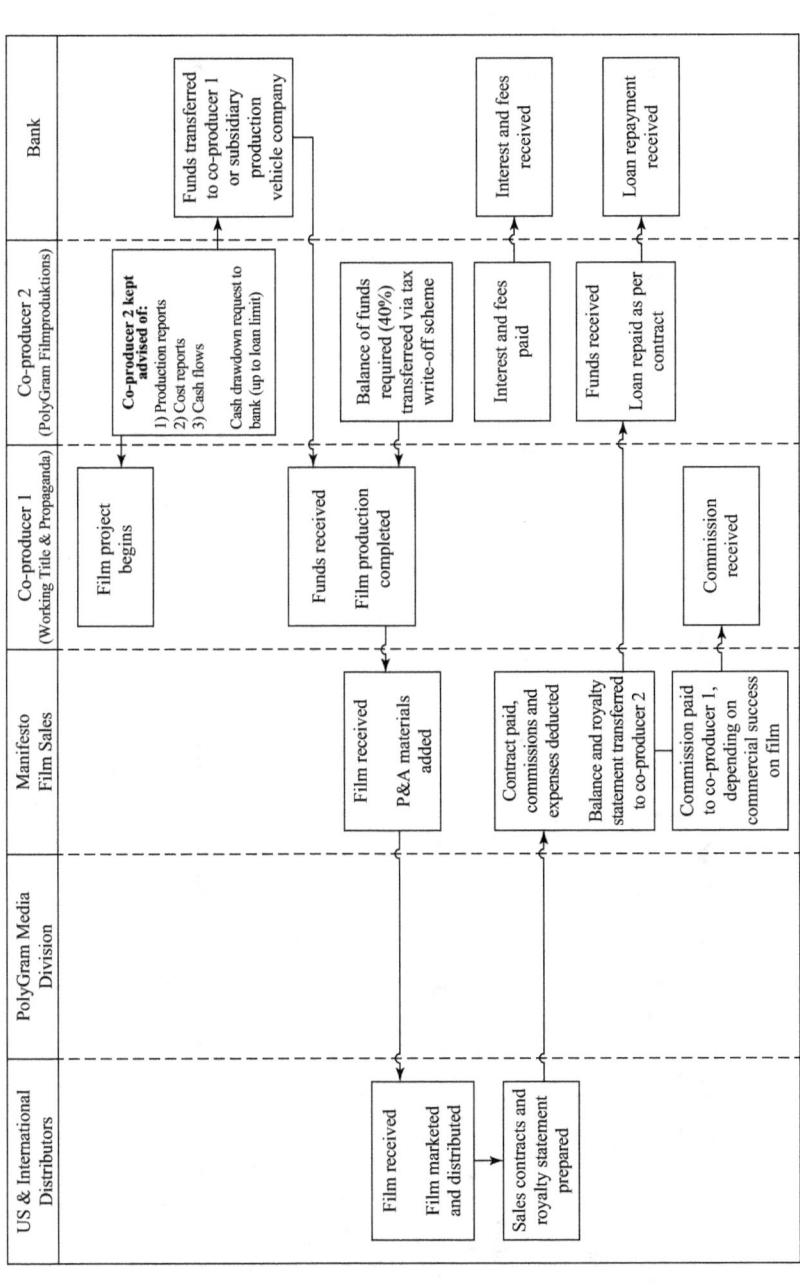

Figure 3.2 PolyGram Film Fund procedures flow chart: production, sales and revenue. Source: PolyGram, 1989, 'PolyGram Film Fund Procedures Flowchart', PFE Archive.

Film	Chicago Joe and the Showgirl	Fools of Fortune	Drop Dead Fred	London Kills Me	Map of the Human Heart	Bob Roberts	Total
Income	5,534	4,554	12,818	3,495	19,218	4,750	50,369
Direct costs							
Production	-5,749	-5,063	-6,414	-2,765	-16,700	-4,172	-40,863
P&A	-1,227	-687	-4,500	-631	-1,500	-500	-9,045
Finance/other	-1,314	-842	-540	-239	-750	-240	-3,925
Amortisation	-8,338	-6,591	-11,454	-3,635	-18,950	-4,912	-53,880
Expenses	-406	-396	-527	-318	-442	-211	-2,310
Operating result	-3,210	-2,432	837	-457	-174	-383	-5,819
Interest/exchange	-69	5	134	-93	-69	-74	-166
Result before tax	-3,279	-2,427	971	-551	-243	-457	-5,986

Figure 3.3 Working Title films funded by PolyGram's Film Fund 1990–2 (all figures $US 000s). Source: PolyGram (1992), 'Media Division: Red Book Consolidated Film Operations Report', PFE Archive.

Several of the films which Working Title had in various stages of development were, however, supported by Channel 4 and British Screen and typically remained in the creative orbit of social art cinema. Channel 4, for example, contributed $1.1 million to *Fools of Fortune* (1990) and $0.9 million to *London Kills Me* (1991).[30] As Kuhn explains, reorienting the company and its output was a long-term project:

> Development takes forever to turn around. It takes a minimum of three, more likely five years if you're starting off to have anything new. So, you had to exist on what you had in the pipeline ... that was stuff that could get made at that time which wasn't necessarily commercial stuff but could help pay your overhead. You did what you had to do, and from a very early stage Tim and I agreed that we almost had to start afresh on development and aim it at a more commercial market. But in the meantime, they had to do what they had to do. They didn't have anything else in the hopper except what they'd had from the past.[31]

The search for more commercial projects at Working Title encouraged expansion in various directions, including a presence in Los Angeles for the first time. In the summer of 1990, Paul Webster moved into a house which Working Title rented on Taft Avenue in the heart of Hollywood. In practice, developing and producing material in the US relied on the same financing model as Working Title's British-based productions. Crucially, however, the development of a US-based slate allowed Working Title to embrace more commercially oriented production from the start. For example, the company's first two US-based films, *Drop Dead Fred* and *Rubin and Ed* (1991), were comedies. Recalling the early years of Working Title's Hollywood outpost, Webster explains:

> Really, I was there to make *Drop Dead Fred*, I went there just to make the movie. They had a kind of assistant type person called Clarissa Troop who lived there and they kept a house there so they could stay when they came out and we all lived there. The office was upstairs and we all lived downstairs. Gradually while I was there I made the decision to stay in America for a while and I said to Tim, 'I can build this up with you, if you like', and he said 'Yes'. We then started exploring other projects, things like *Romeo is Bleeding*, which eventually got made, *Bob Roberts,* which got made, and I hired Liza Chasin, who is still there today, as my assistant. It just kind of grew organically.[32]

During this period, PMD's insistence on viewing projects in development through the prism of the control sheet began to reshape the output of Working Title. Significantly, the transition had a markedly different effect on Working Title's founding partners. 'Tim's films were definitely going in a more commercial direction. I wouldn't have wanted to have made his films,'

Radclyffe explains. 'If you're getting up at 5 o'clock every morning, and you get on set and you're faced with a whole load of problems, and you don't totally believe in the project, you might as well hide under the bedclothes quite frankly. Why bother?'[33] Her insistence on producing films with a personal resonance reunited Radclyffe with Derek Jarman for *Edward II*. 'How he would have coped with today's constraints where you have to make a film for your audience, I don't know,' she muses. 'Derek made his films for himself primarily, but they were much more of a collaborative art form, and that's how they felt.'[34] As she goes on to explain:

> I'm quite sure that I was responsible for not bringing in as much money into Working Title as I should have done, because I was far more interested in the films. I was living the hippy version of it. It was all Derek Jarman's fault for starting me off that way. He was somebody you just bounced off. He was incredibly intelligent. A lot of producers work with just one director and I'm sure I would have wanted to stay and be Derek's producer forever, if he'd still been alive. I loved working with Derek, it was a very different experience. Not that I didn't enjoy working with Stephen Frears and David Leland, but it was different. It was unqualified passion and 'Where there's a will, there's a way', whereas later on I worked with people who were much more capable of seeing the negative side, which is much more balanced and sensible, but Derek would be off shooting a film even if there was no money.[35]

Significantly, Radclyffe's projects, *Edward II* and *Dakota Road*, were respectively funded by BBC Films and Channel 4 and British Screen and thus circumnavigated the involvement of PMD and the control sheet. As Wendy Palmer explains, however, the divergent creative agendas of Working Title's founding partners were highlighted as much by the projects which passed the financial rigours of the control sheet as those which did not:

> Those gritty Channel 4 type of films, they were difficult to sell internationally, that's for sure, so they were difficult to finance under that model we had. That was a time of great frustration for Sarah because the model we had didn't suit the kind of films she wanted to make ... Tim, he really did want to be much more commercial ... He wanted to be in the mainstream, no doubt about it. And I think that was very difficult for their working relationship, Sarah and Tim, because they really were heading off in different directions ... Sarah was a much more instinctive creative producer while Tim ... he was more business-oriented, more structured. Sarah would get incredibly passionate about a project, she would just fall in love with a project and want to get it made at all costs and Tim, he'd be more reflective, more analytical.[36]

PolyGram Media Division's prospects took a decisive turn in January 1991 when David Fine stepped down as CEO and President of PolyGram and was replaced by Alain Levy. Levy, who had previously managed PolyGram's operations in France, was hand-picked by Jan Timmer, who had been appointed President and CEO of Philips the previous year. With new leadership at the helm, Kuhn and Ritchie had reason to hope that PMD's efforts would lead to a more substantial investment in film.

THE LAUNCH OF POLYGRAM FILMED ENTERTAINMENT AND NEW LEADERSHIP AT WORKING TITLE

In August 1991 Kuhn and Levy, with the help of financial expertise from Ritchie, and PolyGram's COO, Jan Cook, presented a business plan to the board of Philips entitled 'PolyGram and Films'. The presentation initially involved reviewing the developments of PolyGram Media Division over the previous four and a half years. 'It was probably not a bad thing that there was a softly, softly, slowly, slowly period as we built up our own experience of the industry and it was just the way that the stars lined up,' Ritchie reflects. 'What we were able to show to PolyGram and Philips is that we'd actually built up a nice business without actually risking a huge amount of money, without investing a huge amount of money.'[37] Thereafter, PMD's plan for the launch of a new film studio was laid out as follows:

> **Stage One** – Establishment of an organisation which has a well-capitalised production unit – envisaged is a 'label' system of production companies achieved by the buy-out of the non-PolyGram shares in Propaganda and Working Title together with the addition of A&M and a further 'mainstream' established producer. The production units should eventually be capable of producing between 8 and 15 'A' movies a year. Establishment of a marketing and sales organisation that allows our production entities to access the distribution margin in each income flow.
>
> **Stage Two** – Medium/long term development of PolyGram's own national film production with distribution worldwide through its own video, theatrical and TV distribution systems. Medium/long term development of a significant movie catalogue by the prudent acquisition and consolidation of quality movie and TV libraries.[38]

With the support of Timmer, the board passed the proposal and the business plan set in motion the creation of PolyGram Filmed Entertainment. The following month, PolyGram announced the $200 million capitalisation of its new film division in the trade press. The new venture would, it was revealed, also increase its stake in both Working Title and Propaganda from 49 per cent to 100 per cent and escalate their combined rate of film production to a minimum of eight films per year – four in the $7–$10 million range and four in the $15–$25 million range (Ajax 1991a: 4). As Ritchie recalls:

> The $200 million figure was the initial cash flow estimate, the total net cash. Net, because obviously we were going to spend much more than $200 million but we were going to start receiving income from the projects that we were producing. It was a combination of everything ... It was for the acquisitions, for the buy-out of Propaganda, for the buy-out of Working Title, for setting up US operations, for setting up US distribution ... [We] envisaged buying a larger entity which ultimately became Interscope and it included, notably, the funding of the projects themselves.[39]

At the time of the announcement PolyGram was the leading member of the so-called 'Big Six' major record companies, a grouping which collectively shared 84 per cent of the worldwide retail market for recorded music. In 1991 this market amounted to $23.8 billion worldwide, with $7.8 billion (33 per cent) of revenue coming from the US 'domestic' market and $16 billion (67 per cent) from the 'international' market, which comprised the rest of the world.[40] Three of the 'Big Six' – PolyGram, EMI and Bertelsmann Music Group (BMG) – were European corporations, while the three remaining majors – Warner Music Group, Sony Music Entertainment (formerly CBS Records) and Music Corporation of America (MCA) – were historically American, although the latter two had been acquired by the Japanese conglomerates Sony and Matsushita in 1988 and 1990 respectively. Figure 3.4 shows these companies according to their respective shares of the worldwide music market in 1991/1992.

Unlike their European counterparts, however, the US-based major record companies were all divisions of larger entertainment conglomerates which also included Hollywood film studios. As a PFE business review acknowledged, the worldwide market for filmed entertainment in 1991 was $51.9 billion, more than double that of the record business. In contrast, however, the ascribed market values were reversed, with the US accounting for $33.2 billion (65 per cent) of the worldwide filmed entertainment market and the rest of the world responsible for $18.7 billion (35 per cent).[41] If successful, the project of building PFE into a major film studio would transform PolyGram into an entertainment conglomerate which, like the major Hollywood studios, was capable of exploiting this vast market.

The pending launch of PFE coincided with the introduction of structural changes at Working Title. In October the company created a low-budget division and Alison Owen, an independent producer, was recruited to manage it (Ajax 1991b: 3). As she explains, the new structure was designed to acknowledge both the history of the company and its future:

> Tim approached me saying that what they wanted to do was restructure. Tim was going to do the big-budget movies, Sarah was going to do 'Rad Films', which was a medium-budget thing, and I was going to fly the Working Title

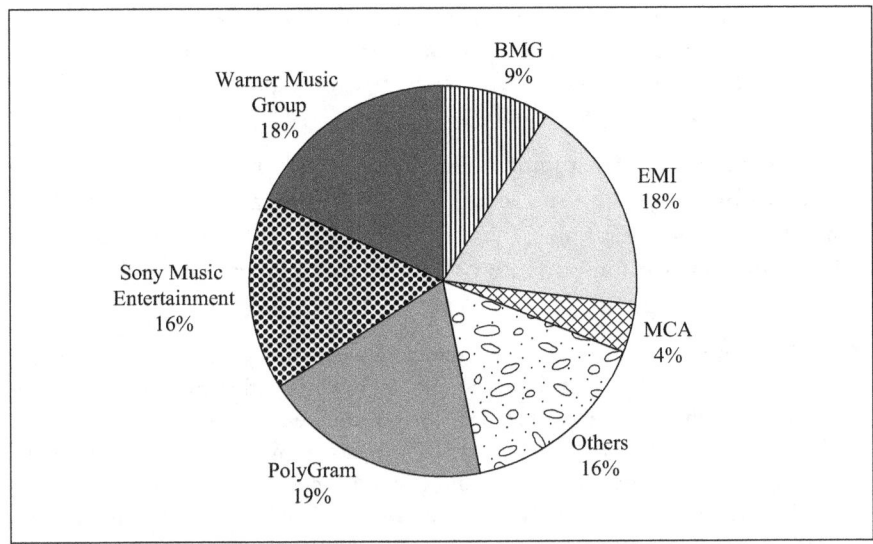

Figure 3.4 World music market: competitor market shares, 1991/1992. Source: PolyGram (1992), 'PolyGram Filmed Entertainment: Presentation to the Group Management Committee (31st August 1992)', PFE Archive.

flag on the kind of movies that they had come to prominence for, the Film Four/British Screen movies ... Almost as soon as I arrived, the cracks in the relationship between Tim and Sarah and Graham were already showing. It was a strange period ... Once PolyGram came in and 100 per cent funded, they didn't really want to do those little films anyway. The whole remit was about growing the company to do films that would appeal much more to an international market.[42]

The reorientation of PFE's production agenda coincided with changes in Working Title's management. In January 1992, Bradstreet incorporated his own film finance company, Bradstreet Media, based at offices in Dean Street. His disentanglement from Working Title was, however, amicably extended over the course of the year, coinciding with the termination of the company's original agreement with PolyGram. As Bradstreet explains, the change in business culture at Working Title over the previous two years was the primary reason for his exit:

> We had been used to doing whatever we liked, quite literally, and we were no longer able to do that ... We had to grow up and conform to a publicly traded very large corporate and their internal requirements and controls and protocols. That was something that none of the three of us had ever been involved with before ... It's just a different culture. When you're used to

being entrepreneurs and the three of you make decisions over a beer or glass of wine, we were now having to report the decision-making process extremely regularly and so we should, they had capitalised the company and were a major financier of ours.[43]

Nonetheless, Bradstreet remembers his time at Working Title fondly. 'For me it was, obviously, a massive learning curve and we all learned on the hoof in order to survive,' he recalls. 'I was lucky to be part of it, and it was vibrant and fun and an enormous amount of hard work and incredible risk taking.'[44] As he goes on to argue:

> Working Title, for me, is the template as to how you create production companies and [how] producers [should] operate within the movie business. I have advised various companies over the years … and it was always a version of the Working Title template because it overtly worked … They still live, independent producers, hand-to-mouth and it's just crazy … This is a business we're in and you've got to create sustainable companies and … that's what Tim and Sarah and I always wanted to do.[45]

Working Title's integration into PFE also took its toll on Radclyffe. Indeed, the creative and commercial imperatives of the control sheet had largely extinguished the Working Title of the 1980s. 'Sarah didn't like the formality of working with PolyGram, she felt they were interfering. She's very, very independent in spirit, and I love her for that,' Bevan recalls. 'She was never going to fit well with this more structured life that we were heading towards and I was desperate for a more structured life.'[46] Having made an initial investment in the company, Kuhn began to seek another producer to partner Bevan at the helm of Working Title. In early 1992, he approached Eric Fellner, the Co-Director of the London-based Initial Film and Television, about the prospect of joining Working Title (Ajax 1992: 2). As Kuhn explains:

> He wanted more money than we were willing to pay at the time and the argument that I used with him was that if you're an independent film producer you get one turn at bat every year to eighteen months but at Working Title he'd get three or four turns at bat every year. It was the year we got going, and if it worked he would quickly build up the most important asset, which is your name, reputation and producing skills, and that would be worth far more than a short-term difference between us on whatever we could afford to pay in cash.[47]

Convinced by the PFE plan, Fellner began working with Bevan shortly thereafter. Fellner had entered the industry at the same time as Bevan, initially working for MGM (Mallet, Godfrey & Mulcahy), one of the largest producers of music videos and commercials. Thereafter, Fellner created his own music video company, Direct Productions, before establishing Initial Pictures with investment from the reconfigured MGMM (Mallet, Grant, Mulcahy & Millaney) (Davies 1986: 26–7). Based at MGMM's offices in Golden Square, Initial largely worked outside the confines of social art cinema, producing more commercially oriented British films like *Sid and Nancy* (1986), *The Rachel Papers* (1989) and *Hidden Agenda* (1990). In 1990 Fellner and his partner, Malcolm Gerrie, organised a management buy-out of the rebranded Initial Film and Television by acquiring the 51 per cent stake in their company which was owned by the ailing MGMM (Moore 1990: 2). Continuing as an independent, Initial also produced American genre films such as *A Kiss Before Dying* (1991) and *Liebestraum* (1991). Recalling the circumstances surrounding Fellner's arrival, Bevan explains:

> What I'd worked out, and what Michael agreed with, is that the best use of me was as [a] film producer. He backed me as a film producer, and he thought the best thing a film producer can do is not worry about distribution all the time, not worry about where the money is going to come from, but worry about developing scripts and then once you've got a decent script, putting a decent team around it … He recognised that's a pretty difficult thing to do, and that there aren't that many people who can do it. I was very lucky. He saw in me someone who might be able to do that, and he thought that I probably wouldn't be able to do it on my own, so wouldn't it be a good idea to find a guy who's had a very parallel career but done exactly the same things, and Sarah and Graham had not done exactly the same things as I had, but Eric had done the same things as I had. Although we're very different people, we have had identical experiences and have very similar abilities.[48]

Fellner's arrival at Working Title coincided with Radclyffe's exit. 'I left because it was all getting too corporate, and I wanted to make films. It was all changing. Michael was really running it, and then Tim and Eric started working closely together,' she recalls. 'I wanted to run the low-budget division, and then Michael didn't want a low-budget division and I didn't want to go backwards and forwards to board meetings.'[49] In July Initial was sold to the media conglomerate Broadcast Communications, freeing Fellner to commit his future to Working Title (Dawtrey 1992: 14), The following month Radclyffe formed a new company, Sarah Radclyffe Productions (SRP), and took up residence in an office on Berwick Street. In the years that followed she remained true to her roots by producing a series of critically acclaimed independent films including *Second Best* (1994), *Bent* (1997) and *The War Zone* (1999) which, like much of Working Title's early work, engage with political and social issues.

With the new management team in place, a new company, Working Title Ltd, was incorporated as a wholly owned subsidiary of PFE in October 1992. Bevan and Fellner were appointed as its directors alongside three senior PFE representatives. Simultaneously, Working Title Films Ltd became dormant, holding the assets and liabilities which the production company had accrued between 1986 and 1992.⁵⁰ In effect, the new company was formed to provide a clean slate for the company's activities going forward. Over the course of the preceding four years, Working Title's integration into PolyGram Media Division, and subsequently PFE, transformed the way in which the company operated. Working within PMD's prototype studio system involved adhering to the creative and commercial demands of the 'control sheet', which effectively reoriented the company's filmmaking activities towards the marketplace. Significantly, the more sophisticated iterations of the control sheet which followed continued to guide Working Title along this trajectory in subsequent years, albeit within a greatly expanded studio system.

Notes

1. PolyGram (1989), 'Movies and Profits', p. 3, PolyGram Filmed Entertainment (PFE) Archive, privately held in Stonehaven and London (hereafter 'PFE Archive').
2. Michael Kuhn, interview with the author, 4-6-2013.
3. Malcolm Ritchie, interview with the author, 10-9-2014.
4. PolyGram (1989), 'Movies and Profits', p. 3, PFE Archive.
5. Malcolm Ritchie, interview with the author, 10-9-2014.
6. Ibid.
7. PolyGram (1989), 'Movies and Profits', Schedule 1A, PFE Archive.
8. Michael Kuhn, interview with the author, 8-2-2013.
9. PolyGram (1988), 'PolyGram: New Business Division', p. 2, PFE Archive.
10. Ibid.
11. PolyGram (1988), 'Business Plan: An Audio Visual Division', PFE Archive.
12. Wendy Palmer, interview with the author, 22-5-2013.
13. Graham Bradstreet, interview with the author, 9-10-2013.
14. Ibid.
15. PolyGram (1989), 'Movies and Profits', PFE Archive.
16. Malcolm Ritchie, interview with the author, 10-9-2014. The three major film sales markets during the 1980s and 1990s were the American Film Market (AFM) in Santa Monica, Le Marché du Film at the Cannes Film Festival and the Mercato Internazionale del Film e del Documentario (MIFED) in Milan.
17. Paul Webster, interview with the author, 10-5-2013.
18. Tim Bevan, interview with the author, 6-8-2013.
19. Malcolm Ritchie, interview with the author, 10-9-2014.
20. Tim Bevan, interview with the author, 6-8-2013.
21. Michael Kuhn, interview with the author, 4-6-2014.
22. PolyGram (1990), 'Proposal for Investment in Working Title Films', PFE Archive.

23 Ibid.
24 Ibid.
25 Malcolm Ritchie, interview with the author, 10-9-2014.
26 Wendy Palmer, interview with the author, 22-5-2013.
27 Ibid.
28 Malcolm Ritchie, interview with the author, 10-9-2014.
29 Ibid.
30 PolyGram (1992), 'Media Division: Red Book Consolidated Film Operations Report', PFE Archive.
31 Michael Kuhn, interview with the author, 8-2-2013.
32 Paul Webster, interview with the author, 10-5-2013.
33 Sarah Radclyffe, interview with the author on 26-3-2015 and email correspondence on 22-4-2015.
34 Ibid.
35 Ibid.
36 Wendy Palmer, interview with the author, 22-5-2013.
37 Malcolm Ritchie, interview with the author, 10-9-2014.
38 PolyGram (1991), 'PolyGram and Films', PFE Archive.
39 Malcolm Ritchie, interview with the author, 10-9-2014.
40 PolyGram (1992), 'PolyGram Filmed Entertainment: Presentation to the Group Management Committee (31st August 1992)', PFE Archive.
41 Ibid.
42 Alison Owen, interview with the author, 26-11-2013.
43 Graham Bradstreet, interview with the author, 30-10-2013.
44 Graham Bradstreet, interview with the author, 9-10-2013.
45 Ibid.
46 Tim Bevan, interview with the author, 6-8-2013.
47 Michael Kuhn, interview with the author, 8-2-2013.
48 Tim Bevan, interview with the author, 6-8-2013.
49 Sarah Radclyffe, interview with the author on 26-3-2015 and email correspondence on 22-4-2015.
50 PolyGram (1995), 'Documents relating to the reorganisation of Working Title Films Limited including the sale of certain assets to Working Title Limited: Volume I', PFE Archive. In February 1995, the dormant assets of Working Title Films Ltd were valued and sold to the wholly owned PFE subsidiary, Working Title Ltd. The ultimate sale price of £798,393 consisted largely of the 'work-in-progress' slate and to a lesser extent the 'movable plant and equipment'. Having acquired the company, Working Title Ltd adopted the original company's name, leaving the former Working Title Films Ltd to continue as a dormant entity under the title Producer Services Ltd.

CHAPTER 4

The PolyGram Years Part II: Development, Green-lighting and Distribution (1993–8)

The launch of PolyGram Filmed Entertainment (PFE) initiated the construction of a European-owned film studio which, over the course of the 1990s, challenged the dominance of the Hollywood industry. In doing so, PFE expanded its production capacity by acquiring three major production 'labels' – Propaganda Films, Working Title Films and Interscope Communications – and signing a host of third-party agreements with independent production companies. Simultaneously, PFE established distribution and marketing operations in fourteen territories worldwide and procured major film and television libraries. Working Title played a crucial role in PFE's development by producing many of the studio's most commercially successful films, including *Four Weddings and a Funeral* (1994), *Bean* (1997), *Elizabeth* (1998) and *Notting Hill* (1999), which helped to redefine expectations about the commercial potential of British films in popular genres. This output was complemented by films from American auteurs such as the Coen brothers (*The Hudsucker Proxy*, 1994; *Fargo*, 1996 and *The Big Lebowski*, 1998), Tim Robbins (*Bob Roberts*, 1992; *Dead Man Walking*, 1995) and Mario Van Peebles (*Posse*, 1993; *Panther*, 1995). Significantly, this eclecticism was underpinned by the company's simultaneous presence in both London and Los Angeles and thus within and between the filmmaking industries and cultures of Britain and Hollywood.

The transatlantic orientation of Working Title's production agenda and operational management was also reflected in the structure of PFE. Michael Kuhn was appointed President and CEO of the new company, which established its headquarters at a series of locations in and around Beverly Hills, close to the heart of the Hollywood film industry. From Los Angeles, Kuhn assumed responsibility for English-language production and 'domestic' distribution and marketing, a designation which entailed the US and Canadian markets. Simultaneously, PolyGram Filmed Entertainment International (PFEI) was established in London, with Kuhn appointing Stewart Till as President. Initially working from PolyGram's International headquarters in Berkeley Square, Till's responsibilities included overseeing the development of 'foreign-language' (non-English) production and 'international' distribution and marketing, a definition which encompassed all territories outside the US and Canada. The long-term strategy of producing British films within this context presented several distinct challenges. As Kuhn points out, the underlying nature of the relationship between the film industries and cultures of Britain and Hollywood placed Working Title in a unique position within PFE's nascent studio system:

> There's an enormous difference between the UK and Europe in several key respects. First of all, language, because we've got the same language as America we compete for talent in a way that European markets don't, because American talent doesn't speak French, Italian, Greek ... but we have to compete with Hollywood ... So that's the first difference, the second difference is that if you have a decent script in European countries you basically get your film made because they have tremendous mandatory TV buys. If you're a French broadcaster or pay TV operator you have to buy a certain number of French-produced, French-language films, the same in Germany, Scandinavia and all that. So, we're disadvantaged in that regard as well, but on the positive side, if you have an English-language film that works, you can sell it anywhere in the world because it's English-language. So, by nature we have to operate in the American world with talent, [but] we don't have the capital base the Americans have to make the films, the studios. We have to be much more inventive as producers to get our films made and we have to know the ways of Hollywood much more intimately than the Europeans do.[1]

Simultaneously, PFE hedged its bets by expanding its supply line of films from a range of LA-based production companies. In 1992, for example, PFE acquired a 51 per cent controlling interest in Interscope Communications for $35 million.[2] Notably, its founder and Chairman, Ted Field, and its President, Robert Cort, had a track record of producing hit films on a Hollywood scale including *Three Men and a Baby* (1987), *Cocktail* (1988) and *The Hand That Rocks the Cradle* (1992). Moreover, the average negative cost of Interscope's films was just $16 million and the company's ongoing contractual obligations to Disney ensured that half of its production costs were offset by the Hollywood studio, which also financed the domestic distribution and marketing of its films.[3] As Malcolm Ritchie, PFE's former COO, explains, buying into Interscope ensured increased diversity within PFE's overall slate:

> They were a different sort of vehicle. They were acquired for their capability, at that time, to produce big pictures, to produce films that could be released through the studio system. A wide release meaning, at that time, over 1,000 prints in the US, which was a different model than the Gramercy one, which, we were probably looking at, generally speaking, no more than 500 prints in the US. So, Interscope was different from the outset. As it turned out ... Interscope was not a success for us, but it had a good track record

of producing films for Disney, the Disney action movies which had done some very credible business immediately prior to [us] acquiring them ... We thought that – and I think that we were right – that you can produce the sort of films that Working Title and Propaganda were doing, but you're going to have to have bigger-budget films with bigger stars and Interscope presented itself as a business that had the ability to produce bigger budget films.[4]

As the project of building a studio got underway, financial discipline was expected of all PFE's production labels, which consistently produced films with budgets substantially below those of the major Hollywood studios. The average negative cost of PFE's films rose from $12 million in 1992 to $28 million in 1997/1998, for example, while the average cost of studio films increased from $28.9 million to $52.7 million in the same period.[5] Bridging the gap between the British and Hollywood industries, then, and simultaneously developing British films that 'work' on a worldwide scale, became key objectives for Working Title. Achieving these goals rested largely with the company's Co-Chairmen, Tim Bevan and Eric Fellner, who were ultimately responsible for directing Working Title's creative and commercial agenda by successfully guiding films through the filmmaking process. The following section explores the roles of Bevan and Fellner within the emerging PFE studio system.

POSITIONING THE PRODUCER

Upon their appointment as Co-Chairmen of Working Title, Bevan and Fellner simultaneously became employees of PFE secured on fixed-term service contracts to the studio. In return, PFE capitalised Working Title with annual overhead and development budgets and permitted the producers creative autonomy at the point of development. In doing so, Working Title's relationship with PFE mirrored the typical arrangement in the contemporary Hollywood industry, in which a studio finances development and production in return for ownership of the resulting intellectual property, and thus the right to exploit it in the marketplace. As Fellner explains, the role of the producer is perhaps best characterised as the intermediary between creativity and commerce:

> A producer is like the chief executive of any business. He has to build the business, come up with the ideas, come up with the money to support those ideas and find the creative and technical talent to make those ideas into reality. He has to finance the business going forward, run the business to a schedule and a budget, and ensure that every single person employed is doing absolutely everything that he or she ought to be doing and support them, in all the ways that you can support them, so they can do their best work. Then, when they've made their product, he ensures that that product is as good as

it possibly can be and that it gets to market, that it's properly marketed and distributed.⁶

The management of Working Title was, however, subject to some experimentation before the two producers settled into the working relationship which would define their partnership. Initially Bevan and Fellner worked together on the development and production of films before dividing this labour between them. As Bevan recalls:

> We realised almost immediately – because we'd both been independent producers beforehand – that that wasn't going to work. One is that we've got slightly different styles, and secondly that it meant that everything was just being doubled up on, and thirdly, for third parties, i.e. creative people like writers and directors, it was an ideal opportunity to divide and rule, basically, because they could come to one of us and then represent to the other one of us ... It became very apparent, very quickly that that wasn't a way to do things. We both already had creative relationships, and so we both built on those creative relationships. We decided that what was important was to pool knowledge about what we were doing ... One is, is it a good idea? Two is, are these good people to ... do it with us? Three, the business side of it, as it were. Pool that knowledge but to run our own projects. Also, what we rapidly realised is that that way we'd be able to do a couple more movies a year.⁷

Significantly, PFE's production companies operated under the same set of principles as the PolyGram 'label system' within which A&R companies functioned as semi-autonomous businesses and developed distinct creative identities. In doing so, the creative sensibilities of Bevan and Fellner came to the fore when guiding the development of the company's slate. As Fellner explains, 'I will probably veer more towards mainstream material, and he will probably veer more towards intellectual [material] or material with artistic integrity, but we can both cross over into those other areas.'⁸ Expanding on this theme, Bevan suggests:

> I'd say that there's a sixty per cent common bandwidth ... there's 20 per cent out there of stuff that I might do that he wouldn't, and there's probably 20 per cent of stuff out there that he might do that I probably wouldn't ... One of the reasons for splitting up the projects too was that you realise in order to get a film produced, you, the lead producer, has to have an immense and tireless passion for it, and you're not going to have the same passion for everything, basically. If he's more passionate about something than me, that I like, that's great. If I'm more passionate about something than him, that he likes, that's fine. It's very, very rare that either of us make a movie that the other actively dislikes, and probably never does that happen ... To the outsider, they wouldn't necessarily know what's an 'Eric film' and what's a 'Tim film' ... so there's a Working Title house style. It's not just us two, it's

the osmosis of the projects coming through the system and similar people are working on the development and the production ... so it's that that makes it a Working Title film.⁹

During the first years of the PFE era, Bevan and Fellner typically took executive producer credits on the films Working Title produced, ostensibly reflecting their new roles within a larger corporate entity. The situation would not, however, continue for long. 'I felt that the people who were ... on the set ... probably deserved the producer credit and that I should take the executive producer credit,' Bevan recalls. 'We were doing all of the producing functions, but we might not be sitting on the set the whole time. There was a sort of inverted snobbery that if you didn't sit on the set you weren't a proper producer, and actually, we thought that was rubbish.'¹⁰ Going forward the producer credit was, however, typically shared with a third-party producer brought in to work on the production of a specific film. As Bevan explains:

> Sometimes there's two films shooting at the same time – it's best if there's not – but there'll always be something in pre-production, something in post-production, something shooting. I don't have time to be on the set the whole time and a film needs to have somebody ... who has producorial authority, producorial creative knowledge who's there all day, every day ... They're the on-set producer. The same names turn up quite often, you'll see on the credits ... They have to have a very good relationship with either one of us, basically, but they also have to have our trust ... I like to say they're in charge of the money ... You'd argue to get it [the film] to whatever the number is that you manage to get it green-lit, but then that third-party producer, I will entrust with spending that.¹¹

Over the years that followed, these names included a host of leading producers in the British film industry such as Jonathan Cavendish, Mark Huffam, Duncan Kenworthy, Alison Owen, Nira Park and Paul Webster. To accommodate such activity, however, Working Title had to significantly reshape its infrastructure. '[We] decided to build a proper business that had departments that operated properly and efficiently ... and had reporting structures,' Fellner confirms. 'Most importantly, we set up the notion of building a slate for development and production, so that each year we were delivering a substantial amount of films into the distribution entity.'¹²

As Figure 4.1 shows, Working Title was promptly organised into six departments: administration, accounts, development, production, the US office and legal and business affairs. The four departments directly involved in filmmaking – development, production, US office and legal and business affairs – were, respectively, run by Debra Hayward, Jane Frazer, Liza Chasin

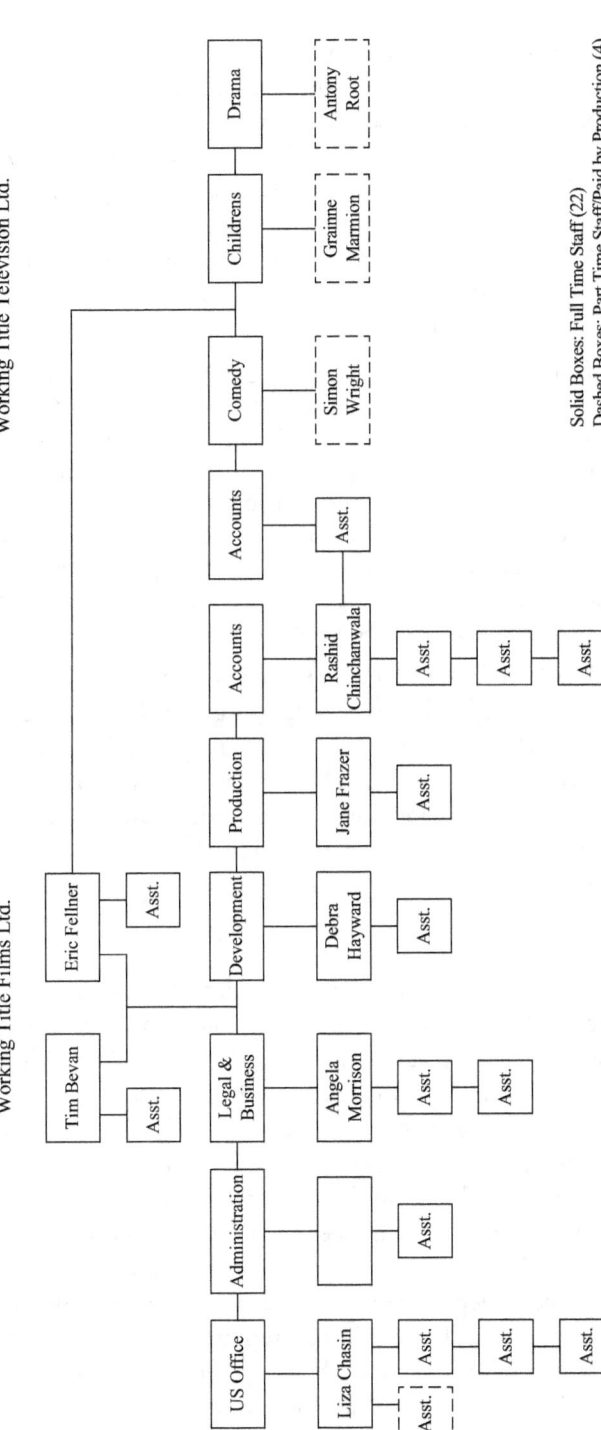

Figure 4.1 Working Title operating framework, 1993. Source: PolyGram (1993), 'PolyGram Filmed Entertainment', PFE Archive.

and Angela Morrison, all of whom were promoted from within. In contrast, Working Title Television (WTTV) consisted of only three members of staff, who were either part-time or paid on commission.

While this basic structure remained in place throughout Working Title's years as a PFE label, the company's headcount rose from twenty-two to thirty-one between 1993 and 1998, in step with the growing ambitions of both parent company and subsidiary.[13] Significantly, this structure allowed Bevan and Fellner to focus their time and energy on the areas of the filmmaking process which surrounded the shoot. As Fellner notes:

> The two critical areas are development and putting the film into production and then post production, marketing and distribution ... Everyone focuses on the shoot, but the shoot is kind of irrelevant, because if you've done your job properly and hired the right camera man, the right director, the script is perfect, [and] you've got the actors – if you've got all those people right – they should create magic. If you've got it wrong, then they won't create magic ... if you've done it right, you're just there to support it and then it's just a physical process of making sure they're on budget and on schedule, and our production team are really good at doing that.[14]

The crucial stages of the filmmaking process identified by Fellner are interpreted here as three key points of gatekeeping: development, green-lighting and distribution. What follows considers the relationship between PFE and Working Title by examining these gates as discrete steps in the filmmaking process which were, in turn, operated by the individual and collective agency of key personnel at both Working Title and PFE.

GATE 1: DEVELOPMENT

The essential role of any development department is to convert original story ideas or existing intellectual property into films by developing them in collaboration with key creative talent. At Working Title, this activity was split between the company's offices in London and Los Angeles, run by Debra Hayward in the former location and Liza Chasin in the latter. In the mid-1990s Working Title's head office moved from Water Lane to Oxford House, a large office building on the east end of Oxford Street. In contrast, Working Title's LA office relocated several times, often residing within the same building as PFE's other LA-based operations. A compelling factor for the development departments in both locations became ensuring that the company's slate would satisfy the requirements of PFE's expanding distribution pipeline. Accordingly, Working Title's development portfolio expanded to include dozens of film projects, ranging from the embryonic to the production-ready.

Crucially, development became a properly resourced stage in the filmmaking process for the first time. Working Title's 1994 budget, for example, included a total development allowance of £2,922,000 ($4.5 million), which allocated up to £324,500 ($500,000) for two 'larger star driven' projects, and up to £162,250 ($250,000) each for twelve 'larger idea driven' projects and a further £324,500 ($500,000) for the acquisition of spec scripts. Working on the expectation that the company would produce four films a year, this amounted to a conversion ratio of 2:1 for 'star driven' projects and 4:1 for 'idea driven' projects.[15] As the ambitions of both PFE and Working Title grew throughout the decade so too did the production company's annual development budget, which reached $11 million in 1998.[16] As Hayward explains, such resources created a working environment which differed substantially from the typical set-up in the British independent sector:

> In America you have all those echelons in the studios and in major production companies – all those creative, executive strata – that didn't exist here. It was very much a cottage producing industry. If you were a producer you did absolutely everything, including pushing it over the final starting line to get your film made ... Through the '90s ... I was very privileged because our films were fully financed ... When it's a one-stop shop like that, when you're not, as a producer, having to go out and piece together bits of funding, it does allow you to be creative and to put all your energies into making the best film possible. I think that obviously accounts for a lot of the success of Working Title. The films were much better ... because ... they were really, really well developed ... well cast [and] well attended to throughout their production.[17]

Despite the benefit of these resources, successfully developing films in-house remained a challenge. 'There has to be a lot of drive and passion behind getting something off the ground because all the way along the chain you're having to convince somebody that they've got to do it,' Hayward explains. 'You're having to convince someone to buy the idea, convince a writer that it's a good idea, then you're having to convince a director of that screenplay.'[18] While Working Title created a development infrastructure in London which began to resemble that of the Hollywood film industry, it was also paramount to maintain a simultaneous presence in Los Angeles. 'It became very apparent, very quickly, that everything we were doing, whether it was strictly a London-based film or not, was coming through LA at some point; through the agencies for talent, or writers or directors,' Chasin recalls. 'Everything was passing through, so having a presence here and having relationships with the agencies and the community here was a necessity really; we couldn't have pushed our movies into being without it.'[19] Doing so as a new entrant into the Hollywood industry, however, required actively establishing a profile for Working Title which also encompassed PFE's overall vision, as Chasin acknowledges:

> We were trying to convince people that we weren't only making beautiful, arty films out of the UK, that we were looking to expand ... We were doing movies that were kind of transitional films ... It was really just convincing people who we were, that this new kind of studio called PolyGram was real and that all of us who were part of that – [Working Title], Propaganda and Interscope ... were forging ahead, convincing the town that this new presence, which everybody only knew as a music company, was making a real foray into film ... There was a lot of outgoing, a lot of outgoing calls. I like to joke that those were the years where we got a lot of scripts from the agents that had a little thin layer of dust on them, that they couldn't get made anywhere else.[20]

The two offices, however, remained distinct in terms of their overall functions. 'I always refer to the LA office as a strictly creative outpost,' Chasin explains. 'We don't house any of our business affairs, our accounting, or physical production team here.'[21] The difference between the British and the Hollywood industries was also clearly felt in terms of scale, as Chasin goes on to point out:

> When we put together those [talent] lists, ours are endless on this end versus the London list because the London pool is so much smaller. Of course, when we're talking about bigger, more studio-minded films, there's a handful of writers you'd go to in London for things like that, but there's pages worth of names you could go to here. With Debra, she and I, for twenty-plus years worked together as though we were in the next room from one another. We had an incredibly close [relationship], both personally and professional[ly] ... and it just meant that we could hand things back and forth easily between one another, which is what we still do now between the two offices ... We could start a project there, and wind up putting a writer on it here, then it comes out of our office, then it flips back there for production. We operate the LA office of Working Title as though it's really embedded, that we're in the same place. We just have the benefit of the eight-hour time difference over here ... so when everyone [in London] goes to bed, we keep going.[22]

Once a project in development reached the latter stages of the process, with a script nearing completion and key creative personnel attached, the project would migrate to the production department for the first time. As Jane Frazer explains:

> You have to do the schedule first. So, you have to schedule the film and work out how long it's going to take. Which scenes [do] you do, when? Where [do] you do them? Are they day or are they night? Who's in them? Which crew do you need? Which specialists do you need? ... Then you break it down in

enormous detail, and then you just cost out that detail ... There has always been a standard, what's known as a chart of accounts, which is how you cost ... What I used to do then, and still do, is prepare a budget and then everyone goes 'It's too much' because it doesn't fit the control sheet figures and then you have to try and bring it down. Then you work with the script, or the producer works with the script, to see whether or not some script amendments can be made.[23]

Script amendments are considered with a keen eye on the 'below-the-line' costs associated with the physical production. 'The most expensive thing is time, so then you try to knock days or weeks off the schedule,' Frazer confirms. 'You try and keep it as contained as possible, you try and put two locations in one location, so you're not travelling between because that wastes time.'[24] Equally, the production budget could be reduced by focusing on the 'above-the-line' costs associated with the key creative players working on the film. 'What you do to bring down costs is you pay people less, pay the actors less, pay the writers less, you pay the producers less,' Frazer explains. 'People often end up deferring their fees.'[25] As she goes on to point out:

> Every single film I've ever done, whether it's Working Title or not, the budget is always higher than it needs to be ... The really big thing that made Working Title so good was the fact that both Tim and Sarah, and then Eric, had come up through independent filmmaking, so no one was used to anything smart or expensive, and they'd actually done it themselves, whereas a lot of producers haven't come up that way any more. They've just done big stuff where there's plenty of money. They forensically understood budgets. They understood what you were talking about when you were doing my job. They knew exactly what was what.[26]

Simultaneously, the legal and business affairs department run by Angela Morrison oiled the wheels of the development and production departments. 'Most of my work was really the heavy lifting on the production side,' she recalls. 'The talent deals, the ... actual production work, so all the agreements relating to locations, clearances, the talent – the actors, the director, the producers, the writers, everything that flowed from that.'[27] As Morrison notes, the management of Working Title's legal and business affairs extended upwards into the PFE corporate hierarchy. 'PolyGram was great at integrating people, individuals, into the organisation so that it never felt that it was them or us,' she explains. 'We were colleagues, we were all working together with the same aim, which was to make films that were successful.'[28] Within the new structure, Alison Owen remained at Working Title but worked on projects directly with Bevan and Fellner, most notably *Elizabeth*, of which she recalls:

> The idea was to do a period movie in the style of *Trainspotting*, that was the brief that we gave to ourselves ... We looked at lots of subjects to see what would best fit that mould. I remember, of all the things we talked about, the two that came down the line were Boudicca and Elizabeth I. In the end we decided to go with Elizabeth I because we felt that it ... had a real resonance with modern women. The choice between the personal life and public life that we felt was a real modern woman's dilemma ... That also informed the choice of Shekhar as director ... because we thought he'd be able to give that chaotic modern style, which was the idea. I don't think that's necessarily what we ended up with – a period movie in the style of *Trainspotting* – but that's how we got to where we got to.[29]

Working Title's movement away from raising production finance from the public sources which had supported the company throughout much of the 1980s was underlined by the arrangement of two 'off balance sheet' film lease agreements which PFE secured in 1994 and 1996 with a consortium led by the Sumitomo and ING investment banks. The deals respectively provided PFE with $200 million and $300 million of capital, which financed the studio's ongoing production slate.[30] A new wave of public investment in film from the National Lottery, however, briefly suggested this might change. In 1997 the Arts Council of England (ACE) used Lottery funds to devise a scheme which awarded grants to UK-based companies which created 'mini studios' by linking production with UK distribution and international sales. In putting a bid together, PFE joined Working Title with Revolution Films and Thejonescompany, two UK-based production companies under 'first-look' deals with the studio, to form a consortium called Double Negative (Dawtrey 1997: 1). As Morrison explains, the bid failed partly because of industry perceptions of PFE:

> I think we were deemed to be not eligible because we had access to what was perceived by the industry as a big corporate backer ... We did on a few occasions successfully persuade the Arts Council on one or two projects that they ought to invest, but generally speaking ... and the grant of that franchise money was a case in point, they weren't going to give it to us. We were already funded by PolyGram and owned by PolyGram, so we were a subsidiary of a major corporation in their minds, so why would they give us the money?[31]

As the years progressed, PFE substantially expanded its production assets beyond its three original labels. As Table 4.1 shows, five of PFE's third-party first-look production deals were with US-based companies, including Scott Free Productions, Havoc Inc., Fincher Films, Egg Pictures and Rumbalara Films. This tendency was further entrenched in January 1998 when PFE

Producer/director	Film credits	Company	Country
Tony Scott, Ridley Scott	*Beverly Hills Cop II, Top Gun, Crimson Tide, Blade Runner, Thelma & Louise, G.I. Jane*	Scott Free Productions	US
Alan Parker	*Evita, The Commitments*	Dirty Hands Productions	UK
Tim Robbins	*Dead Man Walking, Bob Roberts*	Havoc, Inc.	US
David Fincher	*The Game, Seven*	Fincher Films, Inc.	US
Jane Campion	*The Portrait of a Lady, The Piano*	Big Shell Films	Australia
Jodie Foster	*Home from the Holidays, Nell*	Egg Pictures	US
Philip Noyce	*Clear and Present Danger, Patriot Games*	Rumbalara Films	US
Robert Jones	*The Usual Suspects, Sirens*	Thejonescompany	UK
Andrew Eaton, Michael Winterbottom	*Resurrection Man, Jude, Welcome to Sarajevo, Go Now*	Revolution Films	UK
Michael Hamlyn	*Priscilla: Queen of the Desert, U2: Rattle and Hum*	Specific Films	UK
Duncan Kenworthy, Andrew McDonald	*Lawn Dogs, Four Weddings and a Funeral, A Life Less Ordinary, Shallow Grave*	DNA Films	UK

Table 4.1 PFE third-party English-language production deals, 1998. Source: PolyGram (1998), 'Confidential Memorandum: PolyGram Filmed Entertainment', PFE Archive.

raised a further $200 million off balance sheet with Warner Bros. to co-finance the slate of Castle Rock Entertainment, which would be co-distributed by the two studios over a three-year period.[32] Unlike the Hollywood studios, however, PFE invested equally heavily in British-based production, not only through Working Title, but also via third-party production deals with companies such as Dirty Hands Productions, Thejoescompany, Revolution Films, Specific Films and DNA Films. This activity was complemented with high-profile acquisitions from the independent sector including *Shallow Grave* (1994), *Trainspotting* (1996), *Spice World* (1997) and *Lock, Stock and Two Smoking Barrels* (1998). In contrast, PFE's investment in foreign-language production remained limited. Most of this activity was Francophone and mediated through the PFE subsidiary Pan-Européenne (France) and first-look deals with companies like Noe (France) and Cinémaginaire (Canada). As Stewart Till, President of PFEI, observes:

> The only films that travel, really, are Hollywood or American films and British films ... English-language [films] ... The great irony is, if you make a film in France, when you take it to Germany, it's dubbed into German from the French. If you take a film from London, it's dubbed into German, so they're both dubbed into German. So, it's not about the language, it's more about the culture and the storytelling and the filmmaking ... We had some success in France, particularly with a project called *Le huitième jour*, but in the main we didn't spend a lot of time and money on local language films because they didn't travel.[33]

Working Title's final production-related department, Working Title Television, remained an entirely UK-based operation. Shortly before the launch of PFE, WTTV entered the bidding process for one of the fifteen regional ITV franchises which were up for renewal through a consortium called London Independent Broadcasting (LIB). Ultimately, however, the bid was unsuccessful and LIB lost out to the incumbent, London Weekend Television (LWT) (Davidson 1992: 92–108). 'I remember ... talking to Michael Kuhn and it wasn't anticipated that we'd get anywhere with the bid. Nobody ever really seriously thought we'd land it,' recalls Simon Wright, former President of WTTV. 'Life would have been very different had we got it.'[34] As he goes on to explain, the way in which television development and production was funded at WTTV was markedly different from the film model:

> The television side was run just like any other independent company. It would rely on a commission from a broadcaster who would give a licence fee and then the balance of the money would come from ... soft subsidies – in those days we had the sale and leaseback, remember, so you'd get 12 per cent of the budget from that, you'd get the licence fee and then you'd get a distribution advance from a distributor and that would be supplied always by PolyGram ... Very, very few people just fund things without broadcasters attached and there's a simple reason for that as well. The broadcast licence fees are way, way above what you would require to buy a finished programme ... Television only works if you've got the majority of the budget as a licence fee from a single broadcaster.[35]

The activity of WTTV, however, remained relatively limited as its original genre-based structure – 'Comedy', 'Children' and 'Drama' – was collapsed and its staff numbers reduced. Nonetheless, notable productions included *Tales of the City* (Channel 4, 1993), *The Baldy Man* (ITV, 1995–7) and *More Tales of the City* (Channel 4, 1998). The entire feature film development process would, however, only translate into production when a green-light decision was made.

GATE 2: GREEN-LIGHTING

The process for green-lighting films in place at PFE was explicitly designed to avoid top-down decision-making at the studio's head office in Los Angeles, and instead spread the responsibility between various divisions of the studio. Once a project reached the latter stages of development at a PFE label, it was routed through the studio's distribution, marketing and sales divisions which collectively produced a more sophisticated version of the 'control sheet', which was then considered by PFE's senior management. In doing so, the results of the creative autonomy exercised by Working Title at the point of development were examined against various forms of market forecasting. As Ritchie explains:

> It was very simple, they would be working on the development of a project and they would eventually get to the point where they've got a script, they've got talent interested, they've done a budget, they'd put the script and the talent package out to the sales company and some of the key distribution territories to see what sort of interest there might be from them and how the numbers might look: they would put together their control sheet. And then they would come to us, and we would know they were doing it, because they weren't working in isolation ... There was a lot of give and take in the process and Michael would always play an important part although he wasn't nominally the studio head green-lighting films. He was the one that they'd be speaking to, saying 'We're looking at doing a deal here, with this talent, on that project, do you support [this]?'[36]

PFE's distribution infrastructure in the US included Gramercy Pictures, a 'specialty' distribution company for medium- and low-budget films, and eventually a second company, PolyGram Pictures, for big-budget films. In contrast, the infrastructure of PFEI was effectively split between the London-based Manifesto Film Sales, which was rebranded PolyGram Film International (PFI), and a network of operating companies or 'OP COs' which directly handled the distribution and marketing of PFE's films in key international territories. Pointing out the relationship between the two, Stewart Till explains:

> PolyGram Film International did two things. They were the sales company which sold the rights to the territories where we didn't have distribution. Originally that was everywhere except France, then that was everywhere

> except France and the UK, then everywhere except France, the UK and Benelux. So, as we set up more territories the sales company shrank. They also oversaw the theatrical release ... provided the marketing materials, coordinated and had some oversight ... The Hollywood studios had a culture that head office knew best. We had a saying that Hamburg knew best or Rome knew best, and if it didn't know best about the local market, you had the wrong person in there. PFI did more than coordinate, because they could challenge decisions but they didn't control the territories.[37]

In practice, the control sheet was a document which contained all the necessary information to determine the risk and reward profile of each film project in development at PFE's production labels. As the sample control sheet in Figure 4.2 illustrates, input from Working Title's development, production and legal and business affairs departments was used to complete the data in the 'Film Details' and 'Production Budget' sections. The 'Film Details' section also lists the key above-the-line talent (typically the writer, director, producer and lead actors) linked to the project, and the 'participations' that these personnel will receive in relation to the net or gross box office revenue of the film. The initialisms 'BO', 'CBE' and 'IAB' respectively stand for 'Box Office', 'Cash Break Even' and 'Initial Actual Break Even'. The 'Production Budget' section gives a summary of the budget including above-the-line and below-the-line costs as well as contingency, completion bond and financing costs. Thereafter, the production fee and PFE's central fee, charged at 15 per cent and 2.5 per cent respectively, are listed. Finally, the 'Residuals' section lists the various trade guilds which may be involved in the production and the residual benefit payments that may consequently apply. As Ritchie points out, the practice of applying fees was common to all the PFE production, distribution and sales subsidiaries:

> We let the producers take a production fee and the local PFE distributors and PFI take distribution and sales fees. Ideally they would get enough fees in a year to cover their overheads. They were not the ones making the big bucks – this was the ultimate centre of PFE where the film rights are owned and where the profit from a successful film slate sits. From a management point of view, the production companies had to try to break even but we did not want to green-light films and let them earn a production fee so that they could do just this – that would be bad business practice. They had to get good films green-lit and hopefully make a small profit in so doing.[38]

The 'Summary' section presents seven revenue scenarios, marked with 'low', 'medium' and 'high' case outcomes. These figures are based upon the collective revenue forecasts from US distribution (via Gramercy/ PolyGram Pictures), international direct distribution (via the PFE OP COs)

POLYGRAM FILMED ENTERTAINMENT   **CONTROL SHEET MASTER**
Production Control Sheet - Summary

FILM DETAILS		PRODUCTION BUDGET ($000)		DRAFT NOTES		
Director	A. Smithee	Above-the-Line	$3,600			
Cast	A. Starr	Below-the-Line	7,200			
Producer	A. Producer	Sub-Total	10,800			
Start Date	01-Jan-98					
Estimated Release Date	01-Mar-99	Contingence 0.0%	0			
Distributor	Studio	Completion 1.3%	140			
Pay TV Deal?	High	Sub-Total	10,940	**RESIDUALS**		
Network TV Sale?	Yes			Guilds:	SAG	Y
Participations:		Label Fee 15.0%	1,500		WGA	Y
A. Starr: $5M against 5% of 1st Dollar Gross; BO kick		PFE Fee 2.5%	250		DGA	Y
A. Smithee: 5% of CBE w/10% fee; esc. to 7.5% of		Finance Costs	453		AFM	Y
CB esc. to 10% @ IAB.		**Total Negative Cost**	**$13,143**		IATSE	Y

SUMMARY ($000)	LOW		MEDIUM			HIGH	
U.S. Gross Box Office	$20,000	$25,000	$30,000	$35,000	$40,000	$45,000	$50,000
Non U.S. Box Office	85,524	99,446	113,367	127,289	137,546	147,803	158,061
% of U.S. Box Office	427.6%	397.8%	377.9%	363.7%	343.9%	328.5%	316.1%
Income before Fee Contribution	$23,324	$27,300	$30,613	$23,324	$38,805	$43,068	$46,886
Fee Contribution	15,838	17,462	19,045	20,591	21,970	23,464	24,957
Income after Fee Contribution	$39,162	$44,763	$49,658	$43,914	$60,775	$66,531	$71,842
Return before Fee Contribution	68.4%	74.2%	76.6%	55.8%	89.3%	95.5%	100.4%
Return after Fee Contribution	114.8%	121.7%	124.3%	105.0%	139.9%	147.6%	153.8%

NET INCOME ANALYSIS ($000)	LOW			MEDIUM			HIGH
Domestic Gross Box Office	$22,000	$27,000	$33,000	$38,000	$43,000	$49,000	$54,000
U.S. Gross Box Office	$20,000	$25,000	$30,000	$35,000	$40,000	$45,000	$50,000
Rental Rate	40.0%	41.0%	42.5%	42.5%	42.5%	44.0%	45.0%
U.S. Home Video Units - Rental	180	200	215	230	245	260	275
U.S. Home Video Units - Sell-Thru	20	25	30	40	60	80	120
Rental Income	$8,000	$10,250	$12,750	$14,875	$17,000	$19,800	$22,500
Net Home Video Receipts - $41.00	7,380	8,200	8,815	9,430	10,045	10,660	11,275
Net Home Video Receipts - $4.00	80	100	120	160	240	320	480
Pay TV Gross Receipts	4,450	5,643	6,568	7,354	7,840	8,456	9,050
PPV Gross Receipts	156	204	252	288	324	352	379
Network Gross Receipst	1,000	1,250	1,500	2,000	2,500	2,750	3,000
Basic Cable Gross Receipts	450	500	550	600	650	825	1,000
Syndication Gross Receipts	185	195	205	213	225	238	248
Non-Theatrical Receipts	0	0	0	0	0	0	0
Merchandising Receipts	0	0	0	0	0	0	0
International Advance	21,009	21,009	21,009	21,009	21,009	21,009	21,009
International Direct Income	28,270	31,484	34,698	37,911	40,443	42,975	45,507
Total Receipts	70,980	78,834	86,466	93,840	100,276	107,385	114,448
Negative Costs	13,143	13,143	13,143	13,143	13,143	13,143	13,143
U.S. P&A Cost	13,780	15,900	18,550	19,875	21,200	22,525	23,850
International P&A Cost	7,187	7,726	8,264	8,803	9,111	9,419	9,726
Theatrical Distribution Fee 15.0%	1,200	1,538	1,913	2,231	2,550	2,970	3,375
Home Video Distribution Fee 20.0%	1,431	1,592	1,714	1,841	1,978	2,114	2,270
TV Fees (15% except 25% on synd & bank)	1,000	1,238	1,437	1,650	1,818	1,999	2,176
PFI Fee (5% on Direct/15% on Subs)	4,205	4,339	4,473	4,607	4,718	4,829	4,940
PFI Sales Costs	600	600	600	600	600	600	600
Residuals	5,109	5,457	5,759	6,075	6,353	6,615	6,880
Participations	0	0	0	0	0	103	601
Total Disbursements	47,656	51,533	55,853	58,825	61,471	64,317	67,562
Film Income before Fee Contribution	$23,324	$27,300	$30,613	$23,324	$38,805	$43,068	$46,886

Figure 4.2   The control sheet (sample). Source: Kuhn 2002: 130.

and international sales to third parties (via PFI). In the given example, the US gross box office estimate ranges from a low-case scenario of $20m to a high-case scenario of $50m. The same range of scenarios is given for non-US box office, which ranges from a low of $85.5m to a high of $158m.[39] Based on these gross income levels, the net income is then divided to indicate income before fee contribution, fee contribution and income after fee contribution. The income before fee contribution indicates the film's net profit. The 'Fee Contribution' represents the total internal income from all fees charged by PFE production, distribution and sales subsidiaries which, in turn, fund the overheads and margins in these various PFE operations. Significantly, as the number of OP COs expanded, the distribution and marketing expertise available to project the control sheet figures increased. As Julia Short, former Head of Marketing and Publicity at PFE UK, explains:

> We used to supply the numbers that used to get plugged into the control sheet ... we would have to project what box office it would do, how much money we would need to spend to attain that box office, but those two figures would have to take into consideration our TV output deals, because our TV deal with Channel 4 was triggered based on a certain ... P&A spend and our Sky deal was predicated on certain numbers as well ... Because we were always in the same building and the same space as the [PFE UK] video people, we would also find out from them how strong a title it was for home entertainment ... It was a question of understanding all the areas of exploitation.[40]

Next, the 'Net Income Analysis' section demonstrates how the figures in the summary were calculated by presenting a breakdown of receipts and disbursements. As the largest and most diversified entertainment market in the world, the US received the most rigorous breakdown of receipts on the control sheet. The domestic gross box office (US and Canada) is given before the US gross box office is analysed. The rental rate refers to the percentage of box office revenue claimed by the distributor, a figure which, in the example, ranges from 40 per cent to 45 per cent. Thereafter, projected units of rental and sell-through US home video are given before income from rental, home video and the various forms of television – pay TV, pay-per-view, network, basic cable and syndication – are listed. In contrast, international income is presented in consolidated figures, divided only into 'International Advances' or 'International Direct Income'. The former represents sales to third parties via PFI, while the latter indicates income from PFE OP COs. 'Non-Theatrical' and 'Merchandising' receipts are also listed, but have no bearing on this example. The disbursements section begins with the negative cost of the film, before listing the associated US and international P&A costs. Next, the various distribution fees for the PFE distribution/sales companies are listed across the platforms of US theatrical, US home video, US television, PFE OP COs and PFI. Finally, residuals and participations are listed. The total disbursement costs are deducted from the total receipts to give the film income result. This result line therefore shows the 'profit' (or loss) of the film itself after all relevant costs and fees.

While the control sheet presented the commercial case for a given film in black and white, the figures inevitably prompted debate between PFE's production labels, marketing, distribution and sales divisions and senior management. 'It went from coercion to aggression and sometimes neither worked and sometimes both worked,' Fellner joked. 'It was a very good, healthy, discourse and it has taught us right up until today – and it's probably ingrained for the rest of our careers – that you have to make a film at the right budget for the type of film that it is. If you don't, you're just asking for trouble.'[41] Indeed, despite the adversarial nature of the control sheet, the overall working environment at PFE was collaborative. 'We used to refer to the PolyGram family and anyone you speak to who worked at PolyGram would probably say the same, I would think, that it was a family of people who worked very well together,' Morrison explains. 'It was phone calls, it was meetings, it was daily contact, it wasn't ... once every so often and only around the control sheet.'[42] At Working Title, the control sheet was effectively internalised, and became the 'instrument of discipline that the whole company fell in line behind'. As Morrison goes on to point out:

> It brought discipline to the company because the control sheet was revenue, cost, outgoings on third-party participations. What were the deals that we were making? Were they good deals? Were they bad deals? Where should they cut in? ... Part of looking at the control sheet from a cost perspective wasn't just the production budget itself and how much the film would cost to make, but also then what we would have to pay out if it was a success, at what point we were paying that out, and how much we'd have to pay out if it was a success, and what impact that had on the margin that PolyGram needed for its own investment. That, really, was the single most effective tool to bring everybody into line within the decision-making process, and lessons were learned through that that haven't been forgotten.[43]

The control sheet and the international distribution and marketing infrastructure which supported its function were arguably PFE's greatest innovations. As Ritchie explains, the Hollywood film industry within which PFE operated initially viewed the studio's methods with some suspicion:

> There was a snippet that I once cut out from *Variety* about the European company that ran its business through a spreadsheet, and they were speaking about the control sheet ... They thought that this was kind of amusing. In

fact, within a very short period of time, that's exactly what the studios started doing. I'm not saying that we were before them, but they didn't do it to the same extent that we were doing it, because their operations were managed completely differently ... The way that international [at] Warner, UIP, Paramount and all of these companies worked ... They didn't get involved in the selection of the projects, or even giving any input into the projects. They were simply told by Hollywood, 'Here's a film, distribute it'.[44]

Once a green-light decision was made it would, in turn, initiate the final stage of gate keeping: distribution. Following the model in place at the major Hollywood studios, PFE set about establishing distribution and marketing subsidiaries in key markets to coordinate its domestic and international film releases.

GATE 3: DISTRIBUTION

Upon his arrival in Los Angeles, Kuhn's immediate priority was to establish distribution operations in the US. This process had, in fact, begun immediately prior to the launch of PFE with the acquisition of an ongoing output deal from the financially troubled Nelson Entertainment. Nelson was unable to meet its contractual commitments to Columbia, Showtime and Viacom, which were, respectively, due theatrical, pay TV and syndicated TV rights to the company's output. The various deals lasted between two and four years and required four films per year in the $15 million to £25 million budget range (Ilott 1991: 5). This immediate access to comprehensive distribution in the US was complemented by the incorporation of Gramercy Pictures in May 1992 (Farrow 1992: 1). Significantly, Gramercy was set up as a 50:50 joint venture with Universal and was created to distribute and market the low- to medium-budget 'specialty' releases of both its parent companies. Explaining his initial strategy, Kuhn reveals:

> To open up distribution in America is a huge decision and many people, great people ... had tried and failed dismally. It was perceived as a black hole money pit, so it was an extremely nervous-making beginning. We decided insofar as we had big pictures that we'd keep distributing through the studios ... but the smaller ones we'd start on our own ... I wanted to have enough product guaranteed, so I needed another supplier, so that would be cast-offs from Universal ... Hopefully they'd develop some of their own ... [specialty] stuff and ... we'd use their expertise and whatever back office we could and just generally to spread the risk. That was the idea, gain experience of what it means to distribute in North America before you jump in.[45]

In practice, Russell Schwartz, President of Gramercy, was granted day-to-day operational autonomy from both parent companies. 'PolyGram made movies, financed them and put up the P&A and completely controlled their movies and Universal did the same. There were no co-productions that were done,' Schwartz explains. 'It was really about the individual production companies under the PolyGram banner creating product and production execs at Universal [doing the same].'[46] While Gramercy was one of the first specialty distributors to be established or acquired by the major Hollywood studios in the 1990s, it was quickly joined by the likes of Sony Pictures Classics, Miramax, Fox Searchlight and Paramount Classics. As Schwartz points out, the distribution and marketing of 'specialty' films was significantly different from that of major studio releases:

> The movies don't go out wide, they go out in a smaller release pattern and reviews and publicity are very important to engaging an audience. It wasn't about a big TV spend or a big outdoor campaign, or some big commercial idea. Most of these films were not overtly commercial. We have a phrase called POW, which is 'Pay their Own Way'. If they don't work in the beginning you're able to pull back and not spend any more money, whereas with a wide release you're committed from day one and you're spending 90 to 95 per cent of your advertising budget before you even open. With a platform release you can gauge how much money you want to spend to support it depending on how the previous weekend has done.[47]

While the specialty market was positioned outside Hollywood's core business, it was predicated on the expectation that some of these films would cross over to a wider audience. Doing so typically meant bridging the gap between the independent cinema circuit and the multiplexes, an objective that required building momentum behind a release:

> [There were] more individual mom and pop operations besides just a couple of art-house chains that were very dedicated to these kinds of [specialty] movies, so the competition was more amongst companies of similar size [to Gramercy] rather than amongst the studios. What would happen, though, is if one of these movies from either us [Gramercy], or anybody for that matter, looked like it was breaking out, the exhibitors would be the ones who would demand it, because exhibition ... tend to eat their young if they smell a success ... If they had the room to do it, they [the multiplexes] would certainly play it ... Certainly now in the era with so many multi-screen cinemas it's even less of an issue, there's always a screen available if a movie's doing business ... And there's always another film right behind it if the movie's not.[48]

In 1992 PFEI also established OP COs in two major European markets, France and the UK, followed by the Netherlands in 1993. As Stewart Till points out, the studio created a management structure which empowered the OP COs to make decisions at a national level across the platforms of theatrical, home video and television:

> When we set up distribution in every territory, I felt two things. I felt the local managing director should know better than anyone at head office, and if he didn't then you didn't have the right person. Secondly, there was so much overlap between, particularly, theatrical and home video, that the benefits of having one boss [managing] marketing synergies, dating synergies, pricing synergies ... [was that] they could make a decision ... All anyone cares about is 'What's the total revenue?' and 'What's the total marketing spend?' ... I'd worked for Fox Video, I'd seen the studio's departments not talking to each other, let alone not maximising synergy and revenue. To this day, the studios are still hugely horizontally segmented ... It was one of the huge advantages [of PolyGram, because it allowed] ... our general managers to take ownership of a title, because he was responsible for all the revenue in France or all the revenue in Germany, and he was accountable.[49]

Just as PFE fostered an environment of creative autonomy for its production labels, the studio also ensured that its OP COs had the autonomy to pursue distribution and marketing strategies tailored to their own market. In practice, however, the relationship between the OP COs was also collaborative as they grew in number, as Julia Short points out:

> An operational company used to host a four-day conference and over those four days we'd watch the next four months' films. So, we'd watch the films and then the following day we'd all have to present our marketing and distribution plans. So we'd say, 'It's not good enough, it'll have to go straight to video', and we'd look at doing a TV premiere if that was the case, or we'd say 'Loved it! We think it's a 200, 300 print release, and we think this is the target audience' ... The person that was doing the equivalent of my job in Germany and France and Spain and Switzerland, Australia would all be there. So, it was an incredibly collaborative and supportive environment. I've never had it again. There was not a blame culture if something didn't work, there was no blame, so you didn't feel stifled to not try something ... The whole PolyGram philosophy was local knows best. So, we would say, for the UK, this is what we would to do with it and this is how we want to sell it, because these are the selling points in this territory.[50]

The marketing notes from such conferences would, in turn, be used by PFI to develop marketing briefs from which London-based creative agencies designed the marketing materials for PFE's films. The results of this process were typically further refined with input from the OP COs, PFI and PFE's production labels before being finalised. Each OP CO also negotiated output deals with pay TV and free TV broadcasters in their territories for PFE's films. As Simon Wright explains, these output deals also included a quota of television programming which ensured a market for WTTV's production activities in this area:

> The first thing that PolyGram did was negotiate output deals around the world and they were based on the films they were producing, which had escalators tied into them, so if the box office was bigger, you'd pay more as a licence fee ... The value for television showings of films is directly related to how well they've performed in the box office ... On the back of the film deals, they allowed for 100 hours a year of television ... Because everything is driven by Los Angeles and by the American market, to qualify for those output deals we had to have either a US network or a major pay-cable station attached to it ... We took some direct commissions, *Zig and Zag* and things like that, where we just took a licence fee and made it, but most of the bigger stuff all had a US ... [broadcaster] because it then qualified it for our output deals.[51]

Increasing the number of PFEI's operating companies, and thus PFE's direct control of distribution and marketing in key national markets, was considered a priority. As Till explains, however, PolyGram's existing business infrastructure in these territories was a mixed blessing:

> When you arrived there was some infrastructure, some knowledge of the marketplace and some people who could perhaps set up meetings. That was the good news. The bad news was that Alain Levy's vision was to create integrated film and music companies. The reality was that none of the music companies, with the exception of Germany ... knew anything about film but they wanted to be in film. Who doesn't? The advantage of having someone [there], which was not politically correct to say, was hugely outweighed by all the aggravation ... I'd go in the territories and go 'This is the solution I want to pursue' and the local record chief executive would go 'Oh, alright, I want to come to the meeting to make sure ... [of "x"]'. It varied dramatically from country to country but in the main you had to keep quiet about it because the record company was financing everything and, obviously, we made losses so we couldn't get too feisty, but it was a major aggravation.[52]

Despite such complications, the expansion of PFEI was rapid. As Figure 4.3 shows, PFE's international distribution and marketing network grew at an average rate of almost two new territories per year, culminating in a total of ten OP COs covering thirteen national markets. In practice, many of these new subsidiaries were created by acquiring independent distribution companies such as Pan-Européenne (France), Movies Film Productions (Netherlands), Independent Films (Belgium) and Monopole Pathé Films (Switzerland), or occasionally the establishment of a joint venture, as in the case of Sogepaq Distribution (Spain). In contrast, the remaining OP COs in the UK, Canada, Australia/New Zealand, Germany/Austria and Italy were set up from scratch. At the apex of its distribution operations, the studio described its capacity as follows:

	1992	1993	1994	1995	1996	1997	1998
France	•	•	•	•	•	•	•
United Kingdom/Ireland	•	•	•	•	•	•	•
Netherlands			•	•	•	•	•
Spain				•	•	•	•
Canada					•	•	•
Belgium					•	•	•
Australia/New Zealand						•	•
Germany/Austria						•	•
Switzerland						•	•
Italy							•

Figure 4.3 The expansion of PFEI's operating companies by year. Source: PolyGram (1998), 'Confidential Memorandum: PolyGram Filmed Entertainment', PFE Archive.

> PFE has built a fully integrated worldwide distribution network through its US distribution entities, PolyGram Films and Gramercy Pictures for theatrical distribution, PolyGram Video and PolyGram Television, as well as through its operating companies which cover 13 international countries. These worldwide operations reach approximately 85% of the global entertainment market, with plans to commence distribution operations in early 1999 in Latin America (Brazil, Mexico and Argentina). The company provides global distribution in every media segment, including theatrical, video rental, video sell-through, and network, pay and syndicated television. The company's control of its distribution allows it to fully maximise all distribution markets, control the release schedule of its productions, and guarantee strategic marketing uniformity.[53]

Over the same period, PFE also began to invest heavily in expanding its supply line of product. As Table 4.2 shows, PFE acquired film and television libraries with increasing ambition, including the back catalogues of Palace, Virgin, Island/Atlantic and Abbey as well as the substantially larger ITC and Epic libraries. PFE's most ambitious foray into acquisition, however, was the one that failed. In 1996 PolyGram attempted to buy the ailing Hollywood studio, MGM/UA from Crédit Lyonnais. Despite being reported as the front runner, PolyGram ultimately lost to a successful $1.3 billion bid orchestrated by the studio's management (Peers & Busch 1996: 1).

PFE's expansion in the domestic market took shape with the acquisition of Universal's 50 per cent stake in Gramercy in January 1996 (Brown 1996: 2). Over the preceding four years, Universal had produced few specialty films, leaving most of the Gramercy slate to come from PFE. 'They [Universal] just didn't feel they were good at it and didn't have a dedicated team that was doing it. Whereas … PolyGram's business model was specifically geared to making those kinds of movies,' Schwartz explains. 'It takes

Library	Year of acquisition	Acquisition price	Assets	Highlights
Palace	1992	–	10 titles	*The Crying Game, The Pope Must Die, Big Man*
Virgin	1993	–	225 titles	*Drugstore Cowboy, Sex, Lies and Videotape*
Island/Atlantic	1994	$10 million	–	*The Basketball Diaries, Kiss of the Spider Woman, Bagdad Café*
ITC	1995	$156 million	200 films/9,000 hours of TV	*On Golden Pond, Sophie's Choice, Thunderbirds, The Saint*
Abbey	1995	–	55 TV titles	*Enchanted Lands, Bump*
Epic	1998	$225 million	1,051 films	*The Graduate, Terminator, When Harry Met Sally*

Table 4.2 PFE's film and television library acquisitions. Source: PolyGram (1998), 'Confidential Memorandum: PolyGram Filmed Entertainment', PFE Archive.

as much effort and time commitment from a production exec to make a movie that costs $3 million as a movie that costs $200 [million].'[54] In May the following year, PFE launched PolyGram Films, a second US-based distribution company designed to handle big-budget films. Explaining the rationale for the development and some of his reservations surrounding it, Schwartz recalls:

> All of the production entities ... [were] wanting to make bigger movies, which is usually a sign of trouble, and PolyGram was very anxious to establish itself as a studio ... The Gramercy model was quite successful at that point, and I think they felt they could take it to the next level. Now, there's many opinions as to what should have happened next versus what did happen next. It never made any sense to me to start another distribution company when you already had Gramercy that was completely established with an excellent reputation ... I think when you get into making big-budget movies and really starting to compete [with the studios], you've got to have a full slate of movies, ten to twelve titles a year ... It's a very, very big commitment and you've got to be able to make failures ... even back then [it was] 50, 75, $100 million movies.[55]

For many at PFE, the launch of PolyGram Films marked the end of the studio's developmental phase and the beginning of its concerted attempt to rival the major Hollywood studios. As if to underline its maturing status within the industry, all of PFE's LA-based operations were relocated to an elaborate office building on North Crescent Drive. By the end of 1997, however, the senior management at both PolyGram and PFE felt a growing sense of disjuncture between their ongoing efforts to build a major entertainment conglomerate and the long-term strategy of their mutual parent company, Philips. The situation came to a head the following year with profound consequences for both companies.

NOTES

1. Michael Kuhn, interview with the author, 8-2-2013.
2. PolyGram (1992), 'PolyGram Filmed Entertainment: Presentation to the Group Management Committee (31st August 1992)', PFE Archive.
3. Ibid.
4. Malcolm Ritchie, interview with the author, 10-9-2014.
5. Average PFE Budgets: PolyGram (1993), 'PolyGram and Films', and PolyGram (1997), 'Budget 1998: Volume 1 – Overview', PFE Archive. Average Hollywood Budgets: MPAA (2001), '2001 US Economic Review'.
6. Eric Fellner, interview with the author, 14-3-2014.
7. Tim Bevan, interview with the author, 7-12-2016.
8. Eric Fellner, interview with the author, 14-3-2014.
9. Tim Bevan, interview with the author, 7-12-2016.
10. Tim Bevan, interview with the author, 6-8-2013.
11. Tim Bevan, interview with the author, 7-12-2016.
12. Eric Fellner, interview with the author, 14-3-2014.
13. PolyGram (1993), 'PolyGram Filmed Entertainment', PFE Archive and PolyGram (1997), 'Budget 1998 – Volume 1 – Overview', PFE Archive.
14. Eric Fellner, interview with the author, 14-3-2013.
15. PolyGram (1993), 'Working Title Group: Budget 1994', PFE Archive.
16. PolyGram (1997), 'Budget 1998: Volume 1 – Overview', PFE Archive.
17. Debra Hayward, interview with the author, 20-9-2013.
18. Ibid.
19. Liza Chasin, interview with the author, 22-5-2014.
20. Ibid.
21. Ibid.
22. Ibid.
23. Jane Frazer, interview with the author, 18–5–15.
24. Ibid.
25. Ibid.
26. Ibid.
27. Angela Morrison, interview with the author, 26-11-2013.
28. Ibid.
29. Alison Owen, interview with the author, 26-11-2013.
30. PolyGram (1998), 'Confidential Memorandum: PolyGram Filmed Entertainment', p. 80, PFE Archive.
31. Angela Morrison, interview with the author, 26-11-2013.

32 PolyGram (1998), 'Confidential Memorandum: PolyGram Filmed Entertainment', p. 16, PFE Archive.
33 Stewart Till, interview with the author, 24-2–14.
34 Simon Wright, interview with the author, 20-5-2014.
35 Ibid.
36 Malcolm Ritchie, interview with the author, 10-9-2014.
37 Stewart Till, interview with the author, 24-2-2014.
38 Malcolm Ritchie, interview with the author, 10-9-2014.
39 PFE's films in general, and Working Title's films in particular, performed better in the international market than in the domestic market, a fact reflected in the sample control sheet.
40 Julia Short, interview with the author, 6-8-2013.
41 Eric Fellner, interview with the author, 14-3-2014.
42 Angela Morrison, interview with the author, 26-11-2013.
43 Ibid.
44 Malcolm Ritchie, interview with the author, 10-9-14.
45 Michael Kuhn, interview with the author, 8-2-2013.
46 Russell Schwartz, interview with the author, 12-9-2014.
47 Ibid.
48 Ibid.
49 Stewart Till, interview with the author, 27-7-2016.
50 Julia Short, interview with the author, 6-8-2013.
51 Simon Wright, interview with the author, 20-5-2014.
52 Stewart Till, interview with the author, 24-2-2014.
53 PolyGram (1998), 'Confidential Memorandum: PolyGram Filmed Entertainment', PFE Archive.
54 Russell Schwartz, interview with the author, 12-9-2014.
55 Ibid.

'Any idea who the girl in the black hat is?': Fiona (Kristen Scott Thomas) and Charles (Hugh Grant) discuss Carrie in *Four Weddings and a Funeral*.

Matthew (Sean Penn) and Sister Helen (Susan Sarandon) exchange final words in *Dead Man Walking*.

Marge Gunderson (Frances McDormand) detains a man feeding a body through a woodchipper in *Fargo*.

Mr. Bean (Rowan Atkinson) recreates his passport photograph upon entry into the United States in *Bean*.

Marcy (Janeane Garofalo) and Sean (David O'Hara) reconcile in the final scene of *The Matchmaker*.

'The Chinaman is not the issue...': The Dude (Jeff Bridges) argues with Walter (John Goodman) and Donny (Steve Buscemi) at the bowling lanes in *The Big Lebowski*.

'Marry me?' Robert Dudley (Joseph Fiennes) proposes to Queen Elizabeth I (Cate Blanchett) in *Elizabeth*.

'I'm also just a girl, standing in front of a boy …': Anna (Julia Roberts) pleads with Will (Hugh Grant) in *Notting Hill*.

CHAPTER 5

Swapping Studios:
From PolyGram to Universal (1998–9)

The demise of PolyGram Filmed Entertainment (PFE) began a little over a decade after PolyGram's diversification into the film industry started. Just as PFE's project of studio-building was ignited by a change in management, so too was it extinguished. Jan Timmer, the President and Chairman of PolyGarm's parent company, Philips, retired at the end of 1996 and was replaced by Cornelius 'Cor' Boonstra, who was recruited from the food and beverage company, Sara Lee. With no experience of working in the entertainment industry, Boonstra viewed the music and film industries as mercurial and high-risk. Following a period of internal speculation about the future of PolyGram and PFE, the senior management of both companies scheduled a meeting with their opposite numbers at Philips only to have their suspicions confirmed: the hardware company wanted to sell its software subsidiaries. Thereafter, the parties agreed to collectively explore various scenarios under which PolyGram and PFE could be extricated from Philips and thus continue as going concerns

In May 1998, however, it was publicly announced that PolyGram and PFE were for sale, a situation that came as a surprise to the management of both companies. Philips had, in fact, been in confidential negotiations with the Canadian conglomerate, Seagram, for some time. Seagram's Chairman and CEO, Edgar Bronfman Jr, had initiated the diversification of his family's beverage business in 1995 with the acquisition of Music Corporation of America (MCA), the former parent company of Universal. MCA was subsequently reincorporated as Universal Studios, matching the branding of its major divisions: Universal Music Group, Universal Parks & Resorts and Universal Pictures. Seagram and Philips subsequently agreed a $10.6 billion deal for PolyGram and PFE which involved an 80 per cent cash and 20 per cent stock transaction. Significantly, this situation both weakened the Bronfman family's equity position in Seagram to just 29 per cent and increased the company's debt load to $8.5 to $9 billion (Peers 1998a: 1).

The enormous price tag attached to the deal primarily represented the value of PolyGram, the assets of which were promptly merged into Universal

Music Group. In contrast, the fate of PFE was more protracted and complicated. The studio's management negotiated with Philips and Seagram to explore the possibility of selling the entire operation intact. Significantly, the plan was attractive to Seagram because if PFE could be sold, it would help the company's cash position in its acquisition of PolyGram. For PFE, this scenario suggested a way of maintaining the integrity of the studio and thus continuing its long-term ambition of competing with the major Hollywood studios. This arrangement initiated an extended period of uncertainty for both PFE and Working Title during which the fate of both companies hung in the balance.

THE DEMISE OF PFE AND ITS LEGACY

PFE's bid for survival was carried out in a public and ungainly fashion between May and December of 1998. Initial speculation in the trade press suggested Seagram would seek a sale price of $1 billion for PFE, but the figure quickly dropped to $750 million. Despite fielding increasingly successful release schedules, the costs involved in simultaneously building a film studio from scratch ensured that PFE recorded operating losses of $55.5 million, $38.8 million and $78.5 million in 1995, 1996 and 1997 respectively. According to PFE's projected income, however, this figure would fall to $62.3 million in 1998, before making the transition to operating incomes of $13.9 million, $86.4 million, $139.4 million and $250.9 million between 1999 and 2002. Significantly, these outcomes were based on a range of projections over the 1998–2002 period which included the generation of free cash flow of $314 million from the PFE library, $342 million from PFE's immediate release slate and a further $232 million from fourteen subsequently scheduled releases.[1]

In September, it was reported that US independent, Artisan Entertainment, and French media conglomerate, Canal Plus, offered a joint bid of $500 million. The British-based ITV company Carlton Communications also offered $500 million, while MGM offered just $300 million for the PFE film catalogue (Frater 1998: 14). Ultimately, such low bids ensured that PFE would not be sold as a stand-alone entity and triggered the break-up of the company. In October MGM acquired PFE's pre-April 1996 film library of over 1,300 titles for $235 million (Peers 1998b: 8). Canal Plus re-entered negotiations to acquire PolyGram Filmed Entertainment International (PFEI) and Working Title for a combined price of $280 million. The talks, however, ended with Seagram holding out for a price closer to $400 million (Williams & Carver 1998: 7; Dawtrey & Carver 1999: 1). With no prospect of extricating any part of PFE, Michael Kuhn stood down as President and CEO of the company in December 1998. In the same month Seagram completed its acquisition of PolyGram for the revised figure of $10.4 billion and effectively closed the company (Carver & Petrikin 1998: 1). Shortly thereafter Carlton paid $150 million for PFE's ITC film and television catalogue of 300 films and over 5,000 hours of television (Dawtrey 1999a: 8). The remaining PFE assets, including Working Title, were retained by Universal while their future was considered. Contemplating the demise of PFE, Kuhn reflects:

> On the one hand it's not given to many people to have the opportunity to effectively start up a studio from scratch and it was a bloody good ride for ten years. We're all grown up and we know that these things happen in big companies, and you have to go with the flow. It doesn't stop it being annoying at the time, which it was, particularly in those circumstances, when it wasn't as though the management at PolyGram were opposed to letting Philips get out or cashing in, or any of those things. It was done behind our backs for no good reason. There could have been a whole other story. We could have disassembled them from PolyGram in a nice way that would have allowed all those things to continue, and more importantly ... the next step would have been the building up of a European media group, a merger with a Studio Canal or something like that, which would have made a fantastic powerhouse which there has never been in Europe.[2]

The rise and fall of PFE raises questions about how this remarkable narrative of studio-building should be positioned within film history. One answer to this question is found in the 'Key Investment Considerations' section of PFE's final asset portfolio, which describes the studio as follows:

> PFE is the only fully integrated film production and worldwide distribution company to have succeeded in establishing a firm foothold both inside and outside the U.S. in the last 50 years. Its success is unique given that PFE was established less than seven years ago. One of the key factors in this success has been the systematic development of both production and distribution activities on a worldwide basis. This strategy has distinguished PFE from many of its predecessors, which were able to succeed in only one or two of these competencies and eventually failed in successfully challenging the major studios.[3]

In practice, the nature of PFE's challenge was mounted by simultaneously working inside and outside the established structures of the Hollywood industry. PFE was, for example, headquartered in Los Angeles and directly collaborated with the major studios in establishing its domestic distribution operations and co-financing some of its films. Equally, two of its three major production labels, Propaganda and Interscope, were Los Angeles-based companies which made American films. However, PFE also invested heavily in British-based production, not only through Working Title, but also through a range of third-party production deals and acquisitions from the independent sector. Perhaps the clearest illustration of PFE's unique achievements in the British context was inadvertently underlined by the publication of *A Bigger Picture*, a review of the British film industry commissioned by the newly created Department for Culture, Media and Sport (DCMS). Published in the same year as PFE's demise, the report contrasted the British and Hollywood industries as a means of highlighting the essential structural weaknesses associated with the former:

> The US industry is dominated by *distribution-led, integrated structures*, where the processes of development, production and distribution are financed and carried out by a single company. Such firms can use the revenues from distribution to finance production; they have the critical mass to attract finance; they are thus able to make big budget films, write off failures and build up a library of rights. By contrast, the UK industry is *production-led and fragmented*. The production process is separate from the distribution process which is dominated by big US companies. Production remains a 'cottage industry': most producers have no close relationship with a distributor, cannot easily reduce risk or raise finance by developing a slate of films, and have to sell their rights in order to get their films distributed. (DCMS 1998: 4–5)

The omission of PFE as a European-owned counter-argument to these observations is notable in hindsight. Indeed, over the course of the 1990s, PFE was an emphatically 'distribution-led' studio in which the processes of development, production and distribution were integrated under the auspices of a group of PFE-owned or -affiliated companies. On the one hand, such observations align the structure of PFE with those of the major Hollywood studios. On the other, the development of the 'control sheet' proved to be a notable innovation within the studio system which ensured that a distribution-led approach directly informed development and green-lighting decisions. As Stewart Till, former President of PFEI, explains, this circular process had a profound impact upon the roles and responsibilities of all PFE's integrated operations which separated the culture of the company from that of the Hollywood studios:

> What we did brilliantly was the culture we had of empowering ... We empowered everyone. We empowered the territories, we empowered executives, we empowered the producers to make the films ... It's a management style I've taken ... and I [still] apply many of the PolyGram cultures. We were very internationally focused at a time when, even though everyone knew international was at least 50 per cent of the world in terms of box office, the studios were still very domestically driven and we were aggressively ... international. The two smart things we did culturally were empowering people, good people, and being very internationally focused.[4]

Contemplating PFE's position within these various national and international contexts, Till argues, 'We cheated. We tried very hard to be American when we were in America, and European when we were in Europe and British in Britain.'[5] This sense of fluidity was, however, ultimately subsumed beneath a more cohesive sense of national identity. 'Obviously, this is very self-serving, the two most ... senior executives were British, Michael and I, and our most successful production company was British and lots of key executives [were British],' he continues. 'We were absolutely British because I think you ... take it from your management, not your ownership.'[6] As if to underline this sentiment, Kuhn was presented with the Outstanding British Contribution to Cinema Award at the BAFTA ceremony in May 1999 to mark PFE's contribution to the national industry. Yet more unequivocal, Kuhn also ascribes a British identity to the studio:

> What's a British picture? I think so much fuss is made about that and it's just rubbish. No one asks whether ICI or something like that is a British company because most of the share-holders are in America, it never occurs to people. If their heart and soul and mind and everything is here, who owns them is irrelevant ... All the time through PolyGram we had this – 'are we British?' – and it's rubbish. There was a door in London you could go and knock on and get an answer about whether you could make your film, any budget up to $70 million ... In my mind that was a British operation and the fact of who owned it, Philips or their shareholders, or who knows, was irrelevant.[7]

Arguably PFE's greatest achievement was the expansion of a creative space for both British and American films which is at once oriented towards the worldwide commercial market, and yet lies outside the mainstream film culture of the major Hollywood studios. The roots of this legacy are the sum of several overlapping developments which are characterised by a combination of circumstance, design and necessity. Significantly, most of PFE's senior management, and two of its major production labels, Propaganda and Working Title, entered the film industry via the independent sector and were thus not hidebound by the creative and commercial precepts of the studio system. Thereafter, PFE's status as a Hollywood outsider was sustained by the creative autonomy that these labels maintained at the point of development and by a commitment to a production agenda which remained low-budget by studio standards. Simultaneously, however, the development of the control sheet and the expansion of PFE's marketing and distribution network ensured that the results of this autonomy were, in the first instance, constantly informed by assessments of the worldwide marketplace, and in the second instance, capable of effectively exploiting these markets.

THE INTEGRATION OF WORKING TITLE INTO UNIVERSAL AND THE FATE OF PFE'S REMAINING ASSETS

The break-up of PFE continued in earnest in 1999. Without a film library, the value of PFE's production labels was determined by their track record and development slate, factors which suggested the future value of the companies. Significantly, such assessments varied substantially from company to company. 'Interscope made films that didn't work anywhere on a very regular basis and Propaganda made [films that] were more domestic friendly. They didn't have the success of Working Title but had some ... hits,' Till summarises. '[Propaganda] did films with American writers and American directors ... still independent, still not mainstream Hollywood ... but their films had a much better domestic to international ratio.'[8] As Till goes on to argue, the unique strength of Working Title was its successful positioning between the British and Hollywood industries and, in turn, the domestic and international markets:

> They are the only production company outside the US that has consistently made successful films. They're not intimidated by America and they understand international and there aren't many people that's true [of]. Most of the European producers are intimidated by America and a lot of the American producers don't understand international ... They [Working Title] have lots of little skills, or not so little. They work very hard, they're very smart, they get this industry, they've got good contacts, they've formed very important relationships with Richard Curtis, the Coen brothers and [other] people. There is probably a shopping list of twenty things they do well, but the one thing that's made them successful is that they've not been intimidated by America and getting international.[9]

While ownership of Working Title had transferred to Universal following Seagram's acquisition of PolyGram, the continuing commitment of the company's key staff also had to be secured. Initial speculation in the trade press suggested that Working Title's Co-Chairmen, Tim Bevan and Eric Fellner, might seek a deal with another studio (Dawtrey 1999b: 1). Indeed, the particular circumstances surrounding their contractual commitments to PFE ensured that the producers were in a seller's market. As Fellner explains:

> We were very fortunate because our service contracts had expired and so Tim and I were free agents. Working Title had no value outside Tim and I running it, so we were lucky and able to steer the company to where we wanted it to go, regardless of its asset value, whatever that was perceived to be. Wherever we went, the Working Title name and brand would have gone. We did a separate negotiation with Universal, it just so happened that it was the same place as where the PolyGram assets had ended up ... There were a lot of reasons

to do it at Universal but primarily it was the relationship with staff there and the promise that Edgar Bronfman, who owned Seagram and the studio then made us, which was he wanted to set up a company that was additional to the slate, to the core slate, and that additionality meant that he was making films that the studio wouldn't normally have made, and that's what he wanted us to do. Everyone else would have tried to subsume us into the main slate and we'd never have got any films made.[10]

The films that a Hollywood studio 'wouldn't normally have made' were best exemplified by the low- to medium-budget hit films for which the company had become best known, including *Four Weddings and a Funeral* (1994), *Bean* (1997) and *Elizabeth* (1998). In this way, Working Title's years as a subsidiary of PFE demonstrated the worldwide market potential of such films and suggested that they could also be produced within a Hollywood studio. During the months of negotiations with Universal, Working Title's COO, Angela Morrison, took a leading role alongside Bevan and Fellner. As she recalls, the production company proceeded with a clear set of objectives in mind:

We wanted to maintain the degree of autonomy that we had managed to get to with PolyGram. We'd learned the lessons, we'd been through the rigours of the control sheet and green-lighting and we thought that we were at the point in our collective company career that we could make some of our own decisions without having to get approval from LA. We were successful in negotiating a lot of things along those lines to do with what we spent on our overhead, how we managed the business, the staffing, then how we managed production, how much we could spend on productions without a full green-light decision being made with the studio.[11]

In March 1999 Bevan and Fellner committed to a five-year deal with Universal. The agreement permitted the producers to green-light up to five films a year with individual production budgets of up to $25 million without approval from Universal. In contrast, films with budgets over $25 million would be considered on a case-by-case basis with the studio's involvement (Dawtrey 1999c: 1). This unprecedented level of financial backing and creative autonomy immediately made Working Title an unrivalled force in the British film industry. Despite securing such a comprehensive deal, Working Title's Chairmen were also keen to find a co-production partner. 'We were worried about the studio relationship, so we thought if we brought in some money from Europe there'd be more of a focus on trying to get European content made,' Fellner recalls. 'Studios do what studios need to do, and that doesn't really encompass the types of films that we were making.'[12] Having failed to acquire PFEI and Working Title six months earlier, Canal Plus were brought back into the picture. As Morrison explains:

It was part of the strive to maintain autonomy, it was also part of some sort of in-built sense that having a European partner for us was really key because we were based here and there is a different sensibility between the European market and the US market ... I think, ultimately, it was driven by, if we cost [Universal] less, that's got to be good for us in the long term, and the studio, they responded to having a partner and they responded to having a European partner. Partners were, and still are, hard to find and I think because we'd opened that door the studio were very open to having a partner.[13]

In May, Canal Plus agreed to co-finance the operational, development and production costs of Working Title on a 50–50 basis with Universal at a cost of between $50 million and $100 million annually. In return for their contribution, Canal Plus received television rights to all Working Title's films in continental Europe (excluding the UK and Ireland) and French theatrical and video rights for every second film for the first three years of the deal. In the final two years, Canal Plus also received theatrical and video rights in all territories in continental Europe for every second film (Dawtrey 1999d: 8). Significantly, Canal Plus was one of the largest pay-TV operators in Europe, having expanded its network throughout the 1980s and 1990s, as well as establishing French theatrical and home video divisions and an in-house production unit, Canal+ Production (Meir 2016: 50). Notably, the company's deal with Working Title foreshadowed the establishment of Studiocanal in 2000, which was formed from these existing assets. This rebranding was accompanied by the announcement that Canal Plus would double its investment in film production via its new subsidiary with the aim of becoming a 'major' European studio (James 2000: 1).

Of the remaining opportunities for integration, PFE's US-based assets represented the poorest fit. PolyGram Films was closed and Gramercy, along with Universal's specialty US distributor, October Films, was sold to USA Networks for $300 million. Gramercy and October were subsequently merged to form a short-lived mini-major studio, USA Films, into which Propaganda and Interscope were also folded. In reality, the sale did not move PFE's former assets far outside the Universal empire, however, as the studio still owned a 45 per cent stake in USA Networks (Brown 1999: 1–2). The final PFE asset to be considered was PFEI, PFE's network of thirteen international distribution and marketing companies. At the time, Universal distributed its films through United International Pictures (UIP) in international territories. Operating as a joint venture between MGM, Paramount and Universal, UIP was headquartered in London but operated directly in thirty-five 'international' markets. Significantly, Universal's commitment to the UIP consortium was due for renewal in 2001 and MGM had already indicated it would be leaving the partnership (Peers & Petrikin 1999: 14). As

UIP's former COO Andrew Cripps explains, the combination of these events threw the future of UIP into question:

> You had some distinct camps at Universal head office. Some people that, clearly, had worked with UIP for many years, saw the benefit of a joint venture where [you're] not footing 100 per cent of the bill. Then you saw some people that thought 'Wow, this is our opportunity to actually control our own international distribution company'. So you had a real split. So, you had the PolyGram people lobbying ... everybody they could saying, 'You want to be on your own, this is the wonderful PolyGram model that we've set up, it works so much better than UIP.' Then we had the people in the other camp, including us [UIP] lobbying and saying 'It's ridiculous what they're saying, you don't want 100 per cent of the overhead, you want to share your overhead with another studio, so you can continue to have the broad depth of distribution that you enjoy at UIP'.[14]

The PolyGram argument ultimately proved the most attractive for Chris McGurk, President and COO of Universal Pictures. In January 1999 PFEI was renamed Universal Pictures International (UPI) and given the remit of distributing the remaining films which the PFE labels had completed for a two-year period. Thereafter, all of Universal's films would be transferred from UIP to UPI. For Stewart Till, who remained President of the rebranded company, the advantages and disadvantages of each operation were clear cut:

> We were a much better marketing company. UIP's great strength was distribution. They could get good terms and get any screens that they wanted, but because of the sheer number of screens out there, I always thought that any half decent company could get any cinema they wanted if they had the right films and, arguably, our terms weren't much lower than UIP's, maybe one or two percentage points ... We [were] a much leaner company, much leaner overhead, and we were brilliant at marketing ... Some of our campaigns, like *The Usual Suspects* and *Trainspotting*, to this day are still copied and pastiched.[15]

More immediate action was taken in the case of Cinema International Corporation (CIC), the international home entertainment distribution company which Universal shared with Paramount. Universal announced that it was leaving CIC the following month and transferred its home entertainment distribution to PFEI's former video operations (Carver 1999a: 1 & 77). PFEI's Vice President of Continental Europe, Peter Smith, was given the task of managing UPI's new video operations. The rationale for the transition was, he recalls, based partly on the profitable entrepreneurialism that the local PFE OP COs were able to realise with their local acquisition budgets:

> There was only really one ... or two maybe, critical decisions or catalysts to the change. The first was PolyGram had what they called local acquisitions

in their line-up of product. The management of PolyGram managed those relationships ... This business generated ... if I remember rightly, about £30 million of operating profit across the European territories each year which would largely pay for the overhead of the video distribution company, if they [Universal] kept that business ... So, Universal decided to exit CIC, put their own distribution through PolyGram, get PolyGram to continue to invest [in] and grow its local acquisition business, put the two distribution businesses together, and then they had a distribution business that was self-financed ... The second thing that they obviously liked was, we had a good management team in a number of key countries at the time. We had a very good UK team, and a pretty good French team, a pretty good German team, and so on.[16]

In May UPI released *Notting Hill* (1999), which became Working Title's greatest commercial success of the 1990s, making over $300 million worldwide at the box office upon release. In practice, however, UPI's theatrical distribution infrastructure was in operation for only a year. The change in strategy was, once again, due to a change in management. Chris McGurk was replaced by Brian Mulligan and Stacey Snider who became Co-Chairs of Universal following his departure. Unconvinced by the UPI plan, Mulligan negotiated an extension of the UIP contract until 2006 and put the plans for the expansion of UPI in reverse. Having dispensed with the last vestiges of PFE, Mulligan took the position of CFO at Seagram the following month, leaving Snider as the sole Chairman of Universal Pictures. Ultimately UPI's theatrical distribution operations were wound down by the end of the year, and finally closed in January 2000 (Dawtrey 1999e: 22).

SWAPPING PARENT COMPANIES: SEAGRAM, VIVENDI, GENERAL ELECTRIC AND COMCAST

The relationship between Working Title and Universal has proven to be extremely successful and enduring. The initial five-year deal which the two parties agreed upon in 1999 has, at the time of writing, been extended five times over a period of more than twenty years. While the terms of the initial deal have changed significantly, each new contract has ensured the continuing commitment of Working Title's key personnel to the company and, in turn, the company's continuing status as a functioning subsidiary of Universal. In contrast, ownership of the studio has been in near-constant flux, moving between a succession of four multinational conglomerates including Seagram (1995–2000), Vivendi (2000–4) General Electric (GE) (2004–11) and Comcast (2011–present). As Bevan explains, however, the impact of these transitions upon the operation of Working Title was limited:

> On the whole, what's happened is there hasn't been a massive change of management. Ronnie Meyer has been there all the way through our relationship with Universal and the changes of management at Universal between Stacey Snider, then Marc Shmuger and David Linde and now Adam Fogelson have not coincided with the changes of ownership. It's made a lot of difference to ... our accounts department and our business affairs department, because whatever compliance is required and all the rest of it from these various different owners materially affects how our accounts department works and how our business affairs department works, but not on the day-to-day making of the films.[17]

Nonetheless, each of Universal's successive parent companies significantly reconfigured the range and scope of production, marketing and distribution businesses owned by the studio. In turn, several of the new business interrelationships which have emerged from these transitions have had a significant impact upon the way in which Working Title has operated. Indeed, the Universal-Canal Plus co-production deal which initially financed Working Title's operations proved to be prescient. Bronfman's plans to transform Seagram into a media conglomerate waned under the weight of the debt caused by its acquisition of PolyGram. In response, Universal enacted a policy of retrenchment which saw the studio's annual operating budget fall from $1 billion to $600 million in 2000 (McNary 2000: 1). The solution to Seagram's growing debt crisis was found in the form of a three-way merger between Seagram, Canal Plus and Vivendi, the French media conglomerate which owned 49 per cent of Canal Plus. As part of the $33.7 billion reshuffle, Seagram and Vivendi sold their remaining non-media assets, acquired Canal Plus outright and formed a new parent company, Vivendi Universal (Goldsmith & James 2000: 1). The deal, which was announced in the summer of 2000 and completed before the end of the year, saw Bronfman replaced at the top of the conglomerate by the former Vivendi Chairman and CEO, Jean-Marie Messier.

Under the leadership of Messier, Vivendi Universal briefly became the most aggressively acquisitive studio in Hollywood. Vivendi bought the outstanding equity in USA Networks in 2001 for $10.3 billion. The deal gave birth to a new configuration, Vivendi Universal Entertainment (VUE), which was 93.5 per cent owned by Vivendi Universal, with the remaining shares split between USA Networks' parent company, USA Interactive, and its Chairman, Barry Diller, who became CEO of the new holding company as part of the deal (Oppelaar & DiOrio 2001: 1). VUE was, however, also burdened with debt from the merger which formed it, the acquisition of USA Network and other multi-billion dollar investments in media companies like EchoStar and Maroc Telecom in the years that followed. The conglomerate made a loss of

$13 billion in 2001 alone, prompting the fall of its share price by 60 per cent. By the time Messier was removed as President and CEO in July 2002, Vivendi Universal was in the red to the tune of $34 billion (Vaucher & Oppelaar 2002: 1).

Messier's replacement, Jean-René Fortou, was given the immediate task of selling some of the company's assets to reduce its debt position. By March 2004, restructuring and asset sales had reduced the number of individual companies within Vivendi Universal from 6,000 to just 1,000 and lowered the conglomerate's debt load to $6.1 billion (Amdur & James 2004: 1). Having regained control of the operation, VUE sought to consolidate its ownership of certain Universal assets and sell others. Despite an attempt by Bronfman to regain control of the studio, Vivendi elected to sell to General Electric, the parent company of the major American broadcast network, NBC. In the summer of 2004 NBC completed the acquisition of 80 per cent of VUE's film and television assets, for which NBC paid $3.6 billion in cash and assumed $1.8 billion of VUE's debt as part of the deal. Vivendi retained Universal Music Group, Canal Plus, and a 20 per cent stake in the newly merged conglomerate, NBCUniversal (Amdur & McClintock 2004: 4). The Chairman and CEO of GE, Jeffrey Immelt, appointed former NBC CEO Bob Wright as CEO of the combined NBCUniversal. As Thomas Schatz points out, the formation of NBCUniversal marked a significant moment in the unfolding history of 'Conglomerate Hollywood':

> The most salient development in contemporary Hollywood has been the formation of the so-called Big Six media conglomerates and their hegemony over the American film (and TV) industry ... This modern conglomerate era crystallized in the mid-1980s when News Corp purchased 20th Century Fox and launched Fox-TV, and it culminated with the 2003 buyout of Universal Pictures by General Electric (GE) and the subsequent creation of NBCUniversal. At that point a cartel of global media giants – Time Warner, Disney, News Corp, Sony, Viacom and GE – owned all six of the major film studios, all four of the U.S. broadcast TV networks, and the vast majority of the top cable networks, along with myriad other media and entertainment holdings including print publishing, music, computer games, consumer electronics, theme parks, and resorts. (Schatz 2009: 21)

Indeed, NBCUniversal was a relatively modest part of General Electric, which included ten 'GE' prefixed divisions: Advanced Materials, Consumer and Industrial, Infrastructure, Commercial Finance, Consumer Finance, Energy, Healthcare, Transportation, Equipment Services and Insurance. Explaining the impact upon Working Title, Angela Morrison reflects:

> Once GE got involved, with their very strict compliance procedures, our finance and legal side became much more heavily involved with the internal

corporate GE finance and legal. That has dissipated a little bit with Comcast, they have different compliance procedures, but they're not necessarily any more straightforward than GE's were … That's a change in just the world outside as well. Big companies are subject to so many more compliances. For example, the Foreign Corrupt Practices Act, which is American anti-bribery legislation. Because these companies are American companies, they're subject to that, so everything flows from that on the finance side.[18]

Universal further enhanced its reputation as the most bought and sold studio in Hollywood as reports surfaced in late 2009 that General Electric intended to sell NBCUniversal to concentrate on its core industrial businesses. In December GE agreed to acquire Vivendi's 20 per cent stake in the company for $5.8 billion. The announcement also officially stated GE's intention to subsequently sell a 51 per cent controlling interest in NBCUniversal to the telecommunications giant, Comcast. The deal entailed Comcast paying GE approximately $6.5 billion and providing the new joint venture with $7.25 billion worth of its media assets. In the longer term, Comcast reserved the right to acquire yet more of GE's stake under specified conditions (Szalai 2009). In January 2011, Comcast finally acquired a 51 per cent stake in NBCUniversal, at which point Comcast Chairman and CEO Brian Roberts appointed Steve Burke as CEO of NBCUniversal. Two years later, Comcast completed the $16.7 billion buy-out of NBCUniversal by acquiring the remaining 49 per cent of the company. Significantly, Comcast's core business as a cable, internet and telephone service provider had clear synergies with the film industry, most notably its 22 million US cable subscribers (Goldsmith 2013: 1). In recent years, Comcast has continued to expand its media holdings with a number of noteworthy additions, including the acquisition of Dreamworks Animation for $3.8 billion in 2016 (Szalai 2016a). Following the sale of Twentieth Century Fox to Disney two years later, Comcast outbid Fox to seize control of Sky Group for $39 billion, a victory which confirmed the conversion of the 'Big Six' to the 'Big Five' (Chu & Clarke 2018).

NOTES

1. PolyGram (1998), 'Confidential Memorandum: PolyGram Filmed Entertainment', pp. 76–87, PFE Archive.
2. Michael Kuhn, interview with the author, 4-6-2013.
3. PolyGram (1998), 'Confidential Memorandum: PolyGram Filmed Entertainment', p. 8, PFE Archive.
4. Stewart Till, interview with the author, 24-2-2014.
5. Ibid.
6. Ibid.
7. Michael Kuhn, interview with the author, 8-2-2013.

8 Stewart Till, interview with the author, 24-2-2014.
9 Ibid.
10 Eric Fellner, interview with the author, 14-3-2014.
11 Angela Morrison, interview with the author, 26-11-2013.
12 Eric Fellner, interview with the author, 14-3-2014.
13 Angela Morrison, interview with the author, 26-11-2013.
14 Andrew Cripps, interview with the author, 17-9-2015.
15 Stewart Till, interview with the author, 24-2-2014.
16 Peter Smith, interview with the author, 23-3-2016.
17 Tim Bevan, interview with the author, 6-8-2013.
18 Angela Morrison, interview with the author, 26-11-2013.

CHAPTER 6

*The Universal Years Part I:
Development, Green-lighting and Distribution
(1999–2006)*

Working Title's transition from PolyGram Filmed Entertainment (PFE) to Universal is a narrative of both continuity and change. On the one hand, the company remained a subsidiary of a multinational media conglomerate and continued to negotiate the key stages of creative and commercial gatekeeping with its new parent company. On the other, Working Title became a component part of an established Hollywood studio, the scale and resources of which were, and remain, vast. In 1999, for example, Universal's parent company, Seagram, was ranked as the ninth largest entertainment company in the world based on its 1998/99 revenue. Significantly, six of the top ten positions in this listing were occupied by the parent companies of the major Hollywood studios, including Time Warner ($26.8 billion), The Walt Disney Company ($22.9 billion), News Corporation ($13.6 billion), Viacom ($12 billion), Sony ($10.5 billion) and Seagram ($7.2 billion) (*Variety* 1999: 49).

The difference in scale between PFE and Universal is further highlighted by a comparison of the production and distribution resources associated with each. At the height of its development, PFE had fourteen English-language production companies under contract and distributed its own films directly in the US and thirteen international territories. In contrast, Universal had over thirty production companies or individuals under contract in 1999 and distributed directly in the US and thirty-five international territories. Unlike most of the production companies on Universal's books, however, Working Title is a directly owned subsidiary as opposed to an independent. This status was reflected in the business relationship between the two which was exclusive, rather than the more usual 'first-look' deal (Brunet & Gornostaeva 2006: 66). As Working Title's Co-Chairman, Tim Bevan, notes, making the transition between PFE and Universal was initially a source of some concern:

> We were very nervous because when PolyGram stopped we thought we'd had a perfect world. We'd had a great deal of autonomy inside this organisation, and all the rest of it... What we learned very quickly was that they [Universal] were amazing and there was a very good person running the studio, Stacey Snider, and she had a great team there, including Donna Langley actually,

who now runs the studio, but she was a junior then. They were entirely supportive ... and so we were surprised, and we learned, just in the same way that we'd learned with PolyGram, that actually being with one of the 'Big Six' was even better than being with PolyGram because it gave you that much more freedom, their distribution was that much more muscular, they gave us the keys to the kingdom, basically.[1]

Indeed, between 1999 and 2006, Working Title experienced a sustained period of commercial success, at the heart of which was the so-called 'Curtisland' cycle of romantic comedies which included *Notting Hill* (1999), *Bridget Jones's Diary* (2001), *Love Actually* (2003) and *Bridget Jones: The Edge of Reason* (2004). Collectively these films generated more than $1 billion at the worldwide box office and, surrounded by other successful romcoms, including *About a Boy* (2002) and *Wimbledon* (2004), definitively aligned the company with the genre. While the Working Title romcom became a staple of British film culture, the company also launched WT^2, a low-budget subsidiary which largely produced comedy-dramas tinged with social realism such as *Billy Elliot* (2000), *Mickybo and Me* (2004) and *Sixty Six* (2006) and comedies with roots in British television, like *Ali G Indahouse* (2002) and *Shaun of the Dead* (2004). This diversity of output was complemented by the continuation of Working Title's relationship with the Coen brothers on *O Brother, Where Art Thou?* (2000) and *The Man Who Wasn't There* (2001) as well as the production of family films like *Johnny English* (2003) and *Nanny McPhee* (2005).

The terms of the five-year co-production deal which Working Title reached with Universal and Studiocanal in 1999 would not, however, be sustained thereafter. In 2004 Studiocanal agreed to fund Working Title at a reduced rate in the region of $40 million per year (James 2004: 20). This contribution was later reported to cover approximately 25 per cent of Working Title's operational, development and production costs, which brought Studiocanal all French rights and a back-end position in worldwide profits (Dawtrey 2006a: 1). The realignment of Working Title's relationship with its key financiers was partly due to the concurrent change in Universal's corporate ownership, which transferred from Seagram to Vivendi and then to General Electric, sparking a series of downsizing policies at many of Vivendi's subsidiaries, including Studiocanal (Amdur & James 2004: 1). What follows considers the relationship between Working Title and Universal by once again examining the parent company–subsidiary dynamic in terms of creative and commercial gatekeeping. Within this system, the focus remains on the individual and collective agency of the key personnel at both companies who were responsible for operating gates at the stages of development, green-lighting and distribution.

Gate 1: Development

Working Title's relationship with Universal at the point of development is defined by creative autonomy, much as it was during the production company's years as a subsidiary of PFE. Indeed, the four integrated filmmaking departments which were established at the start of the PFE era – development, production, US office and legal and business affairs – remained in place, as did most of the key personnel responsible for their operation. Debra Hayward continued to manage the company's development department in London as President of UK Production, while Liza Chasin remained her opposite number, President of US Production, in Los Angeles. Angela Morrison became the company's COO and continued to oversee the legal and business affairs department in London, while Michelle Wright replaced Jane Frazer as executive in charge of physical production in the same location (Dawtrey 1999f: 27). As Hayward explains, Working Title's multi-year co-production deals with Universal and Studiocanal supported a high level of activity and a wide range of projects:

> When you are lucky enough to see a film from its conception all the way through to its execution, everybody learns that way, everybody that is involved learns. If you are able to do that over and over again, which is what we were doing at Working Title, then you hone your skills and become better and better ... It'll always just keep coming back to material for me, which is, all of a sudden there's resources to develop more material. In developing more material ... you have a number of films hanging over these possible slots and you've got production financing which is allowing you to make a film. You're in a cycle of making films and when you're posting one, you're prepping another. You can keep the machine rolling along when you're capitalised like that, as opposed to raising the money to make a film and then starting that whole process again.[2]

The results of this development activity is, however, constantly channelled through the studio's senior creative executives, who oversee Universal's slate at large and manage its relationships with producers. As Table 6.1 shows, at the point of Working Title's integration into Universal, this included over thirty individuals or production companies, all of which were vying to get their projects green-lit. 'Let's say we've got fifty things in development, the studio is probably across twenty of them,' Bevan explains. 'You want everyone to have ownership on everything, basically, because it's much more likely to get through.'[3] Most notably, this dialogue was mediated through Universal's successive Presidents of Production which included Kevin Misher, Mary Parent and Scott Stuber, and Jon Gordon and Donna Langley. 'They'll know, pretty much, all of the headline stuff that we've got in development. They'll have read all the drafts and all the rest of it. They'll have had input on the drafts,'

Production company/individual	Key personnel
Amblin Entertainment	Steven Spielberg
Beacon Pictures	Armyan Bernstein, Marc Abraham
Castle Rock (distribution deal shared with Warner Bros)	Martin Shafer, Rob Reiner, Andrew Scheinman, Glen Padnick, Alan Horn
Clinica Estetico	Jonathan Demme, Ed Saxon
Dark Horse Entertainment	Mike Richardson
Daybreak Productions	Chuck Gordon
Frankfilm	Scott Frank
Furthur Films	Michael Douglas
Good Machine, Inc.	Ted Hope, James Schamus
Lawrence Gordon Prods.	Lawrence Gordon
Hell's Kitchen	Jim Sheridan, Arthur Lappin
Imagine Entertainment	Brian Grazer, Ron Howard
Jersey Films	Danny DeVito, Michael Shamberg, Stacey Sher
Jersey Shore	Jonathan Weisgal, Dan Levine
Kennedy/Marshall Co.	Kathleen Kennedy, Frank Marshall
Richard LaGravenese	Richard LaGravenese
Larger Than Life Productions	Gary Ross, Jane Sindell, Julie Golden
Lobell Productions	Mike Lobell
Mostow/Lieberman	Jonathan Mostow, Hal Lieberman
Eddie Murphy Productions	Eddie Murphy
Mike Nichols	Mike Nichols
Overbrook Entertainment	Will Smith, James Lassiter
Parkway Productions	Penny Marshall
Marc Platt Productions	Marc Platt
The Playtone Co.	Tom Hanks, Gary Goetzman
Raffaella Productions	Raffaella De Laurentiis
Phil Alden Robinson	Phil Alden Robinson
Shady Acres Entertainment	Tom Shadyac, Jim Brubaker
Shutt/Jones Productions	Buffy Shutt, Kathy Jones
The Robert Simonds Co.	Robert Simonds
Starstruck	Reba McEntire, Shelley Browning
Underworld Entertainment	Albert Hughes, Allen Hughes, Kevin Messick
Telvan Productions	Brian Levant
Working Title	Tim Bevan, Eric Fellner

Table 6.1 Universal's 1999 production deals. Source: Carver 1999b: 84.

Bevan goes on to point out. 'We talk to them all of the time about what we're doing so there's no surprise there. They're laying a foundation all the time as to whether it's something that might go.'[4] The ultimate responsibility for the studio's output, however, rested with Universal Chair, Stacey Snider, and Universal President and COO, Ron Meyer. Throughout this process, Working Title's LA office continued to be vital in bridging the gap between the British and Hollywood industries, as Chasin explains:

> I view my role as the front man to the business on this end ... I have very close twenty plus year relationships with the industry on this end, so I do a lot of the interfacing with the studio, with Universal, and a lot of the day-to-day with the community at large, whether it be directly with the talent that lives here or with the agents, lawyers, managers etcetera who represent the talent ... We run, I would say, not really half the slate, but half the active projects out of the LA office with a view to making probably one to two films a year on this end, versus the numbers on that end. So, there's a lot of managing the actual slate ... we can't make a film over there without it taking up a lot of space over here, it's just the nature of the way it works. It's really liaising with the town and pushing these things forward and, of course, getting the new material and getting people to want to come work here.[5]

The production department maintained its reputation as lavish by the standards of the British film industry, but highly cost-effective by the standards of Hollywood. For Wright, Working Title's ability to consistently realise such economy in production is partly based upon the company's primary location in Britain. 'We stay out of the studio system, we try to keep them at arm's length. Once ... people in Hollywood think you're associated with a big, major studio, they think you've got all the money in the world,' she explains. 'Being over here we're able to say, "Yes we are, they're our distributor, but we're still a UK production company."'[6] Following the introduction of the Section 42 and Section 48 tax relief schemes for film production, Working Title had, like many other UK-based production companies, benefited from the increasingly fertile economic climate which the legislation promoted (Hill 2012: 344–5). In practice, virtually all Working Title's films are official UK productions or co-productions, which typically reflect the national economic inputs of both Universal (US) and Studiocanal (France). As Wright goes on to note, her job is to interrogate all of the production planning from a logistical and economic perspective in collaboration with the principal filmmakers:

> If a movie is worth so much money to the financiers and the producers and the distributors, then how do we make that work? That's the challenge of it and the fun of it ... Once we have a script that everybody likes, that may be in re-writes, but we know pretty much the structure of what the script is going to be, and we have film-makers attached, we have a package. We go in and we break it down. We take the script and we try to turn it into a fine science by breaking it down into a schedule and a budget. It's a management tool to

do so, that's the only way to manage something that's creative like that. We break it down into a schedule: how many days can you shoot it? How do you shoot it? Where do you shoot it? How much will it cost? Once we have that package, we get to work on figuring out that normally it's too much and we figure out how we can make it less.[7]

With Hayward, Chasin, Wright and Morrison at the helm of Working Title's four filmmaking departments, the company continued to be run by women in virtually every significant role below its Co-Chairman, Tim Bevan and Eric Fellner. Reflecting on this situation, Hayward suggests:

> Women are good at multitasking ... or so goes the cliché, and I think it's probably true. When you're doing this job, you are working with a lot of very needy people all the time ... All around you there are writers, directors, producers, executives. You're having to deal with a lot of personalities all the time and I think women are good at that ... At one point we used to call it Working Women, not Working Title. Women have been fundamental to the success of this company.[8]

Amongst the cycle of 'Curtisland' romcoms, Working Title also explored the period drama with *Pride & Prejudice* (2005). The film initiated the company's relationship with Joe Wright, who would go on to direct a series of period films for Working Title, including *Atonement* (2007), *Anna Karenina* (2012) and *Darkest Hour* (2017). Paul Webster, a producer on *Pride & Prejudice*, explains the genesis of the project as follows:

> They were applying a more considered approach to what works in the marketplace and they looked at the tradition of the country house period British movie, adaptations of the classics. I think Deb Hayward said, 'OK, let's look for a classic, let's look at some things that are very obvious and see if there's some mileage in them.' And that's what led them to *Pride & Prejudice*, which is kind of the ultimate love story and, of course, *Bridget Jones's Diary* owes a lot to *Pride and Prejudice* and that's probably not unconnected. I think they thought ... they wanted to make another love story, really, rather than a period piece. They were romantic comedy specialists, so why not go back to the lodestone?[9]

While development remained the key point at which creativity and commerce were reconciled, the extent of Bevan and Fellner's influence on this process could vary widely, with filmmakers like the Coen brothers retaining a high degree of autonomy when working with the company. 'With people like Joel and Ethan, the reason I want to work with them is because they're geniuses. So, I don't want to go around telling them how to be better geniuses, I couldn't even begin to do that,' Fellner explains. 'We raise all the money, do all the marketing, do all the distribution and basically create an environment where they can do what they want to do.'[10] Describing the scope of their influence when working with key creative talent, Bevan adds:

> The Coens are a real exception, because they're auteurs, basically, and they get backed as auteurs. Who's going to tell Joel and Ethan what to do? Nobody. Almost everybody else, they have autonomy, but it's sort of controlled autonomy ... You create a box for any film. You say: 'Stay inside that box, and we want to know everything ... about what's going on inside that box, and we'll make that box really comfortable for you, we'll make it a good box, and we'll let you do what you want to do' ... [However] it's a box that you've all worked out together. It's a box that's got the story we're going to tell [in it], this is what we reckon it's worth when you look at it compared to the market, these are the people who are going to be in it ... It's got the resources that we've all agreed on in the cold calm of day that are applicable to this movie. Now, quite often with us the creative side will probably want more, creative people always want more than is in the box. But we will have been through the process of saying: 'This is the budget that we can achieve for this film'. We've done all the numbers, we've spoken to the financiers, we've worked with Universal, we've worked with Focus, we've worked with the foreign people: *this* is the number that everybody signs off on.[11]

The start of the Universal era also saw the launch of a new Working Title subsidiary, WT^2, which had a creative and commercial agenda which was distinct from that of its parent company. Most significantly, Working Title imposed a $5 million budgetary limit upon the films WT^2 produced, and explicitly set the company the task of attracting new writers and directors, many of whom would make their feature film debut with the subsidiary (Dawtrey 1999g: 12). The staff appointed as joint heads of the new company, Natascha Wharton and Jon Finn, were respectively promoted from positions in Working Title's development and production departments. A significant factor in the establishment of WT^2 was the creation of the New Writers' Scheme, a project which Wharton had initiated while working as a development executive. As she explains:

> One of the things that I really focused on through that time, which in retrospect was fantastically generous of Tim and Eric to let me do, was the New Writers' Scheme. We set up, I think, rather a canny structure to support writers whereby they were allowed to hold onto the copyright in the material. We gave them a set fee, helped them ... [along the] path and then took a view on whether we would develop the project. It was a fantastically rich time because, actually, quite a few of the writers that I worked with at that point went on to have careers ... People who were literally writing their

first scripts: James Watkins, Nick Love, John McDonagh, Rowan Joffe ... It seemed to be less about Tim and Eric finding projects and more about genuinely providing support for emerging talent. At the time, I think, Tim and Eric thought, if out of ten projects one of them came good or there was an interesting relationship that emerged out of one of them, then that would be of value.[12]

WT^2 Ltd was officially incorporated in October 1999 and took up residence in the same offices as Working Title on Oxford Street. Significantly, the new company was provided with a separate overhead and development budget and given a remit to develop its own slate. In doing so, Working Title effectively transferred the developmental autonomy which Universal provided downwards into WT^2. Wharton and Finn were joined by Rachael Prior and Amanda Boyle, who respectively assumed the positions of Head of Development and Company Coordinator, with Prior assisting Wharton and Boyle assisting Finn. In practice, however, the team worked together across all areas of development and production. 'Nat knows her stuff when it comes to production, and I have a lot of opinions on scripts,' Finn confirms. 'In the early stages we did all the meetings together. When people came in to pitch, we did it together, when we decided to pick stuff up, generally we made that decision together.'[13] As Finn makes clear, however, WT^2's agenda was equally about building creative relationships with an eye on the future of Working Title as a whole:

> It was a bit like playing the lottery, because enough of those films did work that you went, 'maybe it's this one'. My feeling about it was what you were really doing there was backing the filmmaker because some of the scripts weren't obvious [commercial successes] ... So, essentially, you go back to the reason we set it up in first place, which was to give people their first break. Give people their first shout, and give it to people who really wanted to make a film. I think there was two agendas going on there, really, and one of them was hoping that one of those films would catch the zeitgeist ... You wanted one in every five, six, seven to make some money but at the same time, with the rest of them, you're giving people a chance to shine or not. You're giving them an opportunity to do what they do, and then maybe feed the bigger company with those sorts of people.[14]

During the development process Finn and Wharton reported to Bevan and Fellner, whose involvement became crucial in the later stages. 'It was really simple. It was whether Tim or Eric wanted to do it, it literally came down to [that],' Finn explains. 'You would go in and show them stuff and go "We want to make this, we want to make this" and quite often they would say "No", but occasionally you'd find something that they also could see something in.'[15] Bevan and Fellner refined the company's remit by aligning its output with 'the three Hs' in the trade press, that is, 'heart, humour and horror' (Dawtrey 2000a: 1). Indeed, the films which WT^2 produced not only mapped onto the genres of comedy-drama, comedy and horror suggested by this slogan, but also conformed to Working Title's broadly commercial house style. As Wharton goes on to point out:

> It's quite rare to be making a film at a $5 million level and assume that it will then play internationally. Bizarrely, sometimes they do, and the ones that you don't expect do ... It was quite a challenge because we were looking at really interesting filmmakers and we always did have an eye on audience as well. Again, when you're making films at that sort of level that is quite a challenge. If you look at most of the British films that are made with emerging talent at the moment, they're much more overtly festival driven films, whereas our agenda was to try to find that talent, and to try and make those films, but for those films to have a similar sort of mainstream appeal as the other Working Title films.[16]

In practice, many of the films that WT^2 produced originated from projects circulating within the independent sector which were already attached to broadcasters or independent production companies. *Billy Elliot*, for example, was initially developed at Tiger Aspect Productions, a company with which Working Title had a first-look deal (Dawtrey 1999h: 7). Similarly, *Ali G Indahouse* and *Shaun of the Dead* originated with FilmFour, while the independents New Moon Pictures and Octagon Films respectively initiated *Mickybo and Me* and *Inside I'm Dancing* (2004) (Hofmann 2003: 6). Significantly, the small scale of WT^2's films helped them attract investment from public sources, including the UK Film Council, the Northern Ireland Film and TV Commission and the Irish Film Board. A second subsidiary, Working Title Australia (WTA), was founded in 2000 and had some early success with *Ned Kelly* (2003) and *Gettin' Square* (2003) under the leadership of the producer, Tim White. The Sydney-based subsidiary, however, proved to be a short-lived venture. The final Working Title film initiated in Australia, *Gone* (2007), was ultimately produced under the auspices of WT^2 following the closure of WTA in 2004 (George 2003; Smith & Kemp 2005).

Working Title's other production subsidiary, Working Title Television (WTTV), was also supplied with a separate overhead and development budget, and was relocated to a separate office from its parent company. As it had done during the PFE years, WTTV continued to work to a business model based on output deals, which were largely driven by the sale of Universal's films to international television broadcasters. The process was organised through Universal Television Distribution (UTD), which also sold broadcasting rights to the Universal film and TV libraries. As former President of WTTV, Simon Wright, explains, the value of programming within this system continued to be determined by the US market, a situation which had a direct effect on the way the company operated:

> It was a completely sure thing. They [Universal] could project within a few dollars what money they would make. So, if it was a $5 million production, they knew through just literally listing the output deals it would go into that they'd ... recoup $8 million, so they'd make $3 million. They called it a licence to print money. They could not get enough TV movies off me ... But it wasn't that simple, because I had to get US broadcasters to make it, we needed [them] attached ... The irony was, and it was one of the problems with my entire career at Working Title, is that we were off the radar in the UK, making British stuff. We didn't even qualify as British because it was technically American programming ... We really were just squashed in between the two markets. We existed for years outside of the mainstream in the UK and certainly outside of the mainstream in the US, just doing what we did.[17]

Other than two series of *Randall and Hopkirk (Deceased)* (BBC, 2000–1), the majority of WTTV's output consisted of made-for-television films such as *The Last of the Blonde Bombshells* (BBC/HBO, 2000), *About a Boy* (Fox/Universal 2003) and *Perfect Strangers* (CBS, 2004). In instances where a UK broadcaster was not attached as a co-producer, these films were seen in Britain through UTD's output deals with Sky and ITV. In many other territories, however, the situation was markedly different. 'The problem I had, and it does bug me even today, is that we would have sold our programmes to thirty, forty countries maybe, but very few of them ever exhibited any of the shows because they were in output deals,' Wright explains. 'There was no obligation on their behalf ever to show them. They were forced to take television in order to get the films, and it was the films they wanted.'[18] Unlike television production, however, the green-lighting process for Working Title's feature films continued to be routed through Universal.

Gate 2: Green-lighting

According to reports in the trade press, the contractual relationship between Working Title and Universal was based upon a high degree of creative and financial autonomy, whereby the production company could green-light up to five films a year with budgets up to $25 million without approval from the studio (Dawtrey 1999c: 1). This legally enshrined autonomy was not, however, enacted in practice. 'Our relationship for green-lighting was channelled through Universal. They were the ultimate decision maker on the big-budget movies,' Morrison explains. 'Going back to the lower-budget movies, even where we had what we called the "puts", we didn't exercise them. We would go through the green-light process and make sure everybody was happy with that.'[19] Within the lexicon of the Hollywood film industry a 'put' deal is so-called because it allows a production company to 'put' a film to a studio, by insisting upon a contractually enforceable green-light. As Fellner explains, however, despite this ability, the fundamental parent company–subsidiary dynamic relied upon consensus building, with the ultimate green-light decision resting with the studio:

> The bottom line is that it didn't mean an awful lot in terms of day-to-day operation, because you can green-light a film but you don't want to green-light it unless the distributor wants to distribute it, because otherwise you green-light a film that gets dumped and there is nothing more depressing than that. If you understand the power of distribution and marketing, you understand that equation, and we understood that. We didn't just immediately go, 'We're making this, we're making that, we're making the other.' We developed a relationship with the studio to try to make sure that everything we wanted to make, they wanted, and that UIP would distribute it properly and that it would get a real life in the marketplace.[20]

The green-lighting process in place at Universal acted as an extension and reiteration of the processes undertaken by Working Title and Universal during development. The discussions leading to a green-light decision ensured that the entire package of the film – script, cast, crew, budget – were discussed collectively by both parties. All such decisions were, however, also directed through a creative and commercial filter which resembled the 'control sheet' that PFE had used throughout the 1990s. This process was initially undertaken within Universal's Business Development and Strategic Planning Group in Los Angeles. Gareth Wilson, who began working within the group in 2003, was responsible for generating revenue forecasts for all the films in development at the various production companies under contract to Universal. 'Working Title films would come through Universal, so I'd work on Working Title films alongside twenty other films and we'd run numbers on maybe fifty-plus movies a year at Universal because, obviously, not everything gets made,' Wilson explains. 'We'd start that process fairly early, as soon as you have the skeleton of a package together from a script to your producer at a very minimum.'[21] As he goes on to note, there are two stages of modelling in place at Universal:

> When it was a young project at Universal we'd run a set of numbers that were effectively driven by a model that has been built up over time. The model aggregates historical film performances and uses that data to forecast future performance at various box office levels. That helps formulate the initial view as to the film's profitability and helps inform decisions about participations, [as] key creative players often get paid based on film performance. As the project takes shape over time, that's when you start going

to all the different distribution departments saying, 'What do you think this film will do?', so you have figures for box office, home video in all its various forms, and TV with corresponding marketing and distribution costs. By the time you get a green-lit film you have, as PolyGram would call it, a 'control sheet' or what Universal calls a 'ten-column'. The ten-column is ten scenarios, from a low-performance scenario to a high-performance scenario, and one of those scenarios will be a green-light case where you have a set of numbers that everyone thinks they can deliver on. That case will build in a return on investment based on various metrics, which differed depending on the owner.[22]

Significantly, the initial modelling process uses comparisons or 'comps' which link the projected commercial performance of a film in development with the established performance of recent films with comparable creative elements. 'Usually it starts with the script and so script will dictate genre, it'll give you a sense of the international capability and then, obviously, that's strongly influenced by your actors attached to it,' Wilson explains. 'The director seems to be the next in line in importance and then ... the producer is obviously a big indicator as well, though maybe less commonly thought about.'[23] The second part of the modelling process refines these numbers with input from Universal's distribution and marketing divisions. The conclusion of this process is the generation of an 'ultimate' which models the studio's anticipated expenditure and revenue for each film throughout its first product lifecycle. Wilson continues:

> For an accounting perspective you'll have your production costs amortised over the lifecycle of eight years, which is how long studios are required to forecast what their films will make. And so, that's what, really, we're looking at when we're looking at a control sheet or you're looking at a ten-column. You're estimating, approximately, the first lifecycle ... Roll forward as the revenue drips in over the course of eight years, obviously most of it in the first two years as your theatrical, video and TV revenues come in and then at the end of the day make sure that on an annualised basis you've made a 7 per cent return. That was the threshold. Seven to ten seems to be the going rate around the industry.[24]

The Working Title films which Universal green-lit were, of course, also partially determined by the wider production strategy of the studio. Speaking in 2005, Snider described the 'portfolio' approach to green-lighting which she had implemented upon her elevation to Chair of Universal Pictures in 1999. As she explains, this strategy involved three levels of production, namely big-budget 'tent-pole' films, medium-budget 'event' films and low-budget 'portfolio' films:

We determine that we can make well about 14 to 16 movies a year. And market and distribute well about 14 to 16 films a year. And within those 16 films or so, we have determined that to have balance and diversity and the size and genre is the key to the portfolio approach, our portfolio approach. So within that diversified play, we've planned to make one or two Tent Pole movies a year. These are the big expensive, special effects generated films like *King Kong*, like *The Mummy*, like *Jurassic Park*. They're released at the highest times of movie going attendance of the summer or the holiday season. And we make about one or two of them a year. Next we make about four or five what we call Event films a year. These are star or story driven. An example of the star driven film will be *The Bourne Identity*, a story driven film might be *Meet the Parents* or *Meet the Fockers*. And these are a little bit less expensive, still pretty pricey. And we make about four or five of these a year. A category of film that we've had real success with, that we have focused on and I think some of the other studios have ignored, are what we call portfolio films. These are low budget, niche films that are geared towards one specific segment of the audience. But we try to make them well enough that hopefully they will cross over. An example of the niche portfolio film is *Bring It On*, which was geared to young girls, and it sort of hit all teenagers. *American Pie*, we thought just boys would go, everybody went. (FD Newswire 2005)

Within this programme of annual output, Working Title contributed between three and seven films a year which typically aligned with the studio's medium-budget 'event' films, like *Bridget Jones's Diary* and *Johnny English*, while low-budget 'portfolio' films such as *Billy Elliot* and *Shaun of the Dead* were typically drawn from the output of WT². The final gate, distribution, propels Working Title's films into the worldwide marketplace and, in doing do, tests the accuracy of the the creative and commercial modelling undertaken at the point of green-lighting.

Gate 3: Distribution

Following the demise of Universal Pictures International (UPI), Working Title's output transferred to Universal's joint-venture international distribution company, United International Pictures (UIP) in 2000. While UIP was headquartered in London, the company operated directly in thirty-five international markets via subsidiaries and licensed its films to third-party distributors in dozens of other territories. From its parent companies, Universal and Paramount, UIP handled between thirty-five and forty films a year, including the output of Dreamworks via a longstanding sub-distribution agreement with Universal. The distribution and marketing strategies which UIP implemented on Universal's behalf, however, began to take shape at the point of green-lighting. Significantly, the 'ten-column' not only projected revenue for each film, but also aligned that projection with the distribution and marketing expenditure required to achieve it. As UIP's former Chairman and CEO, Paul Oneile, explains:

> It was on a film-by-film basis. If you go back to the green-lighting process, obviously Universal was heavily involved in the green-lighting process for Working Title product and that would be all part of it. This is how much the film production was going to cost and on that basis – provided the film turns out as we all hope it will – then we will look at spending 'x' dollars marketing it around the world and 'y' on prints. Once the film has been produced you look at it and say, 'Yes, it has turned out as well as we'd hoped' ... so we'll go ahead with the release strategy as we had anticipated it during the green-lighting process. It never actually worked that way because it became much more complicated and I'd like to think much more business-like.[25]

While an assessment of the completed film could prompt a revision of the initial distribution and marketing budget upwards or downwards, the release strategy was also predicated upon an assessment of the film's market potential on a territory-by-territory basis and, ultimately, the establishment of market success or failure upon release. As UIP's former COO and President, Andrew Cripps, explains:

> We would agree collaboratively with the studio how much we were going to spend. If you were unsure about the international prospects of a film you wouldn't release all your territories day-and-date, you'd go on a staggered release plan and say, 'Here are the three or four markets where the feedback from the territories was the most optimistic' or, 'We think that they can do a good job based on these historical precedents' ... We're going to try it in those markets first, and then we would, and then if they were successful then you roll it out in another sequence of markets. If they weren't successful, you wouldn't spend any more in other markets and you could claw back your losses. Once it was in release it was up to the territory team to push it as hard as they could to make sure they keep it playing on the screen for as long as they can, negotiating with exhibition. Typically, most of your marketing is spent up front anyway with a little bit of sustaining marketing that you would build into the campaign, but once it's in release you're trying to get as much as you can out of it.[26]

In contrast to the PFE approach, which promoted high levels of autonomy within its operating companies, UIP's management strategy was more centralised. In practice, a given release strategy was typically determined in the dialogue between Universal's senior management and UIP's head office before being filtered down to the territories. 'Their budgets were approved, the number of prints that they were going out with was approved, the release date was approved, so everything that they did had to be approved and in line with the strategy that we put in place,' Cripps explains. 'Having said that, they weren't completely powerless in their local territory because we relied on them [for] press relations, third-party promotions, deals with exhibitors. They would have to go out and get the best deal in negotiating the film rental splits.'[27] As Cripps goes on to point out, UIP's ability to negotiate favourable terms with exhibitors was one of its major strengths:

> There were only seven Hollywood studios and UIP represented three of them. So, if you were an exhibitor, the one company you probably didn't want to get off-side was UIP, or whoever happened to have the best line-up of films coming out. But inevitably, what made UIP work so incredibly well was that the movie business is a very cyclical business. So, when Paramount's having a great year, sometimes, Universal wasn't having such a good year. UIP could balance that out and they had a pretty strong slate of films year-in and year-out even though one of the component parts may not be having its best film year ever. If you're an exhibitor you knew, inevitably, 40 per cent of your hit movies were going to come from UIP. UIP was very careful, I would stress, not to abuse it ... but that implied leverage meant that you were probably going to get your films played, you were going to get your trailers played, and you were going to get paid on time.[28]

Significantly, establishing commercial success in the theatrical market bore a direct relation to the prospects of Universal's international sister companies, UPI Home Entertainment, Universal International Television Distribution and Universal Networks International. 'There are very few examples of a failed theatrical movie that went on to be a success in other windows,' Cripps explains. 'In your first window to the consumer, you have to make sure that is a success or everything else suffers ... every movie is its own brand, and you're having to establish that brand every time you go to the marketplace.'[29] As Peter Smith, UPI's former President of International Home Entertainment, explains:

> [The theatrical release] built an awareness for the film beyond theatrical. They would look at it and take the view looking at the ultimate on the film, what would the ultimate revenues be? Both TV, which was driven by box-office, and video, which was driven by box office ... We had regression models based on box-office by genre and we could use that, pretty accurately, to forecast revenues ... We would spend about 10 per cent of our revenues for any release on marketing, 10 to 15 per cent. The bulk of that money was spent on announcing the release date, generally not the storyline, but the release date, because ... people knew by then what ... [the film] was about.[30]

UIP's status as the largest and most powerful of Hollywood's international distribution companies, however, attracted unwanted attention from the European Commission. While it was ultimately determined that the company's business practices and market share were not in breach of antitrust laws, the process of securing exemptions from the Commission proved to be a considerable legal and administrative burden (Stern 1999: 31). A second longstanding issue was the perception that UIP was poor at marketing and distributing medium and low-budget 'specialty' films (Dawtrey 1998: 7). One strategic response to this situation was the continuation of UPI's London-based marketing division following the closure of its theatrical distribution network. UPI's former President of Marketing and Distribution, David Livingstone, and his team were initially given the remit of marketing Working Title's films alongside Universal's specialty output and international acquisitions (Dawtrey 2000b: 16). Recalling the rationale for the arrangement from Working Title's perspective, Livingstone explains:

> I think they'd grown used to being in control of their own destiny and even though I was working for another company, I'd worked very, very closely and very well with them. I think they suddenly thought 'God, if we suddenly end up going through this big faceless company, UIP, we will be one of 35 films they're releasing each year', whereas they'd got used to, with me there, being one of ten films ... [UIP] had so many films to release that it was a slightly homogenised environment. I don't want to be too critical of it, but they had so many films and so many bosses and so many territories that it was quite hard to get attention. We used to, basically, deliver to them what we wanted and try and make it work that way, by basically delivering them a completed package.[31]

In practice, Livingstone worked closely with Bevan and Fellner to produce briefs which were subsequently distributed to third-party creative agencies which designed the marketing materials for Working Title's films. The results were subject to further refinement before being submitted to Universal for approval and ultimately delivery to UIP. Thereafter the UPI team also managed the publicity and promotional campaigns which accompanied the release of Working Title's films. Livingstone was also keen to enhance Working Title's identity as a brand. The company's original logo, which comprised the company name set between two semicircles, was inspired by the London Underground sign. While the connotations of both London and industry were apt, Livingstone felt that a more distinctive image was needed. 'I wanted to show the creative process and I wanted to show it in quite a classical way,' he explains. '[It] went from a drawing, which was meant to be almost like Leonardo da Vinci's sketches to it ... evolving. It was basically a creative idea, the evolution of a creative idea.'[32] The new animated logo, which first appeared on *Bridget Jones's Diary*, showed a black background centrally illuminated with a golden spot of light onto which three concentric circles and a diagonal cross appear to be drawn in chalk. The lines revolve around one another in the motion of a gyroscope before the animation concludes with the formation of a single circle behind the words 'Working Title'.

In 2002, former PFEI/UPI President Stewart Till replaced Paul Oneile as CEO and Chairman of UIP. For Till, the single largest point of contrast between the functions of PFEI/UPI and those of UIP was the latter's lack of involvement in green-lighting. 'Universal and Paramount didn't ask our [opinion] ... I used to attend a Universal weekly green-lighting meeting by phone and then after a bit they asked me not to be on it because I was so opinionated,' he recalls. 'So, we had no input into what films they made, which was in part because they felt we weren't part of them, we were this third-party distribution company.'[33] Instead, Universal continued to generate ten-columns internally by using the expertise of its distribution and marketing executives in Los Angeles. For Till, a second point of contrast between PFEI/UPI and UIP was the difference in corporate culture. '[At PFEI] we had a fabulously competitive attitude as a company, we were creating history, so you got people who worked their socks off, worked all hours,' he recalls. '[At] UIP, the management had been there ten, fifteen years, so I tried to do two things, really. One was [to] make the marketing feistier and better ... and I tried to make the culture a bit more competitive.'[34]

Working Title's films were also subject to studio-level branding at the point of distribution. After pulling out of the Gramercy Pictures partnership with PFE in 1996, Universal founded its own specialty distribution company, Universal Focus, three years later which handled the domestic release of Working Title films like *Billy Elliot* and *The Man Who Cried* (2000) (Goodridge 2000). Universal's 2002 acquisition of USA Networks, however, prompted the reorganisation, expansion and rebranding of Universal's specialty division. In May that year, Universal also acquired Good Machine, Inc., a New York-based independent run by James Schamus, Ted Hope and David Linde (Harris & DiOrio 2002: 1). Good Machine was promptly merged with USA Films and Universal Focus to form Focus Features. In effect, the new company became a mini-major sister studio to Universal which operated three divisions: a New York-based headquarters from which Schamus and Linde oversaw the company's slate; a US-based distribution and marketing company which handled the company's output in the domestic market; and Focus Features International (FFI), a London-based film sales company. As Alison Thompson, former President of FFI, notes:

> We were primarily focused on producing and distributing prestige cinema. I think we were very excited about innovative cinema as well as the more traditional cinema ... We often talked about 'smart-house' audiences ... [to] describe the kind of audience we'd be looking for with our films and so they sat alongside the main studio in a pretty distinctive way because, of course, the main studio was primarily occupied with the bigger, broader films, whereas

the films that Focus was most often involved in were, by-and large, what we describe in the US as platform releases. So, they didn't open on 2,000 prints, they had their roll-out on a smaller number of screens. So, yes, we were primarily focused on prestige and often director or auteur-driven material.[35]

While Working Title's films continued to be developed and green-lit through its deal with Universal, Focus often became involved at the point of marketing and distribution. 'A decision would be made between Working Title, Universal and Focus Features in the US about how best to distribute Working Title films in the US,' Thompson explains. 'Broadly speaking, some of the more specialised, prestige titles were more likely to go through Focus and the broader movies were likely to go through Universal.'[36] In practice, Working Title films such as *The Shape of Things* (2003), *Ned Kelly* and *Pride & Prejudice* were released through Focus as well as WT² titles like *Long Time Dead* (2002), *My Little Eye* (2002) and *Inside I'm Dancing*.

In 2003 another former PFEI executive, David Kosse, was appointed Universal's President of International Marketing and Distribution (Dawtrey & Groves 2003: 1). Significantly, Kosse was based in London and described his role as being akin to that of a 'shadow government' insofar as he provided Universal with enhanced oversight of its international distribution and marketing infrastructure. 'I was in charge of the marketing and distribution of Universal movies via UIP,' he explains. 'I had to approve the marketing spends and I had to approve the dating... on the movie side it was to make sure that a Universal movie wasn't disadvantaged in any way, relative to a Paramount or Dreamworks movie.'[37] Kosse's arrival proved to be the thin end of the wedge and in 2005 it was announced that UIP would restructure its business by ceasing to operate as a joint venture in most of its key territories. As Kosse points out, the decision was predicated on a number of interlocking factors:

> We were making a lot of movies and releasing a lot of movies. So was Paramount, so was Dreamworks. We had a point where in some of the larger territories, you had maybe almost a film a week. So, we felt there was cannibalisation of the screens, as opposed to just [there being an] additive nature of the screens. In other words... it got past the tipping point of... 'We're a big distributor therefore we have clout' to 'We're such a big distributor that we're taking our own films off screen'. That was one element of it. The second element of it was that it felt like the territories, from a studio standpoint, were becoming very cookie cutter. So, the big films were held well, but in a business where surprise hits come out of [different] places, the surprise hit films weren't being given a chance. Next, was generally the perspective that the international market was one that was projected to grow a lot... We felt like it was a core business that we had to be in... To be going through a joint venture really made no sense.[38]

By the beginning of 2007, it was envisaged that fifteen of UIP's major national territories would be divided between Universal and Paramount, while UIP would continue as a joint venture in twenty markets (McNary 2005: 1). The remodelling of Universal's international distribution operation was chiefly orchestrated by Marc Shmuger, Universal's Vice Chairman, who had overall responsibility for worldwide distribution and marketing. Significantly, Stacey Snider left Universal to become Co-Chairman and CEO of Dreamworks in early 2006 and was replaced by Shmuger, who became Co-Chairman alongside David Linde, who was promoted from Focus Features (Snyder 2006: 1). These new appointments, and the simultaneous reorganisation of Universal's international distribution infrastructure, initiated a new phase in Universal's production strategy which had significant consequences for Working Title in the years that followed.

Notes

1. Tim Bevan, interview with the author, 7-12-2016.
2. Debra Hayward, interview with the author, 20-9-2013.
3. Tim Bevan, interview with the author, 7-12-2016.
4. Ibid.
5. Liza Chasin, interview with the author, 22-5-2014.
6. Michelle Wright, interview with the author, 13-7-2014.
7. Ibid.
8. Debra Hayward, interview with the author, 20-9-2013.
9. Paul Webster, interview with the author, 10-5-2013.
10. Eric Fellner, interview with the author, 14-3-2014.
11. Tim Bevan, interview with the author, 7-12-2016.
12. Natascha Wharton, interview with the author, 11-3-2014.
13. Jon Finn, interview with the author, 1-9-2017.
14. Ibid.
15. Ibid.
16. Natascha Wharton, interview with the author, 11-3-2014.
17. Simon Wright, interview with the author, 20-5-2014.
18. Ibid.
19. Angela Morrison, interview with the author, 26-11-2013.
20. Eric Fellner, interview with the author, 14-3-2014.
21. Gareth Wilson, interview with the author, 12-8-2014.
22. Gareth Wilson, interview with the author on 12-8-2014 and subsequent email correspondence on 20-8-2014.
23. Gareth Wilson, interview with the author, 12-8-2014.
24. Ibid.
25. Paul Oneile, interview with the author, 23-2-2016.
26. Andrew Cripps, interview with the author, 17-9-2015.

27 Ibid.
28 Ibid. UIP represented its original three parent companies, MGM, Paramount and Universal until 2001, when MGM left the partnership.
29 Ibid.
30 Peter Smith, interview with the author, 23-3-2016.
31 David Livingstone, interview with the author, 6-5-2014.
32 Ibid.
33 Stewart Till, interview with the author, 24-2-2014.
34 Ibid.
35 Alison Thompson, interview with the author, 31-3-2016.
36 Ibid.
37 David Kosse, interview with the author, 30-6-2014.
38 Ibid.

Billy (Jamie Bell) concentrates in Mrs Wilkinson's ballet class in *Billy Elliot*.

Bridget (Renée Zellweger) and Mark (Colin Firth) look on scornfully at Daniel in *Bridget Jones's Diary*.

Ali G (Sacha Baron Cohen) and Da West Staines Massiv face off against Da East Staines Massiv in *Ali G Indahouse*.

Arch villain Pascal Sauvage (John Malkovich) introduces himself to Lorna Campbell (Natalie Imbruglia) as Johnny English (Rowan Atkinson) makes another faux pas in the film of the same name.

'You have bewitched me, body and soul.' Elizabeth Bennet (Keira Knightley) kisses the hand of Mr Darcy (Matthew Macfadyen) in *Pride & Prejudice*.

Nanny McPhee (Emma Thompson) eyeballs the Brown children in *Nanny McPhee*.

Cecilia (Keira Knightley) and Robbie (James McAvoy) talk in the grounds of the Tallis family estate in *Atonement*.

'You wanna be a big copper in a small town?' Sgt Nicholas Angel (Simon Pegg) and PC Danny Butterman (Nick Frost) chase suspects through Sandford's model village in *Hot Fuzz*.

CHAPTER 7

The Universal Years Part II: Retrenchment and Reorientation (2007–12)

In January 2007, Universal's newly appointed Co-Chairmen, Marc Shmuger and David Linde, secured Working Title's long-term future at the studio. The production company's Co-Chairmen, Tim Bevan and Eric Fellner, signed seven-year contract extensions which suggested Working Title would maintain its exclusive relationship with Universal until at least 2014 (Thompson & Kemp 2007). The lengthy term reflected the remarkable commercial success of the company's films in the preceding eight years, which included both medium-budget 'event' films like *Notting Hill* (1999), *Johnny English* (2003) and *Nanny McPhee* (2005) and low-budget 'portfolio' films, such as *Billy Elliot* (2000), *Ali G Indahouse* (2002) and *Shaun of the Dead* (2004) produced through Working Title's subsidiary, WT^2. In the period between 2007 and 2012, however, the nature of Working Title's output shifted considerably in response to several interlocking factors. Chief amongst these was an industry-wide shift towards big-budget 'tent-pole' production, increased competition from new market entrants and the effects of the 2007–8 global financial crisis. As Bevan explains:

> If you look at the studio system, that's what has happened, it's not peculiar to Universal. What's happened post-2006, post-2008 really, is that they used to make two cornerstone marquee movies a year but now they're making four or six, and those four or six films are costing $150 million to $200 million each and they're then costing another $150 million to release, and they're sucking the resources out of the system, basically ... They also become sort of self-fulfilling prophecies, those films, but also beyond that, when they hit, they hit big. That's the way the studio business has gone. So, the Working Title film is under threat from that on a resource level and it's also under threat from premium television as well, so from your Netflix and your Amazons and all of those guys, who are making these great, very watchable six- to eight- to ten-hour series that are proper competition.[1]

Working Title's response to these developments included the closure of WT^2, the production of big-budget American-set action films and thrillers like *State of Play* (2009), *Green Zone* (2010) and *Contraband* (2012) and the production of sequels, including *Mr. Bean's Holiday* (2007), *Elizabeth: The Golden Age* (2007), *Nanny McPhee and the Big Bang* (2010) and *Johnny English Reborn* (2011). These transitions in the company's production agenda were mirrored by significant industrial changes behind the scenes. Studiocanal, for example, substantially reduced its investment in Working Title's slate, a decision which coincided with Universal's increasing reliance upon a major new financier, Relativity Media. Simultaneously, the reinvention of Universal's international distribution and marketing infrastructure promoted a closer dialogue between studio-owned and operated companies that placed a greater emphasis on marketing and branding within the studio's output.

THE CHANGING CONTEXTS OF DEVELOPMENT, GREEN-LIGHTING AND DISTRIBUTION

While the details of Working Title's seven-year deal with Universal were not publicly announced beyond its duration, little changed in the working relationship between the two, including the continuation of the exclusive 'put' deal that was originally agreed upon in 1999. 'At one point we had up to $35 million as a possibility for one film a year,' explains Working Title's COO, Angela Morrison. 'But to be honest we got to a point where everything was working without the need to have autonomy written in.'[2] Studiocanal's contribution to Working Title's overhead, development and production budgets, however, continued to diminish following the expiration of its second co-financing deal with Universal. Thereafter, the French studio made investments in Working Title's slate on a film-by-film basis. As Morrison points out, Working Title's evolving production strategy under Universal's new leadership was increasingly at odds with that of Studiocanal:

> Their terms changed because they [Studiocanal] didn't want to invest as much. We were making bigger films, they didn't have the balance sheet to support that, so they came down a bit in terms of what they were prepared to fund and then they stopped funding in 2010 ... They had several management changes along the way. The distribution side of it pretty much remained the same, but they were beginning to want to limit their exposure on production cost because, if you look back over the slate, some of the films were $70 million, whereas at the beginning we'd been making much cheaper films, so the studio [Universal] had the appetite to make those big films, they didn't really, so they reduced down and that was negotiated between the studio and Studiocanal.[3]

One of the immediate consequences of this new production agenda was the closure of WT². In practice, there had been a gradual movement of staff and resources away from the company over several years. In 2005 WT²'s Natascha Wharton replaced Debra Hayward at the helm of Working Title's UK development department but also continued to run the subsidiary (Dawtrey 2005: 4). Shortly thereafter, WT² was folded into Working Title and briefly continued as a 'label' before being disbanded (Hofmann 2006: 2). 'I think that the world was in a different place, I think that Tim and Eric felt that they wanted to… keep the focus very much on bigger films,' Wharton recalls. 'They weren't certain that it made sense for them to have multiple executives working across the smaller films … and they've held to that.'[4] Despite its short life-span, WT² succeeded in its role as a creative incubator by forging lasting relationships with emerging talent. Notable examples include Lee Hall, the writer of *Billy Elliot*, *Victoria & Abdul* (2017) and *Cats* (2019); the writing partnership of Edgar Wright and Simon Pegg who were behind *Shaun of the Dead*, *Hot Fuzz* (2007) and *The World's End* (2013); and Sacha Baron Cohen, who eventually followed *Ali G Indahouse* with *Grimsby* (2016). Recalling both the rationale for establishing the company and the decision to shutter it, Bevan notes:

> We felt we were making bigger movies at the studio level and we wanted to stay in touch with younger, developing filmmakers. Now, what we learned in the process of the five or six years that WT² was going, was that actually making those lower budget films … was as time-consuming and angst-ridden and generally as much of a pain … as making a bigger movie. At the end of it we thought 'Why are we doing this? Why don't we choose one or two younger filmmakers in any given film cycle, or a younger filmmaker, and one of us actually produce it and put bigger resources behind them, so that their film stands a better shot?' So, instead of their first film being a $5 million movie, it's a $20 million movie and they can cast people who we know about in it, they can get production value in it, and it stands a chance in the marketplace.[5]

During this period, Working Title built upon its growing success with bigger-budget films, a departure most clearly initiated by the release of *The Interpreter* (2005), an $80 million political thriller starring Sean Penn and Nicole Kidman. 'As a strategy, we absolutely started to steer towards bigger stories [and] bigger worlds to put those stories in, [and] genres we hadn't been in,' explains Liza Chasin, Working Title's President of US Production. '[*The Interpreter*] had an international scope and it was kind of what we call elevated genre – or as Eric has been calling it recently – "intelligent popcorn" … it would be a commercially broad movie but it would have the smarts … that had been important to us in movies up until that point.'[6] In the years that followed, Working Title's 'intelligent popcorn' output largely comprised thrillers, typically featuring American characters, settings and cultural themes including *State of Play*, *Green Zone* and *Contraband*. For Chasin, however, such films often remained European in their creative sensibility and international in their market orientation:

> We always made films worrying more about the international box office than the US domestic box office because that's where our bread and butter was. We knew our films were doing bigger multiples internationally than other movies out of the US were doing. That was something that we really leaned heavily on ... It's the sensibility of a company that's based in Europe, basically, and a desire to feed that side of the world and understand that the rest of the world is equally important ... We don't make anything that feels overly American in that way. You won't see us making an American sports movie. It's a joke I have with Tim and Eric all the time, because it's just not something they're interested in ... We seem like a big company, but we actually function like filmmakers, like we're on the ground producing our movies. The taste of the company inherently is informing the decisions and we're very careful to look at all those decisions both from a creative standpoint and a commercial standpoint ... It's a good checks and balances system for us. We never get into a corner of it being too American, but we do get too into the corner ... where we're being too foreign in some ways, but that's the home base and the area that's important.[7]

Working Title's increasing reliance upon Universal to bankroll its costs during this period was mitigated by a series of high-profile deals between the studio and the Los Angeles-based financier, Relativity Media. In 2006, Relativity struck two separate agreements to co-finance the production of thirty-seven films with Sony and Universal, fifteen of which were Universal films. Under the terms of the agreement, Relativity selected the films in which it wanted to invest at the point of development across the slates of both studios (Kay 2006a; 2006b). By 2008 Universal and Relativity reached a more comprehensive agreement to co-finance approximately forty-five Universal films over a four-year period through its subsidiary, Relativity Capital (Garrett 2008: 1). Across these deals, Relativity's early investments included Working Title films such as *Smokin' Aces* (2006), *Atonement* (2007) and *Wild Child* (2008) and continued with titles like *State of Play*, *Green Zone* and *Johnny English Reborn*. Throughout this period Working Title continued to be self-generative by initiating and then developing ideas with key creative talent in-house. As Bevan explains:

> A good producer ... likely, they'll have been involved in the initiation of the project in the first place, long before a director was involved in it. From an article, a book, or an idea or whatever. They'll have probably developed that idea with a writer. They'll have then picked the right director to come on board to do it. They'll work with that director in creating the vision for it,

and part of that is ensuring that the script is right, the cast is right, the place [where] you're going to make it is right, the cost is right: the elements that are going into it are right ... The shooting of the film is the process that the director is absolutely in charge of, but again, a good producer will be looking at dailies all of the time, [be] on the set every now and again and all the rest of it. But I think a good producer won't get lost in the minutiae of what's happening on the set ... They'll be worried about what is, creatively, being achieved each day because that's what you're left with.[8]

Simultaneously, Working Title's sphere of influence extended beyond the walls of its new offices on Marylebone's Aybrook Street. Indeed, the distribution of its resources amongst the wider British film industry could be measured by the company's cyclical contractual ties with other production companies and individuals. 'We've fallen in and out of deals with Richard Curtis, depending on where we are in a cycle. We'll have a two or three picture deal with him, we've got a several film deal with Joe Wright, we had a several film deal with Edgar Wright,' Bevan explains. 'As part of those first-look deals, there are elements of their lives that come with it. Joe formed Shoebox Films and we fund that, Richard had got his offices over in Portobello and we finance that.'[9] In maintaining production deals with both individuals and independent companies, Working Title began to act like a miniature British-based studio. In doing so, Working Title extended the same level of creative autonomy to the companies and individuals on its books as it was granted by Universal. As Working Title's COO Angela Morrison points out, such deals were, in part, a consequence of the unintegrated structure of the wider UK industry:

It's very hard for an indie producer to have any kind of set-up here, because out there in the local UK business, there aren't many overhead deals. We have had the luxury of having a decent development budget and although it has had some pressures on it, and it has reduced over time, we still feel that if we give these producers some support, that they are going to bring talent relationships, script development, ideas. It's really an expansion of our development department here [at Working Title] and it was perceived to be a good way to bring more ideas in ... We give them a small overhead contribution, we have a first look at their projects. If we want to develop it, we pay for it, and if we don't, they can go somewhere else with it ... [It allows them autonomy] in terms of what ideas they might be generating, and then, once ... something is developed here it enters our system of being just like any other Working Title project.[10]

At the same time, Working Title's ability to assess the market profile of its development slate was enhanced with the arrival of Gareth Wilson from Universal, who was appointed Vice President of Business Development and Production Finance in 2006. Unlike most of Working Title's staff, the changes in Universal's ownership had a direct impact upon Wilson's role. 'GE and Vivendi had different ways of looking at things and Comcast have their own way of looking at things too,' he elaborated. 'You'd have the same comparison to any sort of venture capitalist looking at investing in a new business, everyone has got their different metrics to look at.'[11] Explaining the rationale for his move to Working Title, he elaborates:

> It was a notion of just wanting the capability to look a little bit more closely and have the flexibility to run your own models as opposed to relying on Universal, where you might not be getting the full information, just simply because there is a bit of negotiation there too. For us to get films made, if Universal's going to make them, we have to sell them on the film. Even though we're partners with them in many ways, they're still across the table in some others.[12]

In practice, a major part of Wilson's role remained the production of 'ten-columns'. Assessing the market potential for each film in development continued to involve quantifying the creative elements associated with each. 'In my experience ... the numbers are used to justify creative decisions, not the other way around. It certainly is a creative mentality that drives the process,' Wilson explains. 'You justify things with numbers, but if you look back at people's ability to forecast movie profitability, I think you'll find that history is laden with failures.'[13] From the start of the Shmuger and Linde era, however, there was a growing sense that the application of the 'ten-column' became more exacting. As Chasin recalls:

> [PolyGram's] formula was quite simple and very straightforward. The upside didn't have to be huge, it just had to be a marginal profit in a moderate-case scenario ... whereas I think Universal ... [is] more stringent, their green-light control sheet approach is a little more stringent ... There was a time in the business, remember – which has changed a lot I would say – where heads of the studios could bypass. If you really fell in love with something and the numbers didn't add up you could still say, 'I don't care that the numbers don't add up, I still want to make this film, I believe in this film'. There was a sort of creative gut that ... certainly Stacey Snider had it when she was running Universal, when we got there, and that was very beneficial to us and we certainly had had that experience in the PolyGram days because if there was enough belief, we could make those numbers work, because ... the hurdles weren't as high.[14]

One result was the production of an increasing number of sequels which traded on the established commercial success of Working Title's back catalogue, including *Mr. Bean's Holiday*, *Elizabeth: The Golden Age*, *Nanny McPhee* and the Big Bang and *Johnny English Reborn*. While the commercial evidence base for these films was easier to establish when compared to an entirely new proposition, the task of putting a sequel into production was still reliant upon the right creative elements coalescing, as Fellner explains:

> Franchises ... wasn't like a strategic decision. [We said,] 'Well, that film worked, let's see if we can make another one', if there was a creative reason for it. So that's organic, that just happens, you're crazy not to push when you can push. And the low-budget films, it's just harder and harder to make smaller films get any traction. So, as we go into a world where box sets and digital distribution and high-end TV are raiding the low-hanging fruit of box office receipts, those films are starting to die.[15]

In practice, Working Title banked on sequels while also taking calculated risks on projects which, while still genre- and star-based, were harder to position in the market. 'We've always gone for ... a good story with decent characters, with emotions that we can connect to that make people jump or thrilled or laugh, or whatever they're meant to do in terms of the genre of the movie,' Bevan explains. 'And we've always been very screenplay conscious ... and when we've deviated too much from that we haven't had success.'[16] Bevan encapsulates the process of evaluating the creative and commercial attributes of a project by posing a rhetorical question – 'How big is the bullseye?' – which acts a metaphor for the size of a film's audience. Expanding on this theme, he points to two Working Title films that were released in the same year, but had markedly different public profiles and box office expectations:

> Let's take a film like *Atonement*, if you go back a few years. That is a fairly erudite, weird, book that a few people might have read. You try and make it attractive. Joe Wright had done a decent movie before but wasn't a household [name as a] director, Keira Knightley... [was attached] ... [There's a] pretty small bullseye, you needed to make a really good film for that thing to break through, the film had to be really good to get an audience. Now, a *Mr. Bean* movie, everyone knows what it is, and you can sit here right now and say, 'That film will make £20 million to £25 million in the UK'. On *Atonement*, you say, 'Well, we could make £50 or we could, if we get it *really* good, make £7.5 million.' So, that's all about the elasticity of the bullseye. Because we're always looking at slates, you're always trying to make that bullseye bigger.[17]

During this period, the UK continued to be an attractive destination for filmmaking in no small part because of the introduction of the UK film tax credit in 2007, which became applicable to all certified UK films, and replaced the Section 42 and Section 48 tax relief system (Hill 2012: 345). As Michelle Wright, Working Title's executive in charge of production explains, the legislation has a profound impact upon Working Title's ability to continually produce films economically:

> It's the best tax credit in the world ... that's why you've got every big major over here ... It's straightforward, it's organised, [it delivers] six weeks later, it pays on above-the-line ... Very seldom do we ever go anywhere that doesn't have tax credit. Studios just demand it, it becomes part of your financing plan ... It's huge, it's 25 per cent with certain exclusions, and so it's a big number to get a movie green-lit, without a doubt. That's why you've got all the major Warner Brothers movies over here, that's why you have Disney, that's why you have Lucas[film] ... A lot of places in the States, and around the world, just do below the line, they [the UK] do above the line, which is all the big actors, and producers and directors fees, so it's a huge deal.[18]

Indeed, all of Working Title's films are UK productions or co-productions, many of which also acknowledge the financial inputs of the company's major financiers, Universal (US) and Studiocanal (France), as well as other nations (e.g. Germany, Canada, Ireland, Australia), where production incentives or location shooting further widen the co-production net. Such production arrangements, of course, at once designate the national while also clearly highlighting the transnational. For Fellner, any discussion of British cinema is less important than producing films of global appeal in the UK, regardless of national attributes. 'You try, in your choices, to make films that you think will appeal globally or internationally, not just in the UK,' he explains. 'A lot of people choose to make movies that they feel will just work here, but that's not what we're interested in.'[19] As he goes on to argue:

> The whole nationality issue is a red herring. It's important for two reasons. One, to ensure that we create employment and opportunity here in England, and secondarily so that you qualify for the tax credit to be able to get your films made here. Beyond that, I work in a global business. The fact is, I live here, my family live here, I love this country, I'll never leave. The more I can make here, the happier I am, but I don't think of myself as a British film-maker, I think of myself as a filmmaker.[20]

Significantly, producing films from Working Title's US office often presented more complications. 'The problem with the States is that it's all collective bargaining, so it's all about unions, and teamsters and it makes it just more expensive,' Wright explains. 'A lot of states have tax credits, California doesn't have one that works, which is why all the films left there.'[21] As she goes on to point out:

> You're in Hollywood's back yard, you're in Universal's back yard and it's harder to make deals, and unfortunately the collective bargaining of the unions makes it impossible ... In America when it comes to the cost of labour

> and the cost of things, there is no negotiation. Here [the UK], you still have the ability to make a little movie and you can negotiate for it, but in America it's just all quantified and ... we're all signatories to the contracts for all of the unions ... It's hard for me to explain that sometimes to people because they don't understand that. 'Why can't we make it for less?', because you can't make labour any less, because that is what it is, everybody's unionised.[22]

The fluctuating contexts in which Working Title's films were developed, financed and green-lit was mirrored in the transformation of Universal's international distribution operations. The scope of Universal's longstanding joint venture with Paramount, United International Pictures (UIP), was substantially reduced with the launch of two new theatrical distribution companies, Universal Pictures International (UPI) and Paramount Pictures International (PPI). The move proved to be a moment of personal irony for Stewart Till, who stood down as Chairman and CEO of UIP just as the company adopted the strategy which he had advocated at the end of the 1990s. In turn, Universal's former President of International Marketing and Distribution, David Kosse, was appointed President of UPI. As he explains, Universal's new distribution structure ultimately involved a combination of both UPI and UIP operating companies:

> The parameters of UIP was that if one company left, then the other company would get the operation, and the leaving company would have to pay whatever restructuring costs were in that. So, there was no point in leaving, it was just too much of a poisoned pill ... We realised that we didn't really want to leave UIP per se, we just felt there were a handful of territories that would be better off just releasing the movies of one studio, as opposed to both studios. So, I came up with this idea which was instead of UIP being a joint venture, let's look at it as thirty-six joint ventures and let's take ... the most important sixteen markets and let's split those up, and let's have those go eight and eight to each studio. There was a lot of concern from all of us about what would happen when we left. What if we couldn't set up on our own in the UK or France or whatever quickly? So we had reciprocal distribution arrangements for a few years with the other party. We were able to exit that company, knowing that ... we could always go through them [Paramount] for a few more years while we set up our own company.[23]

As Andrew Cripps, UIP's former COO explains, the division of the company's territories was based upon two distinct rationales. 'Paramount's strategy, as I understood it at the time, was pick the territories where its going to be hardest to set up our own distribution in,' Cripps explains. 'Universal, I think, were more European-focused, obviously, with the territories that they ended up picking up ... they had more of a regional strategy.'[24] As of January 2007, UPI adopted eight UIP operating companies in Germany/Austria, Switzerland, Italy, Spain,

Russia, Belgium, the Netherlands and South Korea. Simultaneously, PPI took five territories including the UK/Ireland, Australia/New Zealand, France, Mexico and Brazil. Distribution in the remaining markets was handled through UIP, which continued as a joint venture between Universal and Paramount in Japan and smaller markets in Scandinavia, Eastern Europe, Latin America and Southeast Asia (Hollinger 2007). As Cripps explains:

> Probably there is some regret on the part of both studios now, the way it's probably worked out, just given the studios are making fewer films again. Sharing overhead and infrastructure is probably a good idea. My personal opinion of what they should have done is they should have kept UIP but set up separate marketing teams, because I think that was always the problem … marketing was always the bottleneck, we had too many films going through the infrastructure. I think the infrastructure was fine, the back office, the finance, the IT, even the distribution side, but they should have set up their own independent marketing groups and really resourced it. They would have been very successful, I think, and they would have saved themselves a lot of money, rather than recreating the whole [operation] twice. But hindsight is 20:20.[25]

Nonetheless, Universal's direct ownership of UPI ensured that the distribution company had a much closer working relationship with the studio. Significantly, this shift in approach mirrored the way in which Working Title's former parent company, PolyGram Filmed Entertainment (PFE), had operated during the 1990s, a fact directly acknowledged by Shmuger in the trade press (Dawtrey 2006b: 10). As if to underline this transformation in perspective, Kosse was subsequently made President of International at Universal with oversight of film across the platforms of theatrical, home entertainment and television; the same set of responsibilities that Stewart Till had assumed at PFE (Jaafar 2009: 1). As Kosse explains, the restructuring paved the way for a much closer dialogue between production and distribution:

> It was much easier for me as I came in as a Universal guy and spent a lot more time at the Universal lot. I became their go-to guy for the information because I'd developed relationships with them … [UPI] are intensely involved [in production] now and have been for a long time. It's an intense process to get involved in, it's a time-consuming process. You can't call and just say, 'Hey, we've got a movie, so-and-so is making it, it's like this, read the script tomorrow, give me a number.' … It's a much more iterative process and a dynamic process and you really need to understand what the movie is going to be *like*, as opposed to making a quick judgement on it … UIP wasn't set up to be that, whereas [at UPI] … you're just part of the company. You see the development slate all the way through the process and you have a constant ebb and flow with those executives working on it and they value your opinion.[26]

The effect on Working Title's green-lighting relationship with Universal was immediate and enduring. 'If we take a picture through Universal ... it used to be the production people would read the script, between you and them you'd come up with a cost, you'd green-light it, you'd set out to make it,' Bevan explains. 'Whereas now, distribution, and particularly foreign distribution – because that's where the growth in the film business is – will be all over the decision of whether the film gets made or not.'[27] Within this new infrastructure, however, responsibility for Working Title's marketing and promotional campaigns continued to rest with David Livingstone, who transferred from UPI to become Working Title's President of Worldwide Marketing. As he explains, effectively marketing Working Title's films became easier with established brand recognition, a factor which applied to an increasing number of the company's titles:

> If you've already had a hit, you don't have to go around proving to people that you can plausibly make a hit. If you come out with ... something with Rowan Atkinson or something with Hugh Grant in, or a Richard Curtis comedy, suddenly everybody, they're all believers. There was a massive conversion. Suddenly [it's] *Trainspotting* versus *Shallow Grave*. The truth is, *Shallow Grave* was also a very good film, but it was a small British film with a cast of unknowns. Suddenly, it became something worth having, *Trainspotting*, because it was from that team that had made a really good, well reviewed film. To a degree, we had the same thing with *Shaun of the Dead*, but this was a long time later ... I was told that it was unreleasable and then it got amazing reviews and, of course, [when] we came out with *Hot Fuzz*, suddenly everybody changed their tune.[28]

The refocusing of Universal's production strategy was accelerated by the forces of the 2007–8 global financial crisis. In December 2008, NBCUniversal cut 500 staff from its payroll and scaled back its expenditure across the board (Szalai & Gough 2008). As Table 7.1 illustrates, Universal also reduced the number of deals it maintained with production companies, which were streamlined from thirty-four to just twenty-two over the course of a decade. Simultaneously, Linde and Shmuger looked towards the successful tent-pole franchises at other studios and began to acquire film options from a range of toy manufacturers, comic books publishers and video games publishers including Hasbro, Mattel, Dark Horse Comics and Take-Two Interactive in the hope of discovering an adaptable property with a 'pre-sold' public profile, synergy in the form of ancillary products and the potential for franchise production (Graser 2009a: 1). In these circumstances, Working Title's ability to economically produce films which lay outside Universal's core slate remained vital. As Bevan notes:

Production company/individual	Key personnel
Apatow Productions	Judd Apatow
Arroyo Films	Scott Frank
Blind Wink Productions	Gore Verbinski
Captivate Entertainment	Jeffrey Weiner, Ben Smith
Dark Horse Entertainment	Mike Richardson
Depth of Field	Chris Weitz, Paul Weitz
Everyman Pictures	Jay Roach
Film 44	Sarah Aubrey, Peter Berg
Hasbro Productions	Brian Goldner, Bennett Schneir
Illumination Entertainment	Chris Meledandri
Imagine Entertainment	Ron Howard, Brian Grazer
Larger Than Life	Gary Ross, Allison Thomas
Mandalay Pictures	Peter Guber
Marc Platt Productions	Marc Platt
Morgan Creek Productions	Jim Robinson, Rick Nicita
Necropia	Guillermo del Toro
Playtone	Gary Goetzman, Tom Hanks, Rita Wilson
Strike Entertainment	Marc Abraham, Tom Bliss, Eric Newman
Stuber Productions	Scott Stuber
Tribeca Films	Robert De Niro, Jane Rosenthal
Wild West Picture Show Productions	Vince Vaughn
Working Title Films	Tim Bevan, Eric Fellner

Table 7.1 Universal's 2009 production deals. Source: *Variety* 2009: 48

> It is very possible to make a film that costs 40, 50, 60, 80 or $100 million dollars that looks exactly the same … It's about properly producing, and a lot of so-called producers in the Hollywood system don't really give a shit about budget. All they care about is what their fee is and then … if somebody asks for more, they shell out for more, basically. They don't take any pride in how the money gets spent and making sure that it's done at a cost. Because we came from independent cinema, where you're very conscious about every penny that you spend, that, again, was in both Eric's and my … DNA.[29]

Despite their efforts to realign Universal's production agenda, Linde and Shmuger were dismissed in October 2009 following a run of poorly performing films. The pair were replaced by incoming Chairman Adam Fogelson, Universal's former President of Marketing, and Co-Chairman Donna Langley, the studio's former President of Production (Graser 2009b: 1). In turn, Langley appointed Debbie Liebling as President of Production before replacing her two years later with Co-Presidents Peter Cramer and Jeffrey Kirschenbaum (*Daily Variety* 2011: 1). With the benefit of hindsight, however, Shmuger and Linde made a substantial contribution to Universal's future prosperity with the 2008 acquisition of Illumination Entertainment, which would underpin Universal's success in the tent-pole family film market throughout the following decade and beyond (Fleming 2008: 1).

The effect of Hollywood's retrenchment was initially felt at Working Title Television (WTTV), which had ostensibly scored its greatest success to date with *The Tudors* (2007–10), a drama series which ran for four seasons on the US premium cable network, Showtime. In practice, however, the programme was largely developed by Michael Hirst, whose prior association with Working Title later became a significant factor in the production. 'It touched upon some of the work that he'd done on *Elizabeth* and there was an agreement to attach Working Title because it was a classic British company and British history,' Simon Wright, former President of WTTV, explains. 'They got a little fee, put the name on it but had nothing to do with it as, indeed, I didn't.'[30] In reality, the final in-house productions at WTTV were the TV movies *The Robber Bride* (CBC, 2007) and *Diana: The Final Journey* (Lifetime, 2007). Recalling the subsequent demise of the company, Wright goes on to note:

> The value of sales of films across the board was diminishing significantly, DVD was looking a bit rockier, people had less money around the world and of course, films are the first to suffer. It all really went from there. It was nothing to do with the performance of Working Title Television at all. It didn't help that coinciding with that Working Title had a few, what I would describe as leaner years … It was a combination of the two, but it was largely the global economy … We closed down over two or three years. First they … cut us back. We lost some film people and half the television people. Then it was about another eighteen months and the writing was on the wall, so they had to close us.[31]

During this period, Working Title also produced its first film, *A Serious Man* (2009), with Focus Features International (FFI) rather than Universal. In contrast to the US-based infrastructure of Focus Features, which was primarily concerned with development, green-lighting and direct distribution in the domestic market, FFI allowed Universal's sister studio to mitigate the risk of investment by pre-selling distribution rights in international territories. As former FFI President, Alison Thompson, explains, the financing and green-lighting process at Focus was distinct from that in place at Universal:

> Focus was very privileged to straddle both the independent and studio world because it allowed us to access both and use both to our advantage … We were often … producing films that were considered relatively risky, and so we were very involved in looking up and analysing and assessing the level of risk that we would want on each and every one of our titles, and along with that, we were also looking about the potential upside that could be

played going through Universal. And by the potential upside I mean that, of course, studios have their great ancillary TV deals and so on, which a lot of independent distributors don't have, and so we were looking at whether there were opportunities in some or all territories to maximise potential through distribution through Universal.[32]

Despite the impact of the global recession on the film industry, the FFI model remained effective. 'The 2000s were a very, very affluent time and a good time for independent cinema and the independent sector was very strong, and we had a really great model,' Thompson recalls. 'We would expect to pre-sell probably about two thirds of the value of our films in international and thereby offset our risk, and then retain the US and maybe one or two other territories to play the upside.'[33] Just as the 'ten-column' continued to assess the worldwide market potential for films in development based on the premise of direct distribution, FFI performed the same risk assessment exercise by combining distribution and sales. As Thompson goes on to point out:

> There was a very good relationship between Focus and Universal, and together we identified territories where, for various reasons – possibly it had something to do with the local market, sometimes it literally had to do with who the people were running that particular division in the particular country – but if we felt there was real opportunity to actually do much better than an independent distributor might do, then we would decide before we even went out to market with a movie and, as we were running green-light plans, we would come up with a plan about which territories to hold back and distribute through Universal. Now, by the same token there were incidents where we knew that for whatever reason the independent sales value of a title in a certain territory would not equate to the value of a movie through that territory at Universal, and I'm talking maybe about some of the less sophisticated markets where prestige cinema doesn't traditionally perform as well.[34]

In 2010, Natascha Wharton left Working Title to take a job as a senior production and development executive at the UK Film Council. Wharton was replaced at the top of Working Title's UK development department by another long-serving member of staff, Amelia Granger. In September the following year, Hayward ended her exclusive executive producing deal at Working Title to form her own production company, Monumental Pictures. 'I wanted to be more autonomous and I also wanted to focus down ... it's hard to be creative when you're jumping from one project on to another, on to another,' she explains. 'Doing a script meeting for three hours here, and then immediately moving into a pitch meeting there ... You can do that for a long time, but it just got to a point where I wanted to focus on fewer things with more concentration.'[35] Monumental would not, however, stray far from

Working Title, taking up residence in its offices and securing a two-year first-look deal with the company (*Variety* 2011a).

These changes in the configuration of Working Title's key personnel coincided with two broader structural realignments in 2010 which ushered in the next era of Working Title's development. In February, WTTV was relaunched as a joint venture between NBCUniversal and Bevan and Fellner, organised through the conglomerate's London-based NBCUniversal International Television Studios. Then in July, it was reported that Working Title was developing a new film, *Tinker Tailor Soldier Spy* (2011) with Studiocanal, despite the four years that remained of the company's exclusive production deal with Universal. Indeed, the following year, the contractual relationship between Working Title and Universal was described as a 'first-look' deal in the trade press (*Variety* 2011b). While this change in status was not made official until 2012, it marked the beginning of a major shift in the relationship between the production company and the studio which profoundly altered the way in which Working Title operated in subsequent years.

Notes

1. Tim Bevan, interview with the author, 7-12-2016.
2. Angela Morrison, interview with the author, 26-11-2013.
3. Ibid.
4. Natascha Wharton, interview with the author, 11-3-2014.
5. Tim Bevan, interview with the author, 7-12-2016.
6. Liza Chasin, interview with the author, 22-5-2014.
7. Ibid.
8. Tim Bevan, interview with the author, 7-12-2016.
9. Tim Bevan, interview with the author, 6-8-2013.
10. Angela Morrison, interview with the author, 26-11-2013.
11. Gareth Wilson, interview with the author, 12-8-14.
12. Ibid.
13. Ibid.
14. Liza Chasin, interview with the author, 22-5-2014.
15. Eric Fellner, interview with the author, 14-3-2014.
16. Tim Bevan, interview with the author, 6-8-2013.
17. Tim Bevan, interview with the author, 7-12-2016.
18. Michelle Wright, interview with the author, 13-7-2014.
19. Eric Fellner, interview with the author, 14-3-2014.
20. Ibid.
21. Michelle Wright, interview with the author, 13-7-2014.
22. Ibid.
23. David Kosse, interview with the author, 30-6-2014.
24. Andrew Cripps, interview with the author, 17-9-2015.

25 Ibid.
26 David Kosse, interview with the author, 30-6-2014.
27 Tim Bevan, interview with the author, 6-8-2013.
28 David Livingstone, interview with the author, 6-5-2014.
29 Tim Bevan, interview with the author, 6-8-2013.
30 Simon Wright, interview with the author, 20-5-14.
31 Ibid.
32 Alison Thompson, interview with the author, 31-3-2016.
33 Ibid.
34 Ibid.
35 Debra Hayward, interview with the author, 20-9-2013.

CHAPTER 8

The Universal Years Part III: New Relationships (2012–)

By the turn of 2012, Working Title had maintained an exclusive contractual relationship with Universal for almost thirteen years, and had a further two years to run on its current deal. The production of the Studiocanal-financed *Tinker Tailor Soldier Spy* (2011) the previous year, however, suggested that change was afoot. In April, it was officially announced that Working Title's Co-Chairmen, Tim Bevan and Eric Fellner, had reached a three-year deal with Universal on a 'first-look' basis (Kilday 2012). The new arrangement underlined Universal's continuing gravitation towards big-budget 'tent-pole' films, an area of production to which Working Title had yet to contribute. Significantly, however, the deal also permitted the production company to work with other studios once Universal declined to green-light a project in development. In doing so, the terms of the deal brought Working Title in line with most of the production companies on the studio's books. Contemplating the transition, Bevan explains:

> It's an ever-evolving relationship, the studio relationship, and I think that if you look at the way the studio business is going, it's polarising towards bigger movies, basically, these gigantic blockbusters ... A low-budget studio film is probably $75 million but an average film is well over $100 million now and their core movies are $200 million plus ... The smaller films that we will have made in the past are just less attractive to them, basically. They may be attractive to their foreign people, they may not be ... The studio recognised that, and we recognised that, and so it didn't make sense because in a Working Title slate, nobody wants to change that. There were always going to be those sorts of movies in an entirely exclusive relationship. For the bigger-budget films, we'll always make them with the studio, and they'll get a first look at everything.[1]

In practice, Universal continued to finance and distribute most of Working Title's films, notably commercially successful sequels like *Bridget Jones's Baby* (2016) and *Johnny English Strikes Again* (2018), while 'specialty' releases such as *The Theory of Everything* (2014) and *Darkest Hour* (2017) continued to be distributed through the studio's sister company, Focus Features. Simultaneously, however, Studiocanal financed and distributed the likes of *I Give It a Year*

(2013), *Legend* (2015) and *King of Thieves* (2018), while other Hollywood studios such as Sony took on projects like *Grimsby* (2016) and *Baby Driver* (2017). During this period, Working Title's output also began to encroach on the periphery of Universal's core tent-pole slate for the first time with the release of *Les Misérables* (2012) and *Cats* (2019) which, despite their very different critical and commercial receptions, drew heavily on their 'pre-sold' status as long-running and highly successful musical theatre productions. Finally, the 2010s saw the re-launch of Working Title Television (WTTV), which began to pursue a more ambitious range of projects while working from bases in both the UK and the US for the first time.

THE RE-EMERGENCE OF STUDIOCANAL, RETRENCHMENT AT UNIVERSAL AND THE RELAUNCH OF FOCUS FEATURES

The re-emergence of Studiocanal as a force in film production took shape following the reorganisation of its parent company, Vivendi, which had also owned Universal between 2000 and 2004. The French media conglomerate began to rebuild its film and television assets closer to home, while also adopting an increasingly 'international' production strategy. In 2006, for example, 90 per cent of Studiocanal's output was French language, however, by 2012, 70 per cent was produced in English (Hopewell 2012: 79). Equally important was the company's investment in its distribution and marketing infrastructure. As Christopher Meir notes, Studiocanal acquired three independent distribution companies in the same period which respectively provided direct theatrical distribution in the UK, Germany and Australia/New Zealand in addition to the studio's existing distribution infrastructure in France (Meir 2019: 93–4). Accordingly, the company was described as 'Europe's nearest equivalent to a major Hollywood studio', in the trade press (Hopewell 2012: 79). From Working Title's perspective, however, a project would only be developed with Studiocanal after Universal passed on it. Explaining the process from that point onwards, Bevan notes:

> It's in what's called turnaround, so they may take an option on it, they'll pick up the costs going forwards and then they'll have to repay the development that's already been spent on it, with a premium, on the first day of principal photography. That's standard, it's called turnaround and it exists anywhere. So if I've spent ten, and then … [Universal tell me that they] don't want to make it, and you find 'y' to make it, I'll probably make 'y' give me one in order to have an option on it while you then go and set it up with 'y'. And then, when 'y' says 'OK, we're going to shoot the movie', on the first day of [principal] photography, 'y' will probably have to pay me twelve, so I'll take a premium … for my risk.[2]

On the one hand, then, a Working Title film which entered turnaround had necessarily failed to pass the creative and commercial rigours of Universal's 'ten-column'. On the other, there was now an opportunity to finance these projects beyond the confines of the studio. The prevailing production agenda at Studiocanal suggested a likely home for projects which typically occupied a creative and commercial terrain outside that of the major Hollywood studios. Indeed, Studiocanal announced an annual production budget of $260 million for the production of ten films with two or three titles in the $40 million to $50 million range beginning in 2013 (Hopewell & Keslassy 2012: 8). As Working Title's COO, Angela Morrison, explains:

> It's enabled us to make some of the films that might not otherwise have been made because Universal didn't want to make them. Before, if Universal really didn't want to make something then that was the end of it. Now … because of the long-term relationship with Studiocanal from the past, we've been able to make some films with them that otherwise wouldn't have been made … *Tinker Tailor*, *I Give It a Year*, then we made *Two Faces of January* with them, which was a project they brought to us. So, it's just freed up the filmmaking process for us on films that the studio don't want to make, which is good because we've been able to keep our production levels at a high level.[3]

In contrast to the global prism through which Universal views the filmmaking process, however, Studiocanal's perspective is influenced by its limited direct distribution and marketing infrastructure, which privileges a small number of key markets. 'They have a mixed model, they distribute in some of their own territories, they distribute in France, Germany, Australia and the UK, so their people put numbers against them, then they have a bunch of sales figures,' Bevan explains. 'They're looking at numbers in just the same way as Universal are, they're just not as sophisticated in many ways … because they're looking for third parties.'[4] As Bevan goes on to note, the strategy of pre-selling films to most of the global marketplace comes with some structural disadvantages:

> One of the reasons that Studiocanal like us is that if they put our name on it, it's worth more on a pre-sale basis, basically, because of our track record and all the rest of it … It's a model that doesn't really work any longer, the pre-sale model, the world's moved beyond that … The problem with the pre-sale model is that in success it covers your downside but it doesn't give you any upside. So, you can get your film made – which is great – and get some fees out of it, but if it's a smash hit, you're unlikely to see any part of it. Whereas a studio model, you're aiming to get the film made and then you want infinite upside by controlling and owning the distribution.[5]

Just as Working Title began to cement its partnership with Studiocanal outside its relationship with Universal, the two studios became embroiled in an acrimonious legal battle. In early 2013, Studiocanal filed a law suit against Universal pertaining to its historical co-financing of Working Title which claimed, amongst other things, breach of fiduciary duty, constructive fraud and breach of contract. This catalogue of alleged wrongdoing included the accusation that Universal had hidden returns from its off balance sheet financing arrangements, reported only 'negligible' revenue from various streams of ancillary income and 'double charged' the partnership for producing and other fees (Johnson 2013: 28). After Universal denied the charges, claiming that they had, in fact, overpaid Studiocanal, the case was finally settled the following year with both sides agreeing to an undisclosed settlement (Gardner 2014).

Over the same period, Universal's co-financing relationship with Relativity Media was substantially revised. While Relativity officially ended its deal with Universal in 2011, the company's logo continued to be applied to Universal films that were green-lit the following year. In practice, however, these titles were financed by Elliott Management, the hedge fund which had previously bankrolled Relativity and retained a stake in the company (Abrams 2012: 1). The last Working Title films funded through this relationship were *Contraband* (2012), *Les Misérables* (2012) and *The World's End* (2013). Two years later, Relativity filed for bankruptcy, citing liabilities of $1.2 billion and assets of just $560 million (Rainey 2015). The gap left in Universal's working capital placed a greater onus on Working Title to co-finance films with third parties, a situation that proved especially true of the company's more expensive film projects. 'You can always tell the films that have been sort of cobbled together, if you like, because there'll be a lot of companies,' Bevan explains. 'It'll be a conglomerate of companies that actually put the money up for the film. One person's not going to write a cheque for $50 million, it'll be a group of them, basically, and they'll each get a production credit.'[6] *Rush* (2013) and *Everest* (2015), for example, each had screen credits split in five directions, including production companies like Imagine Entertainment, Revolution Films and RVK Studios and producer/financiers such as Cross Creek Pictures, Exclusive Media Group and Walden Media. While each deal was unique in its detail, they typically involved dividing domestic and international distribution rights between key financiers. As Bevan goes on to confirm:

> It's best to be within a studio, and it's within a studio where you know all of the ups and downs, where you know all of the creative anomalies, you know the distribution people, so you can drive them a little bit harder. In success, they pay; in failure, you get your wrist slapped. That is definitely the gold standard, but you don't get the gold standard every time. That's just the

way of it. Other films tend to take more time because you're dealing with multiple groups of people, certainly in terms of business affairs and all the rest of it, but also they take more time because they're people that you haven't necessarily worked with before.[7]

At the conclusion of Comcast's acquisition of NBCUniversal in 2013, another shake-up in management occurred when Universal Chairman Adam Fogelson was dismissed in favour of Donna Langley, who had previously acted as Co-Chair. Simultaneously, Jeff Shell was made Chairman of the larger business unit, Universal Filmed Entertainment Group, while Ron Meyer, Universal President and COO, was promoted Vice Chairman of the studio's parent company, NBCUniversal (Masters 2013). By the end of the year, Focus Features' long-serving CEO, James Schamus, was dismissed and its London-based international sales company, Focus Features International (FFI), was closed (McClintock & Roxborough 2014). Significantly, FFI had recently completed pre-sales on *Closed Circuit* (2013), a situation which suggested that the sales company might become a more regular financier of Working Title's films alongside Studiocanal. Explaining the decision to close the company, FFI's former President, Alison Thompson, points to a range of factors:

> By 2013, I think the entire industry was aware that the business model, the old business model, was not going to work for much longer, and Focus had a very particular model that worked successfully for a very long time. It was largely predicated on offsetting risk through international sales, but for many, many reasons, as the market began to falter and as the international sales value of movies began to diminish then, of course, it put pressure on us and it put pressure on the green-lighting process. I think that the entire industry has gone through a very painful process over a number of years and I think in some respects ... Focus was a victim of that ... Comcast had recently bought the company, and wanted results, and I think they were looking at Focus wondering what it should become.[8]

One answer to that question was provided by Focus's incoming CEO, Peter Schlessel. Focus was promptly moved from New York to Los Angeles and merged with Schlessel's company, Film District. Significantly, the latter largely produced genre films of broad commercial appeal such as *Insidious* (2010), *Looper* (2012) and *Olympus Has Fallen* (2013) and thus the reorganisation suggested that Focus might move away from the 'smart-house' territory which it had previously occupied. As Universal once again reoriented its production agenda, the third instalments of Working Title's most commercially successful film series, *Bridget Jones's Baby* and *Johnny English Strikes Again* remained stuck in long-term development. Despite the pressure to continue capitalising on its established hits, the company managed to maintain a relatively diverse slate. As David Kosse, Universal's former President of International explains:

> As with every producer, the first thing they [Working Title] are trying to do is get somebody to say 'Yes' to their movie. And if the people with the purse strings are saying, 'I want Bridget Jones 3' they're going to try to come up with Bridget Jones 3, or Johnny English 3 or Mr. Bean 2, because [for] the movie studios, those are the safer bets. If you take sequels out of the mix, I don't think movie studios make a lot of money, so any movie studio will want what they consider to be a safe bet. So, Working Title are always looking to do those, but at the same time they're looking to do things like *Les Mis* and they're looking to do the smaller movies, like we've got *The Theory of Everything* coming up or *Trash*. So they're looking for movies under $20 million, under $25 million.[9]

In the same period, Working Title's relationship with Universal Pictures International (UPI) also began to change. David Livingstone, Working Title's President of Worldwide Marketing, left the company following its transition to a first-look deal as part of a downsizing strategy. 'In a perfect world, we'd have an in-house marketing person, but it doesn't work like that anymore,' Bevan explains. 'We've got to know all of the marketing people at Universal really well and at Studiocanal, when we work with them, so we don't need that bespoke [arrangement].'[10] In 2014, however, Universal announced its intention to move the headquarters of UPI from London to Los Angeles, prompting the departure of Kosse and the appointment of his successor, Duncan Clark (Bart & Eller 2014). Nonetheless, the decision was soon reversed, much to Bevan's approval:

> The beauty of the studio, and one of the reasons we're with Universal is they run their foreign out of London. None of the other studios do. So, we know the head office guys, like Duncan Clark, Stephen Hewitt, Kate Wyhowska. These are people who are dealing with all of the territories and presenting them with the campaigns and all the rest of it. We will go in depth with [them]. Before each film is released, we'll go through, get a territory presentation where they say, 'This is what we're going to do here, this is what we're going to do here, this is what we're thinking of here' ... They have conferences two or three times a year around the world and if we've got a bunch of films coming up, one of us will go and present to them ... it's a big two-way thing.[11]

In June 2015 Working Title and Universal reaffirmed their commitment to one another with a new five-year deal which extended the company's first-look arrangement until 2020 (Ritman 2015). In the same year, Universal hit a record-breaking run of success led by the release of the tent-pole franchise films *Furious 7*, *Jurassic World* and *Minions*, all of which exceeded $1 billion at the worldwide box office and helped to make it the most commercially successful year in the studio's history (Lang 2015). Simultaneously, however, Universal's new Chair, Donna Langley, began to shift the culture of the studio in a new direction which, in some respects, resembled the Universal regime under Stacey Snider. In early 2016, she appointed Peter Kujawski as Chairman of Focus Features, an executive who had worked at the original incarnation of the company under James Schamus. Simultaneously, Robert Walak was appointed President, dividing his time, and thus the management of the company, between Los Angeles and London (McClintock & Siegel 2016). 'The two best eras [have been] the Stacey Snider era and the Donna Langley era … really, it's because Stacey and Donna both like the sorts of films we make,' Bevan confirms. 'Both Stacey and Donna, as executives, have come up the creative route, the people in between came from marketing.'[12] This commonality of perspective between Universal's senior management and Working Title's Co-Chairmen presented clear advantages for the production company going forward, as Bevan explains:

> It's much more back to the place where the perfect Working Title film in a $15–$25 million range will be distributed by Focus domestically, where it's not over-ambitious in terms of what it needs to achieve, but it will be platformed and it'll be beautifully distributed and the audience will find it, and then it will be whacked out [internationally] … Don't forget, for all of those films, the UK marketplace is more important to us than the US marketplace and it's likely to do as well here, if not better, than it does US domestically … It needs to … [be] properly distributed in America so it gets recognition but also so that the TV deals get triggered in all of the foreign marketplaces because they're all linked back into the domestic release … Studio output deals in, say, France, it's television output deal, will depend on an 'x' print release in the US because that says that the studio are treating it seriously. They will have spent 'y' in P&A and it will have a worldwide profile.[13]

Simultaneously, Universal found a major financier to fill the gap left by the collapse of Relativity. In February 2016 Beijing-headquartered Perfect World Pictures negotiated a $500 million deal with Universal under which the two companies would co-finance the production of fifty Universal films over a five-year period (Brzeski 2016a). In addition to receiving a reported 25 per cent revenue share of specified films, Perfect World's investment was predicated upon several factors, including profiting from the booming Chinese box office for Hollywood films and seizing the opportunity to begin handling the distribution of some Universal titles in the Chinese market (Brzeski 2016b). As Table 8.1 shows, in the same year, the number of Universal's production deals increased modestly from its 2009 levels, moving from twenty-two

Production company/individual	Key personnel
Aggregate Films	Jason Bateman
Apatow Productions	Judd Apatow
Bluegrass Films	Scott Stuber, Dylan Clark
Blumhouse Productions	Jason Blum
Brownstone Productions	Elizabeth Banks, Max Handelman
Captivate Entertainment	Jeffrey Weiner, Ben Smith
Michael De Luca Productions	Michael De Luca
Fake Empire	Josh Schwartz, Stephanie Savage
Gold Circle Entertainment	Paul Brooks
Illumination Entertainment	Chris Meledandri
ImageMovers	Robert Zemeckis, Jack Rapke, Steve Starkey
Imagine Entertainment	Ron Howard, Brian Grazer
Legendary	Thomas Tull
Little Stranger, Inc.	Tina Fey
Chris Morgan Productions	Chris Morgan
One Race Films	Vin Diesel, Samantha Vincent
Will Packer Productions	Will Packer
Penguin Random House	Peter Gethers
Marc Platt Productions	Marc Platt
Scholastic	–
Secret Hideout	Alex Kurtzman
Silvertongue Films	Deborah Forte
Skybound Entertainment	Robert Kirkman, David Alpert
Working Title Films	Tim Bevan, Eric Fellner

Table 8.1 Universal's 2016 production deals. Source: McNary 2016.

to twenty-four. The return of major slate financing at Universal reduced the onus on Working Title to seek co-financing arrangements outside the studio. Instead, the Perfect World logo appeared with increasing regularity on Working Title's films, beginning with *Bridget Jones's Baby* and continuing with the likes of *Victoria & Abdul* (2017), *Darkest Hour* and *Yesterday* (2019).

In 2016, Universal stepped up its tent-pole strategy once again with the acquisition of Dreamworks Animation for $3.8 billion. Significantly, the deal included ownership of a host of highly successful intellectual property such as the multi-billion-dollar film franchises *Shrek* (2001–), *Kung Fu Panda* (2008–), *How to Train Your Dragon* (2010–) and *Madagascar* (2005–), underlining the studio's emphasis on branded family entertainment (Szalai 2016a). The task of convincing Universal to green-light a Working Title project within this context remained demanding. 'The Working Title sort of movie is never a no-brainer, so it's always quite difficult. There is an element of salesmanship and comforting people, if you like, and good sense which goes into it,' Bevan reveals. 'Like every sales person, you're ultimately as good as the last thing that you sold or maybe the one before that if you're lucky.'[14] As he goes on to argue:

> Our job, Eric's and mine, is to keep the pressure on, keep the pressure on, keep the pressure on, keep the pressure on. And one of the reasons that we still are at it is we've still got that bug in us and if we lose that, then we won't be any good at it. You've just got to keep ... the pressure on and forcing those moving parts, because everybody, everyone, conspires to get in your way all the time. It's deciding when you're going to run roughshod over it, when you're going to cajole people into it, when you're going to seduce people into it and when you're going to pay people into it. It's [about] how you get them to get on board and be getting going in the same direction.[15]

While Working Title's films continued to be channelled through Universal for green-lighting, the launch of the new-look Focus Features ensured that the company's specialty titles, including *Victoria & Abdul* and *Darkest Hour* had a place within the studio's overall production strategy. As Bevan explains:

> There's going to be a variable as to where we land on the budget that they feel comfortable green-lighting it at, and that we think that we can actually make the film for. So, there's always downward pressure from the studio, there's upwards pressure from us. We know where the sweet spot on a Focus film is, so we try to cut some corners by saying here 'Don't give me a budget that comes to more than *this*', basically, to our production people, and all the rest of it. 'It's pointless, *this* is the level', [so] we often work backwards into a number ... Our business affairs work very closely with the studio's business affairs on that and it's all about trying to find the right number ... On the Focus level type movie it's quite plain sailing, on the bigger movies it's far less so, and a red flag goes up the flag post quite quickly if you're heading in the wrong direction.[16]

While Working Title continued to produce films which received wide releases through Universal, such as *Bridget Jones's Baby* and *Johnny English Strikes Again*, the company also increasingly looked towards the other Hollywood studios to finance its films. In building these new relationships, Working Title's near thirty-year residency in Los Angeles proved to be an invaluable asset. As Morrison reflects:

> I think we're unique, I don't think there are many other producers who have exactly the same relationship that we have with Hollywood. I think there are a few successful British producers who have, on a few films, done very well ... but sometimes we say we're a little bit of Hollywood in London, because it feels seamless for us, we're part of it ... We have an office in LA, so it's run by Liza Chasin, she manages our relationships out there, but it means it's easy for me to pick up the phone to people there and they'll speak to me, other producers might find that a bit harder ... My guess is, and you'd have

to speak to people outside if you wanted the real truth, I think they probably find it harder to manage. Harder to manage the talent agents and to get into the talent agents, and harder to get attention, whereas I think that's not something that we suffer from.[17]

Films like *Grimsby* and *Baby Driver*, which were respectively financed and distributed by the Sony Pictures subsidiaries Columbia Pictures and TriStar Pictures, reflected Working Title's newfound mobility within the Hollywood industry. At the end of 2017, however, Chasin left Working Title and started her own production company, 3dot Productions, the following year (Hazelton 2018). Nonetheless, Working Title continued to operate simultaneously from offices in London and Los Angeles, actively combining the film industries and cultures of Britain and Hollywood. This situation was underlined in December 2020 when the production company renewed its first-look deal with Universal for a further five years (Kay 2020). Indeed, the essential function of Working Title remained its ability to successfully reconcile the demands of creativity and commerce presented by each film project. Reflecting on the role of the producer, Fellner argues:

> It has a creative [role] and a business role. In every decision I make with Stephen Daldry or Richard Curtis or the Coen brothers, or whomever it may be – Paul Greengrass, Edgar Wright, Joe Wright – you're having to consider both sides of the equation. The trick is how to work with creative talent and at the same time run an efficient business. That's the line we straddle. It would be far easier if you were making widgets because they don't answer back, they don't have opinions ... You just make 50,000 of them or 100,000 or a million of them or whatever and ship them out, but that's not what we do.[18]

Alongside the changes induced by Working Title's transition from an exclusive to a first-look deal with Universal, the company also substantially expanded its interest in television production in the 2010s. The following section explores this development

THE REINVENTION OF WORKING TITLE TELEVISION

The relaunch of Working Title Television in 2010 marked a substantial shift in Working Title's interest in television production. The new venture was underpinned by NBCUniversal's aggressive expansion into the international television market. By 2011, NBCUniversal Television Group had formed three distinct content production divisions, Universal Television, Universal Cable Productions (later Universal Content Productions) and NBCUniversal International Studios. The first two are based in the US and produce television primarily for the NBC terrestrial network and NBC's cable and satellite channels. In contrast, NBCUniversal International Studios is based in London and has the remit to invest in the growth of the international market for original programming, particularly the development and production of content that can be exported to the US and other international markets. Under the leadership of successive Presidents of International Television Production, Angela Bromstad and Michael Edelstein, the division's expansion included the acquisition of UK-based companies such as Carnival Film and Television in 2008 and Monkey Kingdom in 2010 (Littleton 2012: 2).

Significantly, the new formulation of WTTV was established as a joint venture between NBCUniversal International and Bevan and Fellner. As part of the deal, NBCUniversal International effectively maintained a first-look deal with WTTV under which the production company was provided with an overhead and development budget in exchange for which the studio retained the right to acquire all available distribution to its output. For the first time, WTTV also began to mirror the transatlantic orientation of its parent company, with WTTV President, Shelley McCrory, based in the US, and Head of Television, Juliette Howell, based in the UK (Andreeva 2010). Staff turnover at both WTTV offices, however, saw McCrory replaced by Daniel Pipski, before the arrival of Andrew Stearn in 2015, while Howell was eventually replaced by Andrew Woodhead in 2016 (Szalai 2016b).

The new WTTV also differed from the original company in its relationship with the UK television industry. Rather than prioritising commissions from US broadcasters, the London-based arm began to work with major UK broadcasters as a first port of call. Simultaneously, developing television at WTTV was slowly uncoupled from the development slate of its parent company. 'The rationale behind the new company was having the muscle of NBC alongside them, [and saying] "Let's really start to be a company in our own right" and there was that fantastic branding to use and launch yourself with,' Howell notes. 'Television needed to be television, rather than just … [being] something that we couldn't get made with film.'[19] Nonetheless, the first projects to emerge from the new WTTV, *The Borrowers* (BBC, 2011) and *Birdsong* (BBC, 2012) originated with Working Title Films. As Howell explains:

> In your first year you're looking to just get into production quickly and the way in which you do that is to have short-form pieces because they're much easier to get commissioned and you can turn them around much more quickly. It takes a year to write a ten-parter and a year to film it, and so even if you get the commission straight away you're in year three of your business before anyone's seeing it and certainly before there's any revenue from that. I think the agenda up front was, production, and then, absolutely, you're looking for long-running pieces.[20]

WTTV's first efforts in this regard were two five-part dramas, *True Love* (BBC, 2012) and *The Secrets* (BBC, 2014). These shows, however, proved to be unusual within the overall output of the company. '[They] were very low budget, overtly domestic pieces that didn't really have an eye on the international, but they were about supporting very specific talent,' Howell explains. 'Because they were very low cost, and pretty much fully funded by the BBC, it was less of a concern, but I think core business always aimed at the US as well.'[21] Indeed, the typical approach of the WTTV's UK operations was to target a commission from a major UK broadcaster as the starting point of a larger package of financing which typically also included a US broadcaster. As Howell goes on to point out, the company's deal with NBCUniversal international remained an integral part of closing the financing package of most productions:

> What the BBC will do is say, 'We will give you half or two thirds of the budget that you require as a licence and you need to go and raise the rest of that money', and so typically we would either go back to NBC and say, 'Do you want to deficit finance the remainder?' and then it would be as simple as that. Or it may be, [as] in the case of *London Spy*, we went to BBC America who gave us additional licence money and then that closed the gap, so there was a very small advance that we needed from NBC … As part of the agreement NBC have the right to distribute and then it's a conversation with them as to whether it's, 'Should we enter into a co-production with HBO because that gives us "x" amount of money?' or 'Do you want to give us the money?'.[22]

Beyond the deficit financing that NBCUniversal International provided for WTTV's productions, the UK office operated largely independently of its parent and sister companies. 'We didn't have a slate that we cleared with NBC or anything like that, we operated as our own entity,' Howell explains. 'Those big shows that were co-productions with HBO or with NBC network or … ABC, those were relationships that we managed ourselves, so we didn't club together with our US arm for that.'[23] There was, however, one notable exception, as she goes on to explain:

> The project that probably sat slightly outside of that was *You, Me and the Apocalypse* which was a big show that we just did for Sky where NBC network were also involved and so that meant that NBC International had a rather different role from any that they'd had on previous shows, also partly driven by the fact that the show itself was set half in America, had a number of big American stars and so was very different from anything we had done before that had been much more domestic in its set-up.[24]

In 2013 NBCUniversal International established an office in Los Angeles to support its US-based infrastructure, from which JoAnn Alfano acted as Executive Vice President of Scripted Entertainment and, in turn, liaised with

NBC's Vice President of Scripted Programming, Scott Herbst (Szalai 2013). Indeed, WTTV's initial US commissions came through NBC, including *Love Bites* (NBC, 2011) which aired for eight episodes as a summer replacement series and *About a Boy* (NBC, 2014–15) which ran for thirty-three episodes over two seasons. In contrast to the commissioning process in the UK, US network television runs to a definitive schedule according to which new series are pitched between July and October. Explaining the typical process in place when working with US networks, former WTTV President Andrew Stearn reveals:

> I come up with an idea with a writer and we come up with a pitch ... I go to JoAnn and Scott and I say 'This is the pitch', they say 'We like it, let's move forward with it', going with that or this. The next thing we do is put a deal in place. You make the deals in America, in this case usually I would make it an 'if come' deal, which means you put all the numbers in place, but the writer only gets paid if it sells. So, then we decide, once we have a meeting, what territories we should pitch to, by that I mean which networks. So, we have a discussion about where we should take it ... Usually broadcast is very straightforward ... I'd go to Fox, CBS, NBC and ABC and we see who wants it. Then you make a deal with them to buy it from you and then the next step is a story document, and you go from a story document to an outline, from an outline to a script. Then they make a decision whether or not they're going to make the pilot come January, February of ... [the following year]. Once you make the pilot, then it goes through the process and they decide whether or not they're picking up the series.[25]

Developing shows for US network television, however, means working within well-established creative parameters. 'Usually they like a closed ended story every week, even if it's a soap opera they still want something that closes up, so that viewers have ... a feeling of satisfaction within the hour,' Stearn explains. 'It's definitely more mainstream and that's across the board ... It's that conundrum of they still want it to stand out, yet they're constantly trying to make it flatter.'[26] Successfully launching and subsequently returning a network series, however, remains a difficult task which is highly dependent upon audience ratings. As Stearn goes on to note:

> Sometimes the show just doesn't do well. You debut with your thirteen [episodes], the ratings are bad, you know the handwriting is on the wall and you're not going to get picked up. That's the difference, I think, nowadays between broadcast and S-VOD, because S-VOD, they keep the numbers a secret so you really don't know where you stand, where in broadcast or basic cable you see the numbers every week, so you have an idea whether you're an automatic pickup, whether you're on the fence, or you're going to get cancelled. The numbers can tell their story unless, for some reason, there's always the wildcard of critical acclaim.[27]

In practice, WTTV had more success with S-VOD (Subscription Video on Demand) platforms in the years that followed, beginning with *Gypsy* (Netflix, 2017). Working with Netflix, however, involved markedly different forms of commissioning and deal-making. 'They pick it up for series, they base it on a script and a pitch and they decide to go straight to ten [episodes] in a room, where in broadcast you're always making a pilot,' Stearn explains. 'They buy out for the world, so you don't have the opportunity to sell it internationally and really in syndication, so there isn't that back end that you would normally get on a broadcast show.'[28] In contrast, WTTV's UK operations continued to receive the majority of its commissions from UK broadcasters, including *Yonderland* (Sky, 2013–16), *London Spy* (BBC, 2015) and *The Luminaries* (BBC, 2020). As Howell explains, while the UK industry has also experienced the impact of S-VOD commissioning, the major public service broadcasters still have a powerful influence on the creative and commercial agenda of the national TV landscape:

> There are certainly so many more buyers and I think for UK producers there is a way of pitching direct to some of those US buyers that certainly didn't happen in the past, and that's a good thing. You want to feel there are as many opportunities to try and sell your product as possible. But I think, in terms of UK buyers, I still think there is an inherent conservatism, I don't think they're massive risk takers ... I think there is an obsession with ratings which is slightly outmoded. I think it depends on who your commissioners are ... If you look at the BBC now, there's a nervousness around charter renewal which means: 'Well, let's just repeat patterns'. That's not conducive to risk-taking when budgets are at stake and I think Channel 4 is in a not dissimilar position. I think Sky certainly spend more money and, perhaps, do take a few more risks but they will also think about their audience, who I'm not sure are that brave ... We haven't made shows for ITV recently, but I have found them quite hard to sell to.[29]

In practice WTTV continued to work in the S-VOD arena with the production of *Hanna* (Amazon, 2019–), based on the Joe Wright-directed feature film of the same name. Despite the difference between the US and UK television industries, the essential brand identity of WTTV remained consistent across both offices and continued to be strongly associated with its parent company. As Howell confirms:

> It's not dissimilar from the output of Working Title Films in as much as they had those broader comedies, those *Atonement, Tinker Tailor* high-end pieces, and those slightly different more commercial, international [films] ... They were always quite a good model, in a way, as to how you can cover all those bases, yet still retain a really strong brand ... I think as long as the production values are high enough ... [if] they feel like they are quality shows that are the

best of the genre that they inhabit, then they feel like they can be a Working Title show. What we always tried not to do was ape what other people did or inhabit that middle ground.[30]

The sense of brand identity associated with WTTV was further enhanced with the development and production of projects that exploited Working Title's back catalogue. 'The whole idea would be to take that same brand of quality, of character-driven features, and take that into the TV space,' Stearn explains. 'Hopefully sometimes it'll be exploiting the library and taking some of those titles and maybe making them into television shows. It could be just working with some of the similar talent that we've worked with in features.'[31] This scenario played out with *Tales of the City* (Netflix, 2019) which built on WTTV's *Tales of the City* (Channel 4, 1993) and *More Tales of the City* (Channel 4, 1998). Similarly, *Four Weddings and a Funeral* (Hulu, 2019) is loosely based on the original feature film, but was not directly produced by WTTV despite the involvement of Bevan and Fellner in the early stages of its development (Tingley, 2019).

Notes

1. Tim Bevan, interview with the author, 6-8-2013.
2. Tim Bevan, interview with the author, 7-12-2016.
3. Angela Morrison, interview with the author, 26-11-2013.
4. Tim Bevan, interview with the author, 7-12-2016.
5. Ibid.
6. Ibid.
7. Ibid.
8. Alison Thompson, interview with the author, 31-3-2016.
9. David Kosse, interview with the author, 30-6-2014.
10. Tim Bevan, interview with the author, 7-12-2016.
11. Ibid.
12. Ibid.
13. Ibid.
14. Ibid.
15. Ibid.
16. Ibid.
17. Angela Morrison, interview with the author, 26-11-2013.
18. Eric Fellner, interview with the author, 14-3-2014.
19. Juliette Howell, interview with the author, 25-2-2016.
20. Ibid.
21. Ibid.
22. Ibid.
23. Ibid.

24 Ibid.
25 Andrew Stearn, interview with the author, 29-8-2017.
26 Ibid.
27 Ibid.
28 Ibid.
29 Juliette Howell, interview with the author, 25-2-2016.
30 Ibid.
31 Andrew Stearn, interview with the author, 29-08-2017.

'Put up a note? Highly classified shit found?': Chad (Brad Pitt) and Linda (Frances McDormand) plan their next move at Hardbodies gym in *Burn After Reading*.

George Smiley (Gary Oldman) considers the identity of the mole in *Tinker Tailor Soldier Spy*.

Niki Lauda (Daniel Brühl) confronts James Hunt (Chris Hemsworth) in *Rush*.

Stephen Hawking (Eddie Redmayne) ponders the mysteries of the universe in *The Theory of Everything*.

Reggie and Ronnie Kray (Tom Hardy) await Reggie's bride in *Legend*.

Debora (Lily James) and Baby (Ansel Elgort) discuss music in *Baby Driver*.

'What is our aim? I can answer in one word: victory. Victory at all costs.' Winston Churchill (Gary Oldman) addresses parliament in *Darkest Hour*.

'A great guitar requires a great song': Jack (Himesh Patel) plays *Yesterday* to Ellie (Lily James) in the film of the same name.

CHAPTER 9

The Global Market for Working Title's Films

A crucial question for any commercially oriented film production company is the size and location of the audience for its output. Such factors have a profound effect upon the entire filmmaking process along the circuit of development, green-lighting and distribution. An assessment of the market profile for Working Title's films inevitably relies on publicly available information, namely box office data. Such data, however, needs to be used advisedly.[1] Box office figures, of course, indicate only the gross revenue derived from the theatrical release of each film. Accordingly, these figures do not indicate profit because they do not account for the production cost of each film, the costs associated with distribution and marketing or the division of gross revenue between the distributor and exhibitor. Equally, they do not indicate the revenue derived from subsequent release windows, including home video and various forms of pay and free television, which are typically more predictable and lucrative streams of income. These variables are, of course, exactly the factors which PolyGram Filmed Entertainment (PFE) quantified with the 'control sheet' and Universal continues to quantify with the 'ten column' in order to forecast profitability across the initial product life cycle of each film.

Despite these limitations, analysing box office data paints a useful picture of the initial gross revenue generated by each film and therefore broadly indicates the relative success or failure of films in the worldwide marketplace. Before turning to such an analysis, however, it is useful to examine the distribution and marketing of Working Title's first worldwide hit, *Four Weddings and a Funeral* (1994), in some detail. The film is, of course, remarkable for its critical and commercial success, winning both Golden Globe and BAFTA awards and grossing over $250 million worldwide by the end of its theatrical run. Beyond this, however, *Four Weddings* can also be seen as an important precursor to Working Title's creative trajectory in later years. Indeed, the romcom subsequently formed the backbone of the company's commercial success in the 1990s and 2000s, with films like *Notting Hill* (1999), *Bridget Jones's Diary* (2001), *About a Boy* (2002), *Love Actually* (2003) and *Bridget Jones: The Edge of Reason* (2004). Given this extraordinary run, it is tempting to see the success of *Four Weddings and a Funeral* as almost inevitable. In reality, however, the film was a surprise hit, and emerged at a time when Working Title was still in the process of reorienting its activities towards the worldwide market under the newly launched PFE.

THE IMPACT OF *FOUR WEDDINGS AND A FUNERAL*

Prior to its US theatrical release in March 1994, *Four Weddings and a Funeral*, a low-budget British romantic comedy starring Hugh Grant and Andie MacDowell, was not viewed by many as a potential hit. 'The perception of the movie was that it was a small British movie with an unknown British actor and a somewhat known American actress and a whole bunch of quirky British people who were well-known in their native country but not very well-known in America,'[2] explains Russell Schwartz, the former President of Gramercy Pictures. Indeed, the marketing campaign which David Livingstone, PolyGram Film International's former President of International Marketing and Publicity, devised for the film drew inspiration from the limited pool of successful films with comparable creative elements:

> The only film that I remember that had been successful for some time that was a British comedy was *A Fish Called Wanda*, and to a degree, there was an element of looking at the *A Fish Called Wanda* poster and campaign and me going, 'Look, you know, at least there'll be some recognition here, some familiarity from people that makes them go, "This could be a hit, this feels like it's in the zone of something that I've enjoyed before" ... [That was] one of the things that became what was considered the Working Title look – and I wasn't really aware I was particularly creating a look, but it became the look that we did ... constantly. This white poster campaign where a lot of the comedies were against white backgrounds ... At the time, something I was told by people that had worked in the business a lot longer than me [was that this was something] that you shouldn't do. Apparently white posters would get dirty on the underground and nobody did white posters. The philosophy was ... not knowing the rules ... to a degree, but to do things differently to the way other people had done them before.[3]

The US release, however, proved remarkably successful. 'We decided to open the movie and got an opening date and we gave it a classic ... platform release,' Schwartz recalls. 'It opened up quite well, and by the second weekend we realised that the movie was going up on the same number of screens and we realised how strong the word of mouth was.'[4] The initial platform locations of New York and Los Angeles showed strong per-screen averages, and promoted demand from exhibitors, at which point the film was rolled out to other cities. Six weeks after its release, the film reached number one at the US box office, a feat which also established a platform for the subsequent international release (Kuhn 2002: 67). '[*Four Weddings*] was a hit and got to the number 1 position, which was a miracle ... That became a marketing element and a news story ... "The British film *Four Weddings* has become the number 1 film in the US" – and it felt very exciting,' Livingstone explains. 'It was really the moment that we got it right, the moment where we said "this is how we do it". We threw everything into it and we spent loads, which we could afford to do.'[5] As Stewart Till, former President of PolyGram Filmed Entertainment International (PFEI) explains, the impact upon PFE was transformative:

> In the film business, there's three types of films. There are the films that are never going to work and fail and lose lots of money, films that break even, make a little bit of money, got close to working, and there's the blow out hits ... You can't make only blow out hits, the skill is only making [films in] the second two categories. It's [like] football – wins, draws and defeats – the skill is, you draw a load and occasionally you win a big game. *Four Weddings*, it was immeasurable what it did for the company. I don't know how Philips reacted, but certainly the record company went 'Wow', and more importantly, in fact, the whole industry went 'Wow'. Suddenly, it was easier to attract people, get attention ... In the States, obviously, it did $50 million, so for Gramercy to have a hit ... all the territories where we released it, it was a hit. People who bought the film from us made immeasurable money and so wanted to buy more films from us. We went from overnight being a really interesting player to a major player.[6]

On the one hand, the extraordinary critical and commercial success of *Four Weddings and a Funeral* reassured both PolyGram and Philips that PFE's strategy was working. On the other hand, directly comparing the operational infrastructure of PFE to its Hollywood counterparts also served as a sobering experience. As former PFE COO, Malcolm Ritchie, recalls:

> Just after we did *Four Weddings* Michael and I went for lunch with Tom Pollack, who was then the President of Universal, on the Universal lot. It was a nice chat and he was speaking about *Four Weddings* and congratulating us on the success ... The worldwide box office, he knew that it was up to well over $200 million. He said, 'You must have made about $120 million profit on this', and Michael said, 'Well, maybe not quite as much as that.' After we came out, Michael said, 'How did he get that figure?' ... The studio heads had a rough idea that if a film did 'x' at the worldwide box office, how that would translate by the time you took into account video and television, the cost of the release and the cost of the film, what he would make in his worldwide distribution system. We made a good profit on *Four Weddings* but it was nowhere near that, and the difference, of course, was because Universal had a worldwide distribution system. At that time we had very few territories ... and the rest were pre-sold, so the upside for us was limited. It was just an

interesting conversation that brought home to us why it was important to get into as much distribution as possible.[7]

Perhaps the most significant legacy of *Four Weddings* was the way in which it altered industry perceptions about the worldwide market potential of British films in popular genres. Its release was, however, met with some criticism for the stereotypical version of white middle and upper-class Britishness on offer in the film (Street 2002: 205). Nonetheless, for Working Tittle's Co-Chairman, Tim Bevan, the film succeeded as culturally valid on its own terms. 'One of the things that ... in terms of British film, works very well is when you're culturally specific,' he argues. 'There's something honest about those films and people connect to them.'[8] In particular, he singles out Richard Curtis's films as an example of this strategy:

> People would hate to ... admit this but there is cultural specificity ... in Richard's movies as well, which is about a particular class, if you like, of British society that does reflect Britain. I remember reading an editorial that some Labour politician had written after the success of *Four Weddings*, being absolutely furious that this was a reflection of British culture, and you thought, 'Well, actually mate, it is, and there's nothing you can do about it and $250 million worth of people around the world would agree with me on that.' It's all very well writing that in *The Guardian*, but it's sort of meaningless ... It's a strand of British society, it's not British society, it is a strand, you may like it, you may hate it ... but it is a strand of Britishness.[9]

Four Weddings remained the most successful Working Title release of the PFE era, eventually being displaced as the company's top grossing film by *Notting Hill* at the start of the Universal era. Significantly, however, *Four Weddings* established a market profile for Working Title's films that continues to this day. Most notably this involved its remarkable success in the international market, where the film made just over $205 million, compared to the $52 million it accrued in the domestic market.[10] The following sections explore this trend during Working Title's years as both a PFE and Universal subsidiary and, in turn, places the company's output in context by comparing it with that of its successive parent companies.

THE MARKET FOR WORKING TITLE'S FILMS IN THE PFE ERA

Over the course of the 1990s the films that PFE released achieved substantially greater returns in the international market than the domestic market. As Table 9.1 shows, the top fifteen films released by the studio generated just over $550 million (37.3 per cent) from the domestic market (i.e. the US and Canada) and $1 billion (62.7 per cent) from the international market (i.e.

Rank	Film	Year	Transatlantic British Cinema?	Estimated Budget	Domestic Box Office	%	International Box Office	%	UK Box Office	%	Worldwide Box Office
1	Four Weddings and a Funeral	1994	Yes	4.4	52.6	20.4	205.1	79.6	41.3	16.0	257.7
2	Bean	1997	Yes	18	42.5	18.1	192.0	81.9	24.9	10.6	234.4
3	Sleepers	1996	No	44	53.3	29.4	127.7	70.6	14.6	8.0	181.0
4	The Game	1997	No	50	46.4	41.7	64.9	58.3	3.3	2.9	111.3
5	Nell	1994	No	31	33.6	31.4	73.3	68.6	3.1	2.9	106.9
6	Mr Holland's Opus	1995	No	23	82.6	77.3	24.3	22.7	1.2	1.2	106.9
7	What Dreams May Come	1998	No	85	53.3	53.6	46.1	46.4	2.4	2.4	99.4
8	French Kiss	1995	No		38.9	39.6	59.4	60.4	4.9	4.9	98.3
9	Dead Man Walking	1995	No	11	42.9	49.8	43.2	50.2	4.3	5.0	86.1
10	Elizabeth	1998	Yes	30	28.9	39.4	44.4	60.6	8.8	12.1	73.3
11	The Borrowers	1997	Yes	29	22.0	43.1	29.1	56.9	12.5	24.4	51.1
12	Fargo	1996	No	7	24.5	48.0	26.5	52.0	N/A		51.0
13	The Big Lebowski	1998	No	15	17.0	38.4	27.3	61.6	2.9	6.5	44.2
14	The Adventures of Priscilla, Queen of the Desert	1994	No		11.2	28.0	28.9	72.0	2.5	6.1	40.1
15	La huitième jour	1996	No		0.5	1.3	37.9	98.7	N/A		38.4
	Total				550.1	37.3	1,030.0	62.7	126.5	7.9	1,580.1

Table 9.1 PFE slate: box office top fifteen (excluding acquisitions), 1992–8 (all figures $US millions). Source: box office data, PFE Archive. Estimated production budgets: IMDb.[11]

the rest of the world). Within this overall slate, Working Title became by far the most commercially successful PFE label and produced eight of the top fifteen PFE films, collectively contributing $896.1 million in worldwide box office revenue, over half of the $1.58 billion total. Within this grouping, the Transatlantic British Cinema produced by Working Title – *Four Weddings and a Funeral*, *Bean* (1997), *Elizabeth* (1998) and *The Borrowers* (1997) – collectively contributed $616.5 million (68.8 per cent), while its American films – *French Kiss* (1995), *Dead Man Walking* (1995), *Fargo* (1996) and *The Big Lebowski* (1998) – accumulated $279 million (31.2 per cent). Significantly, when considered collectively, these eight films drew $269.2 million (30 per cent) of their gross box office receipts from the domestic market and $626.9 million (70 per cent) from the international market. Within this international figure, the UK market accounted for $99.5 million (11 per cent) overall.

These commercial returns were achieved largely through PFE's 'specialty' distribution company, Gramercy Pictures, in the US and PFEI, the studio's international distribution and marketing network, which operated directly in thirteen territories at its peak. For Stewart Till the market profile of PFE's films was the result of a combination of factors which included both the studio's production agenda and the strength of its distribution and marketing infrastructure, both of which made the domestic market more of a challenge:

> It's uphill. America is a very inward-looking culture – notwithstanding Miami and LA and New York and Chicago – but mainstream America. The number of successful foreign films you can count on one hand. Every now and again something breaks out, like a *Slumdog* [*Millionaire*], and pushes through ... British films are on a gradient, it's not so much a ceiling, but they're trying to run uphill ... In the US the studios conspired to stop us. They would say to exhibitors at one stage, that if you give PolyGram screens you won't get our next film, so they really tried to stop us ... It was illegal, so they couldn't do it ... in the open and therefore not so effectively ... Internationally we didn't have that resistance at all ... It was harder domestically. It's harder because there's huge P&A budgets ... Obviously it's the biggest market, but even pro rata they'll spend two or three times the marketing money domestically, so it's a much scarier marketplace.[12]

Indeed, it is interesting to consider further the market profile of Working Title's films when the company's Transatlantic British Cinema is separated from its American films. Just 23.7 per cent ($146 million) of the collective revenue of *Four Weddings and a Funeral*, *Bean*, *Elizabeth* and *The Borrowers* came from the domestic market, while 76.3 per cent ($470.6 million) came from international and $88.9 million (14.4 per cent) was from the UK market. In contrast, the company's American films – *French Kiss*, *Dead Man Walking*,

Fargo and *The Big Lebowski* – derived $123.2 million (44.1 per cent) from the domestic market, $156.3 million (55.9 per cent) from international and just $12 million (4.3 per cent) from the UK markets. This swing in market share underlines the fact that the Transatlantic British Cinema produced by Working Title is substantially more popular in the international market than in the domestic market and particularly so in the UK market. This realisation played into the release strategy of *Bean*, for example, which reversed the approach taken with *Four Weddings*. As Livingstone explains:

> [Rowan Atkinson] was a big star across much of the world and he wasn't a big star in America ... The plan wasn't 'OK, we'll do America last', it was the fact that America just wasn't desperately interested in it, and so we had no choice ... It was one of those occasions where people really liked what they saw. It was just a slightly better, longer version of the TV show and the TV show hadn't exhausted itself so that people absolutely adored it. That was unusual, but then also I think it gave us a bit of confidence with some of these other films we said, 'Let's release it first [internationally]' ... and we did on a lot of occasions and did extremely well out of it ... It was very useful because the rest of the world always looked to America to go, 'How is this film going to do?' ... Working Title changed that by making it a hit in the UK ... films like *Bean* would go to America already having grossed $200 million and suddenly the tables were turned. The onus was on the US to have a hit. Prior to that, it was always: 'How has it done in the US? How many screens has it got? Who's the distributor in America'?[13]

Significantly, the international market profile that Working Title established during its years as a PFE label has continued throughout its years as a subsidiary of Universal. Moreover, the company's films are distributed and marketed by an established Hollywood studio that operates through Universal and its 'specialty' sister studio, Focus Features, in the domestic market and through its international distribution companies United International Pictures (UIP) and Universal Pictures International (UPI) in as many as thirty-five territories in the international market.

THE MARKET FOR WORKING TITLE'S FILMS IN THE UNIVERSAL ERA

During Working Title's years as a subsidiary of Universal, the company's most commercially successful films typically conform to Universal's 'event' category of medium budget production. Table 9.2 shows the top twenty Working Title films distributed by Universal in the domestic market and UIP/UPI in international territories ranked according to worldwide box office performance.[14] These titles are typically the most expensive productions on Working Title's slate, with an average estimated budget of $42 million. One notable exception, however, is Working Title's most commercially successful

Rank	Film	Year	Transatlantic British Cinema?	Estimated Budget	Domestic Box Office	%	International Box Office	%	UK Box Office	%	Worldwide Box Office
1	Les Misérables	2012	No	61	148.8	33.7	293.0	66.3	63.2	14.3	441.8
2	Notting Hill	1999	Yes	42	116.1	31.9	247.8	68.1	49.3	13.5	363.9
3	Bridget Jones's Diary	2001	Yes	25	71.5	25.4	210.4	74.6	60.3	21.4	281.9
4	Bridget Jones: The Edge of Reason	2004	Yes	40	40.2	15.3	222.3	84.7	68.2	26.0	262.5
5	Love Actually	2003	Yes	40	59.7	24.2	187.2	75.8	62.7	25.4	246.9
6	Mr Bean's Holiday	2007	Yes	25	33.3	14.5	196.4	85.5	44.0	19.1	229.7
7	Bridget Jones's Baby	2016	Yes	35	24.3	11.4	187.7	88.6	60.4	28.5	212.0
8	Everest	2015	No	55	43.5	21.4	159.9	78.6	15.8	7.8	203.4
9	The Interpreter	2005	No	80	72.7	44.6	90.2	55.4	13.7	8.4	162.9
10	Johnny English	2003	Yes	40	28.1	17.5	132.5	82.5	31.2	19.4	160.6
11	Johnny English Reborn	2011	Yes	45	8.3	5.2	151.8	94.8	33.1	20.7	160.1
12	Johnny English Strikes Again	2018	Yes	25	4.4	2.8	154.6	97.2	23.2	14.6	159.0
13	Yesterday	2019	Yes	26	73.3	47.7	80.4	52.3	17.8	11.6	153.7
14	About a Boy	2002	Yes	30	41.4	31.7	89.2	68.3	24.3	18.6	130.5
15	Nanny McPhee	2005	Yes	25	47.1	38.5	75.3	61.5	29.2	23.8	122.5
16	Paul	2011	Yes	40	37.4	38.2	60.6	61.8	23.3	23.8	98.0
17	Contraband	2012	No	25	66.5	69.1	29.7	30.9	3.3	3.4	96.3
18	40 Days and 40 Nights	2002	No		38.0	39.9	57.2	60.1	7.7	8.1	95.1
19	Green Zone	2010	No	100	35.1	36.9	59.8	63.1	8.3	8.7	94.9
20	Nanny McPhee and the Big Bang	2010	Yes	35	29.0	31.1	64.2	68.9	23.6	25.3	93.3
	Total				1,018.7	27.0	2,750.4	73.0	662.6	17.6	3,769.1

Table 9.2 Working Title's Universal slate: box office top twenty, 1999–2019 (all figures $US millions). Source: box office data courtesy of Box Office Mojo. Used with permission. Estimated production budgets: IMDb.

film, *Les Misérables* (2012), which arguably belongs to Universal's 'tent-pole' category of production. Like most other films within this grouping, it is based upon an internationally 'pre-sold' intellectual property, in this case a long-running and highly successful stage musical.

The majority of Working Title's films, however, remain within Universal's medium-budget 'event' category of production. The most commercially successful in this grouping are the company's romantic comedies, including *Notting Hill*, *Bridget Jones's Diary*, *Bridget Jones: The Edge of Reason*, *Love Actually*, *Bridget Jones's Baby* (2016), *Yesterday* (2019), *About a Boy* (2002) and *40 Days and 40 Nights* (2002). Collectively, this grouping accounts for over $1.7 billion in worldwide revenue and forms the most commercially successful genre grouping in Working Title's output. Thereafter, the company's family films form a second tier of commercial success, led by the Rowan Atkinson vehicles *Mr. Bean's Holiday* (2007) and the *Johnny English* trilogy (2003-2018), and followed by *Nanny McPhee* (2005) and *Nanny McPhee and the Big Bang* (2010), which collectively generated over $920 million worldwide. Finally, Working Title's 'intelligent popcorn' thrillers and action/adventure films such as *Everest* (2015), *The Interpreter* (2005), *Contraband* (2012) and *Green Zone* (2010) complete the list, collectively contributing just over $550 million in worldwide box office revenue.

Significantly, the audience for Working Title's Universal slate remained largely in the international market, which accounts for just over $2.7 billion (73 per cent) of revenue with domestic market taking just over $1 billion (27 per cent). Within the gross international figure, the UK is by some measure the largest national market, accounting for $662.6 million (17.6 per cent) of box office revenue. When Working Title's Transatlantic British Cinema is considered separately, however, the proportional market configuration of Working Title's films shifts considerably, with domestic revenue falling to 23 per cent and international and UK revenue rising to 77 per cent and 20.6 per cent respectively. Thus, despite the vast difference in size between the US and the UK markets, Working Title's Transatlantic British Cinema almost reaches market parity in these territories, with titles such as *Bridget Jones: The Edge of Reason*, *Love Actually*, *Mr. Bean's Holiday* and *Johnny English* recording higher box office grosses in the UK than the US. Perhaps unsurprisingly, the remaining Working Title films (which are typically American in terms of character, setting or cultural theme) show a market shift in the opposite direction, with an increased domestic revenue of 37 per cent, while international and UK revenue fall to 63 per cent and just 10.2 per cent respectively. Contemplating the overall market profile for the films that Working Title produces, the company's Co-Chairman, Eric Fellner, explains:

> We're making international films as opposed to making domestic-centric films. American film producers, predominantly, [make domestic centric

films]. It's just because of who they are and where they're based and because of who we are and where we're based. I believe that in a multiplex in Europe, if there are two good films and one has a slightly European sensibility and one has an American sensibility – and they're both good – I think people will choose the European one and in America the opposite ... You try to make everybody feel that they're getting what they want. Ultimately, in America, it's very, very hard to make them feel like they're getting what they want because what they really want is what they really want, and that's American films. They don't want foreign films. Even though our films are made in English, they're perceived as foreign films.[15]

A second grouping of Working Title films was distributed through Focus Features in the US. Significantly, Focus typically uses platform releases that target a smaller number of cinemas in specific locations and attempts to build an audience for its 'specialty' product outside the 'wide release' strategies of Universal. 'It meant there was somebody that actually cared about smaller films and was in the art-house business, which a lot of British films – to Americans – look like they should be in,' explains David Livingstone, Working Title's former Head of Worldwide Marketing. 'If a film only did $12 million or $15 million it was a success to them, whereas Universal was such a huge machine, they wanted the film that did $80 or $100 million.'[16] Table 9.3 shows the top fifteen Working Title films distributed by Focus Features in the domestic market and UIP/UPI internationally, ranked according to worldwide box office performance.[17] In contrast to the company's top releases through Universal, which have an average estimated production budget of $42 million, this grouping comprises considerably less expensive films, with estimated average budgets of just $23 million.

Working Title's releases through Focus are dominated by examples of Transatlantic British Cinema, and more specifically historical dramas including *Darkest Hour* (2017), *Atonement* (2007), *The Theory of Everything* (2014), *Pride & Prejudice* (2005), *Billy Elliot* (2000), *Tinker Tailor Soldier Spy* (2011), *Victoria & Abdul* (2017) and *Mary Queen of Scots* (2018). Collectively, this grouping of films accounts for over $825 million in worldwide revenue, with those period dramas set elsewhere in Europe, *Anna Karenina* (2012) and *The Danish Girl* (2015), contributing a further $133 million. Two comedy films, *The World's End* (2013) and *The Boat that Rocked* (2009), added just over $82 million in revenue, while the remaining Coen brothers titles, *Burn After Reading* (2008), *A Serious Man* (2009) and *The Man Who Wasn't There* (2001), together added just over $214 million worldwide.

Once again, the audience for Working Title's Focus Features slate is largely found in the international market, which accounts for $855 million (68 per cent) of revenue with the domestic market taking just over $400 million

Rank	Film	Year	Transatlantic British Cinema?	Estimated Budget	Domestic Box Office	%	International Box Office	%	UK Box Office	%	Worldwide Box Office
1	*Burn After Reading*	2008	No	37	60.4	36.9	103.4	63.1	12.7	7.8	163.7
2	*Darkest Hour*	2017	Yes	30	56.5	37.4	94.4	62.6	33.4	22.1	150.8
3	*Atonement*	2007	Yes	30	50.9	39.4	78.3	60.6	24.1	18.6	129.3
4	*The Theory of Everything*	2014	Yes	15	35.9	29.0	87.8	71.0	31.9	25.8	123.7
5	*Pride & Prejudice*	2005	Yes	28	38.4	31.7	82.7	68.3	26.6	21.9	121.1
6	*Billy Elliot**	2000	Yes	5	22.0	20.1	87.3	79.9	25.2	23.1	109.3
7	*Tinker Tailor Soldier Spy*	2011	Yes	20	24.1	20.0	56.5	70.0	22.6	28.0	80.6
8	*Anna Karenina*	2012	No		12.8	18.6	56.1	81.4	8.7	12.7	68.9
9	*Victoria & Abdul*	2017	Yes	15	22.2	34.0	43.2	66.0	14.0	21.4	65.4
10	*The Danish Girl*	2015	No	15	11.1	17.3	53.1	82.7	10.8	16.9	64.2
11	*Mary Queen of Scots*	2018	Yes	25	16.5	35.3	30.2	64.7	12.1	25.9	46.7
12	*The World's End*	2013	Yes	28	26.0	56.4	20.1	43.6	13.4	29.0	46.1
13	*The Boat That Rocked*	2009	Yes	50	8.0	22.1	28.3	77.9	10.1	27.9	36.3
14	*A Serious Man*	2009	No	7	9.2	29.4	22.2	70.6	2.4	7.6	31.4
15	*The Man Who Wasn't There***	2001	No	20	7.5	39.7	11.4	60.3	2.4	12.5	18.9
	Total				401.6	32.0	855.0	68.0	250.4	19.9	1,256.6

*Released by Universal Focus **Released by USA Films

Table 9.3 Working Title's Focus Features slate: box office top fifteen, 1999–2019 (all figures $US millions). Source: box office data courtesy of Box Office Mojo. Used with permission. Estimated production budgets: IMDb.

(32 per cent). Within the gross international figure, the UK accounts for just over $250 million (19.9 per cent) of box office revenue. When Working Title's Transatlantic British Cinema is considered separately, however, the proportional market configuration shifts modestly, with domestic revenue rising to 33.1 per cent and international falling to 66.9 per cent, despite UK revenue increasing to 23.5 per cent. Accordingly, the majority of Working Title's 'specialty' Transatlantic British Cinema, including titles like *Darkest Hour*, *Atonement*, *The Theory of Everything* and *Pride & Prejudice* attained better box office returns in the US than the UK. Conforming to expectation, the American Working Title films distributed by Focus – *Burn After Reading*, *A Serious Man* and *The Man Who Wasn't There* – show a proportionally increased domestic revenue of 36 per cent, with international and UK revenue standing at 64 per cent and just 8.2 per cent respectively.

Unsurprisingly, the commercial success of the films produced by Working Title's low-budget subsidiary, WT^2, is limited when compared to Working Title's Universal and Focus Features slates. As Table 9.4 shows, the slate comprises ten films which cost $5 million or less and belong to Universal's third tier of production, the so-called 'portfolio' category. They can be grouped into genre categories when aligned with the company's 'heart, humour and horror' creative remit, with heart exemplified by the drama *Billy Elliot*, and three comedy-dramas, *Inside I'm Dancing* (2004), *Mickybo and Me* (2004) and *Sixty Six* (2006); humour is found in the comedies *Ali G Indahouse* (2002*)*, *Shaun of the Dead* (2004) and *The Calcium Kid* (2004), while *Long Time Dead* (2002), *My Little Eye* (2002) and *Gone* (2007) sit within the horror genre. The entire slate grossed $186.1 million worldwide, of which $33.8 million (19.2 per cent) is domestic revenue, $150.3 million (80.8 per cent) is international revenue and $62.4 million (33.5 per cent) is UK revenue. This trend was, however, distorted by a number of UK-only releases (*The Calcium Kid*, *Mickybo and Me*) or international-only releases (*Long Time Dead*, *My Little Eye*, *Ali G Indahouse*).

By far the company's greatest critical and commercial success was WT^2's debut film, *Billy Elliot*. 'It did make things a little bit hellish, I suppose, because everything after it seemed a dismal failure, given that it had Oscar nominations and BAFTA wins,' recalls Natascha Wharton, former head of WT^2. 'I don't think it actively changed things but it did put, I suppose, a certain kind of pressure on ... I don't think we did ever deliver something subsequently which had that box office success.'[18] *Billy Elliot* is followed by *Shaun of the Dead* and *Ali G Indahouse*, which respectively grossed $30 million and $23.3 million worldwide. This was supported by relative success in the horror genre with *Long Time Dead* and *My Little Eye* taking $13.1 million and $6.8 million respectively.[19] The remaining four WT^2's films, however, all failed to reach $2 million at the box office, collectively grossing just $3.7 million.

Rank	Film	Year	Transatlantic British Cinema?	Estimated Budget	Domestic Box Office	%	International Box Office	%	UK Box Office	%	Worldwide Box Office
1	Billy Elliot	2000	Yes	5	22.0	20.1	87.3	79.9	25.2	23.1	109.3
2	Shaun of the Dead	2004	Yes	4	13.5	45.1	16.5	54.9	12.3	41.1	30.0
3	Ali G Indahouse	2002	Yes	5			23.3	100.0	14.8	63.8	23.3
4	Long Time Dead	2002	Yes				13.1	100.0	2.6	19.6	13.1
5	My Little Eye	2002	No	2			6.8	100.0	4.0	59.3	6.8
6	Sixty Six	2006	Yes		0.2	12.0	1.6	88.0	1.6	85.3	1.9
7	Inside I'm Dancing	2004	Yes		0.0	1.9	1.2	98.1	1.2	98.1	1.2
8	Mickybo and Me	2004	Yes	5			0.5	100.0	0.5	100.0	0.5
9	The Calcium Kid	2004	Yes				0.1	100.0	0.1	100.0	0.1
10	Gone	2007	No		—		—		—		—
	Total				35.8	19.2	150.3	80.8	62.4	33.5	186.1

Table 9.4 WT²'s slate: box office top ten, 1999–2007 (all figures $US millions). Source: box office data courtesy of Box Office Mojo. Used with permission. Estimated production budgets: IMDb.

Successfully distributing and marketing low-budget British films to a global audience proved to be a difficult task according to UIP's former Chairman, Stewart Till. 'I honestly believe that UIP ... had the expertise and the resources to market all the great films they were given, large and small. I've always said that great distribution and marketing can add 30 per cent to the box office and bad marketing and distribution can lose 30 per cent,' he argues. 'What it can't do ... [is] take a film that hasn't got an audience and just by brilliant marketing make people want to go and see it.'[20] As he goes on to contend, the barrier which prevented many of WT²'s films reaching a wide audience through UIP was a matter of cultural specificity:

> *Shaun of the Dead* is a good case in point. It was a huge success in the UK, and didn't really travel outside, didn't work in any other territories. Working Title at the time – and probably still do – maintained that it didn't work because we didn't give it the marketing support, and it could have worked ... We didn't give it the marketing support, not because we said, 'Look guys, we haven't got the time or the resources.' I said, 'I don't think this film will work outside the UK. It's a very UK-centric humour' ... [Similarly] Ali G compared to ... Sacha Baron Cohen's subsequent films, it is very, very British and low-budget and very few production values, and obviously, the character wasn't known outside the UK as a television character. So, that's another one where it wasn't like we didn't have capacity, the film was inherently a very UK-centric film.[21]

It is also useful to compare Working Title's output with that of its current parent company, Universal, to position the company's production agenda within the slate of the studio at large. Table 9.5 shows the top twenty films released by Universal since Working Title's integration into the studio, ranked in order of worldwide box office performance. The average estimated budget of these films is $116 million and the majority belong to Universal's first tier tent-pole production category. Significantly, fourteen of Universal's top twenty films are instalments of three highly successful film franchises. *Jurassic World* (2015) and *Jurassic World: Fallen Kingdom* (2018) alone account for almost $3 billion in worldwide revenue. Thereafter, the five *Fast & Furious* films (2011–19) add just under $5 billion, while the seven Illumination Entertainment animations (*Despicable Me*, 2010; *Despicable Me 2*, 2013; *The Secret Life of Pets*, 2016; *Sing*, 2016; *Despicable Me 3*, 2017; *Minions*, 2015; *Dr Seuss' The Grinch*, 2018) generated $5.7 billion in worldwide box office. Beyond these franchises, outliers in the tent-pole area include *King Kong* (2005) and *How to Train Your Dragon: The Hidden World* (2019), the film which marks the beginning of Universal's Dreamworks Animation slate. These box office juggernauts are complemented by several highly successful 'event' films, including *Mamma Mia!* (2008), *Fifty Shades of Grey* (2015), *Ted* (2012) and *Meet the Fockers*

Rank	Film	Year	Transatlantic British Cinema?	Estimated Budget	Domestic Box Office	%	International Box Office	%	UK Box Office	%	Worldwide Box Office
1	*Jurassic World*	2015	No	150	652.3	39.0	1,019.4	61.0	99.7	6.0	1,671.7
2	*Fast & Furious 7*	2015	No	190	353.0	23.3	1,163.0	76.7	59.9	4.0	1,516.0
3	*Jurassic World: Fallen Kingdom*	2018	No	170	417.7	31.9	890.7	68.1	54.7	4.2	1,308.5
4	*The Fate of the Furious*	2017	No	250	226.0	18.3	1,010.0	81.7	37.5	3.0	1,236.0
5	*Minions*	2015	No	74	336.0	29.0	823.4	71.0	72.7	6.3	1,159.4
6	*Despicable Me 3*	2017	No	80	264.6	25.6	770.2	74.4	62.9	6.1	1,034.8
7	*Despicable Me 2*	2013	No	76	368.1	37.9	602.7	62.1	72.3	7.4	970.8
8	*The Secret Life of Pets*	2016	No	75	368.4	42.1	507.1	57.9	45.0	5.1	875.5
9	*Fast & Furious 6*	2013	No	160	238.7	30.3	550.0	69.7	38.3	4.9	788.7
10	*Fast & Furious Presents: Hobbs & Shaw*	2019	No	200	174.0	22.9	585.1	77.1	26.2	3.5	759.1
11	*Sing*	2016	No	75	270.4	42.6	363.8	57.4	36.1	5.7	634.2
12	*Fast & Furious 5*	2011	No	125	209.8	33.5	416.3	66.5	30.2	4.8	626.1
13	*Mamma Mia!*	2008	No	52	144.2	23.6	465.7	76.4	94.4	15.5	609.9
14	*Fifty Shades of Grey*	2015	No	40	166.2	29.1	404.8	70.9	51.6	9.0	571.0
15	*King Kong*	2005	No	207	218.1	38.8	344.3	61.2	52.6	9.4	562.4
16	*Ted*	2012	No	50	218.8	39.8	330.6	60.2	48.9	8.9	549.4
17	*Despicable Me*	2010	No	69	251.5	46.3	291.6	53.7	32.3	5.9	543.1
18	*How to Train Your Dragon: The Hidden World*	2019	No	129	160.8	30.9	359.1	69.1	25.8	5.0	519.9
19	*Meet the Fockers*	2004	No	80	279.3	54.1	237.4	45.9	54.4	10.5	516.6
20	*Dr. Seuss' The Grinch*	2018	No	75	270.6	52.9	241.0	47.1	35.6	7.0	511.6
	Total				4,936.1	32.3	10,356.7	67.7	931.4	6.1	15,292.8

Table 9.5 Universal's slate: box office top twenty, 1999–2019 (all figures $US millions). Source: box office data courtesy of Box Office Mojo. Used with permission. Estimated production budgets: IMDb.

(2004), which, despite exceeding worldwide grosses of $500 million, are steadily being replaced in the top twenty by Universal's tent-pole franchises.

While there are no examples of Transatlantic British Cinema in Universal's top twenty grossing films, it is interesting to note the popularity of these titles in the domestic, international and UK markets compared to Working Title's films. Universal's top twenty films made over $15 billion worldwide, of which $4.9 billion (32.3 per cent) was from the domestic market and $10.3 billion (67.7 percent) was from the international market. Within this international figure, the UK market contributed just over $931 million (6.1 per cent) in gross theatrical revenue. In contrast, Working Title's top twenty releases via Universal made just under $3.8 billion, of which $1 billion (27 per cent) was derived from the domestic market, $2.7 billion (73 per cent) from the international market and $662.6 million (17.6 per cent) from the UK. While this underlines the international market profile of Working Title's films, it also highlights the contribution of the UK towards it. Indeed, while Working Title's films regularly outperform Universal's in the UK market on a proportional basis, there are several (e.g. *Bridget Jones's Diary*, *Bridget Jones: The Edge of Reason* and *Love Actually*) that generate greater revenues outright than all but the most successful Universal titles (e.g. *Jurassic World*, *Minions* and *Despicable Me 2*). As Bevan reflects, the strength of the UK theatrical market is one of several factors that make the British film industry distinctive:

> We've got a great domestic marketplace, because we have a fantastic audience base. We're third in the world behind America and China, so people in Britain like going to the cinema … Of the 'foreign' territories, i.e. every territory outside America, we tend to produce two or three or four movies a year – as opposed to maybe one – that's seen on a worldwide basis … In any given year there's maybe one French film, but there are going to be four or five British films you'll see all around the world. We punch above our weight in terms of developing talent, that's because we have a very healthy and interrelated television industry. So, in terms of developing writers and directors … and actors … we punch above our weight. Then we have the English language, which is a colossal advantage because it is the worldwide language of cinema.[22]

Following Working Title's transition to a 'first-look' deal with Universal in 2012, the company's films have, however, also been financed and distributed by other studios, most notably Studiocanal. Table 9.6 shows the seven films that were produced from this relationship between 2011 and 2019, ranked according to worldwide box office performance. With an average estimated budget of $21 million, the studio's films occupy a similar commercial terrain as the output of Focus Features, albeit with a reduced emphasis on the so-called 'smart-house' audience. Indeed, Working Title's Studiocanal slate is

Rank	Film	Year	Transatlantic British Cinema?	Estimated Budget	Domestic Box Office	%	International Box Office	%	UK Box Office	%	Worldwide Box Office
1	*Tinker Tailor Soldier Spy*	2011	Yes	20	24.1	30.0	56.5	70.0	22.6	28.0	80.6
2	*Legend*	2015	Yes	30	1.9	4.4	41.1	95.6	28.0	65.1	43.0
3	*I Give it a Year*	2013	Yes		0.0	0.1	28.2	99.9	9.5	33.5	28.2
4	*The Two Faces of January*	2014	No	31	0.5	3.7	13.0	96.3	2.7	19.8	13.6
5	*King of Thieves*	2018	Yes		0.0	0.1	11.3	99.9	7.8	68.5	11.3
6	*We Are Your Friends*	2015	No	2	3.6	32.3	7.5	67.7	0.8	7.5	11.1
7	*The Program*	2015	No		0.0	0.4	3.3	99.6	0.6	17.3	3.3
	Total				30.2	15.8	161.0	84.2	71.8	37.6	191.2

Table 9.6 Working Title's StudioCanal slate: box office top films, 2011–19 (all figures $US millions). Source: box office data courtesy of Box Office Mojo. Used with permission. Production budgets: IMDb.

populated by crime films and thrillers such as *Tinker Tailor Soldier Spy*, *Legend* (2015), *The Two Faces of January* (2014) and *King of Thieves* (2018) as well as a romantic comedy, *I Give it a Year* (2013), a drama, *We Are Your Friends* (2015) and a biopic, *The Program* (2015).

The audience for Working Title's Studiocanal slate is, once again, predominantly found in the international market, which accounts for $161 million (84.2 per cent) of revenue, with the domestic market taking just over $30.2 million (15.8 per cent). Within the gross international figure, the UK accounts for more than $71 million (37.6 per cent) of box office revenue. The proportion of revenue accruing from the international and UK markets is unsurprising given Studiocanal's distribution and marketing infrastructure, which supports direct operations in only the UK, France, Germany and Australia/New Zealand, of which the UK is the largest national market. Notably, the only substantial revenue from the domestic market was achieved through a distribution and marketing arrangement with Focus Features on *Tinker Tailor Soldier Spy*. As Bevan points out, distributing films outside the Hollywood studio system comes with disadvantages of both scale and market leverage:

> Studiocanal ... distribute in four of the big territories, they're not worldwide yet. And also, you see, ... from our point of view... that they do not have the power. When you see Universal put a picture out in the UK, and the muscle they have with exhibition, because you'll sit in between *Fast and the Furious* and *Despicable Me* ... that makes a substantive difference in terms of getting your film into the market, keeping it there, holding the cinemas, the business that you're able to do. Now, if that's branded Hollywood, that's fine by me. It's a good thing that some British films can get distributed like that.[23]

Finally, the market profile of Working Title's films also needs to be understood in the context of the shifting complexion of the worldwide market for films in general. Figure 9.1 uses data from the Motion Picture Association of America (MPAA) to show changing domestic and international market profiles for films distributed by its members, the major Hollywood studios (Disney, Fox, Paramount, Sony, Universal, and Warner Bros.). Overall the pattern is towards substantial growth with gross worldwide revenues increasing from $16.7 billion to $41.1 billion between 2001 and 2018. The driver of this change is, however, the remarkable growth of the international market.

In 2001, for example, the domestic and international markets were at near parity, with domestic revenue of $8.1 billion (49 per cent) and international revenue at $8.6 billion (51 per cent). Over the subsequent years, however, domestic revenue rose slowly and international revenue rose sharply. The former reached just $10.6 billion (34 per cent) in 2010, while the latter increased to $21 billion (66 per cent). This trend continued and by 2018 domestic revenue reached $11.9 billion (29 per cent), and international hit

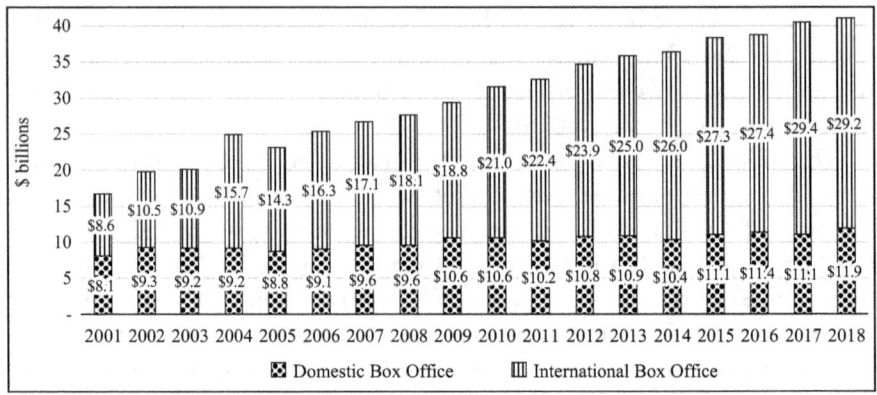

Figure 9.1 Domestic vs international box office for Hollywood films, 2001–18.
Source: MPAA 2007, 2012, 2018.

29.2 billion (71 per cent). Significantly, this remarkable shift in market composition has had implications for the way in which the Hollywood studios think about the audiences for their films. As Universal's former President of International, David Kosse, explains:

> The overall international market is so much more important and gets so much more focus from all of the top management … International was just called 'foreign', and it was an insignificant part of the business and it wasn't part of the strategic planning … It's gone from being just a small outlier to being really a focal point of the business. Within that … what is 'international'? International is a composite of a lot of countries. The relative importance and the mix of those countries has dramatically shifted from France, Germany, the UK and Japan – which is probably what it was fifteen years ago, that was what you wanted to focus on [by asking] 'Will it work there?' – to now, is it going to work in Brazil, Mexico, the UK, China, Korea, and Germany and France? … Where the audience is internationally is shifting, which will shift and define the kinds of movies that are being made.[24]

It is unsurprising, then, that Universal's most commercially successful films in the international market are those which are most readily transferable to other cultures insofar as their appeal lies primarily in spectacle and/or the seamless dubbing that is possible with animated family films. In contrast, the culturally specific elements on display in most of the Transatlantic British Cinema produced by Working Title, such as humour, cultural mores and historical figures and eras, ensure that such films generate most of their revenue from anglophone and non-anglophone European markets. In these ways, Working Title's films remain separate from Universal's core slate which is defined by the most globally oriented forms of filmmaking.

Notes

1. Figures sourced from Box Office Mojo/IMDb were recorded in February 2020. It should be noted that Box Office Mojo intermittently updates its box office data online and, accordingly, some of the figures listed in this chapter are slightly different from those online at the time of publication, including both recent and historic releases. All figures have been rounded to one decimal point.
2. Russell Schwartz, interview with the author, 12-9-2014.
3. David Livingstone, interview with the author, 6-5-2014.
4. Russell Schwartz, interview with the author, 12-9-2014.
5. David Livingstone, interview with the author, 6-5-2014.
6. Stewart Till, interview with the author, 24-2-2014.
7. Malcolm Ritchie, interview with the author, 10-9-2014.
8. Tim Bevan, interview with the author, 6-6-2013.
9. Ibid.
10. The international figure of $205 million was inaccurately stated to be $211 in Townsend (2018b), which was the box office estimate.
11. The box office data available from Box Office Mojo for films released during the 1990s is typically much more limited that that available from the 2000s onwards. For this reason, I have used a box office report from the PFE Archive as the source for the data reproduced here. Unfortunately, however, this report did not include UK box office data for two films, *Fargo* (1996) and *Le huitième jour* (1996).
12. Stewart Till, interview with the author, 24-2-2014.
13. David Livingstone, interview with the author, 6-5-2014.
14. There are occasional exceptions to this rule, such as *Bridget Jones's Diary*, which was distributed by Miramax in the US.
15. Eric Fellner, interview with the author, 14-3-2014.
16. David Livingstone, interview with the author, 6-5-2014.
17. The exception to this is *Tinker Tailor Soldier Spy*, which was released by Focus in the US, but was released by Studiocanal internationally (in the UK, France, Germany and Australia/New Zealand) or sold for third-party release in other territories.
18. Natascha Wharton, interview with the author, 11-3-2014.
19. Box Office Mojo originally indicated a worldwide box office of $13.1 million for *Long Time Dead*, but this was subsequently updated with a figure of $22.6 million, listing a second release of the film. It is not clear which of these is accurate.
20. Stewart Till, interview with the author, 17-7-2014.
21. Ibid.
22. Tim Bevan, interview with the author, 7-12-2016. According to the Motion Picture Association of America (MPAA 2016: 5), the UK accounted for $1.9 billion in box office revenue in 2015, second only to China within the international territories with $6.8 billion in revenue.
23. Tim Bevan, interview with the author, 2-8-2013.
24. David Kosse, interview with the author, 30-6-2014.

CHAPTER 10

Transatlantic British Cinema:
Creative Risk, Commercial Risk and the
Issue of Diversity

This book has offered a history of Working Title Films which charts the company's journey between opposite ends of the British film industry and British film culture. Throughout this narrative of near-constant transition, the focus has remained on both the creative and commercial aspects of the company's development, specifically the ways in which creativity and commerce have been reconciled within successive industrial contexts. This began in the independent sector during the 1980s within which Working Title produced low-budget 'social art cinema', primarily supported by public funding. In the following decade, the company was integrated into a nascent film studio, PolyGram Filmed Entertainment (PFE), which briefly operated as a European-owned competitor to the major Hollywood studios. Following PFE's demise, however, Working Title became a subsidiary of Universal and thus a component part of the contemporary Hollywood studio system. Since the 2010s, the company has formed new industrial partnerships beyond its relationship with Universal which have included working with other Hollywood studios and so-called 'mini-major' studios.

In the interest of positioning this historical trajectory within a wider framework of ideas, this book has favoured a contextual, rather than a celebratory approach. Initially, this involved aligning Working Title's operation and output with the concept of Transatlantic British Cinema during its years as a subsidiary of PFE and Universal. Here, economic transnationalism describes an industrial strategy which links British studios or production companies to the financing, distribution and marketing functions of multinational media conglomerates, the subsidiaries of which are typically the major Hollywood studios. In contrast, globalising transnationalism is a production strategy which involves British producers drawing on these resources to make films in popular genres which feature star actors and high production values. Finally, affinitive transnationalism is a second production strategy which forges links, implicitly or explicitly, between British and American culture onscreen through the representation of characters and/or settings and/or cultural themes which draw on and enhance the existing affinities between the two nations. Significantly, these strategies are transatlantic in the first instance and global in the second. Accordingly, their use in combination underlines the creative and commercial ambition of Transatlantic British Cinema, namely that it should both appeal to and reach the markets of Hollywood's global operations.

This book has, however, also viewed the concept of Transatlantic British Cinema through the lens of political economy, which sees films as commodities which are produced, distributed and consumed within a capitalist industrial system. In turn, this initially entailed focusing on the macro-level issues of national and international economy and policy. Doing so paints a picture of increasing Hollywood domination of the British film industry along the circuit of production, distribution and exhibition. Moreover, the prevailing 'market-friendly' film policies supported by successive UK governments over the last thirty years have enhanced the disparity of public resources available to Transatlantic British Cinema and its conceptual other, independent British cinema. The result has entrenched and perpetuated Hollywood dominance, helping to ensure that Transatlantic British Cinema is positioned at the centre of British and global film culture, while independent British cinema occupies the periphery.

The examination of Transatlantic British Cinema through the lens of political economy is resumed here at the 'mid level' of analysis. This initially involves aligning the industrial structures, processes and strategies which have defined the operation of Working Title during its years as a subsidiary of PFE and Universal with their overarching function, namely the creative and commercial management of risk. When applied to filmmaking, the mitigation of risk becomes analogous with audience familiarity. Expressed in the terms of Working Title's Co-Chairman, Tim Bevan, this situation can be assessed by asking the rhetorical question 'How big is the bullseye?' The bullseye can, of course, be enlarged by pursuing the strategies of economic, globalising and affinitive transnationalism which respectively work to reduce the industrial, formal and cultural distance between British and Hollywood cinema. As a research approach, however, political economy requires more than an account of the ways in which a combination of creative and commercial strategies respond to and shape market forces. Rather, it demands that these industrial dynamics are placed within the wider social, economic and political contexts from which they emerged and are critiqued in relation to their role in maintaining the power relations inherent within these contexts.

Viewing Transatlantic British Cinema through the lens of political economy, then, involves examining the conversion of creative and commercial risk management into cultural power and the ways in which this translation is bounded by the concomitant forces of social power. Initially, this entails considering the films produced by Working Title at a textual level by exploring the versions of Britain and Britishness which have emerged in the company's output over time, ranging from the production of 'social art cinema' as an independent to the production of Transatlantic British Cinema as a subsidiary of PFE and Universal. In doing so, Janet Wasko's (2003) remaining film industry 'illusions' – 'There's no business like show business' and 'That's entertainment!' – are invoked to highlight the misconceptions that the film business is uniquely and inherently risky and that the commodities it produces merely entertain audiences, rather than functioning as ideological products. Finally, this leads to the pressing issue of diversity within the British film industry and within British film culture, the ways in which film policy has intervened in these areas, and the consequences of these interventions for both Transatlantic British Cinema and independent British cinema.

CREATIVE RISK, COMMERCIAL RISK AND THE REPRESENTATIONAL RANGE OF TRANSATLANTIC BRITISH CINEMA

As an independent production company, the commercial risk of filmmaking at Working Title was, to a greater or lesser degree, managed by investment from publicly owned institutions like Channel 4, the British Film Institute (BFI) Production Board and British Screen. Collectively, these organisations supported the independent sector by correcting 'market failure' and thus ensuring the continuation of low-budget indigenous film production. During the mid-1980s, the levels of funding available from these sources meant that filmmaking at Working Title was largely or entirely shielded from market forces. By the end of the decade, however, the company had to attract an increasing proportion of funding from commercial sources. This situation entailed moving from a producer-for-hire business model to operating as a production company which developed projects in-house. Throughout this period, Working Title was sustained in a hand-to-mouth fashion primarily through the receipt of production fees while contending with an undercapitalised development infrastructure, increasing production costs and capricious financing arrangements in both the public and private sectors.

While the aims of Channel 4, the BFI Production Board and British Screen during the 1980s were not identical, the collective effect of the commissioning and investment practices in place at these institutions encouraged creative risk-taking and helped to produce diverse and challenging visions of Britain and Britishness. It is worth invoking Christopher Williams' definition of 'social art cinema' (1996) once again as a means of positioning the creative orientation of Working Title's output during much of the 1980s and early 1990s. Here, the preoccupations of European art cinema including, amongst other things, sexuality, psychological complexity, interiority and ambiguity are foregrounded alongside the depiction of social issues and the use of realism as a representational mode. Many of these features are readily observable in films like *My Beautiful Laundrette* (1985), *Wish You Were Here* (1987), *Sammy and Rosie Get Laid* (1987), *London Kills Me* (1991) and *Edward II* (1991), which engage with a range of social and political issues including social inequality, racism, homophobia, homelessness and substance abuse in striking ways.

Working Title's integration into PolyGram Media Division and subsequently PolyGram Filmed Entertainment profoundly altered the company's orientation vis-à-vis the marketplace and the ways in which it was exposed to risk. Firstly, as a subsidiary of a multinational media conglomerate, Working Title became an internal business within a studio system and was provided with annual overhead and development budgets while a worldwide distribution and marketing infrastructure was built around it. Secondly, PFE managed risk by routing Working Title's development slate through the so-called 'control sheet', which produced worldwide commercial forecasts for each film project. Thereafter, the control sheet became a crucial factor in determining each green-light decision, effectively aligning PFE's production agenda with data-based assessments of commercial potential. In turn, the control sheet was subject to constant adjustment to accommodate both the success and failure of the films PFE released but also the profit margins attainable across its growing distribution and marketing infrastructure on a platform-by-platform and territory-by-territory basis. Finally, risk was also mitigated at the studio level by defraying the cost of investment amongst a range of financial partners, including the major Hollywood studios and the Sumitomo and ING investment banks which co-financed PFE's slate.

By the time Working Title was integrated into Universal, control sheet-like practices were common currency in the Hollywood film industry. Indeed, the company's transition between the two studios was defined by continuity as much as change. Retaining its status as a subsidiary of a multinational media conglomerate, Working Title also received annual overhead and development budgets from its new parent company. Similarly, Universal initially manages risk by modelling historical film performance data to produce 'comps' before creating a so-called 'ten-column' to fully assess the market potential of any given project in development. Like the control sheet, the ten-column is a dynamic instrument which quantifies the creative inputs of each development project in relation to their value in the marketplace and builds this assessment into an 'ultimate' which forecasts the initial product life cycle of a film across its successive windows of release. In contrast to PFE, Universal was at a considerable advantage in this respect due to the scale of its distribution and marketing infrastructure and its associated market leverage across each release window. Like PFE, however, Universal also relied on financial partners to co-produce

Working Title's slate, including a longstanding partnership with Studiocanal and more recent deals with Relativity Media and Perfect World Pictures.

Significantly, the creative and commercial risk environments within which Working Title has operated have also responded to managerial and strategic changes over time at the studio level. PFE's attempt to compete directly with the Hollywood studios during the latter stages of its development, for example, was reflected in both the expansion of the studio's distribution and marketing network and the increasing budgets associated with its films. In contrast, Universal's transition from a 'portfolio' to a 'tent-pole' oriented production strategy in the late-2000s was motivated by the studio's marketing-oriented management team, the effects of the global financial crisis and new market entrants. Working Title's subsequent transition from an exclusive to a 'first-look' deal with the studio in the 2010s marked a continuation of this process, and underlined the ongoing movement of the company's output towards the periphery of Universal's production agenda, which is increasingly dominated by branded tent-pole franchises. Simultaneously, however, this direction of travel is curbed by the operation of Universal's sister studio, Focus Features, which has ensured a continuous home for Working Title's 'specialty' output.

As I have suggested throughout this book, the fundamental parent company–subsidiary dynamic at play in both the PFE and Universal eras of Working Title's history can be conceptualised in terms of creative and commercial gatekeeping. The gates in place at the stages of development, green-lighting and distribution equate to key points of control within these studio systems. In development, Working Title has always maintained creative autonomy and uses its multi-million-dollar development budgets to pursue a range of film projects initiated both inside and outside the company. In contrast, green-light decisions have always been dictated by the studio, even during the extended period of Working Title's 'put' deal with Universal. Equally, the final gate, distribution, is controlled by the studio, which determines the scale and focus of the distribution and marketing campaigns that propel Working Title's films into the worldwide marketplace. The operation of each gate, however, remains linked to a central creative and commercial filter. While the control sheet/ten-column is primarily used to inform green-light decisions, the creative autonomy Working Title maintains in development is, of course, exercised with its commercial demands in mind. In turn, this situation shapes the 'controlled autonomy' which Working Title's Co-Chairmen, Tim Bevan and Eric Fellner, afford to the key creative players who are directly responsible for making the company's films. Finally, box office targets and corresponding distribution and marketing budgets for each film are initially predicated upon the forecasting produced by the control sheet/ten-column and thus shape the early stages of planning around each theatrical release.

So, while each film commodity is a unique cultural product, there is a clear industrial process at work in the relationship between studio and production company which manages creative and commercial risk along the circuit of development, green-lighting and distribution. Accordingly, the entire gatekeeping process should be conceptualised as circular rather than linear over time. In this way, each gate is calibrated in response to the commercial performance of previously released films and, more broadly, to the rising or falling market values ascribed to various creative inputs. This situation, of course, encourages the repetition of creative forms which achieve commercial success and discourages the repetition of those that do not. From this perspective, then, the logic of the marketplace appears to self-select the direction of creativity in a democratic way. The validity of such a claim, however, rests on the assumption that equal resources are directed towards the development, production, distribution and marketing of all types of film. In practice, however, the dice are loaded in favour of creative forms which are, to a greater or lesser degree, risk-averse at every stage of the gatekeeping process. This situation underlines the ways in which Working Title has operated with relative autonomy within two successive studio systems which have effectively circumscribed the company's agency by ensuring that its activities are consistently aligned with assessments of the marketplace.

These industrial structures, processes and strategies, however, do much more than manage creative and commercial risk. In practice, they also circumscribe the representational boundaries of Transatlantic British Cinema and thus the versions of Britain and Britishness which circulate within popular film culture. In doing so, they convert industrial power into cultural power by determining which stories are worth telling and, as importantly, which stories are not. Given that Transatlantic British Cinema is the most heavily capitalised and the most widely distributed, marketed and exhibited version of British cinema, its representational boundaries also have a profound influence upon which stories are seen and heard and which stories are not. What, then, is the impact of Transatlantic British Cinema upon British and global film culture at large? Which versions of Britain and Britishness are most familiar to audiences, generate the greatest commercial returns, and thus present the least creative risk? Equally, which versions of the nation are less familiar, generate limited commercial returns, and thus present greater creative risk?

A substantial set of answers to these questions can, of course, be found by surveying the Transatlantic British Cinema produced by Working Title. Doing so suggests a hierarchy of representational risk which can be conceptualised as a centre-periphery model. Positioned at the centre, the commercial 'bullseye' is defined by white middle- and upper-class characters in privileged, often idyllic, settings in metropolitan and rural England who are gender-normative, heteronormative and able-bodied. In contrast, the periphery of this model is populated by films which offer versions of the nation which, to varying degrees, depart from this homogeneity. Significantly, this situation reorients the propositions outlined above. What is determined by the industrial structures, processes and strategies which shape Transatlantic British Cinema, then, is not merely which stories are worth telling and which are seen and heard, but rather, *whose* stories are worth telling and *whose* stories are seen and heard.

The centre of Working Title's representational range is most emphatically embodied in the conceptual construction of so-called 'Curtisland', a term which originated in the broadsheet press to describe a range of commonalities between the social and geographical milieus represented in films written by Richard Curtis (Crompton 2001: 9). These tropes include, amongst other things, idealised versions of London and rural England, an abundance of spacious period housing and an array of eccentric supporting characters, all of which are evident in romcoms such as *Four Weddings and a Funeral* (1994), *Notting Hill* (1999), *Bridget Jones's Diary* (2001), *Love Actually* (2003), *Bridget Jones: The Edge of Reason* (2004) and *About Time* (2013). Writing in *The Observer*, for example, Tim Adams describes the emergence and development of Curtisland by suggesting:

> *Four Weddings* located a different kind of Britain to any that had been filmed before. It was neither kitchen-sink gritty nor carry-on smutty. It was an apolitical place, full of can-do possibility, obsessed with the educated middle class, perfectly relaxed about the filthy rich, much more in love with sentiment than ideas, and insatiable in its optimism; it was also in thrall to the idea of happy endings ... As the Blair years unfolded, so did Curtisland become more populous. Looked at one way, Britain became the broken-home and teenage-pregnancy capital of Europe; looked at another, it was the subject of ever more feel-good, confetti-strewn, loved-up films. If they were not always from Curtis's pen, then at least they followed his winning formula. (Adams 2009: 12)

In this way, the boundaries of Curtisland can be extended to encompass other Working Title romcoms such as *About A Boy* (2002), *Wimbledon* (2004) and *Bridget Jones's Baby* (2016), which share common representational features. In turn, these films have received significant academic interest from various perspectives. Michael Wayne, for example, suggests that Working Title's films have developed a 'brand identity' which foregrounds 'neo-heritage locations' and 'white middle-class characters' (Wayne 2006: 59). Elsewhere Robert Murphy (2001) describes Working Title's romcoms as 'urban fairy-tales' in which London becomes an enchanted 'city of delights'. Extending the fairy-tale theme, Paul Dave (2006) notes the construction of a middle-class 'metropolitan idyll' which is exclusive and privileged yet omits visible enclosure or contestation. The term 'Curtisland' itself has been taken up in film scholarship by James Leggott (2012), who, like Jay Bamber (2020) and William Brown (2020), explore the various combinations British and American representations that intersect in Curtis's oeuvre.

The core ingredients which define the centre of Working Title's representational range also extend to the majority of Working Title's historical dramas, including *Elizabeth* (1998), *Pride & Prejudice* (2005), *Elizabeth: The Golden Age* (2007) and *Emma* (2020). This is equally true of the company's period dramas set in the twentieth century which embrace representations that are, in various ways, 'neo-heritage'. Examples range from the Oxbridge-educated journalists, intelligence agents and scientists which respectively populate *Frost/Nixon* (2008), *Tinker Tailor Soldier Spy* (2011) and *The Theory of Everything* (2014) to the aristocratic ownership of the Hesketh Racing team in *Rush* (2013); and from the landed gentry of *Atonement* (2007), to the parliamentary debates of the ruling class in *Darkest Hour* (2017). Similar visions of the nation pervade many of Working Title's family films, including *Nanny McPhee* (2005) and *Nanny McPhee and the Big Bang* (2010), and *Johnny English* (2003), *Johnny English Reborn* (2011), and *Johnny English Strikes Again* (2018).

There are, however, films at the periphery of Working Title's representational range which offer versions of Britain and Britishness beyond these creative precepts. In this respect, the brief rise and fall of Working Title's former low-budget subsidiary, WT^2, has had a lasting impact upon diversity within the company's output overall. Films such as *Billy Elliot* (2000), *Mickybo and Me* (2004), *Inside I'm Dancing* (2004) and *Sixty Six* (2006), for example, mix the conventions of British social realism with comedy-drama and are set in social and geographical milieus far removed from Curtisland. Similarly, the talent and humour behind *Ali G Indahouse* (2002) and *Shaun of the Dead* (2004) originated on British television and feature characters who, in terms of social class positioning at least, are decidedly ordinary. Despite the company's closure, the talent associated with WT^2's most commercially successful films maintained a space for such representations in Working Title's subsequent output such as *Hot Fuzz* (2007), *Paul* (2011), *The World's End* (2013) and *Grimsby* (2016). Elsewhere, the likes of *Legend* (2015) and *King of Thieves* (2018) appropriate the criminal archetypes of London's East End. Racially diverse representations have, however, been much slower to appear. In this regard, some of the company's more recent output, including *The Kid Who Would Be King* (2019) *Yesterday* (2019) and *Cats* (2019) are notable exceptions to the rule.

Significantly, however, the centre-periphery model of Working Title's representational range correlates closely with the centre and periphery of the company's commercial success, albeit with some noteworthy trends and anomalies. The relative underperformance of *Wimbledon* and *About Time* within the extended Curtisland canon, for example, are also notable for the absence of Working Title's archetypal male romcom leads, Hugh Grant and Colin Firth. Equally, the critical acclaim and major awards received by *Pride & Prejudice*, *Atonement*, *The Theory of Everything* and *Darkest Hour* helped to elevate the commercial returns of these films amongst the company's 'specialty' output. Elsewhere, the Rowan Atkinson vehicles, *Bean* and *Mr. Bean's Holiday*, achieved extraordinary commercial success based on the popularity of a largely mute and strangely classless character, albeit one already known to television audiences worldwide. Despite the diminished resources afforded to the output of WT^2, the subsidiary produced some significant commercial successes, although on a more modest scale than those of its parent company. While *Billy Elliot* remains the most remarkable example in this regard, films like *Ali G Indahouse* and *Shaun of the Dead* also highlight how alternative versions of Britain and Britishness found a degree of traction in the global marketplace. More recently, two Working Title films which prominently feature racially diverse casts, *The Kid Who Would Be King* and *Cats*, were notable commercial failures, while a third, *Yesterday*, continued the general trend towards box office success which accompanies the Curtisland canon.

Significantly, the white middle- and upper-class characters and privileged settings which dominate the centre of Working Title's representational range also define contemporary Transatlantic British Cinema at large. Collectively these creative precepts constitute the route of least cultural resistance and serve as a highly effective shorthand for the most familiar and risk-averse version of Britain and Britishness which circulates in global film culture. Prominent examples include the most recent instalments of the James Bond cycle (1962–), as well as other action-adventure fare such as the *Tomb Raider* (2001–), *Sherlock Holmes* (2009–) and *Kingsman* (2014–) film series. Equally, family movies such as the *Harry Potter* (2001–11) and *Chronicles of Narnia* (2005–10) film series and titles like *Cinderella* (2015), *Mary Poppins Returns* (2018) and *Christopher Robin* (2018) add significantly to this trend. The billions of dollars in revenue collectively generated by these films are, of course, divided between the Hollywood studios – Disney, Paramount, Sony, Twentieth Century Fox, Universal and Warner Bros. – which financed their production, distribution and marketing. In reference to the Harry Potter, James Bond and Kingsman films, for example, James Russell argues:

> Each of these films or franchises was made in the UK, pitched at the largest possible global audience, and rooted in a relatively conservative vision of British culture. The Harry Potter films, for instance, bring together a long-standing tradition of public school stories, with gothic fantasy, concerns over class prejudice, nostalgia for a medieval and Victorian past, and a

focus on British youth. The films rarely depicted Britain as it is. Instead they provided a CGI-augmented vision of Britain (or the 'Wizarding world') as it might have been if post-war modernity had never occurred. The Britain of Harry Potter is the fantasy that flutters to life in tourist attractions like Salisbury Cathedral, or the Shambles in York, or the Cotswolds. The same is true of James Bond's stoic, colonial masculinity, or *Kingsman*'s knowing mishmash of Arthurian idealism with Savile Row tailoring. They are precisely the kinds of films that overseas viewers might comprehend as quintessentially British, in the same way that buddy action movies and westerns seem quintessentially American to European eyes. (Russell 2017: 384)

This situation has prompted Michael Wayne to argue that 'the integration and subordination of British cinema into Hollywood and the American market provides massively diminished conditions within which British filmmakers could explore the diversity and complexity of life within the United Kingdom' (Wayne 2006: 63). Indeed, the assertion that Hollywood dominates British cinema and that 'massively diminished conditions' apply to filmmaking beyond the ambit of Transatlantic British Cinema is supported by all the available evidence. Wayne's arguments, however, draw attention to a fundamental consequence of Hollywood domination, namely a contraction of the creative conditions within which 'diversity and complexity' can be explored. A common counter-argument to this position might run as follows: audiences seeking to engage with the diversity and complexity of British life are unlikely to turn to James Bond, Bridget Jones or Harry Potter for answers. The films which feature these characters are produced with the creative ambition to entertain audiences and the commercial ambition to realise a profit in doing so. This line of thinking, however, fails to acknowledge that films are highly symbolic commodities with important ideological implications. As Douglas Kellner argues:

> Radio, television, film, digital media, and the other products of media culture provide materials out of which individuals in contemporary media and consumer societies forge their very identities, including sense of self, notion of what it means to be male or female, and conception of class, ethnicity and race, nationality, and sexuality. Media culture helps shape both an individual's and a society's view of the world, defining good or evil, their positive ideals and sense of who they are, as well as who and what are seen as threats and enemies, creating, in some cases, sharp divisions between 'us' and 'them'. Media stories provide the symbols, myths, and resources through which individuals constitute a common culture and through their appropriation become part of the culture and society. (Kellner 2009: 95)

How, then, does Transatlantic British Cinema help to shape the versions of Britain and Britishness which circulate in popular culture? What symbols, myths and resources does it provide for individuals seeking to constitute a common culture? Which identities does it help forge? Despite occasional counter-examples, the narrow representational range which defines the vast majority of Transatlantic British Cinema perpetuates a divide between 'us' and 'them' along the lines of race, social class, gender-normativity, heteronormativity, able-bodiedness and geographical location. This situation has a clear bearing on the maintenance of hegemony, because within this division it is predominantly the stories of those who are positioned towards the top of societal power structures that are seen and heard. This situation is, of course, further underlined in the case of Working Title because of the company's journey from the independent to the studio sector, and from the production of 'social art cinema' to the production of Transatlantic British Cinema.

Transatlantic British Cinema, Independent British Cinema and the Issue of Diversity

While the many films identified above highlight the narrow representational range of Transatlantic British Cinema, they do not account for the dominance of these representations in sociohistorical terms. The short explanation is, of course, that the white middle and upper classes have always dominated British society, and thus the dominant culture which it produces. Inevitably, there are myriad historical explanations for this state of hegemony which measure their influence in centuries and cannot possibly be accounted for here. In these ways Transatlantic British Cinema did not create these representational power divides but merely reinforces and perpetuates them. Or, as Michael Wayne has it vis-à-vis the relationship between the British and Hollywood film industries: 'the dominant external other reinforces internal relations of domination' (Wayne 2006: 60). Unsurprisingly, however, the centre–periphery model which defines the representational range of Transatlantic British Cinema also defines the workforce within the British film industry, underlining the ways in which an industrial culture is reproduced in an image culture. As a 2018 review of diversity in the UK screen sector summarised:

- Women, disabled workers, workers from working-class and ethnic minority backgrounds, carers and individuals living outside London/South East England are significantly less likely to establish and maintain a career in the UK screen sector.
- Many workers have to overcome more than one barrier to workforce participation, e.g. women from working-class backgrounds or disabled workers who also have caring responsibilities.
- Particularly powerful obstacles to workforce participation are the screen sector's reliance on personal networks for allocating work and business

opportunities; a 'white, male, middle-class'-dominated industry culture; working conditions characterised by long working hours, flexible and mobile working and income insecurities; and an underlying acceptance of these conditions as diversity-unfriendly but necessary and unchangeable. (CAMEo 2018: 6–7)

Significantly, the task of combating these systemic inequalities has rested largely with public bodies. As John Hill notes, the UK Film Council (UKFC) combined the industrial dimensions of film policy with 'socially utilitarian concerns', including the promotion of 'social inclusion' and 'diversity' from the time of its establishment in 2000. Given the UKFC's commitment to working with 'the grain of the market', these objectives were not only aligned with the principle of social equality, but also with a 'business imperative' which suggested that diversity also makes good commercial sense (Hill 2004: 35–6). As Jack Newsinger notes, the trajectory continued throughout the lifetime of the UKFC, during which links were often made between diversity and innovation in the context of business success. 'Cultural and social aims were fine, but only in so far as they could be justified in terms of training, infrastructure development, tourism and so on, and only in so far as they did not interfere with commercial interests,' he argues. 'As in New Labour cultural policy more generally, the UKFC was unable to make a case for "diversity" that was not based on commercial criteria, as opposed to a moral or political argument' (Newsinger 2012: 142). Furthering this line of thinking Clive Nwonka suggests:

> Whilst the UKFC rode on a wave of political imperatives, their diversity policy lacked a broad political underpinning to infuse the diversity project with some form of conceptual authority, becoming a moral reflex rather than a political action. So from the beginning the UKFC's diversity policies possessed very paradoxical features, demonstrating a commitment to social inclusion but also a reluctance to take responsibility for that exclusion. In a moment of what the UKFC perceived to be industrial change [it] at the same time rejected the fundamental sociological narratives that any diversity policy concerned with social exclusion should have constructed its legitimacy on. (Nwonka 2015: 87–8)

The failure of these policies to enhance diversity over the lifetime of the UKFC has been noted. Paul Moody, for example, points to a decline in workforce diversity during this period, noting an overall decrease in the number of people from ethnic minority backgrounds and those with a disability working in the industry (Moody 2017: 404). Moreover, he suggests that this 'damningly negative data' highlights the UKFC's 'failure to tackle the endemic problem of privilege throughout the industry' and 'provided the main barrier to entry and the unifying factor across all aspects of exclusion' (ibid.: 417–18).

Despite these failings, Moody notes that BFI rhetoric surrounding diversity represents a continuation of the pronouncements initiated during the UKFC era. The BFI's 2017–2022 strategy document, for example, continues to argue that 'diversity is good for creativity, supports economic growth, taps into underserved audiences and makes good business sense'(ibid.: 419).

Since 2014, the major policy initiative in this area has been the implementation of the BFI's 'Three Ticks' system which was subsequently rebranded as the BFI 'Diversity Standards' in 2016. In practice, the framework requires all recipients of BFI funding to meet specified diversity obligations in at least two of four areas, including 'on-screen representation, themes and narratives'; 'creative leadership and project team'; 'industry access and opportunities'; and 'audience development' (BFI 2019b: 3–6). The filmmaking arms of Channel 4 and the BBC, Film4 and BBC Films, signed up to the Standards in 2016 and 2018 respectively, effectively aligning the vast majority of 'selective' public funding for filmmaking in Britain with these measures. In these ways, many of the principles which underpinned the commissioning and investment practices of Channel 4, the BFI Production Board and British Screen during the 1980s have been sustained under a more formalised and contractually enforceable commitment to diversity. This is evidenced onscreen in recent films such as *Peterloo* (2018), *Wild Rose* (2018) and *Been So Long* (2018), which received investment from the BFI and Film 4, and *Yardie* (2018), *Sorry We Missed You* (2019) and *Misbehaviour* (2020), which were supported by both the BFI and BBC Films.

The impact of BFI's Diversity Standards is, however, directed almost exclusively towards the production of independent British cinema and circumscribed by both the scale of the resources available to the films which adhere to them and the effectiveness of the Standards in enhancing diversity. In 2018, for example, the BFI distributed £30.9 million in National Lottery awards to 302 recipients across the areas of Production (£14.3 million), Audiences (£7.2 million), Heritage (£4.1 million), Development (£2.2 million), International (£1.9 million) and Talent Development (£1.2 million). The available production funding, for example, supported thirty-nine feature films, only two of which received awards in excess of £1 million (BFI 2019a: 199). In the same period, the annual budgets of BBC Films and Film 4 stood at £11.3 million and £25.4 million respectively. This combined figure of £67.6 million represents just over 40 per cent of the total £164.7 million of 'selective' public funding for film in the UK in 2017/18, and the vast majority alloted to film production (ibid.: 194). Significantly, a recent report which focuses upon the issues of race and ethnicity in the UK film industry, describes the Diversity Standards as the 'most ambitious and wide-ranging attempt to respond to the issues of diversity', while also offering a number of reservations about the overall effectiveness of the measures:

> At present, the Diversity Standards do not yet respond to the complexity and nuances of diversity within the film sector, and a more targeted strategic range of criteria is required to produce the kind of sophisticated workforce data that will allow forthcoming research to accurately assess the on-screen and off-screen inclusion of racial difference. (Nwonka 2020: 19)

Ironically, the same level of scrutiny is almost never directed towards the vast majority of public funding for film in the UK, which continues to be distributed by the BFI in the form of UK film tax relief. This 'automatic' funding amounted to £469 million in 2017/18, which accounted for almost three quarters of all public investment in film (BFI 2019a: 194). As the tax credit is an inducement to attract inward investment to the UK as a whole, this 'corporate welfare system', provides public funds which flow overwhelmingly to the largest investors in UK film production: the major Hollywood studios (Newsinger & Presence 2018). While films in receipt of tax relief must pass the decidedly lax requirements of the 'Cultural Test' or meet the requirements of a co-production agreement to qualify, the BFI's Diversity Standards remain voluntary, rather than compulsory. Consequently, the prevailing tax system helps to finance the production of both Transatlantic British Cinema and Hollywood cinema with no commitment towards diversity. To date Paramount Pictures is the first and only Hollywood studio to sign up to the BFI's Diversity Standards for its UK-based productions; however, the BFI maintains an 'active dialogue' with the other major studios on the issue (BFI 2020a: 7).

Without the explicit policy directives of publicly funded institutions, private sector involvement in matters of diversity has depended largely upon notions of good citizenship. Working Title's Co-Chairmen have been active in this area for some time. Tim Bevan was Chair of the UK Film Council's Leadership on Diversity in Film Group, for example, before becoming the organisation's Chairman. Considering the issue in relation to the British film industry at large, Bevan reflects: 'We're appalling at diversity – appalling, appalling, appalling ... we live in a multi-cultural, multi-linguistic, multinational society now and, basically, film sets are full of white posh people, and most of our films and television programmes are too ... that's the one thing that really something needs to happen about.'[1] For its part, Working Title made a substantial intervention in this area by jointly establishing the London Screen Academy (LSA) with Heyday Films and Eon Productions, the companies respectively behind the Harry Potter and James Bond films. The state-funded college, which opened in 2019, offers a two-year programme of study for sixteen- to nineteen-year-old students designed to prepare them for careers in the film and television industries. Significantly, the issues of diversity, inclusion and access are stressed throughout the LSA's first prospectus:

> The screen industries are often seen as inaccessible; it's hard to know where to start and training is expensive. LSA will change this. LSA is committed to giving talented young people, no matter their background, the opportunities to build a successful creative career. LSA is free to attend and dedicated to building more diverse, sustainable and valuable screen industries that are open to everyone. (LSA 2019: 4)

This is, of course, a positive development which seeks to initiate change from the ground up based on the expectation that increased diversity in the workforce will lead to increased diversity onscreen through a process of osmosis. As a relatively laissez-faire intervention, however, it fails to directly address the industrial structures, processes and strategies which collectively determine the complexion of Transatlantic British Cinema. At the centre of this observation is an uncomfortable but inescapable truth: the market value of a film project within this system, and therefore the likelihood that it will pass through the stages of development, green-lighting and distribution, is inextricably bound up with the agency of 'white posh people' on both sides of the camera. This situation is a reminder that such determinations take place within an industrial context defined by relative autonomy in which activity is constantly circumscribed by assessments of the marketplace. Within this environment, a commitment to diversity does not unproblematically make 'good business sense', as suggested by prevailing film policy in the UK. Rather, it involves actively introducing creative and commercial risk into a system which is predicated upon its mitigation.

In recent years, the pressure to do so has been heightened by a series of high-profile social media campaigns which have addressed the issue of diversity in the media industries from various perspectives. #OscarsSoWhite and #BritsSoWhite, for example, drew attention to the underrepresentation of non-white workers. In contrast, #Actorawareness underlines the barriers faced by actors from working-class backgrounds, while the #MeToo movement continues to highlight the issue of gender-based power imbalances in the workplace (Newsinger & Eikhof 2020: 48). Simultaneously, the Black Lives Matter movement has focused the spotlight on the issue of racial inequality on an unprecedented international scale. Significantly, these developments have begun to have an impact inside film institutions. This was exemplified within the Hollywood studio system, for example, by the launch of Universal's Global Talent Development & Inclusion (GTDI) initiative in 2017. More recently, the BFI released a statement in which it acknowledged that, while the organisation was united against racism, it had not been 'actively antiracist'. Moreover, the statement declared a 'doubling-down on our duty as a public organisation', with an acknowledgement that 'the status quo in the film community is undoubtedly still a system that privileges whiteness, and it has persisted for too long' (BFI 2020b).

Operating within this changing social and political landscape, Working Title demonstrated an increasing commitment to diversity in its output with the release of three films in 2019 – *The Kid Who Would be King*, *Yesterday* and *Cats* – which prominently feature racially diverse casts. It is interesting to note that in addition to the economic, globalising and affinitive transnationalism which defines Transatlantic British Cinema, each film also features a prominent 'pre-sold' element. *The Kid Who Would be King*, for example, draws on the Arthurian legend, *Yesterday* is based upon the music of The Beatles and *Cats* is an adaptation of a long-running and highly successful stage musical. Simultaneously, the adaptation of *Four Weddings and a Funeral* into an equally diverse television show underlined this trend, albeit outside Working Title's direct influence. In these ways, the negotiation of risk can be viewed as a balancing act onscreen in which diversity has finally become another element to be reconciled in the interplay between creativity and commerce.

The strategies of creative and commercial risk management which define Transatlantic British Cinema, however, continue to sit uneasily alongside the social and political imperatives of diversity and inclusion. In practice, these impulses often remain siloed at opposite ends of the British film industry and British film culture. Within this dichotomy, Transatlantic British Cinema benefits from the market-friendly fiscal incentives designed to attract Hollywood investment without a necessary commitment to diversity, while independent British cinema is supported by interventionist film policies which work to preserve a space for diverse versions of Britain and Britishness onscreen. This situation effectively ensures that the former occupies the mainstream of British and global film culture, while the latter remains at the periphery. These distinctions have, however, been complicated by recent examples of Transatlantic British Cinema which, in various ways, demonstrate the compatibility of diversity with the creative and commercial management of risk. While these breakthroughs do not, of course, mean that the lack of diversity on display in the vast majority of Transatlantic British Cinema is an issue consigned to the past, they do at least suggest that progress is being made. The future is, of course, unwritten and it remains to be seen whether such progress is sustained long-term, and what Working Title's role in these unfolding developments may be. Nonetheless, the current direction of travel suggests that a transition is under way from an industrial context in which a commitment to diversity was too risky, to one in which a failure to embrace diversity presents new forms of risk.

Note

1 Tim Bevan, interview with the author, 7-12-2016.

Bibliography

Abrams, Rachel (2012), 'U renews its Elliott coin pact; But studio seeks new deal for 2013', *Daily Variety*, 1 October, p. 1.
Adams, Tim (2009), 'A shiny, happy place, relaxed about the filthy rich, insatiable in its optimism, in love with happy endings, and very New Labour. Welcome to Curtisland. . .', *The Observer* (Observer Film Quarterly), 22 March, p. 12.
Ajax, Scott (1991a), 'PolyGram plans $200m Expansion', *Screen International*, 27 September, p. 4.
Ajax, Scott (1991b), 'Working Title Creates Low-Dough Division', *Screen International*, 18 October, p. 3.
Ajax, Scott (1992), 'PolyGram/Palace pact awaits auditor's nod', *Screen International*, 27 March, p. 2.
Amdur, Meredith and Alison James (2004), 'Gauls tout big u-turn', *Daily Variety*, 18 March, p. 1.
Amdur, Meredith and Pamela McClintock (2004), 'Feds Bless NBC-U Wedding Plan', *Daily Variety*, 21 April, p. 4.
Andreeva, Nellie (2010), 'Working Title Launching TV Division', *The Hollywood Reporter*, 16 February, <https://www.hollywoodreporter.com/news/working-title-launching-tv-division-20722> (last accessed 23 August 2020).
Andrew, Dudley (2009), 'Time Zones and Jet Lag: The Flows and Phases of World Cinema', in Nataša Ďurovičová and Kathleen Newman (eds), *World Cinemas, Transnational Perspectives*, London: Routledge, pp. 59–89.
Bakker, Gerban (2006), 'The Making of a Music Multinational: PolyGram's International Businesses, 1945–1998', *Business History Review*, 80: 1, pp. 81–123.
Bamber, Jay (2020), '"American, a Slut, and Out of Your League": Working Title's Equivocal Relationship with Americanness', in Barbara Jane Brickman, Deborah Jermyn and Theodore Louis Trost (eds), *Love Across the Atlantic: US–UK Romance in Popular Culture*, Edinburgh: Edinburgh University Press, pp. 159–75.
Bart, Peter and Claudia Eller (2014), 'Inside Jeff Shell's First Year at Universal', *Variety*, 23 September, <https://variety.com/2014/film/news/jeff-shell-universal-chairman-first-year-1201312010/> (last accessed 23 August 2020).
Bevan, Tim (1985), 'Business or Charity?', *AIP & Co.*, 70, p. 32.
BFI (2011) *BFI Statistical Yearbook 2011*, British Film Institute. Available online, see BFI 2019a.
BFI (2012), *BFI Statistical Yearbook 2012*, British Film Institute. Available online, see BFI 2019a.
BFI (2013), *BFI Statistical Yearbook 2013*, British Film Institute. Available online, see BFI 2019a.
BFI (2014), *BFI Statistical Yearbook 2014*, British Film Institute. Available online, see BFI 2019a.
BFI (2015), *BFI Statistical Yearbook 2015*, British Film Institute. Available online, see BFI 2019a.
BFI (2016), *BFI Statistical Yearbook 2016*, British Film Institute. Available online, see BFI 2019a.

BFI (2017), *BFI Statistical Yearbook 2017*, British Film Institute. Available online, see BFI 2019a.
BFI (2018), *BFI Statistical Yearbook 2018*, British Film Institute. Available online, see BFI 2019a.
BFI (2019a), *BFI Statistical Yearbook 2019*, British Film Institute, <https://www.bfi.org.uk/industry-data-insights/statistical-yearbook> (last accessed 23 August 2020).
BFI (2019b), *BFI Diversity Standards Criteria*, British Film Institute, <https://www.bfi.org.uk/inclusion-film-industry/bfi-diversity-standards> (last accessed 23 August 2020).
BFI (2020a), *BFI Diversity Standards Initial Findings*, British Film Institute, <https://www.bfi.org.uk/industry-data-insights/reports/bfi-diversity-standards-initial-findings> (last accessed 23 August 2020).
BFI (2020b), 'A letter from Ben Roberts, BFI Chief Executive', British Film Institute, 17 June, <https://www.bfi.org.uk/news/letter-from-ben-roberts-bfi-chief-executive> (last accessed 23 August 2020).
Blanchard, Simon and Sylvia Harvey (1983), 'The Post-war Independent Cinema – Structure and Organisation', in James Curran and Vincent Porter (eds), *British Cinema History*, London: Weidenfeld and Nicolson, pp. 226–41.
Bradstreet, Graham (1988), 'Casebook 1: Sammy and Rosie Get Laid', *Screen International*, 14 May, p. 50.
Brown, Colin (1996), 'PolyGram picks up Gramercy', *Screen International*, 12 January, p. 2.
Brown, Colin (1999), 'Diller hunts down foreign sales pipeline for start-up USA Films', *Screen International*, 16 April, pp. 1–2.
Brown, William (2020), 'Bridget Jones's Special Relationship: No Filth, Please, We're Brexiteers', in Barbara Jane Brickman, Deborah Jermyn and Theodore Louis Trost (eds), *Love Across the Atlantic: US–UK Romance in Popular Culture*, Edinburgh: Edinburgh University Press, pp. 53–68.
Brunet, Johanne and Galina Gornostaeva (2006), 'Company profile: Working Title Films, independent producer: internationalization of the film industry', *International Journal of Arts Management*, 9: 1, pp. 60–9.
Brzeski, Patrick (2016a), 'Universal Finalises $250m Slate Deal with China's Perfect World, Plans to Raise Debt', *The Hollywood Reporter*, 17 February, <https://www.hollywoodreporter.com/news/universal-finalizes-250m-slate-deal-866613> (last accessed 23 August 2020).
Brzeski, Patrick, (2016b), 'China Exec who put $500m into Universal Pictures says "More to Come"', *The Hollywood Reporter*, 21 April, <https://www.hollywoodreporter.com/news/general-news/china-exec-who-put-500m-884961/> (last accessed 23 August 2020).
CAMEo (2018), *Workforce Diversity in the UK Screen Sector: Evidence Review*, Leicester: CAMEo Research Institute.
Carver, Benedict and Chris Petrikin (1998), 'U takes a Giant Gulp', *Daily Variety*, 11 December, p. 1.
Carver, Benedict (1999a), 'U abroad: A not-so-simple plan', *Variety*, 15–21 February, pp. 1 & 77.
Carver, Benedict (1999b), 'Variety facts on pacts', *Variety*, 28 June–11 July, p. 84.
Chapman, James (2005), *Past and Present: National Identity and the British Historical Film*, London: I.B. Tauris.
Chu, Henry and Stewart Clarke (2018), 'Sky Auction: Comcast Beats Fox with $39 billion bid', *Variety*, 22 September, <https://variety.com/2018/tv/news/comcast-wins-battle-sky-bid-defeats-fox-1202952781/> (last accessed 23 August 2020).
Crofts, Stephen (1993), 'Reconceptualising National Cinema/s', *Quarterly Review of Film and Video*, 14: 3, pp. 49–67.
Crompton, Sarah (2001), 'Curtis Land in 10 steps: Alluring weather, vast houses, backdrops

like a florists' convention … and look – here's lovely Hugh Grant! In *Bridget Jones's Diary*, Richard Curtis returns us to his fairy-tale vision of England', *The Daily Telegraph*, 7 April, p. 9.

Daily Variety (2011), 'U toppers shake up exec tier', *Daily Variety*, 3 May, p. 1.

Dave, Paul (2006), *Visions of England: Class and Culture in Contemporary Cinema*, Oxford: Berg.

Davidson, Andrew (1992), *Under the Hammer: Inside Story of the ITV 1991 Franchise Battle*, London: William Heinemann.

Davies, Nina (1986), 'I Did it my Way', *AIP & Co.*, 73, pp. 26–7.

Dawtrey, Adam (1988), 'Financing of Channel Four films hit as interest of US distributors dries up', *Screen Finance*, 5 October, pp. 1–2 & 17–19.

Dawtrey, Adam (1989), 'British Screen joins Channel Four in giving distribution cash for two films', *Screen Finance*, 12 July, pp. 1–2.

Dawtrey, Adam (1992), 'Initial Sold to B'cast, Will Quit Film Prod'n', *Daily Variety*, 27 July, p. 14.

Dawtrey, Adam (1997), 'Bidders ask UK to give 'em lots drawn to UK Pic Lottery', *Daily Variety*, 27 April, p. 1.

Dawtrey, Adam (1998), 'Can Old Distrib Learn New Tricks?', *Variety*, 15–21 June, p. 7.

Dawtrey, Adam (1999a), 'Late Library Liaison: Carlton gets U's ITC package in overdue deal', *Daily Variety*, 20 January, p. 8.

Dawtrey, Adam (1999b), 'Working Title duo to stay', *Daily Variety*, 26 March, p. 1.

Dawtrey, Adam (1999c) 'Working, U toiling for Canal cash', *Daily Variety*, 29 March, p. 1.

Dawtrey, Adam (1999d), 'U Nails Plus Pact', *Daily Variety*, 14 May, p. 8.

Dawtrey, Adam (1999e). 'The Till is gone as UPI unwinds its operation', *Daily Variety*, 13 December, p. 22.

Dawtrey, Adam (1999f), 'Working Title Taps Vets, Wright, Granger', *Daily Variety*, 9 July, p. 27.

Dawtrey, Adam (1999g), 'Working Title bows WT2', *Daily Variety*, 18 May, p. 12.

Dawtrey, Adam (1999h), 'Brit Wits Dig Mitts into Pix', *Variety*, 12–18 July, p. 7.

Dawtrey, Adam (2000a), 'Heavyweight helmers head to Working Title', *Daily Variety*, 8 December, p. 1.

Dawtrey, Adam (2000b), 'SPECIAL ASSIGNMENT: UPI's London marketing team gets reprieve', *Daily Variety*, 9 February, p. 16.

Dawtrey, Adam (2005), 'Working Title Shuffles Crew', *Daily Variety*, 21 June, p. 4.

Dawtrey, Adam (2006a), 'Euros buy creative freedom', *Variety*, 23–9 October, p. 1.

Dawtrey, Adam, (2006b), 'U's New Arm Accents Foreign Clout', *Variety*, 9–15 October, p. 10.

Dawtrey, Adam and Benedict Carver (1999), 'Canal Plus near deal to join Working Title, U', *Daily Variety*, 10 May, p. 1.

Dawtrey, Adam and Don Groves (2003), 'Exex top build London bridge for Universal', *Daily Variety*, 11 September, p. 1.

DCMS (1998), *A Bigger Picture: The Report of the Film Policy Review Group*. London: Department for Culture, Media and Sport.

Decker, Lindsey (2016), 'British cinema is undead: American horror, British comedy and generic hybridity in *Shaun of the Dead*', *Transnational Cinemas*, 7: 1, pp. 67–81.

Dickinson, Margaret and Sarah Street (1985), *Cinema and State: The Film Industry and the British Government 1927–84*, London: BFI Publishing.

Dickinson, Margaret and Sylvia Harvey (2005), 'Film policy in the United Kingdom: New Labour at the movies', *Political Quarterly*, 76: 3, pp. 420–9.

Doyle, Gillian (2014), 'Film support and the challenge of "sustainability": on wing design, wax and feathers, and bolts from the blue', *Journal of British Cinema and Television*, 11: 2–3, pp. 129–51.

Dupin, Christophe (2012), 'The BFI and Film Production: Half a Century of Innovative Independent Film-making', in Geoffrey Nowell-Smith and Christophe Dupin (eds), *The British Film Institute, the Government and Film Culture, 1933–2000*, Manchester: Manchester University Press, pp. 197–218.

Ezra, Elizabeth and Terry Rowden (2006), 'General Introduction: What is Transnational Cinema?', in Elizabeth Ezra and Terry Rowden, *Transnational Cinema: The Film Reader*, Abingdon: Routledge, pp. 1–12.

Farrow, Boyd (1992), 'Gramercy set for Autumn Bow', *Screen International*, 22 May, p. 1.

FD Newswire (2005), 'NBC Universal Analyst Meeting – Final', *FD (Fair Disclosure) Newswire*, 15 February.

Fleming, Michael (2008), 'U puts focus on family pix', *Daily Variety*, 6 March, p. 1.

Frater, Patrick (1998), 'Four Bidders and a Funeral', *Screen International*, 25 September, p. 14.

Freeman, Matthew (2016), *Industrial Approaches to Media: A Methodological Gateway to Industry Studies*, London: Palgrave MacMillan.

Gardner, Eriq (2014), 'Universal Studios, Studiocanal Settle Multimillion-Dollar Lawsuit', *The Hollywood Reporter*, 6 January, <https://www.hollywoodreporter.com/thr-esq/universal-studios-studiocanal-settle-multimillion-668572> (last accessed 23 August 2020).

Garrett, Diane (2008), 'U's banking on Relativity', *Daily Variety*, 28 February, p. 1.

George, Sandy (2003), 'Working Title readies New Zealand Number', *Screen International*, 27 October, n.p.

Goldsmith, Jill and Alison James (2000), 'Fait Accompli: French conglom, Canal Plus & Seagram boards OK merger', *Daily Variety*, 20 June, p. 1.

Goldsmith, Jill (2013), 'Die is Comcast; Cable giant, looking to expand content offerings, cements status as sole owner of NBCU entertainment assets with $16.7 billion deal buyout of GE', *Daily Variety*, 13 February, p. 1.

Goodridge, Mike (2000), 'Universal dubs specialised arm Universal Focus', *Screen Daily*, 29 June, <https://www.screendaily.com/universal-dubs-specialised-arm-universal-focus/402834.article> (last accessed 23 August 2020).

Graser, Marc (2009a), 'U's brand new world', *Variety*, 27 April–3 May, p. 1.

Graser, Marc (2009b), 'Two swaps at the top', *Daily Variety*, 6 October, p. 1.

Groves, Don (1989) 'PolyGram, Working Title and Propaganda form Manifesto, global sales firm in London', *Variety*, 19–25 July, pp. 3 & 7.

Harris, Dana and Carl DiOrio (2002), 'Good Machine Buy Alters Focus at U', *Daily Variety*, 3 May, p. 1.

Harvey, Sylvia (1989), 'Deregulation, Innovation and Channel Four', *Screen*, 30: 1–2, pp. 60–79.

Havens, Timothy, Amanda D. Lotz and Serra Tinic (2009), 'Critical Media Industry Studies: A Research Approach', *Communication, Culture & Critique*, 2: 2, pp. 234–53.

Hazelton, John (2018), 'Ex-Working Title executive Liza Chasin launches 3dot Productions', *Screen Daily*, 21 March, <https://www.screendaily.com/news/ex-working-title-executive-liza-chasin-launches-3dot-productions/5127687.article> (last accessed 23 August 2020).

Hedling, Erik (1997), 'Lindsay Anderson and the Development of British Art Cinema', in Robert Murphy (ed.), *The British Cinema Book*, London: BFI Publishing, pp. 178–86.

Higson, Andrew (1989), 'The Concept of National Cinema', *Screen*, 30: 4, pp. 36–46.

Higson, Andrew (1995), *Waving the Flag: Constructing a National Cinema in Britain*, Oxford: Oxford University Press.

Hill, John (1993), 'Government Policy and the British Film Industry 1979–90', *European Journal of Communication*, 8: 2, pp. 203–24.

Hill, John (1996). 'British Television and Film: The Making of a Relationship', in John Hill and Martin McLoone (eds), *Big Picture, Small Screen: The Relations between Film and Television*, Luton: University of Luton Press, pp. 151–76.

Hill, John (1997), 'British Cinema as National Cinema: Production, Audience and Representation', in Robert Murphy (ed.), *The British Cinema Book*, London: BFI Publishing, pp. 244–54.

Hill, John (2004), 'UK film policy, cultural capital and social exclusion', *Cultural Trends*, 13: 2, pp. 29–39.

Hill, John (2012), '"This is for the *Batmans* as well as the *Vera Drakes*": Economics, Culture and UK Government Film Production Policy in the 2000s', *Journal of British Cinema and Television*, 9: 3, pp. 333–56.

Hill, John (2016), 'Living with Hollywood: British film policy and the definition of "nationality"', *International Journal of Cultural Policy*, 22: 5, pp. 706–23.

Hjort, Mette (2009), 'On the Plurality of Cinematic Transnationalism', in Nataša Ďurovičová and Kathleen Newman (eds), *World Cinemas, Transnational Perspectives*, London: Routledge, pp. 12–33.

Hochscherf, Tobias and James Leggott (2010), 'Working Title Films: from mid-Atlantic to the heart of Europe?', *Film International*, 8: 6, pp. 8–20.

Hofmann, Katja (2003), 'WT2's the "baby" label, from genre pix to Ali G', *Variety*, 10–16 November, p. 6.

Hofmann, Katja (2006), 'Working hard for the money: A who's who of company principals: Natascha Wharton', *Variety*, 23–9 October, p. 2.

Hollinger, Hy (2007), 'PPI, UPI: New era for o'seas output', *The Hollywood Reporter*, 2 January, <https://www.hollywoodreporter.com/news/ppi-upi-new-era-oseas-127037> (last accessed 23 August 2020).

Holt, Jennifer and Alisa Perren (2009), 'Does the World Really Need One More Field of Study?', in Jennifer Holt and Alisa Perren (eds), *Media Industries: History, Theory, and Method*, Malden: Wiley-Blackwell, pp. 1–16.

Honess Roe, Annabelle (2009), 'A special relationship? The coupling of Britain and America in Working Title's romantic comedies', in Stacey Abbott and Deborah Jermyn (eds), *Falling in Love Again: Romantic Comedy in Contemporary Cinema*, London: I. B. Tauris, pp. 79–91.

Hopewell, John (2012), 'Creative punch meets biz savvy; Studiocanal topper changed the company into international film and TV powerhouse', *Daily Variety*, 14 May, p. 79.

Hopewell, John and Elsa Keslassy (2012), 'Ace deal for gaul; Studiocanal reups slate financing', *Daily Variety*, 28 November, p. 8.

Ilott, Terry (1986), 'British Screen, Palace and Zenith set joint sales arm', *Screen International*, 5 July, pp. 1–2.

Ilott, Terry (1991), 'PolyGram buying Nelson's deal', *Variety*, 7 October , pp. 5 & 29.

Isaacs, Jeremy (1989), *Storm Over 4: A Personal Account*, London: Weidenfeld and Nicolson.

Jaafar, Ali (2009), 'U gives exec a global gig', *Daily Variety*, 22 July, p. 1.

James, Alison (2000), 'Canal changes name, ups coin for pic prod'n', *Daily Variety*, 20 April, p. 1.

James, Alison (2004), 'Studiocanal restructures with focus on more mainstream fare', *Variety*, 10–16 May, p. 20.

Johnson, Ted (2013), 'Studiocanal Sues Universal', *Daily Variety*, 1 March, p. 28.

Jones, Huw (2017), 'The box office performance of European films in the UK market', *Studies in European Cinema*, 14: 2, pp. 153–71.

Kay, Jeremy (2006a), 'Sony, Universal hatch co-financing pacts with Relativity', *Screen Daily*, 19 January, <https://www.screendaily.com/sony-universal-hatch-co-financing-pacts-with-relativity/4025811.article> (last accessed 23 August 2020).

Kay, Jeremy (2006b), 'Relativity sets up Gunn Hill Road II co-financing with Sony, Universal', *Screen Daily*, 12 May, <https://www.screendaily.com/relativity-sets-up-gun-hill-road-ii-co-financing-with-sony-universal/4027161.article> (last accessed 23 August 2020).

Kay, Jeremy (2020), 'Universal, Working Title renew first-look deal through 2025', *Screen Daily*, 11 December, <https://www.screendaily.com/news/universal-working-title-renew-first-look-deal-through-2025/5155651.article> (last accessed 6 January 2021).

Kellner, Douglas (2009), 'Media Industries, Political Economy, and Media/Cultural Studies: An Articulation', in Jennifer Holt and Alisa Perren (eds), *Media Industries: History, Theory, and Method*, Malden: Wiley-Blackwell, pp. 95–107.

Kent, Nicolas (1987), 'Commissioning Editor', *Monthly Film Bulletin*, Autumn, 56: 4, pp. 260–3.

Kilday, Gregg (2012), 'Universal Extends its Pact with Working Title Films Through 2015', *The Hollywood Reporter*, 27 April, <https://www.hollywoodreporter.com/news/universal-extends-pact-working-title-films-les-miserables-317579> (last accessed 23 August 2020).

Kuhn, Michael (2002), *One Hundred Films and a Funeral*, London: Thorogood.

Kureishi, Hanif (1986), *My Beautiful Laundrette and The Rainbow Sign*, London: Faber and Faber.

Lambert, Stephen (1982), *Channel 4: Television with a Difference?* London: BFI Publishing.

Lang, Brent (2015), 'Universal Boss Jeff Shell Leads Studio to Its Best Year Ever — Without Superheroes', *Variety*, 17 November, <https://variety.com/2015/film/features/jeff-shell-universal-2015-jurassic-world-furious-7-pitch-perfect-1201641846/> (last accessed 23 August 2020).

Lay, Samantha (2007), 'Good Intentions, High Hopes and Low Budgets: Contemporary Social Realist Film-making in Britain', *New Cinemas: Journal of Contemporary Film*, 5: 3, pp. 231–44.

Leggott, James (2012), 'Travels in Curtisland: Richard Curtis and British Comedy Cinema', in I.Q. Hunter and Laraine Porter (eds), *British Comedy Cinema*, London: Routledge, pp. 184–95.

Littleton, Cynthia (2012), 'NBCU Intl. unity mighty from Blighty', *Daily Variety*, 29 May, p. 2.

Lotz, Amanda, D and Horace Newcomb (2011), 'The Production of Entertainment Media', in Klaus Bruhn Jensen (ed.), *A Handbook of Media and Communication Research: Qualitative and Quantitative Methodologies*, 2nd Edition, Abingdon: Routledge, pp. 71–86.

LSA (2019), 'London Screen Academy 2019/20 Prospectus', London Screen Academy, <https://lsa.ac.uk/admissions> (last accessed 23 August 2020).

Mackie, Lindsay (1986), 'Thou Shalt Not Be Profligate With Thy Budget', *AIP & Co.*, 71, pp. 22–3.

Magor, Maggie and Philip Schlesinger (2009), '"For this relief much thanks." Taxation, film policy and the UK government', *Screen*, 50: 3, pp. 299–317.

Masters, Kim (2013), 'Jeff Shell Moving to Universal Studios Job; Adam Fogelson Out', *The Hollywood Reporter*, 9 September, <https://www.hollywoodreporter.com/news/jeff-shell-moving-universal-studios-624678> (last accessed 23 August 2020).

Mayne, Laura (2012), '"Creative Commissioning": Examining the Regional Aesthetic in the Work of Channel 4's First Commissioning Editor for Fiction, David Rose', *Journal of British Cinema and Television*, 9: 1, pp. 40–57.

McClintock, Pamela and Scott Roxborough (2014), 'Cannes: Market to Open with Few Stars,

Less Buzz', *The Hollywood Reporter*, 13 May, <https://www.hollywoodreporter.com/news/cannes-market-open-few-stars-703739> (last accessed 23 August 2020).

McClintock, Pamela and Tatiana Siegel (2016), 'Focus Features Shake-Up: What's Behind Peter Schlessel's Abrupt Exit', *The Hollywood Reporter*, 9 February, <https://www.hollywoodreporter.com/news/focus-features-shake-up-whats-862969> (last accessed 23 August 2020).

McDonald, Paul (2008), 'Britain: Hollywood, UK', in Paul McDonald and Janet Wasko (eds), *The Contemporary Hollywood Film Industry*, Malden: Blackwell Publishing, pp. 220–31.

McDonald, Paul (2013), 'Introduction', *Cinema Journal*, 52: 3, pp. 145–9.

McGahan, A. M. (1993), 'The Incentive Not to Invest: Capacity Commitments in the Compact Disc Introduction', *Research on Technological Innovation, Management and Policy*, 5, pp. 177–97.

McNary, Dave (2000), 'Black Tower Tries U Turn', *Variety*, 8–14 May, p. 1.

McNary, Dave (2005), 'U-Par divorce decree', *Daily Variety*, 7 September, p. 1.

McNary, Dave (2016), 'Facts on Pacts: Studio-Producer Deals Retreat as Sony, Warner Bros. Pull Back', *Variety*, 24 March, <https://variety.com/2016/film/news/studio-producers-deals-1201736686/> (last accessed 23 August 2020).

Meehan, Eileen R. and Janet Wasko (2013), 'In Defence of a Political Economy of the Media', *Javnost – The Public*, 20: 1, pp. 39–53.

Meir, Christopher (2016), 'Studiocanal and the Changing Industrial Landscape of European Cinema and Television', *Media Industries*, 3: 1, pp. 49–64.

Meir, Christopher (2019), *Mass Producing European Cinema: Studiocanal and its Works*, London: Bloomsbury Academic.

Moody, Paul (2017), 'The UK Film Council and the "Cultural Diversity" Agenda', *Journal of British Cinema and Television*, 14: 4, pp. 403–22.

Moore, Oscar (1990), 'Initial Executives Close Buyout Deal', *Screen International*, 30 June, p. 2.

Mosco, Vincent (2009), *The Political Economy of Communication*, 2nd Edition, London: Sage Publications.

MPAA (2001), *2001 US Economic Review*, Motion Picture Association of America.

MPAA (2007), *Theatrical Market Statistics 2007*, Motion Picture Association of America.

MPAA (2012), *Theatrical Market Statistics 2012*, Motion Picture Association of America.

MPAA (2016), *Theatrical Market Statistics 2015*, Motion Picture Association of America.

MPAA (2018), *2018 THEME REPORT*, Motion Picture Association of America.

Murphy, Robert (2001), 'Citylife: urban fairy-tales in late 90s British cinema', in Robert Murphy (ed.), *The British Cinema Book*, 2nd Edition, London: BFI Publishing, pp. 292–300.

Newsinger, Jack (2012), 'British Film Policy in an Age of Austerity', *Journal of British Cinema and Television*, 9: 1, pp. 133–44.

Newsinger, Jack and Steve Presence (2018), 'United Kingdom: Film Funding, the "Corporate Welfare System" and its Discontents', in Paul Clemens Murschetz, Roland Teichmann and Matthias Karmasin (eds), *Handbook of State Aid for Film: Finance, Industries and Regulation*, New York: Springer, pp. 447–62.

Newsinger, Jack and Doris Ruth Eikhof (2020), 'Explicit and Implicit Diversity Policy in the UK Film and Television Industries', *Journal of British Cinema and Television*, 17: 1, pp. 47–69.

North, Alex (1986), 'Comrade Relph: The State in the Industry', *AIP & Co.*, 73, pp. 10–11.

Nwonka, Clive James (2015), 'Diversity pie: rethinking social exclusion and diversity policy in the British film industry', *Journal of Media Practice*, 16: 1, pp. 73–90.

Nwonka, Clive James (2020), 'Race and Ethnicity in the UK Film Industry: An Analysis of the BFI Diversity Standards', British Film Institute, <https://www.bfi.org.uk/industry-data-insights/reports/diversity-reports> (last accessed 23 August 2020).

Oppelaar, Justin and Carl DiOrio (2001), 'Vivendi pens first page of synergy saga', *Daily Variety*, 18 December, p. 1.

Paterson, Richard (1992), 'Changing Conditions of Independent Production in the UK', in Duncan Petrie (ed.), *New Questions of British Cinema*, London: BFI Publishing, pp. 40–51.

Peake, Tony (1999), *Derek Jarman*, London: Little, Brown and Company.

Pearson, Nichola (1988), 'Of Credits and Titles', *Producer*, Spring: 3, pp. 22–3.

Peers, Martin and Anita Busch (1996), 'Kirk's the Lion King Again: Mancuso team victorious with $1.3 billion bid', *Daily Variety*, 17 July, p. 1.

Peers, Martin (1998a), 'Seagram Sings New Tune: PolyGram deal transforms firm', *Daily Variety*, 22 May, p. 1.

Peers, Martin (1998b), 'MGM seals PFE library pact', *Daily Variety*, 12 November, p. 8.

Peers, Martin and Chris Petrikin (1999), 'MGM exits UIP but Par, U stay true', *Variety*, 28 June–11 July, p. 14.

Petley, Julian (1985a), 'Experience Preferred and Essential', *AIP & Co.*, 67, pp. 14–15.

Petley, Julian (1985b), 'Which Way for the Board?', *AIP & Co.*, 64, pp. 16–17.

Petrie, Duncan (1991), *Creativity and Constraint in the British Film Industry*, London: Macmillan.

Producer (1988), 'Levelling out the terms', *Producer*, Winter: 6, pp. 24–5.

Pym, John (1992), *Film on Four: A Survey 1982/1991*, London: BFI Publishing.

Rainey, James (2015), 'Ryan Kavanaugh Left Adrift in Hollywood as Relativity Implodes', *Variety*, 5 August, <https://variety.com/2015/biz/news/ryan-kavanaugh-relativity-adrift-1201556461/> (last accessed 23 August 2020).

Ritman, Alex (2015), 'Universal, Working Title Extend Production Deal Through 2020', *The Hollywood Reporter*, 5 June, <https://www.hollywoodreporter.com/news/universal-working-title-extend-production-800326> (last accessed 23 August 2020).

Romer, Stephen (1992), 'Production Strategies in the UK', in Duncan Petrie (ed.), *New Questions of British Cinema*, London: BFI Publishing, pp. 65–75.

Russell, James (2017), 'Hollywood Blockbusters and UK Production Today', in I.Q. Hunter, Laraine Poter and Justin Smith (eds), *The Routledge Companion to British Cinema History*, London: Routledge, pp. 377–86.

Ryall, Tom (2001), *Britain and the American Cinema*, London: Sage Publications.

Schatz, Thomas (2009), 'New Hollywood, New Millenium', in Warren Buckland (ed.), *Film Theory and Contemporary Hollywood Movies*, New York: Routledge, pp. 19–46.

Screen International (1985), 'New Trade Body for Music Video Industry', *Screen International*, 7 December, p. 34.

Screen International (1987a), 'Gavin Films Ears Pricked for Prizes', *Screen International*, 2 May, pp. 61 & 229.

Screen International (1987b), 'Atlantic Pays Top Price for C4 film', *Screen International*, 16 May, p. 2.

Smith, Bec and Stuart Kemp (2005), (no headline in original), *The Hollywood Reporter*, 19 May, n.p.

Snyder, Gabriel (2006), 'Pair has Universal appeal', *Daily Variety*, 17 March, p. 1.

Stern, Andy (1999), 'EU to renew 5-year UIP exemption', *Daily Variety*, 7 September, p. 31.

Street, Sarah (1997), *British National Cinema*, London: Routledge.

Street, Sarah (2002), *Transatlantic Crossings: British Feature Films in the USA*, London: Continuum.

Szalai, Georg (2009), 'Comcast, NBC Universal deal announced', *The Hollywood Reporter*, 3 December, <https://www.hollywoodreporter.com/news/comcast-nbc-universal-deal-announced-91948> (last accessed 23 August 2020).

Szalai, Georg (2013), 'NBCUniversal International TV Production Hires JoAnn Alfano to Run Scripted Business', *The Hollywood Reporter*, 4 September, <https://www.hollywood

reporter.com/news/nbcuniversal-international-tv-production-hires-620710> (last accessed 23 August 2020).

Szalai, Georg, (2016a), 'NBCUniversal to Acquire Dreamworks Animation in $3.8B Deal', *The Hollywood Reporter*, 28 April, <https://www.hollywoodreporter.com/news/comcast-acquire-dreamworks-animation-888103> (last accessed 23 August 2020).

Szalai, Georg (2016b), 'Working Title Television U.K. Names Andrew Woodhead Managing Director', *The Hollywood Reporter*, 9 March, <https://www.hollywoodreporter.com/news/working-title-television-uk-names-873792> (last accessed 23 August 2020).

Szalai, Georg and Paul Gough (2008), 'Layoffs pile up at media firms', *The Hollywood Reporter*, 5 December, <https://www.hollywoodreporter.com/news/layoffs-pile-up-at-media-123949> (last accessed 23 August 2020).

Tingley, Anna (2019), 'TV News Roundup: "Veronica Mars", "Four Weddings and a Funeral" Set Hulu Premiere Dates', *Variety*, 12 April, <https://variety.com/2019/tv/news/veronica-mars-four-weddings-and-a-funeral-premiere-date-hulu-1203188580/> (last accessed 23 August 2020).

The Stage and Television Today (1984), 'Comic Doc from Working Title', *The Stage and Television Today*, 26 July, p. 16.

Thompson, Anne and Stuart Kemp (2007), 'Working Title re-ups with Universal', *The Hollywood Reporter*, 15 January, <https://www.hollywoodreporter.com/news/working-title-ups-universal-127951> (last accessed 23 August 2020).

Townsend, Nathan (2014), 'The Trans/national Divide: Towards a Typology of "Transatlantic British Cinema" during the 1930s and 1940s', in Laura Mee and Johnny Walker (eds), *Cinema, Television & History: New Approaches*, Newcastle upon Tyne: Cambridge Scholars Publishing, pp. 121–41.

Townsend, Nathan (2018a), 'PolyGram Filmed Entertainment and Working Title Films: The making of a film studio and its production label', *Historical Journal of Film, Radio and Television*, 38: 3, pp. 555–83.

Townsend, Nathan (2018b), 'Working Title Films and Universal: The integration of a British production company into a Hollywood studio', *Journal of British Cinema and Television*, 15: 2, pp. 179–203.

Townsend, Nathan (2019), 'WT^2: a low budget experiment in "heart, humour and horror"' *Studies in European Cinema*, 16: 1, pp. 38–54.

Townsend, Nathan (2020), 'PolyGram Filmed Entertainment and Working Title Films Part II: The rise and fall of a film studio', *Historical Journal of Film, Radio and Television*, 40: 4, pp. 772–803.

UKFC (2002), *UK Film Council Statistical Yearbook 2002*, UK Film Council. Available online, see UKFC 2010.

UKFC (2009), *UK Film Council Statistical Yearbook 2009*, UK Film Council. Available online, see UKFC 2010.

UKFC (2010), *UK Film Council Statistical Yearbook 2010*, UK Film Council, <https://www.bfi.org.uk/industry-data-insights/statistical-yearbook> (last accessed 23 August 2020).

Variety (1999) 'Variety's Global 50', *Variety*, 23–9 August, p. 49.

Variety (2009), 'Facts on Pacts', *Variety*, 14 September, p. 48.

Variety (2011a), 'Going it on her own; Working Title exec launches shingle', *Daily Variety*, 17 June, p. 12.

Variety (2011b), 'Focus spies "Tinker" date', *Daily Variety*, 2 June, p. 2.

Vaucher, Andrea and Justin Oppelaar (2002), 'Viv topper is French toast', *Daily Variety*, 2 July, p. 1.

Wasko, Janet (2003), *How Hollywood Works*, London: Sage Publications.
Wasko, Janet and Eileen R. Meehan (2013), 'Critical Crossroads or Parallel Routes? Political Economy and New Approaches to Studying Media Industries and Cultural Products', *Cinema Journal*, 52: 3, pp. 150–7.
Wayne, Michael (2006), 'Working Title Mark II: a critique of the Atlanticist paradigm for British cinema', *International Journal of Media and Cultural Politics*, 2: 1, pp. 59–73.
Wilkinson, Kenton T. and Patrick F. Merle (2013), 'The Merits and Challenges of Using Business Press and Trade Journal Reports in Academic Research on Media Industries', *Communication, Culture and Critique*, 6: 3, pp. 415–31.
Williams, Christopher (1996), 'The Social Art Cinema: A Moment in the History of British Film and Television Culture', in Christopher Williams (ed.), *Cinema: the Beginnings and the Future*, London: University of Westminster Press, pp. 190–200.
Williams, Michael and Benedict Carver (1998), 'Canal Plus quits PolyGram talks', *Variety*, 23–9 November, pp. 7 & 11.

Filmography

The Independent Years (1984–8)

Title	Year	Director	Writer	Producer	Cast
My Beautiful Laundrette	1985	Stephen Frears	Hanif Kureishi	Tim Bevan, Sarah Radclyffe	Daniel Day-Lewis, Gordon Warnecke, Saeed Jaffrey
Caravaggio*	1986	Derek Jarman	Nicholas Ward-Jackson, Derek Jarman	Sarah Radclyffe	Nigel Terry, Sean Bean, Tilda Swinton
Personal Services**	1987	Terry Jones	David Leland	Tim Bevan	Julie Walters, Shirley Stelfox, Alec McCowen
Wish You Were Here	1987	David Leland	David Leland	Sarah Radclyffe	Emily Lloyd, Tom Bell, Jesse Birdsall
Sammy and Rosie Get Laid	1987	Stephen Frears	Hanif Kureishi	Tim Bevan, Sarah Radclyffe	Ayub Khan Din, Frances Barber, Shashi Kapoor
A World Apart	1988	Chris Menges	Shawn Slovo	Sarah Radclyffe	Barbara Hershey, Jodhi May, David Suchet

* Produced by the BFI
** Produced by British Screen/ Zenth Entertainment

The PolyGram Years (1988–98)

Title	Year	Director	Writer	Producer	Cast
Paperhouse	1988	Bernard Rose	Matthew Jacobs	Tim Bevan, Sarah Radclyffe	Charlotte Burke, Glenne Headly, Ben Cross
For Queen & Country	1989	Martin Stellman	Martin Stellman, Trix Worrell	Tim Bevan	Denzel Washington, Dorian Healy, Amanda Redman

Title	Year	Director	Writer	Producer	Cast
The Tall Guy	1989	Mel Smith	Richard Curtis	Paul Webster	Jeff Goldblum, Emma Thompson, Rowan Atkinson
Diamond Skulls	1989	Nick Broomfield	Tim Rose-Price	Tim Bevan	Gabriel Byrne, Amanda Donohoe, Struan Rodger
Chicago Joe and the Showgirl	1990	Bernard Rose	David Yallop	Tim Bevan	Kiefer Sutherland, Emily Lloyd, Liz Fraser
Fools of Fortune	1990	Pat O'Connor	Michael Hirst	Sarah Radclyffe	Julie Christie, Iain Glen, Mary Elizabeth Mastrantonio
Drop Dead Fred	1991	Ate De Jong	Carlos Davis, Anthony Fingleton	Paul Webster	Phoebe Cates, Rik Mayall, Marsha Mason
Rubin and Ed	1991	Trent Harris	Trent Harris	Paul Webster	Crispin Glover, Howard Hesseman, Karen Black
Edward II	1991	Derek Jarman	Derek Jarman, Stephen McBride, Ken Butler	Stephen Clark-Hall, Anthony Root	Steven Waddington, Andrew Tiernan, Tilda Swinton
Robin Hood	1991	John Irvin	Sam Resnick, John McGrath	Tim Bevan, Sarah Radclyffe	Patrick Bergin, Uma Thurman, Jürgen Prochnow
London Kills Me	1991	Hanif Kureishi	Hanif Kureishi	Tim Bevan, Graham Bradstreet	Justin Chadwick, Steven Mackintosh, Fiona Shaw
Dakota Road	1991	Nick Ward	Nick Ward	Donna Grey	David Bamber, Amelda Brown, Jason Carter
Bob Roberts	1992	Tim Robbins	Tim Robbins	Forrest Murray	Tim Robbins, Giancarlo Esposito, Alan Rickman
Map of the Human Heart	1992	Vincent Ward	Louis Nowra	Tim Bevan, Vincent Ward	Patrick Bergin, Anne Parillaud, Jason Scott Lee

(continued)

Title	Year	Director	Writer	Producer	Cast
The Young Americans	1993	Danny Cannon	Danny Cannon, David Hilton	Alison Owen, Paul Trijbits	Harvey Keitel, Iain Glen, Viggo Mortensen
Romeo is Bleeding	1993	Peter Medak	Hilary Henkin	Paul Webster, Hilary Henkin	Gary Oldman, Lena Olin, Annabella Sciorra
Posse	1993	Mario Van Peebles	Sy Richardson, Sario Scardapone	Preston L. Holmes, Jim Steele	Mario Van Peebles, Stephen Baldwin, Charles Lane
The Hudsucker Proxy	1994	Joel Coen	Joel Coen, Ethan Coen, Sam Raimi	Ethan Coen	Tim Robbins, Jennifer Jason Leigh, Paul Newman
Four Weddings and a Funeral	1994	Mike Newell	Richard Curtis	Duncan Kenworthy	Hugh Grant, Andie MacDowell, Kristin Scott Thomas
That Eye, The Sky	1994	John Ruane	John Ruane, Jim Barton	Grainne Marmion, Peter Beilby	Peter Coyote, Lisa Harrow, Amanda Douge
Panther	1995	Mario Van Peebles	Melvin Van Peebles	Mario Van Peebles, Melvin Van Peebles, Preston L. Holmes	Kadeem Hardison, Bokeem Woodbine, Courtney B. Vance
French Kiss	1995	Lawrence Kasdan	Adam Brooks	Tim Bevan, Eric Fellner, Kathryn F. Galan, Meg Ryan	Meg Ryan, Kevin Kline, Timothy Hutton
Moonlight and Valentino	1995	David Anspaugh	Ellen Simon	Tim Bevan, Eric Fellner, Alsion Owen	Elizabeth Perkins, Whoopi Goldberg, Gwyneth Paltrow
Dead Man Walking	1995	Tim Robbins	Tim Robbins	Tim Robbins, Jon Kilik, Rudd Simmons	Susan Sarandon, Sean Penn, Robert Prosky
Loch Ness	1996	John Henderson	John Fusco	Tim Bevan, Eric Fellner, Steve Ujlaki	Ted Danson, Joely Richardson, Ian Holm
Fargo	1996	Joel Coen	Joel Coen, Ethan Coen	Ethan Coen	Frances McDormand, William H. Macy, Steve Buscemi

Title	Year	Director	Writer	Producer	Cast
The Matchmaker	1997	Mark Joffe	Greg Dinner, Karen Janszen, Louis Nowra, Graham Linehan	Tim Bevan, Eric Fellner, Luc Roeg	Janeane Garofalo, David O'Hara, Milo O'Shea
Bean	1997	Mel Smith	Richard Curtis, Robin Driscoll	Peter Bennett-Jones, Tim Bevan, Eric Fellner	Rowan Atkinson, Peter MacNicol, Burt Reynolds
The Borrowers	1997	Peter Hewitt	Gavin Scott, John Kamps	Tim Bevan, Eric Fellner, Rachel Talalay	John Goodman, Jim Broadbent, Celia Imrie
The Big Lebowski	1998	Joel Coen	Joel Coen, Ethan Coen	Ethan Coen	Jeff Bridges, John Goodman, Julianne Moore
What Rats Won't Do	1998	Alastair Reid	Steve Coombs, Dave Robinson, William Osborne	Tim Bevan, Eric Fellner, Simon Wright	James Frain, Natascha McElhone, Parker Posey
Elizabeth	1998	Shekhar Kapur	Michael Hirst	Tim Bevan, Eric Fellner, Alsion Owen	Cate Blanchett, Geoffrey Rush, Joseph Fiennes

WT² (1999–2007)

Title	Year	Director	Writer	Producer	Cast
Billy Elliot	2000	Stephen Daldry	Lee Hall	Greg Brenman, Jon Finn	Jamie Bell, Gary Lewis, Julie Walters
Long Time Dead	2002	Marcus Adams	Marcus Adams	James Gay-Reed	Alec Newman, Marsha Thomason, Joe Absolom
Ali G Indahouse	2002	Mark Mylod	Sacha Baron Cohen, Dan Mazer	Tim Bevan, Eric Fellner, William Green, Dan Mazer	Sacha Baron Cohen, Kellie Bright, Charles Dance
My Little Eye	2002	Marc Evans	David Hilton, James Watkins	Jon Finn, Alan Greenspan, David Hilton, Jane Villiers	Sean Cw Johnson, Laura Regan, Bradley Cooper

(continued)

Title	Year	Director	Writer	Producer	Cast
Shaun of the Dead	2004	Edgar Wright	Simon Pegg, Edgar Wright	Nira Park	Simon Pegg, Nick Frost, Kate Ashfield
The Calcium Kid	2004	Alex De Rakoff	Alex De Rakoff, Raymond Friel, Derek Boyle	Tim Bevan, Eric Fellner	Orlando Bloom, Michael Peña, Billie Piper
Mickybo and Me	2004	Terry Loane	Terry Loane	Mark Huffam, Mike McGeagh	John Jo McNeill, Niall Wright, Julie Walters
Inside I'm Dancing	2004	Damien O'Donnell	Jeffrey Caine	James Flynn, Juanita Wilson	James McAvoy, Steven Robertson, Romola Garai
Sixty-six	2006	Paul Weiland	Bridget O'Connor, Peter Straughan	Tim Bevan, Eric Fellner, Elisabeth Karlsen	Gregg Sulkin, Eddie Marsan, Helena Bonham Carter
Gone	2007	Ringan Ledwidge	James Watkins, Andrew Upton	Deborah Balderstone, Nira Park	Shaun Evans, Scott Mechlowicz, Amelia Warner

The Universal Years (1998–)

Title	Year	Director	Writer	Producer	Cast
The Hi-Lo Country	1998	Stephen Frears	Walon Green	Tim Bevan, Eric Fellner, Barbra Da Fina, Martin Scorsese	Woody Harrelson, Billy Crudup, Patricia Arquette
Notting Hill	1999	Roger Michell	Richard Curtis	Duncan Kenworthy	Julia Roberts, Hugh Grant, Rhys Ifans
Plunkett & Macleane	1999	Jake Scott	Selwyn Roberts, Neal Purvis, Robert Wade, Charles McKeown	Tim Bevan, Eric Fellner, Rupert Harvey	Robert Carlyle, Jonny Lee Miller, Liv Tyler
High Fidelity	2000	Stephen Frears	D.V. DeVincentis, Steve Pink, John Cusack, Scott Rosenberg	Tim Bevan, Rudd Simmons	John Cusack, Jack Black, Iben Hjejle

Title	Year	Director	Writer	Producer	Cast
O Brother, Where Art Thou?	2000	Joel Coen	Joel Coen, Ethan Coen	Ethan Coen	George Clooney, John Turturro, Tim Blake Nelson
The Man Who Cried	2000	Sally Potter	Sally Potter	Christopher Sheppard	Christina Ricci, Cate Blanchett, Johnny Depp
Captain Corelli's Mandolin	2001	John Madden	Shawn Slovo	Tim Bevan, Eric Fellner, Mark Huffam, Kevin Loader	Nicolas Cage, Penélope Cruz, John Hurt
Bridget Jones's Diary	2001	Sharon Maguire	Richard Curtis, Helen Fielding, Andrew Davies	Tim Bevan, Eric Fellner, Jonathan Cavendish	Renée Zellweger, Colin Firth, Hugh Grant
The Man Who Wasn't There	2001	Joel Coen	Joel Coen, Ethan Coen	Ethan Coen	Billy Bob Thornton, Frances McDormand, James Gandolfini
40 Days and 40 Nights	2002	Michael Lehmann	Rob Perez	Tim Bevan, Eric Fellner, Michael London	Josh Hartnett, Shannyn Sossamon, Vinessa Shaw
About a Boy	2002	Chris Weitz, Paul Weitz	Peter Hodges, Chris Weitz, Paul Weitz	Tim Bevan, Eric Fellner, Robert Di Niro, Brad Epstein, Jane Rosenthal	Hugh Grant, Nicholas Hoult, Toni Collette
The Guru	2002	Daisy von Scherler Mayer	Tracey Jackson	Tim Bevan, Eric Fellner, Michael London	Jimi Mistry, Heather Graham, Marisa Tomei
Johnny English	2003	Peter Howitt	Neal Purvis, Robert Wade, William Davies	Tim Bevan, Eric Fellner, Mark Huffam	Rowan Atkinson, John Malkovich, Natalie Imbruglia
Ned Kelly	2003	Gregor Jordan	John Michael McDonagh	Lynda House, Nelson Woss	Heath Ledger, Orlando Bloom, Naomi Watts
Love Actually	2003	Richard Curtis	Richard Curtis	Tim Bevan, Eric Fellner, Duncan Kenworthy	Hugh Grant, Liam Neeson, Colin Firth

(continued)

Title	Year	Director	Writer	Producer	Cast
Thirteen	2003	Catherine Hardwicke	Catherine Hardwicke, Nikki Reed	Jeffrey Levy-Hinte, Michael London	Holly Hunter, Evan Rachel Wood, Nikki Reed
Gettin' Square	2003	Jonathan Teplitzky	Chris Nyst	Martin Fabinyi, Timothy White, Trisha Lake	Sam Worthington, David Wenham, Gary Sweet
The Shape of Things	2003	Neil Labute	Neil Labute	Neil Labute, Andrew Lipson, Gail Mutrux, Philip Steuer, Rachel Weisz	Paul Rudd, Rachel Weisz, Gretchen Mol
Wimbledon	2004	Richard Loncraine	Jennifer Flackett, Mark Levin, Adam Brooks	Tim Bevan, Eric Fellner, Mary Richards, David Livingstone	Kirsten Dunst, Paul Bettany, Sam Neill
Thunderbirds	2004	Jonathan Frakes	Michael McCullers, William Osborne	Tim Bevan, Eric Fellner, Mark Huffam	Bill Paxton, Anthony Edwards, Ben Kingsley
Bridgit Jones: The Edge of Reason	2004	Beeban Kidron	Richard Curtis, Helen Fielding, Andrew Davies	Tim Bevan, Eric Fellner, John Cavendish	Renée Zellweger, Colin Firth, Hugh Grant
The Interpreter	2005	Sydney Pollack	Charles Randolph, Scott Frank, Steven Zallian	Tim Bevan, Eric Fellner, Kevin Misher	Nicole Kidman, Sean Penn, Catherine Keener
Pride & Predjudice	2005	Joe Wright	Deborah Moggach, Emma Thompson	Tim Bevan, Eric Fellner, Paul Webster	Keira Knightley, Matthew Macfadyen, Brenda Blethyn
Nanny McPhee	2005	Kirk Jones	Emma Thompson	Tim Bevan, Eric Fellner, Lindsay Doran	Emma Thompson, Colin Firth, Angela Lansbury
United 93	2006	Paul Greengrass	Paul Greengrass	Tim Bevan, Eric Fellner, Paul Greengrass, Lloyd Levin	Christian Clemenson, Cheyenne Jackson, David Alan Basche

Title	Year	Director	Writer	Producer	Cast
Catch a Fire	2006	Philip Noyce	Shawn Slovo	Tim Bevan, Eric Fellner, Anthony Minghella, Robyn Slovo	Derek Luke, Tim Robbins, Bonnie Henna
Smokin' Aces	2006	Joe Cranahan	Joe Cranahan	Tim Bevan, Eric Fellner	Ben Affleck, Ryan Reynolds, Andy Garcia
Hot Fuzz	2007	Edgar Wright	Edgar Wright, Simon Pegg	Tim Bevan. Eric Fellner, Nira Park	Simon Pegg, Nick Frost, Jim Broadbent
Mr Bean's Holiday	2007	Steve Bendelack	Hamish McColl, Robin Driscoll	Peter Bennett-Jones, Tim Bevan, Eric Fellner	Rowan Atkinson, Emma de Caunes, Max Baldry
Atonement	2007	Joe Wright	Christopher Hampton	Tim Bevan, Eric Fellner, Paul Webster	James McAvoy, Keira Knightley, Saoirse Ronan
Elizabeth: The Golden Age	2007	Shekhar Kapur	William Nicholson, Michael Hirst	Tim Bevan, Eric Fellner, Jonathan Cavendish	Cate Blanchett, Geoffrey Rush, Clive Owen
Definitely, Maybe	2008	Adam Brooks	Adam Brooks	Tim Bevan, Eric Fellner	Ryan Reynolds, Isla Fisher, Derek Luke
Wild Child	2008	Nick Moore	Lucy Dahl	Tim Bevan, Eric Fellner, Diana Philips	Emma Roberts, Alex Pettyfer, Natasha Richardson
Burn After Reading	2008	Joel Coen, Ethan Coen	Joel Coen, Ethan Coen	Joel Coen, Ethan Coen	George Clooney, Frances McDormand, John Malkovich
Frost/Nixon	2008	Ron Howard	Peter Morgan	Tim Bevan, Eric Fellner, Brian Grazer, Ron Howard	Frank Langella, Michael Sheen, Matthew Macfadyen
The Boat that Rocked	2009	Richard Curtis	Richard Curtis	Tim Bevan, Eric Fellner, Hilary Bevan-Jones	Philip Seymour Hoffman, Bill Nighy, Rhys Ifans
State of Play	2009	Kevin Macdonald	Matthew Carnahan, Tony Gilroy, Billy Ray	Tim Bevan, Eric Fellner, Andrew Hauptman	Russell Crowe, Ben Affleck, Rachel McAdams

(continued)

Title	Year	Director	Writer	Producer	Cast
The Soloist	2009	Joe Wright	Susannah Grant	Gary Foster, Russ Krasnoff	Jamie Foxx, Robert Downey Jr, Catherine Keener
A Serious Man	2009	Joel Coen, Ethan Coen	Joel Coen, Ethan Coen	Joel Coen, Ethan Coen	Michael Stuhlbarg, Richard Kind, Fred Melamed
Green Zone	2010	Paul Greengrass	Brian Helgeland	Tim Bevan, Eric Fellner, Paul Greengrass, Lloyd Levin	Matt Damon, Greg Kinnear, Brendan Gleeson
Nanny McPhee and the Big Bang	2010	Susanna White	Emma Thompson	Tim Bevan, Eric Fellner, Lindsay Doran	Emma Thompson, Maggie Gyllenhaal, Rhys Ifans
Senna	2010	Asif Kapadia	Manish Pandey	Tim Bevan, Eric Fellner, James Gay-Rees	Ayrton Senna, Alain Prost, Frank Williams
Paul	2011	Greg Mottola	Simon Pegg, Nick Frost	Tim Bevan, Eric Fellner, Nira Park	Simon Pegg, Nick Frost, Seth Rogen
Johnny English Reborn	2011	Oliver Parker	Hamish McColl, William Davies	Tim Bevan, Eric Fellner, Chris Clark	Rowan Atkinson, Gillian Anderson, Dominic West
Tinker Tailor Soldier Spy	2011	Tomas Alfredson	Bridget O'Connor, Peter Straughan	Tim Bevan, Eric Fellner, Robyn Slovo	Gary Oldman, Colin Firth, Mark Strong
Contraband	2012	Baltasar Kormakur	Aaron Gazikowski	Tim Bevan, Eric Fellner, Baltasar Kormakur, Stephen Levinson, Mark Whalberg	Mark Wahlberg, Kate Beckinsale, Ben Foster
Big Miracle	2012	Ken Kwapis	Jack Amiel, Michael Begler	Tim Bevan, Eric Fellner, Liza Chasin, Steve Golin, Michael Sugar	Drew Barrymore, John Krasinski, Kristen Bell
Anna Karenina	2012	Joe Wright	Tom Stoppard	Tim Bevan, Eric Fellner, Paul Webster	Keira Knightley, Jude Law, Aaron Johnson

Title	Year	Director	Writer	Producer	Cast
Les Miserables	2012	Tom Hooper	William Nicholson	Tim Bevan, Eric Fellner, Debra Hayward, Cameron Mackintosh	Hugh Jackman, Russell Crowe, Anne Hathaway
I Give it a Year	2013	Dan Mazer	Dan Mazer	Tim Bevan, Eric Fellner, Kris Thykier	Rose Byrne, Rafe Spall, Simon Baker
The World's End	2013	Edgar Wright	Edgar Wright, Simon Pegg	Tim Bevan, Eric Fellner, Nira Park	Simon Pegg, Nick Frost, Paddy Considine
Closed Circuit	2013	John Crowley	Steven Knight	Tim Beven, Eric Fellner, Chris Clark	Eric Bana, Rebecca Hall, Riz Ahmed
About Time	2013	Richard Curtis	Richard Curtis	Tim Bevan, Eric Fellner, Nicky Kentish Barnes	Domhnall Gleeson, Rachel McAdams, Bill Nighy
Rush	2013	Ron Howard	Peter Morgan	Tim Bevan, Eric Fellner, Andrew Eaton, Brian Grazer, Ron Howard, Peter Morgan, Brian Oliver	Chris Hemsworth, Daniel Brühl, Alexandra Maria Lara
The Two Faces of January	2014	Hossein Amini	Hossein Amini	Tim Bevan, Eric Fellner, Robyn Slovo, Tom Sternberg	Viggo Mortensen, Kirsten Dunst, Oscar Isaac
Trash	2014	Stephen Daldry	Richard Curtis	Tim Bevan, Eric Fellner, Kris Thykier	Rooney Mara, Martin Sheen, Wagner Moura
The Theory of Everything	2014	James Marsh	Anthony McCarten	Tim Bevan, Eric Fellner, Anthony McCarten, Lisa Bruce	Eddie Redmayne, Felicity Jones, Charlie Cox
We Are Your Friends	2015	Max Joseph	Max Joseph, Meaghan Oppenheimer	Tim Bevan, Eric Fellner, Liza Chasin	Zac Efron, Wes Bentley, Emily Ratajkowski

(continued)

Title	Year	Director	Writer	Producer	Cast
Legend	2015	Brian Helgeland	Brian Helgeland	Tim Bevan, Eric Fellner, Chris Clark, Quentin Curtis, Brian Oliver	Tom Hardy, Emily Browning, Christopher Eccleston
Everest	2015	Baltasar Kormákur	William Nicholson, Simon Beaufoy	Tim Bevan, Eric Fellner, Baltasar Kormákur, Nicky Kentish Barnes, Tyler Thompson, Brian Oliver	Jason Clarke, Josh Brolin, Jake Gyllenhaal
The Program	2015	Stephen Frears	John Hodge	Tim Bevan, Eric Fellner, Tracey Seaward, Kate Solomon	Ben Foster, Chris O'Dowd, Guillaume Canet
The Danish Girl	2015	Tom Hooper	Lucinda Coxon	Tim Bevan, Eric Fellner, Anne Harrison, Tom Hooper, Gail Mutrux	Eddie Redmayne, Alicia Vikander, Ben Whishaw
Hail, Caesar!	2016	Joel Coen, Ethan Coen	Joel Coen, Ethan Coen	Joel Coen, Ethan Coen, Tim Bevan, Eric Fellner	Josh Brolin, George Clooney, Alden Ehrenreich
Grimsby	2016	Louis Leterrier	Sacha Baron Cohen, Phil Johnston, Peter Baynham	Sacha Baron Cohen, Nira Park, Peter Baynham, Ant Hines, Todd Schulman	Sacha Baron Cohen, Mark Strong, Rebel Wilson
Bridget Jones's Baby	2016	Sharon Maguire	Helen Fielding, Dan Mazer, Emma Thompson	Tim Bevan, Eric Fellner, Debra Hayward	Renée Zellweger, Colin Firth, Patrick Dempsey
Baby Driver	2017	Edgar Wright	Edgar Wright	Tim Bevan, Eric Fellner, Nira Park	Ansel Elgort, Kevin Spacey, Lily James

Title	Year	Director	Writer	Producer	Cast
Victoria & Abdul	2017	Stephen Frears	Lee Hall	Tim Bevan, Eric Fellner, Beeban Kidron, Tracey Seaward	Judi Dench, Ali Fazal, Eddie Izzard
The Snowman	2017	Tomas Alfredson	Hossein Amini, Peter Straughan, Søren Sveistrup	Tim Bevan, Eric Fellner, Robyn Slovo, Peter Gustafsson	Michael Fassbender, Rebecca Ferguson, Charlotte Gainsbourg
Darkest Hour	2017	Joe Wright	Anthony McCarten	Tim Bevan, Lisa Bruce, Eric Fellner, Anthony McCarten, Douglas Urbanski	Gary Oldman, Kristin Scott Thomas, Lily James
Entebee	2018	José Padilha	Gregory Burke	Tim Bevan, Eric Fellner, Ron Halpern, Kate Solomon, Michelle Wright	Rosamund Pike, Daniel Brühl, Eddie Marsan
Johnny English Strikes Again	2018	David Kerr	William Davies	Tim Bevan, Eric Fellner, Chris Clark	Rowan Atkinson, Olga Kurylenko, Emma Thompson
Mary Queen of Scots	2018	Josie Rourke	Beau Willimon	Tim Bevan, Eric Fellner, Debra Hayward	Saoirse Ronan, Margot Robbie, Jack Lowden
The Kid Who Would Be King	2019	Joe Cornish	Joe Cornish	Tim Bevan, Eric Fellner, Nira Park	Louis Ashbourne Serkis, Rebecca Ferguson, Patrick Stewart
Yesterday	2019	Danny Boyle	Richard Curtis	Tim Bevan, Eric Fellner, Bernie Bellew, Matthew James Wilkinson, Richard Curtis, Danny Boyle	Himesh Patel, Lily James, Joel Fry

(continued)

Title	Year	Director	Writer	Producer	Cast
Cats	2019	Tom Hooper	Lee Hall, Tom Hooper	Tim Bevan, Eric Fellner, Tom Hooper, Debra Hayward	Judi Dench, James Corden, Idris Elba
Radioactive	2019	Marjane Satrapi	Jack Thorne	Tim Bevan, Eric Fellner, Paul Webster	Rosamund Pike, Sam Riley, Anya Taylor-Joy
Emma	2020	Autumn de Wilde	Eleanor Catton	Tim Bevan, Eric Fellner, Graham Broadbent, Peter Czernin	Anya Taylor-Joy, Johnny Flynn, Mia Goth
The High Note	2020	Nisha Ganatra	Flora Greeson	Tim Bevan, Eric Fellner	Dakota Johnson, Tracee Ellis Ross, Kelvin Harrison Jr
Rebecca	2020	Ben Wheatley	Jane Goldman, Joe Shrapnel, Anna Waterhouse	Tim Bevan, Eric Fellner, Nira Park	Lily James, Armie Hammer, Kristin Scott Thomas

Index

Note: f indicates a figure, n indicates note, t indicates table, *italic* indicates illustration

About a Boy, 20, 139, 190, 198, 205t, 206, 224
About Time, 20, 22, 224, 226
Academy Awards, 1, 53
action/adventure films, 162–3, 206
Adams, Tim, 224
Aldabra (music video production company), 5, 49, 50, 56
Alfano, JoAnn, 189–90
Ali G Indahouse, 6, 21, 139, 146, *159*, 162, 209, 210t, 211, 225, 226
American Film Market (AFM), 92n16
Amoo, Shola, 28
Andrew, Dudley, 12–13
Anna Karenina, 143, 207, 208t
Arnold, Andrea, 12
art cinema, 15, 28, 38
    European-model, 14, 220–1
    see also social art cinema
art-house films, 14, 38, 42, 207
Arts Council of England (ACE), 32–3, 35, 104
Atkinson, Rowan, 20, 21, *121*, *159*, 204
Atlantic Entertainment, 60, 75
Atonement, 20, 21, 23, 143, *161*, 165, 168, 208t, 209, 225, 226
avant-garde films, 15, 47

Baby Driver, 1, 7, 179, 187, *196*
BAFTAs, 1, 198
Bamber, Jay, 225
Bamborough, Karin, 50, 52
Barber, Frances, *65*
Barnard, Clio, 28
Baron Cohen, Sacha, 21, *159*, 164
BBC, 43–4, 51, 189, 191

BBC America, 189
BBC Films, 35, 36, 86, 230
Bean, 1, 6, 20, 21, 22, 94, *121*, 130, 168, 202t, 203, 204, 226
Bell, Jamie, 21, *158*
Bertelsmann Music Group (BMG), 88, 89f
Bevan, Tim, 5, 6
    on British film industry, 213
    on Channel 4, 42–3
    'Charity or Business?' manifesto, 53–4
    on co-financing, 181–2
    on distribution, 215
    on diversity, 231
    on *Four Weddings and a Funeral*, 201
    and funding, 58
    and PolyGram, 68, 75, 76–7, 78, 85, 86, 90, 91, 96–100, 103
    on producer's role, 97–8, 144, 165–66, 173, 186, 222
    and Studiocanal, 179, 180, 183, 215
    and Universal, 129, 130, 133–4, 138–9, 140–1, 144, 162, 165–6, 172–3, 178, 184, 185–6
    on Working Title's origins, 48, 49, 50, 52, 56, 57, 59, 61–2
    and WT^2, 145–6, 164
Big Lebowski, The, 1, 94, *122*, 202t, 203–4
Billy Elliot, 1, 6, 21, 24, 139, 146, 150, 154, *158*, 162, 164, 207, 208t, 209, 210t, 225, 226
Birdsong, 188
Blanchett, Cate, *123*
Boat that Rocked, The, 20, 207, 208t
Bob Roberts, 1, 69, 84f, 85, 94, 105t

Boonstra, Cornelius 'Cor', 124
Borrowers, The, 20, 188, 202t, 203
box office, 1, 110, 168, 198, 200, 206, 209, 215, 222
    Focus Features slate top fifteen 1999–2019, 208t
    Hollywood films domestic vs international, 2001–18, 216f
    PFE, 109f, 202t
    Studiocanal top films, 2011–19, 214t
    UK and ROI, 2002–18, 36f, 37f, 39t, 40t
    Universal slate top twenty, 1999–2019, 205t, 211, 212t, 213
    WT² top ten, 199–2006, 210t
Boyd, Don, 48
Boyle, Amanda, 145
Bradstreet, Graham, 5, 56–7, 60, 73, 77, 78, 89–90
Bridges, Jeff, *122*
Bridget Jones: The Edge of Reason, 20, 139, 198, 205t, 206, 213, 224
Bridget Jones's Baby, 7, 20, 21, 22, 178, 185, 186, 205t, 206, 224
Bridget Jones's Diary, 1, 6, 20, 139, 143, 150, *158*, 182, 198, 205t, 206, 213, 224
Britain and Britishness, 23, 40–1, 200, 201, 220, 223, 226–7
British cinema, 12
    and American cinema compared, 127, 128
    box office 2018, 38
    Cultural Test, 33
    government policies, 31–4, 45
    independent, 27–8, 29, 37, 58–9
    investment, 29, 30–3, 39, 46, 230, 231
    as national cinema, 13–16
    production categories, 29–31
    public expenditure, 34, 35–6, 39–40
    taxation, 32, 33–5, 39, 60, 62
    see also British New Wave; Transatlantic British Cinema
British Documentary Film Movement, 12, 14
British Film Commission, 33
British Film Institute (BFI), 48
    and diversity, 230–1, 232
    and funding, 33, 34, 35, 54
    Library, 9
    Production Board, 5, 43, 46–7, 60, 62, 220, 230
    Research and Statistics Unit (RSU), 9, 29
British New Wave, 12
British Screen Finance Ltd, 5, 32, 43, 45, 47, 48, 56, 58, 59, 60, 85, 86, 220, 230
Britishness *see* Britain and Britishness
Bromstad, Angela, 188
Bronfman, Edgar, Jr, 124, 130, 134, 135
Brown, William, 225
Brühl, Daniel, *195*
Burke, Steve, 136
Burn After Reading, 2, *194*, 208t, 209
Buscemi, Steve, *122*

Calcium Kid, The, 209, 210t
Canal Plus, 125, 130–1, 134, 135; *see also* Studiocanal
Cannes Film Festival, 59, 62
capitalism, 3, 24, 25, 27
Caravaggio, 15, 54, 57, 61t
Carlton Communications, 125, 126
Carnival Film and Television, 188
Castle Rock Entertainment, 104–5
Cates, Phoebe, *67*
Cats, 7, 23, 164, 179, 225, 226, 233
Cavendish, Jonathan, 98
Central Independent Television, 54–5
Channel 4
    challenge of, 43
    filmmaking remit, 46–8, 54, 55–6, 59, 60, 61t, 62, 75, 85, 86, 220, 230
    and funding, 5, 36, 42, 45, 47–8, 51, 55
    investment, 2
    as a public service broadcaster, 44–5, 51–2
    see also Film Four/Film4; Film on Four
Channel 4 Films, 42, 50
Chapman, James, 23
Chasin, Liza, 85, 98, 99f, 100, 102, 140, 142, 143, 164, 165, 167, 186, 187
Chicago Joe and the Showgirl, 5, *66*, 69, 82, 84f
China, 184
Cinecom, 58, 75
Cinema International Corporation (CIC), 132
Cinematograph Exhibitors' Association (CEA), 45

Index

Clark, Duncan, 183
Closed Circuit, 182
Coen, Joel and Ethan, 1, 94, 139, 143–4
Columbia, 112, 187
Comcast, 6, 19, 133, 136, 167, 182
comedies, 12, 14, 20, 21, 85, 199, 209, 225
    romantic, 7–8, 20, 22, 139, 143, 198, 206, 215; *see also* Curtisland
comedy dramas, 139, 209
Comic Strip Presents, The, 48
commercial cinema, 14, 28, 85–6
commercials, 43, 49
compact discs (CDs), 70
competition, 25–6, 33, 39, 40, 44, 113, 162
conglomerates, 18, 19, 69–70, 78, 88, 91, 118, 124, 125, 133, 134–5
Contraband, 1, 181, 205t, 206
Cook, Jan, 87
Cort, Robert, 95
crime films, 28, 215; *see also* thrillers
Cripps, Andrew, 132, 151–2, 170–1
Crofts, Stephen, 13–14, 28
Curtis, Richard, 20, 75, 76, 166, 201
Curtisland, 7–8, 139, 143, 224–5
Curzon (distributors), 39, 59

Dakota Road, 69, 86
Danish Girl, The, 207, 208t
Darkest Hour, 7, 12, 20, 21, 23, 38, 39t, 41n5, 143, 178, 186, *197*, 207, 208t, 209, 225, 226
Dave, Paul, 224–5
Day-Lewis, Daniel, *64*
Dead Man Walking, 1, 94, 105t, *120*, 202t, 203
Decker, Lindsey, 23
Denton, Charles, 54
Diamond Skulls, 75
Dickinson, Margaret, 33
Diller, Barry, 134
Direct Productions, 91
directors, 15, 42, 46, 48, 49, 61, 97, 100, 105t, 108, 144, 149, 165–6
Disney, 19, 37, 38, 96, 135, 136
distribution, 18, 19, 77, 79, 82, 87, 94–5, 100
    global, 211
    independent companies, 115
    theatrical, 46, 52, 58–9, 76, 108, 111, 112, 116

United States, 58, 60, 76, 204
    see also markets/marketing; Universal Television Distribution
diversity, 228–33
    gender, 232
    racial, 225, 226
    see also social class
documentaries *see* British Documentary Film Movement
Donohue, Walter, 50
Double Negative consortium, 104
Dreamworks Animation, 19, 136, 150, 185
Drop Dead Fred, 5, *67*, 69, 84f, 85
dubbing, 106, 216

Ealing Studios, 12, 14
Edelstein, Michael, 188
Edinburgh Film Festival, 52
Edward II, *67*, 69, 86, 221
Egg Pictures, 104, 105t
Elgort, Ansel, *196*
Elizabeth, 1, 6, 20, 21, 23, 94, 103–4, *123*, 130, 202t, 203
Elizabeth: The Golden Age, 20, 23, 163, 167–8, 225
Elliot, Nick, 76
Elliott Management, 181
EMI, 88, 89f
EMI Films, 12, 14
Emma, 20, 23, 225
Entebbe, 2
Entertainment (distributors), 38, 40t
Entertainment One, 28
Eon Productions, 12, 231
eOne Films, 38, 40t
European Commission, 33, 152–3
European Convention on Cinematographic Co-production, 29
European Union (EU) MEDIA programme, 35, 36
'event' films, 6, 150, 204, 206
Everest, 2, 181, 205t, 206
Ezra, Elizabeth, 11

family films, 20, 139, 174, 185, 206, 225, 226
fantasy films, 12, 75; *see also* Harry Potter films

Fargo, 1, 94, *121*, 202t, 203
feature films, 1, 42, 46, 47, 50, 55, 70, 72, 107, 230
Fellner, Eric, 5, 6, 90–1, 143
    on appeal of films, 169
    on franchises, 168
    on green-lighting, 148
    on market profile, 206–7
    and PFE, 96–100, 111, 129–30
    on producer's role, 96–7, 187, 222
    and Universal, 162
    and WT², 145–6
Field, Ted, 95
Fiennes, Joseph, *123*
Film District, 182
Film Four/Film4, 35, 36, 89, 146, 230
Film Four International, 48, 52–3, 59–60
film libraries, 87, 94, 116, 117t
Film on Four, 50–1, 53, 59
Fincher Films, 104, 105t
Fine, David, 72, 86
Finn, Jon, 144, 145
Firth, Colin, 21, *158*, 226
Fish Called Wanda, A, 199
Focus Features, 6, 7, 19, 154, 178, 184, 186, 204, 207, 215, 222
Focus Features International (FFI), 154–5, 174–5, 182
Fogelson, Adam, 134, 174, 182
Fools of Fortune, 84f, 85
foreign-language productions, 94, 105–6
Fortou, Jean-René, 135
40 Days and 40 Nights, 1, 205t, 206
Four Weddings and a Funeral, 1, 6, 7, 20, 22, 94, 105t, *120*, 130, 192, 198–201, 202t, 203, 224, 233
Fox TV, 135
France
    distribution to, 108, 115, 116f
    Le huitième jour project, 106
    PFI operating companies (OP COs), 113, 114
    production, 41n2, 106
franchises, 104, 106, 168, 172, 222
Frazer, Jane, 98, 99f, 102–3
Frears, Stephen, 51, 58
Freeman, Matthew, 3

French Kiss, 202t, 203
Frost, Nick, *161*
Frost / Nixon, 20, 22, 225
Frye brothers, 57
Fugitive Films, 49

Gainsborough Pictures, 12, 14
Garofalo, Janeane, *122*
gatekeeping, 6, 48, 100, 138, 139, 222–3
General Electric (GE), 6, 19, 133, 135–6, 139, 167
genre films, 14, 182, 209
genre parody, 23
Gerrie, Malcolm, 91
Goldblum, Jeff, *66*
Golden Globes, 198
Goliń, Steve, 72
Gone, 146, 209, 210t
Good Machine, Inc., 154
Goodman, John, *122*
Gordon, Jon, 140
Gramercy Pictures, 6, 19, 95, 107, 112, 113, 116, 117, 131, 200, 203
Grammophon-Philips Group, 69
Granger, Amelia, 175
Grant, Hugh, 21, *120*, *123*, 199, 226
Green Zone, 7, 21, 163, 165, 205t, 206
Grimsby, 7, 20, 164, 179, 187, 207, 225
Gypsy, 191

Hall, Lee, 164
Handmade Films, 73
Hanna, 191
Hardy, Tom, 21, *196*
Harry Potter films, 12, 226–7
Harvey, Sylvia, 33
Havens, Timothy, 26
Hayward, Debra, 98, 99f, 100, 101, 102, 140, 143, 175
Hemsworth, Chris, *195*
'heritage' films, 15
    'neo-heritage' films, 225
    see also historical dramas
Hershey, Barbara, *65*
Heyday Films, 12, 231
Higson, Andrew, 11, 15, 16–17
Hill, John, 14, 15, 16, 28, 31, 33, 229
Hirst, Michael, 174

historical dramas, 12, 225; *see also* 'heritage' films; period dramas
Hjort, Mette, 16, 17, 21–2
Hochscherf, Tobias, 22
Hollywood
  conglomerates, 135
  domestic vs international box office, 2001–18, 216f
  dominance of, 12, 28, 31, 36–8, 39t, 58, 227
  studio culture, 108
  and Transatlantic British Cinema, 13–14, 15–17, 18, 19, 226–7
  and Working Title, 101–2, 186–7
Holt, Jennifer, 3
Honess Roe, Annabelle, 22
Hope, Ted, 154
horror films, 22, 146, 209
Hot Fuzz, 1, 20, 23, *161*, 164, 172, 225
Howell, Juliette, 188, 189, 191–2

I Give It a Year, 7, 20, 22, 178–9, 180, 214t, 215
Illumination Entertainment, 173, 174
Imbruglia, Natalie, *159*
Independent Broadcasting Authority (IBA), 44
Independent Filmmakers' Association (IFA), 46
independent films, 45, 56, 75, 175; *see also* 'specialty' films
Initial Film and Television, 73, 91
Inside I'm Dancing, 21, 24, 146, 155, 209, 210t, 225
Interpreter, The, 21, 164, 205t, 206
Interscope Communications, 88, 94, 95–6, 102, 126, 129, 131
Ireland, Republic of (ROI), 36–7, 38, 39–40
Isaacs, Jeremy, 45, 51
ITV, 43–4, 75, 191; *see also* Central Independent Television

James, Lily, 21, *196*, *197*
James Bond films, 12, 23, 226, 227
Jarman, Derek, 15, 48, 49, 54, 86
Johnny English, 1, 6, 20, 21, 23, 139, 150, *159*, 162, 205t, 206, 225

Johnny English Reborn, 7, 20, 163, 165, 168, 205t, 206, 225
Johnny English Strikes Again, 7, 20, 39t, 41n5, 178, 182, 186, 205t, 206, 225
Jones, Robert, 105t
  Thejonescompany, 104, 105t

Kapur, Shekhar, 104
Kellner, Douglas, 227
Kenworthy, Duncan, 98, 105t
Khan-Din, Ayub, *65*
Kid Who Would Be King, The, 20, 23, 225, 226, 233
King of Thieves, 7, 38, 39t, 40t, 179, 214t, 215, 225
Kingsman films, 226, 227
Knightley, Keira, 21, *160*, *161*, 168
Kosse, David, 155, 170, 183, 216
Kuhn, Michael, 50, 68, 70, 72, 74, 77, 81, 85, 87, 90, 94, 95, 107, 112, 126
Kujawski, Peter, 184
Kureishi, Hanif, 51, 58

Langley, Donna, 138–9, 140, 174, 182, 184
language, 95; *see also* foreign-language productions
Lay, Samantha, 24
Legend, 1, 7, 179, *196*, 214t, 215, 225
Leggott, James, 22, 225
Leigh, Mike, 12, 15, 28, 51
Leland, David, 55
Levy, Alain, 86–7, 115
Linde, David, 134, 154, 156, 162, 172, 173–4
Lionsgate, 28–9, 38, 40t
Livingstone, David, 153, 172, 183, 199, 200, 204, 207
Lloyd, Emily, *66*
Loach, Ken, 12, 15, 28
London Kills Me, 69, 84f, 85, 221
London Screen Academy (LSA), 231–2
London Spy, 189, 191
London Weekend Television (LWT), 75–6, 106
Long Time Dead, 155, 209, 210t
Lotz, Amanda D., 4, 26
Love Actually, 20, 22, 139, 198, 205t, 206, 213, 224
Love Bites, 190

low-budget films, 2, 5, 6, 28, 46, 47, 72, 88–9, 91, 107, 128, 130

McAvoy, James, 21, *161*
McCrory, Shelley, 188
McDonald, Paul, 3, 16
McDormand, Frances, *121*, *194*
MacFadyen, Matthew, *160*
McGurk, Chris, 132, 133
Malkovich, John, *159*
Man Who Wasn't There, The, 2, 139, 208t, 209
Manifesto Film Sales, 74, 78, 79, 82, 107
Map of the Human Heart, 5, 82, 84f
markets/marketing
  and competition, 215–17
  and distribution, 18, 19, 94, 114–15, 153, 154, 180, 211, 222
  forecasting, 6, 107
  recorded music, 88, 89f
Mary Queen of Scots, 20, 23, 207, 208t
Matchmaker, The, 122
Matheson, Margaret, 54, 55
May, Jodhi, *65*
Mayall, Rik, *67*
Meadows, Shane, 12, 15
media culture, 227
media economics, 26–7
Media Industry Studies, 3–4, 26
Meehan, Eileen R., 26–7
Meir, Christopher, 179
melodrama, 12, 14
Merle, Patrick, 8
Messier, Jean-Marie, 134, 135
Meyer, Ron, 134, 141, 182
MGM, 125, 131
MGM-British, 18
MGM (Mallet, Godfrey & Mulcahy), 90
MGMM (Mallet, Grant, Mulcahy & Millaney), 49, 90, 91
Mickybo and Me, 21, 24, 139, 146, 209, 210t, 225
MIFED (Mercato Internazionale del Film e del Documentario), 53, 92n16
Miramax, 58, 113
Misérables, Les, 7, 179, 181, 204, 205t, 206
Misher, Kevin, 140
Monumental Pictures, 175–6

Moody, Paul, 229–30
More Tales of the City, 107, 192, *see also Tales of the City*
Morrison, Angela, 99f, 100, 103, 111, 130–1, 135–6, 140, 143, 147–8, 163, 166, 180, 186–7
Mosco, Vincent, 24–5
Mr. Bean's Holiday, 7, 20, 21, 163, 167–8, 205t, 206, 226
Mulligan, Brian, 133
multiplexes, 113, 207
Murphy, Robert, 224
Music Corporation of America (MCA), 88, 89f, 124
Music Film and Video Producers' Association, 49
musical films, 70, 164, 179; *see also Cats*; *Misérables, Les*
My Beautiful Laundrette, 1, 5, 42, 51–3, 54, 57, 60, 61t, 62, *64*, 210t, 221
My Little Eye, 155, 209
Myer, Carole, 53, 59

Nanny McPhee, 6, 20, 23, 139, *160*, 162, 205t, 206, 225
Nanny McPhee and the Big Bang, 7, 20, 21, 23, 163, 167–8, 205t, 206, 225
national cinema, 11–15; *see also* British cinema
NBCUniversal, 19, 135, 136, 172, 182
NBCUniversal International Studios, 176, 187, 188
NBCUniversal Television Group, 187
Ned Kelly, 146, 155
Nelson Entertainment, 112
Newcomb, Horace, 4
News Corporation, 135, 138
Newsinger, Jack, 34–5, 229
Notting Hill, 1, 20, 21, 22, 94, *123*, 133, 139, 162, 198, 201, 205t, 206, 224
Nwonka, Clive, 229, 231

O Brother, Where Art Thou?, 1–2, 139
O'Hara, David, *122*
Oldman, Gary, 21, *194*, *197*
Oneile, Paul, 151
Orion Classics, 53, 58
Owen, Alison, 88–9, 98, 103–4

Palace Pictures, 58–9, 76
Palmer, Wendy, 73, 74, 79, 86
Paramount, 12, 19, 37, 112, 131, 156; *see also* United International Pictures (UIP)
Paramount Pictures International (PPI), 170, 171, 231
Parent, Mary, 140
Patel, Himesh, *197*
Paul, 20, 21, 22, 205t, 225
Pegg, Simon, 21, *161*, 164
Penn, Sean, *120*, 164
Perfect World Pictures, 6, 184, 185, 222
period dramas, 20, 23, 143, 225; *see also* historical dramas
Perren, Alisa, 3
Personal Services, 54, 55, 57, 60, 61t
Petrie, Duncan, 42, 48
Philips, 69, 124, 200
Pitt, Brad, *194*
political economy of film, 24–8, 41, 219–20
Pollack, Tom, 200
PolyGram Film International (PFI), 105, 107–8, 131
PolyGram Filmed Entertainment (PFE), 2, 5–6, 18–19, 68, 94–118, 124, 132, 200
   budget, 96
   demise, 124–9
   distribution, 94, 106, 107, 112–18, 132–3, 138–9
   green-lighting, 107–12, 221
   investment, 105–6, 116, 126–7, 133
   launch, 87–92
   label system, 87, 97
   marketing, 87, 201–4
   operating companies, 108, 110, 111, 114–15, 132–3
   producer placement, 96–100
   production deals, 105t
   and risk, 221
PolyGram Filmed Entertainment International (PFEI), 94
   distribution, 6, 203
   operating companies (OP COs), 107, 113–14, 115–16
   renamed as Universal Pictures International (UPI), 132
   and Universal compared, 154

PolyGram Filmproduktion GmbH, 74, 79, 82
PolyGram Films, 6, 116, 117, 131
PolyGram Media Division (PMD)
   business plans, 71, 77–8, 87
   control sheets, 5, 68, 81, 85, 92, 108–12, 127, 128, 132, 149, 150–1, 167, 198, 221
   expansion, 72–87
   funding, 78, 79, 80f, 82, 83f, 84f
   investment, 72–3, 74, 77–8, 87
PolyGram Music Video Ltd (PMV), 49–50, 68, 72
PolyGram Pictures, 69–72, 107
PolyGram Television, 116
PolyGram Video, 116
'portfolio' films, 6, 150, 162, 209
postmodern films, 15
Powell, Nik, 58
Presence, Steve, 34–5
Pride & Prejudice, 20, 21, 23, 143, 155, *160*, 207, 208t, 209, 225, 226
Prior, Rachael, 145
producers, 73
   budgets, 173
   fees, 56, 108
   and finance, 96, 101
   roles, 53–4, 75, 96–100, 101, 165–6, 187
Program, The, 2, 214t, 215
Propaganda Films, 72, 73, 74, 79, 87, 88, 94, 102, 126, 129, 131

racial diversity, 225, 226
racism, 232
Radclyffe, Sarah, 5, 42
   on *Caravaggio*, 54
   on Channel 4, 52
   creative role of, 57
   on investment, 55–6
   on *My Beautiful Laundrette*, 51, 54
   and PolyGram, 77, 78, 90
   and production, 86, 91
   on profit participation, 61
   and Working Title's origins, 48–9, 50, 103
   on *A World Apart*, 60
Rank Organisation, 12, 14, 18, 46
realism, 14, 15, 47, 221; *see also* social art cinema; social realism
record industry, 69–70, 88, 89f

Redmayne, Eddie, 21, *195*
Relativity Media, 6, 163, 165–6, 181, 222
Relph, Simon, 46, 52
Revolution Films, 104, 105t, 181
risk, 174–5, 191, 219, 221–8, 233
Ritchie, Malcolm, 68, 71, 74, 76, 78, 81, 87–8, 95–6, 107, 111–12, 200–1
Robbins, Tim, 1, 94, 105t
Roberts, Brian, 136
Roberts, Julia, *123*
Roeg, Luc, 56
Roeg, Nic, 56
romcoms *see* comedies: romantic
Rose, David, 50, 51, 52, 59
Rowden, Terry, 11
RSO Records, 69–70
Rumbalara Films, 104, 105t
Rush, 20, 181, *195*, 225
Ryall, Tom, 15

Sales Company, The, 59
Sammy and Rosie Get Laid, 1, 5, 42, 58, 60, 61t, 62, *65*, 221
Sarandon, Susan, *120*
Schamus, James, 154, 182
Schatz, Thomas, 135
Schlessel, Peter, 182
Schwartz, Russell, 112–13, 116–17, 199
Scott Thomas, Kristin, 21, *120*
scripts, 29, 51, 52, 58, 79, 91, 95, 101, 102, 103, 142, 149
Seagram, 19, 124, 125, 133, 134, 138
Second Best, 91
Secrets, The, 189
sequels, 167–8, 178, 183
Serious Man, A, 2, 174, 208t, 209
Shallow Grave, 105, 105t, 172
Shape of Things, The, 155
Shaun of the Dead, 6, 21, 23, 139, 146, 150, 162, 164, 172, 209, 210t, 211, 226
Shmuger, Marc, 72, 134, 156, 162, 171, 172, 173–4
Shoebox Films, 166
Short, Julia, 110, 114
Siemens, 69
Sighvatsson, Sigurjón 'Joni', 72
Sixty Six, 21, 24, 139, 209, 210t, 225
Sky Group, 19, 136, 191

Slovo, Shawn, 60
Smith, Peter, 132–3, 152
Smith, Tony, 47
Smokin' Aces, 7, 165
Snider, Stacey, 133, 134, 138, 141, 149–50, 156, 184
social art cinema, 47, 54, 56, 60–1, 62, 69, 74, 220
social class, 22, 23, 58, 201, 223–5, 226, 228
social inclusion *see* diversity
social realism, 12, 21, 24, 139, 225
Sony, 37, 38t, 70, 135, 138, 165, 226
Sony Music Entertainment, 88, 89f
Sony Pictures, 2, 7, 179, 187
Sony Picture Classics, 113
'specialty' films, 7, 113, 116–17, 178, 203, 209, 222, 226
State of Play, 1, 7, 21, 163, 165
Stearn, Andrew, 188, 190, 191, 192
Street, Sarah, 15
Stuber, Scott, 140
Studiocanal
   box office share, 38, 40t
   budget, 180
   co-production, 139–40, 142, 176, 180
   distribution, 7, 38, 178–9, 180, 215
   funding, 139, 163
   investment, 131, 163, 179
   transnationalism, 28–9
   and Universal, 181, 222
   and Working Title, 2, 213, 214t, 215
Sutherland, Kiefer, *66*

Tales of the City, 192; *see also More Tales of the City*
Tall Guy, The, *66*, 75–6
television
   Britain, 44–5
   cable, 71, 110, 115, 135, 136, 190
   libraries, 87, 94, 116, 117t
   licensing, 44, 75–6, 106, 114–15, 189
   made-for television film, 45, 174
   network, 190
   see also BBC; Canal Plus; Channel 4; Fox TV; ITV; London Weekend Television; NBCUniversal Television Group; PolyGram Television; Working Title Television Ltd

Tempest, The, 48–9
'tent-pole' films, 6, 7, 149, 150, 162–3, 178, 183–4, 185, 206, 222
theatrical / literary adaptations, 12, 14–15
theatrically released film, 45
Theory of Everything, The, 1, 7, 20, 21, 178, *195*, 207, 208t, 209, 225, 226
Thompson, Alison, 154–5, 174–5, 182
Thompson, Emma, 21, *66*, *160*
'Three Flavours Cornetto Trilogy' *see Hot Fuzz*; *Shaun of the Dead*; *World's End, The*
thrillers, 162–3, 164–5, 206, 215; *see also* crime films
Tiernan, Andrew, *67*
Tiger Aspect Productions, 146
Till, Stewart, 94, 106, 107–8, 113–14, 127–8, 129, 154, 170, 200, 203, 211
Time Warner, 135, 138
Timmer, Jan, 70, 71–2, 87, 124, 128
Tinic, Serra, 26
Tinker Tailor Soldier Spy, 1, 20, 176, 178, 180, *194*, 207, 208t, 214t, 215, 217n16, 225
trade unions, 43, 44
Trafford, Elizabeth, 56
Trainspotting, 105, 105t, 132
Transatlantic British Cinema, 13
  and affinitive transnationalism, 21–4
  and capitalism, 27
  commercial success of, 203, 204, 206, 209, 213
  and diversity, 228–33
  genres of, 20
  and independent British cinema, 28–41, 228–33
  and risk, 219, 220–8
  typology of, 16–18
transnational cinema, 11, 13
transnationalism, 11, 28–9
  affinitive, 17, 18, 21–4, 218–19
  economic, 17, 18–19, 28, 218, 219
  globalising, 17, 18, 19–21, 218, 219
  opportunistic, 17
True Love, 189
Tudors, The, 174
Twentieth Century Fox, 19, 37, 38t, 135, 136
Two Faces of January, 180, 214t, 215

United 93, 163, 165
United International Pictures (UIP), 6, 7, 112, 131–2, 150–6, 170, 204, 211
United Kingdom
  Annan Report, 44
  box office 2002–18, 36–7, 38
  Broadcasting Act (1980), 44
  Broadcasting Act (1990), 72
  Broadcasting Bill (1978), 44
  Department for Culture, Media and Sport (DCMS), 32, 35, 127
  as a filmmaking destination, 168–9, 170
  Films Act (1985), 32, 45
  Finance Acts, 32, 142
  funding: BFI, 33, 34, 35, 54; broadcasting, 43–4; Eady Levy, 31–2, 45, 46, 47
  public, 32–6, 39–40, 47, 54, 104, 218
  National and Regional Development Agencies, 35, 36
  National Film and Television School (NFTS), 35–6
  National Film Finance Corporation (NFFC), 31, 32, 45
  National Lottery, 32, 33, 35, 104, 230
  Studio-Backed films, 36f, 37, 40
  Thatcher administration/Thatcherism, 31–2, 43, 44, 45
  UK Film Council (UKFC), 32–3, 146, 229
United States
  distribution to, 116f, 203, 204
  films, 36, 127, 169–70; *see also* Hollywood
  Foreign Corrupt Practices Act, 136
  Four Weddings and a Funeral in, 199–200
  marketing to, 211
  network television, 190
  and Transatlantic British Cinema, 206–7
Universal, 12
  budget, 134, 207
  development, 140–7
  distribution, 138, 50–6, 172, 178, 184
  funding, 181
  and Gramercy Pictures, 112, 116
  green-lighting process, 140, 147–50, 151, 154, 167, 170, 172, 185–6
  marketing, 204–17
  ownership, 19
  production deals, 141t, 173t, 185t
  production department, 142

Universal (cont.)
  production strategy, 6, 7
  ten-columns, 6, 149, 150–1, 154, 167, 175, 180, 198, 221
  and theatrical market, 37
  and Working Title, 2, 19, 131, 138–56
  see also NBC Universal International Television Production; United International Pictures
Universal Focus, 154
Universal Global Talent Development & Inclusion (GTDI), 232
Universal International Television Distribution, 152
Universal Music Group, 124–5, 135
Universal Pictures International (UPI), 7, 132, 135, 170–1, 183, 204
Universal Studios, 19, 124
Universal Television Distribution (UTD), 146
Universal Television Group, 187
USA Films, 131, 154; see also Focus Features
USA Networks, 131, 134, 154
Usual Suspects, The, 132

Van Peebles, Mario, 1, 94
Vestron Pictures, 58, 75
Viacom, 112, 135
Victoria & Abdul, 7, 12, 20, 23, 164, 185, 186, 207, 208t
Video Arts, 49
videos
  distribution, 70, 116
  income from, 109f
  markets, 71, 110
  music, 43, 49–50, 56; see also PolyGram Music Video (PMV)
  rights, 76, 131
  S-VOD (subscription video on demand), 190, 191
Vivendi, 6, 19, 133, 136, 139, 167, 179
Vivendi Universal Entertainment (VUE), 134–5

Waddington, Steven, *67*
Walak, Robert, 184
War Zone, The, 91
Ward-Jackson, Nicholas, 54
Warnecke, Gordon, *64*

Warner Bros., 12, 19, 37, 38t, 104, 112; see also Time Warner
Warner Music Group, 88, 89f
Wasko, Janet, 25, 26–7, 220
Wayne, Michael, 224, 227, 228
We Are Your Friends, 214t, 215
Webster, Paul, 58, 75, 85, 98, 143
Wharton, Natascha, 144, 164, 175
White, Tim, 146
Wild Child, 20, 165
Wilkinson, Kenton, 8
Williams, Christopher, 47, 220
Wilson, Gareth, 148–9, 166–7
Wimbledon, 20, 22, 139, 224, 226
Wish You Were Here, 1, 5, 55, 57, 60, 61t, *64*, 221
Wolf, Rita, *64*
Woodhead, Andrew, 188
Woolley, Stephen, 58
Working Title
  actors, 20–1
  affinitive transnationalism, 22–4
  background, 1–2
  brand identity, 153–4, 181, 224
  budget, 21, 101, 103, 111, 162, 173, 178, 186
  business models/plans, 57–62, 72–3, 76
  co-productions, 2, 54, 55, 60–1, 134, 139, 142, 169, 174, 176, 178, 181
  cultural impact, 1
  development, 48–62, 218
  diversity, 1–2
  finance, 7, 12, 53–4, 60, 75–6, 78–9, 82, 104, 131, 134, 163, 165, 170, 174, 178–9, 181, 184–5, 186–7, 189, 213, 221–2
  funding, 2, 5, 57, 60, 61t, 62, 86, 220
  genre output, 20, 21, 22, 130
  green-lighting process, 222
  and Hollywood, 101–2, 186–7
  incorporation, 2, 50, 56
  independence, 42
  investment, 2, 55–6, 57, 58, 60, 62, 75, 76–7, 163, 165, 220, 221
  marketing, 37–8, 40, 45, 52, 71, 114, 183; global, 198–217
  offices, 2, 50, 69, 78, 85, 100, 102, 141–2, 166

and PolyGram, 18, 68–9, 72–92, 94–107, 108–12, 125–6, 201–4, 221, 222
   production: costs, 139; strategies, 7, 186; values, 21, 22, 191–2
sales, 59–60, 73, 74
sphere of influence, 166
strength, 129
and Transatlantic British Cinema, 27
and Universal, 19, 129–34, 138–56, 162–76, 178–92, 221–2
women's roles, 143
see also WT²
Working Title Australia (WTA), 146
Working Title (Developments) Ltd, 57
Working Title Films Ltd, 56–7, 77, 92, 99f
Working Title Group Ltd, 77, 92
Working Title Ltd, 42, 50, 91–2
Working Title Television Ltd (WTTV), 5, 7, 106–7, 146, 174, 176, 179, 187–92
   brand identity, 191–2
   funding, 106
   incorporation, 72
   and NBCUniversal International, 188–90
   and S-VOD (subscription video on demand), 191

World Apart, A, 1, 42, 60, 61t, 62, *65*, 75t
World's End, The, 20, 23, 164, 181, 207, 208t, 225
Wright, Edgar, 164, 166
Wright, Joe, 143, 166, 168, 191
Wright, Michelle, 140, 142–3, 168–9
Wright, Simon, 99f, 106, 114–15, 146–7, 174
WT², 6, 139, 155
   closure, 7, 162, 164
   commercial success, 209, 210t
   development process, 145
   and diversity, 225
   incorporation of, 145
   investment in, 146
   New Writers' Scheme, 144–5
   and transnationalism, 24
Wyhowska, Kate, 183

Yesterday, 1, 20, 22, 23, 185, *197*, 205t, 206, 225, 226, 233
You, Me and the Apocalypse, 189

Zellweger, Renée, *158*
Zenith Entertainment, 54–5, 59

EU representative:
Easy Access System Europe
Mustamäe tee 50, 10621 Tallinn, Estonia
Gpsr.requests@easproject.com

www.ingramcontent.com/pod-product-compliance
Lightning Source LLC
Chambersburg PA
CBHW052105230426
43671CB00011B/1943